RIVERSIDE TEXTBOOKS
IN EDUCATION
EDITED BY ELLWOOD P. CUBBERLEY
PROFESSOR OF EDUCATION
LELAND STANFORD JUNIOR UNIVERSITY

PUBLIC EDUCATION IN THE UNITED STATES

A STUDY AND INTERPRETATION OF AMERICAN EDUCATIONAL HISTORY

AN INTRODUCTORY TEXTBOOK DEALING WITH
THE LARGER PROBLEMS OF PRESENT-DAY
EDUCATION IN THE LIGHT OF THEIR
HISTORICAL DEVELOPMENT

BY

ELLWOOD P. CUBBERLEY

DEAN OF THE SCHOOL OF EDUCATION
LELAND STANFORD JUNIOR UNIVERSITY

HOUGHTON MIFFLIN COMPANY

BOSTON · NEW YORK · CHICAGO · DALLAS
SAN FRANCISCO
The Riverside Press Cambridge

The Riverside Press
CAMBRIDGE · MASSACHUSETTS
PRINTED IN THE U.S.A.

TO

MY MANY FORMER STUDENTS

WHOSE HELPFUL CRITICISMS OF THE COURSE

HAVE SERVED TO

MAKE THIS BOOK OF GREATER VALUE

AUTHOR'S PREFACE

THE history of education as an introductory subject for students in normal schools and colleges has recently received much criticism, largely because it has, as usually written and taught, had so little relation to present-day problems in education, and because it has failed to "function," to use a common expression, in orienting the prospective teacher. The truth of such criticisms was brought out forcibly by a recent study which showed that, of the dozen most commonly used textbooks, only three gave as much as twenty-five per cent of their space to the developments of the past fifty years; that most of them devoted the great bulk of their space to ancient and mediæval education and European development; that most of them were cyclopædic in character, and seemed constructed on the old fact-theory-of-knowledge basis; that only two or three attempted to relate the history they presented to present-day problems in instruction; that only one made any real connection between the study of the history of education and the institutional efforts of the State in the matter of training; and that practically none treated the history of education in the light of either the recent important advances in educational practice and procedure or the great social, political, and industrial changes which have given the recent marked expansion of state educational effort its entire meaning.

That the history of education, as usually taught, needs reorganizing, there can be little question. That for beginners, at least, much old subject-matter should be eliminated and much new subject-matter added, also seems to be accepted without much question. That it is too valuable a subject to lose entirely also seems to most teachers to be true. What the beginning teacher needs, though, it seems to be somewhat generally conceded, is not a long course covering either the history of the evolution of our higher civilization or the various attempts of educational reformers to propose ideal solutions for the educational problem. On the contrary, what is offered to beginning students should be very practical, should be closely tied up with the social, political, and industrial forces which have shaped the nineteenth century, and should help the teacher to see the problems of the twentieth century in the light of their historic evolution and the probable lines of their future development.

Education, with us, was a fruit of the movements which resulted from the Protestant Revolt of the sixteenth century, and the general awakening of Europe which was at that time taking place. Back beyond this historic event the beginning student scarcely need go. One short chapter will give the beginner the necessary historic background, and the study can then begin with the transfer of European civilization and educational zeal to our shores. Much time, too, need not be spent on our development before the first quarter of the nineteenth century, when the forces — national, state, philanthropic, social, political, and economic — which were potent in our educational development first began to find expression. The battle for taxation for education; the battle to eliminate the pauper-school idea; the battle to do away with the rate bill and the fuel tax, and make the schools entirely free; the battle to establish supervision; the battle to eliminate sectarianism; the battle to extend and complete the system by adding the high school and the state university; the struggle to establish normal schools, and begin the training of teachers; the gradual evolution of the graded system of instruction; and the opening of instruction of all grades to women; — these are the great milestones in our early national educational history which are of real importance for the beginning student of education to know. Of the educational reformers, the beginning can be made with Rousseau, as the inspirer of Pestalozzi's labors. Then Pestalozzi, Fellenberg, Froebel, and Herbart are the Europeans whose main ideas the student needs to grasp, and it was not until near the middle of the nineteenth century that the work of the first two of these began to be made known to us by returning travelers and to influence the current of our national educational progress. The other educational reformers with whom the beginning student should become familiar are the practical constructive American thinkers who fought through our early state educational battles and shaped the traditions of our American state school systems.

Up to the time of our Civil War we were engaged in laying foundations and establishing principles of action. The great period of our educational development and expansion has been since 1860, since which time we have twice reorganized our elementary instruction, first in the light of the "faculty" psychology which came in with Pestalozzian ideas, and again in the light of the vast and far-reaching social and industrial changes of the past fifty years. We probably are now at the beginnings of a third reorganization, this time to include the high school as well. The kindergarten, manual training, domestic arts, Herbartian ideas have also come from abroad since 1860, and been incorporated into our educational theory and practice. The great stream of immigration which has come to our shores, the vast industrial revolution which has taken place, the destruction of the old-type home, the virtual disappearance of the apprenticeship system of training, the institution of compulsory education, new conceptions as to the education of delinquents and defectives, new child-welfare legislation, and the rise of a rural-life problem of great dimensions, — these are the more important changes and forces of the past three decades which have necessitated extensive modifications in almost every aspect of our educational service. To enable our schools to meet these new problems of our changing democratic life, we have been forced to change the direction of our schools and to adapt the instruction given

to the new needs and conditions of society. A new educational theory has been evolved, adjustments and differentiations in school work have had to be worked out, the education of defectives and delinquents has required new
classes and new state institutions, child-welfare work has
been given an importance before unknown, the high school
has had to be made over, vocational education and the
improvement of agriculture and rural-life conditions have
recently been made great national undertakings, the education of adults for literacy and intelligent citizenship has
recently awakened a wide national interest, and the original one-course colleges have been transformed into great
universities, training leaders for and ministering unto the
needs of the State. The new problems in education have
developed so rapidly, and have become problems of such
national importance, that questions of educational reorganization and educational readjustment — the curriculum, the organization of the school, city education, rural
and village education, county organization, state organization, national aid and oversight, and the study of education
as a science — these and others have now everywhere been
pushed to the front, and are matters of everyday discussion
with which teachers and students of education should be
familiar. Within the past quarter of a century we have
come to see, with a clearness of vision not approached before, that education is our Nation's greatest constructive
tool, and that the many problems of national welfare which
education alone can solve are far greater than the schoolmaster of two or three decades ago dreamed.

To be familiar with recent development, to be able to
view present-day educational problems in the light of their
historical evolution and their political and social bearings,
and to see the educational service in its proper setting as a
great national institution evolved by democracy to help it
solve its many perplexing problems, the writer holds to be
of fundamental importance to the beginning student of education and the teacher in our schools. Such a study offers

for education what a beginning course in history or economics or science does, in that it gives the student the cardinal points of the compass for the journey in the study of the subject, gives the larger problems of the field their proper historical setting, states the problems of the present and near future in terms which give them significance, reveals the ignorance and prejudice against which those who labored to make possible the educational organization which we inherit worked, shows the relations existing between the different institutions of society engaged in the educational service, reveals the forces which circumscribe and condition and direct and limit all our educational endeavors, and sets forth the fundamental principles in the light of which we labor.

It is from such a point of view that this book has been written. The first chapter gives the needed European background; the next two describe the establishment of education on our shores, and trace its development through the colonial and early national periods; the next four trace the half-century of struggle to establish education as a function of the State, and cover the period up to about 1850; the next two chapters give the background, in the work of Rousseau and Pestalozzi, needed to understand the great reorganization of elementary education traced in the chapter which follows, and which covered the period from 1860 up to about 1890; the far-reaching consequences of the vast social and industrial changes of the latter half of the nineteenth century are traced in Chapter XI; and the four remaining chapters deal with the twentieth-century problems which have arisen as a result of the social and industrial and political changes of the nineteenth century, and the attempts which have been made and are being made to find a solution for them. All but the first two chapters deal with educational development since the beginning of our national period; two fifths of the book deal with the period since 1860; and one third of the book with the problems which have arisen since about 1890, the attempts we have made to find solutions for them, and a look ahead.

This book is the outgrowth of many years of work in introducing beginning students to a study of the subject of education. For the past twenty-one years I have given the introductory course in the work of the Department of Education at the Leland Stanford Junior University. This course has been open to students of sophomore grade. At first I gave a course in the general history of education, beginning with the ancient civilizations and carrying the subject along to modern times. I soon came to feel that such a course, while of large value to the more advanced student of education, if made other than a fact course involves too mature thinking to be suitable to the needs of the beginning student. Then for a time I gave an introductory course on present-day educational theory and problems, but without the historical perspective. Then I changed again, and for the past dozen years have given the course substantially as presented in the present volume. In this last type of introductory course I have obtained an interest not awakened by either of the other plans. The course as at present given has been listed and described in the university announcements as follows:

1. *Public Education in the United States.* A consideration of the more important present-day problems in the organization, administration, and adjustment of public education in the United States, studied in the light of their historical development. An introductory course. Lectures, following a syllabus, with assigned readings. *3 units, Autumn quarter. (Cubberley.)*

After the completion of this course the student, at Stanford, passes to a second elementary and introductory course, dealing with present-day educational practice, and entitled "Introduction to the Study of Education." A text covering the work of this second course is now in preparation.

A number of my former students, who are now in college and normal-school positions as teachers of education, have taken my syllabus and have established similar courses in the institutions to which they have gone. They have repeatedly urged me to write up the course in book form, in part that they might use such a text with their classes, and in part that the course might find a wider place in normal schools and colleges as an introductory course. This I have not found time to do until now. In this new form I have revised and expanded the old syllabus outline, and have tried to make a text which would be a still more useful introduction to the study of education than my course has been. In particular I have tried to catch the spirit of our American educational development, and to use the facts as a background upon which to paint the picture which our national evolution presents. I have also tried to make the book a history of administrative progress rather than of theories about education.

To make the volume of greater teaching value I have appended to the chapters a series of questions for discussion, and to most of the chapters a short list of topics for investigation and report. To make the references given of greater value I have selected them carefully, prefixed an asterisk to the more important ones, tried to indicate their length and value to the student, and have omitted all, regardless of value, not likely to be found in a small normal-school or college library. The text of the volume as it is, with the questions for discussion and collateral reading selected from the references given, makes a very satisfactory four- or five-unit course for a period of twelve weeks, or a three-unit course for a period of sixteen weeks.

ELLWOOD P. CUBBERLEY

Stanford University, Cal.,
November 30, 1918.

CONTENTS

CONTENTS

FIGURES IN THE TEXT

PORTRAITS
AND OTHER ILLUSTRATIONS

PUBLIC EDUCATION IN THE UNITED STATES

CHAPTER I

OUR EUROPEAN BACKGROUND

Sources of our civilization. The problems which we are to-day facing in our American education have not come about by accident, but are the result of a long historical evolution, and are best understood if considered in the light of their historical development. The history of education is essentially a phase of the history of civilization. School organization and educational theory represent but a small part of the evolution, and must be considered after all as but an expression of the type of civilization which a people has gradually evolved. The road that man has traveled since the days when might made right and children had no rights which even parents were bound to respect, to a time when the child is regarded as of first importance and adults represented in the State declare by law that the child shall be cared for and educated for the welfare of the State, is a long road and at times a very crooked one. Its ups and downs have been those of the progress of civilization itself, and in consequence any history of education must be in part a history of the progress of the civilization of the people whose educational history is being traced.

The civilization which we to-day enjoy is a very complex thing, made up of many contributions, some large and some small, and from people in many different lands and ages. To trace even the different educational contributions back to their sources might be interesting, but it would take too long, and for our purposes would not be important. All *insight*

we need is sufficient background to give perspective and
color to the sketch of the development of our American
history and problems which it is here proposed to give.
Even this takes us back to European lands, and especially
to the later Middle Ages.

The civilization which we have inherited has come down
to us from three main sources, and in a fairly continuous
stream. The Greeks, the Romans, and the Christians laid
the foundations, and in the order named. On these three
foundation stones, superimposed upon one another, our
modern European and American civilization rests. We
have made many additions in modern times, building an
entirely new superstructure on these old foundations, but
the foundations for the structure of our civilization nevertheless were laid by Greece and Rome and Christianity.

The three foundation elements. The work of Greece
underlies all else. This wonderful people introduced a new
force into the world by placing a premium on personal and
political freedom and initiative, and by developing a literature, an art, and a philosophy which was to be a heritage
to all succeeding civilizations. In the lines of culture and
philosophic thought the world will always remain debtor
to this small but active, imaginative, artistic, and creative
people. To the Romans we are indebted for an entirely
different type of inheritance. They were weak where
Greece was strong, and strong where Greece was weak.
Their strength lay in law and government and the practical
arts. Rome absorbed and amalgamated the whole ancient
world into one Empire, to which she gave a common language, dress, manners, religion, literature, and government.
By imposing law and order and government on an unruly
world, and unifying the ancient civilizations into one organized whole, Rome laid the necessary basis for the success of
Christianity, and thus saved civilization from a great dis-
aster when the Germanic hordes poured over her Empire.

Into this Roman world, united by Roman arms and
government, came the first of the modern forces of our

present-day civilization — that of Christianity. Building
on Greek philosophic ideas and Roman governmental forms,
and with its new message for an old world, (Christianity
forms the connecting link and the preserving force between
the old and the new civilizations.) A new ethical force of
the first importance was by it added to the effective energies
of mankind, and a basis for the education of all, not to be
realized for centuries, to be sure, was laid for the first time
in the history of the world.

Christianity, too, came at just the right time to enable it
to organize and establish itself to meet and in time overcome and civilize the barbarian deluge from the North
which, in the fifth and sixth centuries, poured over the
boundaries of the Empire and almost obliterated the ancient
civilizations. The fall of the Roman Empire, and the long
struggle of the Christian Church to preserve civilization
from complete destruction at the hands of the Germanic
barbarians, is a story with which almost every one is
familiar. Progress ceased in the ancient world. The
creative force of antiquity seemed exhausted. The diges-
tive and assimilative powers of the old world were gone.
Greek was forgotten. Latin was corrupted. The knowledge of the arts and sciences was lost. Schools disappeared. Only the Christian Church remained to save
civilization from the wreck, and it too almost went under.
It took ten centuries to partially civilize, educate, and
reduce to national order this heterogeneous horde of new
peoples, and to preserve enough of the ancient civilization
so that the modern world has been able to reconstruct its
main outlines from the fragments which remained.

The period of the awakening. Finally, however, first in
Italy, and later in the new nations formed from the tribes
which raided the ancient Empire, there came a period of
awakening and discovery which led to a wonderful revival
of ancient learning, a great expansion of men's thoughts,
a general questioning of all ancient authority, a great religious awakening, a wonderful period of world exploration

and discovery, the founding of new nations in new lands, the reawakening of the old Greek spirit of scientific inquiry, and the evolution of our modern civilization. It was out of these new impulses and forces that America was discovered; out of the contests incident to the great revolt against religious authority, known among Protestants as the Reformation, that America was in large part colonized; and out of the rediscovery of the ancient literature and learning in the days of the Renaissance, and the Protestant belief in general education as a means to salvation, that the early traditions of American education were derived. The three main forces to which we owe our settlement and educational beginnings were the Renaissance, the Protestant Revolt, and the beginnings of scientific inquiry and world exploration and trade. Let us examine each of these, briefly, in order.

The thirteenth century has often been called the wonderful century of the mediæval world. It was wonderful largely in that the forces struggling against the oppressive mediævalism which had grown up as a result of the long effort of the Church to Christianize the barbarian and reduce him to some form of civilized order, in this century first find clear expression. It was a century of rapid and unmistakable progress in every line. It saw the evolution of the first of the universities, the beginnings of modern scholarship, the great era of guild-hall and cathedral building, a rapid expansion of reviving commerce, the rise of a burgher and lawyer class, distinct from the clergy and the nobility on the one hand and the craftsmen and apprentices on the other, and the evolution of modern States and modern languages as expressive of the new feeling of nationality which was beginning to pervade Europe. The fourteenth century was a period of even more rapid change. New objects of interest were brought to the front, and new standards of judgment were applied. The mediæval man, with his feelings of personal insignificance and lack of confidence, began to give way to men possessed of the modern spirit — men conscious of a past behind and a future before them, and capable of independence, action, initiative, and enjoyment. With this transformation in the character of life and change in the nature of human interests, Europe was ready for a revival of learning.

The Revival of Learning. The revival began in Italy, Petrarch (1304–1374) being regarded as the first modern scholar and man of letters in the Western World. In time the old monastic treasures were brought to light, the study of Greek was revived in the West, the first modern libraries and scientific academies were founded, and the history, literature, religion, and political and social life of the ancient world were reconstructed. In 1396 the first professorship of Greek in a university was created at Florence, then the center of art and literature and learning in the Western World.

So slowly did new ideas travel at that time that it was nearly a century before this revival began to be heard of north of the Alps. A professorship of Greek was created at Paris, in 1458; one at Seville in Spain, in 1473; and one at Vienna, in 1523. The German university of Erfurt established a professorship of Poetry and Eloquence, in 1493. Greek came to Oxford about 1490. Very fortunately for the spread of the new learning, an important process and a great invention now came at a most opportune time. The new process was the manufacture of paper, obtained from Mohammedan sources, the first paper-mill being set up in Italy, in 1276. By 1450 paper was in common use throughout Europe, and the way was open for one of the world's greatest inventions. This was made in German lands, the first engraved page dating from 1423, the first movable types from 1438, and the first printed book from 1456. By 1475 the printing-press had been set up in the leading cities of Europe. From then on the way was open for a rapid extension of schools and learning, and the press was destined in time to surpass in importance the pulpit and the sermon, and to become one of the world's greatest instruments for human progress and individual liberty.

The new classical secondary school. The important and
outstanding educational result of the revival of ancient
learning by Italian scholars was that it laid the basis for a
new type of school below that of the recently created colleges and universities, and one destined in time to be much
more widely opened to promising youths than the cathedral
and monastic schools of the Middle Ages had been. This
new school, basing its curriculum on the intellectual inheritance recovered from the ancient world by Italian scholars, dominated the secondary-school training of the middle
and higher classes of society for the next four hundred years.
This type of school was well under way by 1450, and it
clearly controlled education until after 1850. Out of the
efforts of Italian scholars to resurrect, reconstruct, understand, and utilize in education the fruits of our inheritance
from the Greek and Roman worlds, modern secondary education, as contrasted with mediæval church education,
arose. Classical schools, known as Court Schools in Italy,
Collèges and Lycées in France, Gymnasia in German lands,
and Latin Grammar Schools in England, were founded.
The reformed Latin Grammar School, founded by Dean
Colet, at St. Paul's in London, in 1510, thoroughly established the type, and was copied throughout England during
the succeeding century. Many of the old cathedral and
monastic schools of England were made over, after his
model, into reformed Latin Grammar Schools to teach pure
Latin and Greek and some elementary mathematics. In
particular these schools were to teach Latin as a restored
and living tongue. This type of secondary school had become common all through England by 1600, and it was the
type our early New England settlers knew and brought to
and set up in the American colonies.

The revolt against authority. Another outgrowth of the
Italian Renaissance, and for the history of education in
America a much more important development, was the
change in attitude toward the dogmatic and repressive rule
of the Church which came as a somewhat natural result of

the work of the Renaissance scholars, the new life in Christendom consequent upon the Crusades, the revival of commerce, the rise of city governments, the formation of lawyer
and merchant classes, the founding of new States, the evolution of the university organizations, and the discovery and
spread of the art of printing. All these forces united to
awaken a new attitude toward the old religious problems,
and to prepare Western Europe for a rapid evolution out
of the mediæval conditions which had for so long dominated
all action and thinking. Had the Church realized this, and
assumed a tolerant attitude toward the many progressive
tendencies of the time, the whole history of modern life.
and particularly the history of educational development in
America, with which in this volume we are to be particularly concerned, might have been different. But it did not,
and whether we be Catholic or Protestant makes no difference with the facts of history. So far as the Protestant
Reformation is concerned, we may believe that Luther and
Zwingli and Calvin and Knox were merely ambitious and
selfish disturbers who made trouble without cause, or we
may go to the opposite extreme and believe that they were
inspired men, leading the world back to a truer religion.
The facts of history remain the same in either case, and our
religious beliefs need in no way enter into the problem.
The great outstanding fact remains that one Martin Luther,
in 1517, disputed the practices of the Church, later defied
its authority, and was excommunicated by it in 1520; that
the German people, and especially the German princes,
largely adopted Luther's point of view and revolted; and
that the revolt spread to other countries in the North and
West of Europe, and as a result the Western or Roman
Catholic Church, which had remained one for so many
centuries and been the one great unifying force in Western
Europe, was permanently divided. How much of Europe
was lost to the Church is shown by the map on the following
page.

The resulting conflict. Of course the revolt against the authority of the Church, once inaugurated, could not be easily stopped. This is nearly always the case when revolution has to be resorted to to secure progress or reform. The same right of freedom in religious belief which Luther claimed for himself and his followers had of course to be

FIG. 1. RESULTS OF THE PROTESTANT REVOLTS

extended to others. This the German, the English, and other Protestants were not much more willing to do than had been the Catholics before them. The world was not as yet ready for such rapid advances, and religious toleration, though established in principle by the revolt, was an idea to which the world required a long time to accustom itself. It took a century and a half of intermittent religious warfare, during which Catholic and Protestant waged war on one another, plundered and pillaged lands, and killed each other for the salvation of their respective souls, before the people of Western Europe were willing to stop fighting and recognize for others that for which they were fighting for themselves. For still another century the world was divided into hostile camps as a result of the hatreds engendered by this religious warfare. When religious toleration became established by law, civilization had made a tremendous advance. The result of this long religious strife was to check the orderly progress of civilization, spread misery and suffering abroad, and drive from the countries persecuted those who would rather leave than conform. It was from among these irreconcilable non-conformists that the early settlers of most of our American colonies were drawn. The early educational history of America is hardly to be understood without some knowledge of the different religious forces and hatreds awakened as a result of the Protestant Revolt.

The dominant idea, and its educational consequences. What we are primarily concerned with, however, are the educational consequences of this break with authority. To understand this we need to know the dominant idea underlying Luther's action, and for that matter the action of Zwingli, Calvin, and Knox as well. The idea was that of substituting the authority of the Bible in religious matters for the authority of the Church, and was in turn one of the results of the revival of the study of Greek and the recovery of the Gospels in the original. This meant the substitution of individual responsibility for salvation for the collective responsibility of the Church, and meant that those who were to be saved, in theory at least, must be able to read the word of God, participate intelligently in the Church service, and shape their lives in accordance with the commands of the Heavenly Father. Whether one accepts the Protestant position as sound or not depends largely on one's religious training and beliefs, and need not concern us here, as it makes no difference with the course which history has actually taken. We can believe either way, and the course of history remains the same.

The educational consequences of this position, though, were important, and are our chief concern. Under the older religious theory of collective judgment and collective responsibility for salvation — that is, the judgment of the Church rather than that of individuals — it was not important that more than a few be educated. Under the new theory of individual responsibility promulgated by the Protestants the education of all became a vital necessity. To provide this meant the creation of an entirely new type of school — the elementary, for the masses, and in the native tongue — to supplement the secondary Latin schools of the Renaissance and the still older cathedral and monastic Latin schools for the education of those who were to become the leaders in Church and State. These schools were in time created, and the result of the evolution in the centuries since has been the development, all through Europe, of a double school system, the two parts of which — an elementary school system for the masses, and a secondary school system for the classes — have but little in common. We in America started this way also, but before such a development had made much headway it was turned aside by the rise of a distinctively American and democratic spirit, as will be explained in subsequent chapters, which in time demanded one common school system for all.

The modern elementary vernacular school then may be said to be essentially a product of the Protestant Reformation. This is true in a special sense among those peoples which embraced some form of the Lutheran or Calvinistic faiths. These were the Germans, Moravians, Swedes, Norwegians, Danes, Dutch, Walloons, Swiss, Scotch, Scotch-Irish, French Huguenots, and the English Puritans. As the Renaissance gave a new emphasis to the development of secondary schools by supplying them with a large amount of new subject-matter and a new motive, so the Reformation movement gave a new motive for the education of children not intended for the service of the State or the Church, and the development of elementary vernacular schools was the result. Only in England, of all the revolting countries, did this Protestant conception as to the necessity of education for salvation fail to take root, with the result that elementary education in England awaited the new political and industrial impulses of the latter half of the nineteenth century for its development. These educational attitudes were all faithfully reflected in the settlement of the American colonies, as we shall see in the next chapter.

The discovery and settlement of America. The discovery of America was another development of the desire for travel and discovery awakened by the Crusades, the revival of commerce which now sought a sea-route to the riches of the Indies, and the new intellectual life in Christendom which stimulated thinkers to question the old theories as to the shape and position of our earth. These impulses led to the perfecting of the compass in the fourteenth century, the revival of geographical discovery, the rounding of the Cape of Good Hope (1487), the discovery of the new world (1492), and the circumnavigation of the globe by Magellan (1519–21).

After the first century of exploration of the new continent had passed, and after the claims as to ownership had been largely settled, colonization began. The first, that of Virginia, was actuated wholly by gain, and rested on a commercial basis. This was also largely true of the other southern colonies. To the northward, however, the settlements were mostly due to the desire to secure religious freedom, and resulted from the warfare and persecution following the Protestant Revolt in Europe. Those who came to establish new homes along the bleak Atlantic coast did so that here, in a new land, they might establish their churches, order their civil life, and bring up their children to worship God after the dictates of their own conscience. It took a high degree of courage and deep religious conviction to cause men, at that time, to take such a step, as it meant the giving up of all the associations of a lifetime and the bringing of their families to a new and unbroken land to start life over again. The result was that the American colonies settled from religious motives were from the first peopled by a splendid stock, and the character of this stock has repeatedly shown itself in the history of the different colonies and later in the history of our Nation.   Just what our different colonists came for, what they tried to do by means of education, what types of schools and educational attitudes they established here, and how their belief in education for salvation or lack of such has colored our whole colonial and national history, it will be the purpose of the chapters which follow to set forth.

QUESTIONS FOR DISCUSSION

1. Would any type of general education be possible among a people where might made right?
2. Give a number of illustrations to show the presence of Greek and Roman elements in the foundations of our civilization.
3. Compare the barbarian invasions of the fifth and sixth centuries with the Bolshevik destructions of the twentieth.
4. Why did it take so long for the revival of the study of Greek to extend over Western Europe?
5. Show how the evolution of Latin higher schools for the education of boys from the middle and higher classes of society was a perfectly natural evolution.
6. Show how the elementary vernacular school was a natural outgrowth of the Protestant Revolts and the invention of printing.
7. Show that a class, instead of a common or mass system of education, has been perfectly natural for European states.

CHAPTER II

THE BEGINNINGS OF AMERICAN EDUCATION

I. ORIGIN OF OUR TYPE ATTITUDES TOWARD EDUCATION

Religious origin of our schools. Schools, with us, as with the older European countries from which our early settlers came, arose as children of the Church. From instruments of religion they have been gradually changed into instruments of the State. The first schools in America were clearly the fruits of the Protestant Revolt in Europe. The reformers everywhere had insisted upon the necessity of the Gospels as a means to personal salvation. This meant, carried to its logical conclusion, that each child, girls as well as boys, should be taught to read so that they might become acquainted with the commandments of God and learn what was demanded of them. Not being able to realize their ideals of life and worship in the old home lands, large numbers of religious congregations left Europe and came as bodies to America. Here they settled in the wilderness and began life anew. Among other things they brought with them their European ideas as to religion and the training of children, and hence a European background lies behind all the beginnings of American education.

Practically all of the early settlers of America came from among those people and from those lands which had embraced some form of the Protestant faith, and most of them came to America to enjoy a religious freedom impossible in the countries from which they came. This was especially true of the French Huguenots, who settled along the coast of the Carolinas; the Calvinistic Dutch and Walloons, who settled in and about New Amsterdam; the Scotch and Scotch-Irish Presbyterians, who settled in New Jersey, and later extended along the Allegheny Mountain ridges into

all the southern colonies; the English Quakers about Philadelphia, and a few English Baptists and Methodists in

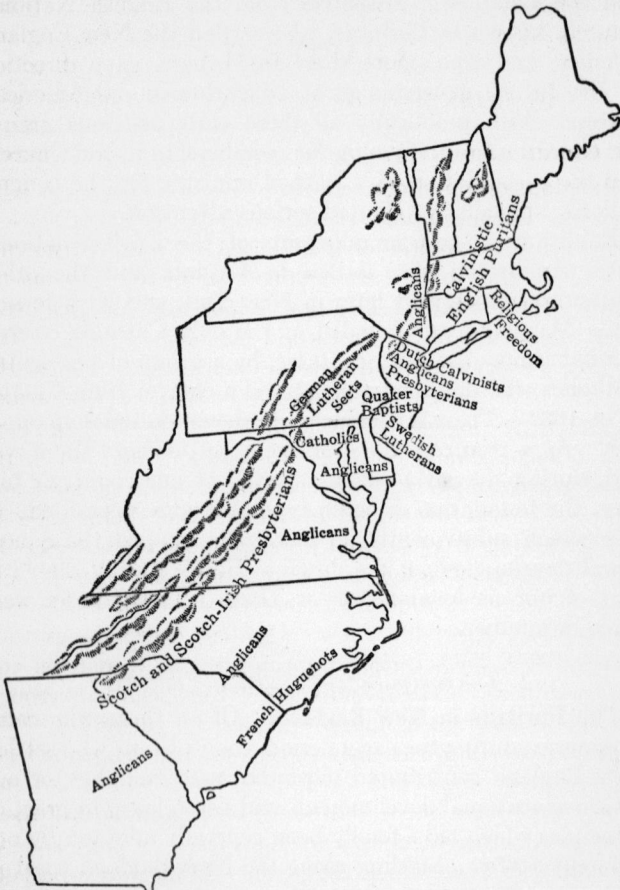

FIG. 2. SHOWING THE RELIGIOUS FAITHS OF THE EARLY COLONISTS IN
AMERICA

eastern Pennsylvania; the Swedish Lutherans along the
Delaware; the German Lutherans, Moravians, Mennonites,

Dunkers, and Reformed-Church Germans who settled in
large numbers in the mountain valleys of Pennsylvania;
and the Calvinistic dissenters from the English National
Church, known as Puritans, who settled the New England
colonies, and who, more than any others, gave direction
to the future development of education in our American
States.   With practically all these early religious groups
the education of the young for membership in the Church,
and the perpetuation of a learned ministry for the congregations, immediately elicited serious attention.

Englishmen who were adherents of the English national
faith (Anglicans) also settled in Virginia and the other
southern colonies, and later in New York and New Jersey,
while Maryland was founded as the only Catholic colony,
in what is now the United States, by a group of persecuted
Catholics who obtained a grant and a charter from Charles
I, in 1632.   These settlements are shown on the map opposite.   As a result of these different settlements there was
laid, during the early colonial period of our country's history, the foundation of those type attitudes toward education which subsequently so materially shaped the educational development of the different States during the early
part of our national history.   These type attitudes were
three in number.

1. The compulsory-maintenance attitude

The Puritans in New England.   Of all those who came
to America during the early period, the Puritans who settled
New England contributed most that was valuable for our
future educational development, and established in practice
principles which have finally been generally adopted by our
different States.   Settling along the New England coast in
little groups or congregations, they at once set up a combined
civil and religious form of government which became known
as a New England town.   The "Meeting House" was the
center of their civil and religious life, and in it they met
both as a religious congregation and as a civil government.

The two were one in membership and spirit. Being deeply imbued with Calvinistic ideas as to religion and government, the Puritans founded here a series of little town governments, but loosely bound together in Colony federations, the corner stones of which were religion and education. The attitude of the early Puritans toward religion and learning is well expressed in the following extract from an early New England pamphlet, *New England's First Fruits*, printed in London in 1643:

> After God had carried vs safe to New England
> And wee had builded ovr hovses
> Provided necessaries for ovr liveli hood
> Reard convenient places for Gods worship
> And setled the civill government
> One of the next things we longed for
> And looked after was to advance learning
> And perpetvate it to posterity
> Dreading to leave an illiterate ministry
> To the churches when ovr present ministers
> Shall lie in the Dvst.

At first home instruction and apprenticeship training were depended upon to furnish the necessary ability to read and to participate in the home and church religious services, the great religious purpose which had brought the colonists to America being the motive which was to insure such instruction. In addition, the town religious governments began the voluntary establishment of town Latin Schools to prepare boys for the college (Harvard) which the colonial legislature had established, in 1636. In this establishment in the wilderness of New England of a typical English educational system of the time — that is, private instruction in reading and religion in the homes and by the master of apprentices, Latin grammar schools in the larger towns to prepare boys for the colony college, and an English-type college to prepare ministers for the churches — we see manifested the deep Puritan-Calvinistic zeal for education as a bulwark of Church and State. As in England, the system was voluntary, and clearly subordinate to the Church.

The Massachusetts Law of 1642. It early became evident, however, that these voluntary efforts on the part of the people and the towns would not be sufficient to insure that general education which was required by the Puritan religious theory. Under the hard pioneer conditions and the suffering which ensued, many parents and masters of apprentices apparently proved neglectful of their educational duties. Accordingly the leaders in the Puritan Church appealed to what was then their servant, the State as represented in the colonial legislature, to assist them in compelling parents and masters to observe their obligations. The result was the famous Massachusetts Law of 1642, which directed the officials of each town to ascertain, from time to time, if parents and masters were attending to their educational duties; if all children were being trained "in learning and labor and other employments profitable to the Commonwealth"; and if the children were being taught "to read and understand the principles of religion and the capital laws of the country." The officers were empowered to impose fines on those who failed to give proper instruction, or to report to the officer when required. This Law of 1642 is remarkable in that, for the first time in the English-speaking world, a legislative body representing the State ordered that all children should be taught to read. This was a distinctively Calvinistic contribution to our new-world life, and a contribution of large future importance.

The Massachusetts Law of 1647. The Law, however, did not establish schools, nor did it direct the employment of schoolmasters. After true English fashion, the provision of education was still left with the homes. The results still continuing unsatisfactory, five years later the colonial legislature enacted the famous Law of 1647, by means of which it has been asserted that "the Puritan government of Massachusetts rendered probably its greatest service to the future." After recounting in a preamble that it had in the past been "one chief point of that old deluder, Satan, to keep men from a knowledge of the Scriptures . . . by keeping them in an unknown tongue," so now "by persuading from the use of tongues," . . . learning was in danger of "being buried in the grave of our fathers in church and commonwealth," the Law then ordered:

1. That every town having 50 householders should at once appoint a teacher of reading and writing, and provide for his wages in such manner as the town might determine; and

2. That every town having 100 householders must provide a (Latin) grammar school to fit youths for the university, under a penalty of £5 for failure to do so.

This Law represents a distinct advance over the Law of 1642. The State here, acting again as the servant of the Church, enacted a law for which there were no English precedents. Not only was a school system ordered established — elementary for all towns and children, and secondary for the youths in the larger towns — but, for the first time among English-speaking people, there was the assertion of the right of the State to require communities to establish and maintain schools, under penalty of a fine if they refused to do so.

Importance of these two laws. It can safely be asserted that these two Massachusetts laws of 1642 and 1647 represent not only new educational ideas in the English-speaking world, but that they also represent the very foundation stones upon which our American public school systems have been constructed.

Mr. Martin, the historian of the Massachusetts public school system, states the fundamental principles which underlie this legislation as follows:

1. The universal education of youth is essential to the well-being of the State.
2. The obligation to furnish this education rests primarily upon the parent.
3. The State has a right to enforce this obligation.
4. The State may fix a standard which shall determine the kind of education, and the minimum amount.

5. Public money, raised by a general tax, may be used to provide such education as the State requires. This tax may be general, though the school attendance is not.

6. Education higher than the rudiments may be supplied by the State. Opportunity must be provided, at public expense, for youths who wish to be fitted for the university.

Mr. Martin then adds the following significant comment:

It is important to note here that the idea underlying all this legislation was neither paternalistic nor socialistic. The child is to be educated, not to advance his personal interests, *but because the State will suffer if he is not educated*. The State does not provide schools to relieve the parent, nor because it can educate better than the parent can, but because it can thereby better enforce the obligation which it imposes.

These laws became the basis for legislation in all the other New England colonies, except Rhode Island, which had been founded on the basis of religious freedom, and the conceptions as to the establishment and maintenance of schools which they embodied deeply influenced the educational development of all the States to which New England people later migrated in any numbers.

In New England, then, was established the first of the three important type attitudes to which we earlier referred, — that of the State compelling the towns to establish schools, and

FIG. 3. TOWN SCHOOL AT DEDHAM, MASSACHUSETTS, BUILT IN 1648

parents to send their children to school to learn to read and to receive instruction in religion. The State here, acting as the servant of the Church, enacted legislation which formed a precedent and fixed a tradition as to school management and support which was retained long after State and Church had parted company.

2. The parochial-school attitude

Pennsylvania as a type. In New England the Puritan-
Calvinists had had a complete monopoly of both Church
and State. Into the middle colonies, best represented by
Pennsylvania, there had come a mixture of peoples representing different Protestant faiths, and no such monopoly
was possible in these colonies. The English and Dutch had
mixed in New York; the English, Dutch, Swedes, Scotch-
Irish, and Germans had settled in New Jersey; while in
Pennsylvania, which Penn had founded on the basis of
religious freedom, a large number of English and German
Protestant sects had settled. All were Protestant in faith,
though representing different creeds and nationalities; all
believed in the importance of being able to read the Bible as
a means to personal salvation; and all made efforts looking
toward the establishment of schools as a part of their church
organizations. Unlike New England, though, no sect was in
a majority. Church control by each denomination was, as a
result, considered to be most satisfactory, and hence no appeal to the State was made by the churches for assistance
in carrying out their religious purposes. The clergymen
were usually the teachers in the parochial schools established, while private pay schools were opened in a few of the
larger towns. These, as were the church services, were conducted in the language of the different immigrants. Girls
were educated as well as boys, the emphasis being placed
on reading, writing, counting, and religion, rather than
upon any form of higher training.

The result was the development in Pennsylvania, and to
some extent in the other middle colonies as well, of a policy
of depending upon Church and private effort for educational advantages, and the provision of education, aside
from certain rudimentary and religious instruction thought
necessary for religious purposes, was left largely for those
who could afford to pay for the privilege.

Under the freedom allowed many communities made but

indifferent provisions, or allowed their schools to lapse
entirely. In the primitive conditions of the time the interest even in religious education frequently declined almost to
the vanishing point. Two attempts were made, later on,
to enforce the maintenance of schools in the colony; but one
was vetoed by William and Mary as foreign to English practices, and the other proved unenforceable. In consequence,
Pennsylvania settled down to a policy of leaving education
to private and parochial effort, and in time this attitude
became so firmly established that the do-as-you-please idea
persisted up to 1834, and was only overcome then after
bitter opposition. In New Jersey and New York this same
policy prevailed during the whole of the colonial period.
Each parochial group did as it wished, and private and
church effort, in pay and charity schools, provided practically all the educational facilities available until well into
our national period.

3. The pauper-school non-state-interference attitude

Virginia as the type. In the settlement of Virginia and
the southern colonies, almost all the attending conditions
were in contrast with those of the New England colonies.
The early settlers were from the same class of English
people, but with the important difference that, whereas the
New England settlers were dissenters from the English
National Church and had come to America to obtain freedom in religious worship, the settlers in Virginia were adherents of that Church and had come to America for gain.
The marked differences in climate and possible crops led to
the large-plantation type of settlement, instead of the compact little New England town; the introduction of numbers
of "indentured white servants," and later negro slaves, led
to the development of classes in society instead of to the
New England type of democracy, making common schools
impossible; and the lack of any strong religious motive for
education naturally led to the adoption of English practices
instead of the development of distinctively colonial schools.

The tutor in the home, education in small private and select pay-schools, or education in the mother country for the
sons of the well-to-do planters were the prevailing methods
adopted among the wealthier people, while the poorer
classes were left with only such advantages as apprenticeship training and the few pauper schools of the time might
provide.

Practically all the Virginia colonial legislation relating
to education refers either to William and Mary College,
founded in 1693, or to the education of orphans and the children of the poor. Both these interests were typically English. The seventeenth-century legislation included the compulsory apprenticeship of the children of the poor, training in
a trade, the requirement that the public authorities must
provide opportunities for this type of education, and the use
of both local and colony funds for the purpose — all, as the
Statutes state, "according to the aforesaid laudable custom
in the Kingdom of England." It was not until 1705 that
Virginia reached the point reached by Massachusetts in
1642 of requiring that "the master of the [apprenticed]
orphan shall be obliged to teach him to read and write."
During the entire colonial period the indifference of the
mother country to general education was steadily reflected
in Virginia and the other colonies which followed the English example. As in the mother country, education was not
considered as any business of the State, nor did the Church
give any great attention to it. Virginia thus stands as
the clearest example of the third type of colonial attitude
toward education, — viz., tutors and private schools for
those who could afford them, church charity schools for
some of the children of the poorer members, but no State
interest in the problem of education except to see that
orphans and children of the very poor were properly apprenticed and trained in some useful trade, which in Virginia usually was agriculture.

This type in other colonies. In the other American colonies which followed the example of Virginia — New

York, New Jersey, Delaware, Maryland, the Carolinas, and
Georgia — the English charity-school idea largely dominated such education as was provided, with the apprenticing of orphans a prominent feature. The "Society for the
Propagation of the Gospel in Foreign Parts," an English
society, chartered in 1701, to act as an auxiliary of the
Church of England "to train children in the tenets and worship of the Church, through the direct agency of schools,"
provided for these Anglican colonies probably the best
charity schools in America during the later colonial period.
The work of this Society in New York was specially noteworthy, though valuable work was done in other colonies.
Its schoolmasters were well selected and sound in the faith,
and the children were taught reading, writing, a little arithmetic, the catechism, and the religious observances of the
English National Church. The church charity schools of
this Society furnished the nearest approach to a free school
system found in the Anglican colonies before the Revolution.
They were, though, only for a class, being usually open only
to the children of the poorer communicants in the Anglican
Church.

Type attitudes represented by 1750. The seventeenth
century witnessed the transplanting of European ideas as to
government and religion and education to the New American colonies, and by the eighteenth century we find three
clearly marked types of educational practice or conceptions
as to educational responsibility established on American soil.

The first was the strong Calvinistic conception of a religious State, supporting a system of common schools,
higher Latin schools, and a college, both for religious and
civic ends. This type dominated New England, and is
best represented by Massachusetts. From New England
it spread westward, and deeply influenced the educational
development of all States to which New England people
migrated. It was the educational contribution of Calvinism
to America. Out of it, by the later separation of Church and
State, our modern state school systems have been evolved.

The second was the parochial school conception of the Dutch, Moravians, Mennonites, German Lutherans, German-Reformed Church, Quakers, Presbyterians, Baptists, and Catholics. This type is best represented by Protestant Pennsylvania and Catholic Maryland. It stood for church control of all educational effort, resented state interference, was dominated only by church purposes, and in time came to be a serious obstacle in the way of state organization and control.

The third type, into which the second type tended to fuse, was the attitude of the Church of England, which conceived of public education, aside from collegiate education, as intended chiefly for orphans and the children of the poor, and as a charity which the State was under little or no obligation to assist in supporting. All children of the upper and middle classes in society attended private or church schools, or were taught by tutors in their homes, and for such instruction paid a proper tuition fee. Paupers and orphans, in limited numbers were, for a limited time, provided with some form of useful education at the expense of either the Church or the State.

These three types or attitude toward public education became fixed American types, and deeply influenced subsequent American educational development, as we shall see in the chapters which follow.

II. Types of Schools transplanted and developed

Transplanting the old home institutions. At the time the early colonists came to America the parish elementary school for religious training had become an established institution in German lands, while in England three main types of schools had been developed. All of these were transplanted to America, and established here in much the same form that they had developed in the home lands. The Dutch in New Amsterdam, the Swedes along the Delaware, and the different German sects in Pennsylvania and the other colonies where they settled, reproduced in America the

Lutheran parish school of Europe, with its instruction in reading, singing, religion, and sometimes writing, and taught usually by the pastor, but sometimes by the sexton or other teacher. This type of school continued largely unchanged throughout the whole of the colonial period. The English, who formed the great bulk of the early immigrants to the American colonies, reproduced in the different colonies the main types of schools at that time existing in the mother country. These were the petty or dame school, the writing school, and the Latin grammar school for those who could afford to pay for education; the charity or pauper elementary school for a limited number of indigents; and apprenticeship training for orphans and the children of pauper parents. The first three became the characteristic schools of New England, and the last two largely characterized the English educational work in the central and southern colonies. It was these English-type schools, rather than the continental European type of parochial school of the central colonies, which exerted the greatest influence on our early American educational development.

The petty or dame school. The dame school was a very elementary school, kept in a kitchen or living room by some woman who, in her youth, had obtained the rudiments of an education, and who now desired to earn a pittance for herself by imparting to the children of her neighborhood her small store of learning. For a few pennies a week the dame took the children of neighbors into her home and explained to them the mysteries connected with learning the beginnings of reading and spelling. Occasionally a little writing and counting also was taught, but not often. Originating in England after the Reformation, and introduced into New England by the early colonists, it flourished greatly in America during the eighteenth century, while in England it continued popular until well into the nineteenth. While men teachers were employed at first in the town schools, the dame school soon became the primary school of colonial New England, and instruction in the A B Cs and the elements of reading and writing in it became a prerequisite for admission to the town grammar school.

Origin of the school of the 3-Rs. The second type of school brought over was the writing school, a school in which writing, reckoning, and the simplest elements of merchants' accounts were taught. The masters in this also gave instruction in writing to the boys in the third type of school brought over — the Latin grammar school. Sometimes the instruction was given in a separate school, taught by a "scrivener" and arithmetic teacher, and sometimes the writing and reckoning were taught by a peripatetic scrivener, who moved about as business seemed to warrant. The writing school never became common in New England, as the exigencies of a new and sparsely settled country tended to force a combination of the dame and the writing school into one, thus forming the school of the so-called 3-Rs — "Readin, Ritin, and Rithmetic" — from which our elementary schools later were evolved. Among the Dutch, Quakers, and Germans of the middle colonies as well this combination was commonly found in their parochial schools, and from it their elementary schools also evolved.

The Latin grammar school. The third type of school brought over, and for New England the important school of the early period, was the Latin grammar school. In this the great teachers of the early time were found. By this was meant a school for beginners in Latin, still the sacred language of religion and learning, and upon the study of which the main energy of the schools was spent. The school took the boy from the dame school at the age of seven or eight, and prepared him for entrance to college at fifteen, or thereabout, the boy in the meantime having learned to read, write, and make his own quill pens, and having mastered sufficient Latin to enter the college of the colony. He was usually ignorant of numbers, and was usually unable to write English with any degree of fluency or accuracy. He was, however, well schooled in the Latin tongue, and usually in the elements of Greek as well. The purpose of the

FIG. 4. A DAME SCHOOL.

Latin school is well stated by the admission requirements of Harvard College, in 1642, which read:

When any Scholler is able to understand Tully, or such like classicall Latine author extempore, and make and speake true Latine in verse and prose, *suo ut aiunt Marte:* and decline perfectly the paradigms of nounes and verbes in the Greek tongue: let him then, and not before, be capable of admission into the Colledge.

The Latin grammar school attained its greatest development in New England, where such schools had been required by the law of 1647, and where the attitude toward classical study was distinctly more friendly than in the colonies to the southward. Latin grammar schools were, however, found here and there in the few large towns of the middle and southern colonies, though in these the commercial demands early made themselves felt, and the tendency in the higher schools was toward the introduction

Fig. 5. The Boston Latin Grammar School

Showing the school as it was in Cheever's day, with King's Chapel on the left, the school facing on School Street.

of more practical studies, such as merchants' accounts, navigation, surveying, and the higher mathematics. This in time led to the evolution of a distinctively American type of higher school, with a more practical curriculum — the Academy — and this in time displaced the Latin grammar school, even in New England.

III. General Character of the Colonial Schools

Dominance of the religious purpose. The most prominent characteristic of all the early colonial schooling was the predominance of the religious purpose in instruction. One learned to read chiefly the Catechism and the Bible, and to know the will of the Heavenly Father. There was scarcely any other purpose in the maintenance of elementary schools. In Connecticut colony the law required that the pupils were to be made "in some competent measure to understand the main grounds and principles of Christian Religion necessary to salvation," and "to learn some orthodox catechism." In the grammar schools and the colleges students were instructed to consider well the main end of life and studies. These institutions existed mainly to insure a supply of learned ministers for service in the Church and the State. Such studies as history, geography, science, music, drawing, secular literature, and physical training were unknown. Children were constantly surrounded, week days and Sundays, by the somber Calvinistic religious atmosphere in New England, and by the careful religious oversight of the pastors and elders in the colonies where the parochial school system was the ruling plan for education. Schoolmasters were required "to catechise their scholars in the principles of the Christian religion," and it was made "a chief part of the schoolmaster's religious care to commend his scholars and his labors amongst them unto God by prayer morning and evening, taking care that his scholars do reverently attend during the same." Religious matter constituted the only reading matter, outside of the instruction in Latin in the grammar schools. The Catechism was taught and the Bible was read and expounded. Church attendance was required, and grammar school pupils were obliged to report each week on the Sunday sermon. This insistence on the religious element was more prominent in Calvinistic New England than in the colonies to the south, but everywhere the religious purpose was dominant. The church parochial and charity schools were essentially schools for instilling the church practices and the beliefs of the churches maintaining them. This state of affairs continued well toward the beginning of our national period.

This dominance of the religious purpose was well shown

in the textbooks used for instruction.   Down to the time
of the American Revolution these were English in their
origin and religious in their purpose.   The *Hornbook*, the
Primer, the *Psalter*, the *Testament*, and the *Bible* were the
books used.   It was not until about the time of the Revolution that the first American secu-
lar textbook appeared.

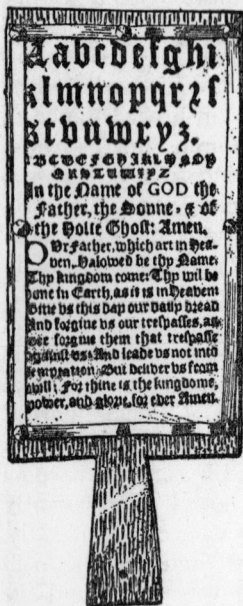

FIG. 6. A HORNBOOK

The textbooks used.   Instruction at first everywhere began with
the *Hornbook*, from which children
learned their letters and began to
read.   This was a thin board on
which a printed leaf was pasted,
and this was covered with a thin
sheet of transparent horn to protect it from dirty fingers.   Figure 6
shows a common form of this
early type of primer, the mastery
of which usually required some
time.   Cowper thus describes this
little book:

Neatly secured from being soiled or torn
Beneath a pane of thin translucent horn,
A book (to please us at a tender age
'T is called a book, though but a single page)
Presents the prayer the Savior designed to
    teach,
Which children use, and parsons — when
    they preach.

Having learned to read, the child next passed to the *Catechism* and the *Bible;* these constituted the entire range of
reading in the schools.

The New England Primer.   In 1690 there appeared a wonderful little volume, known as *The New England Primer*,
which at once leaped into popularity and soon superseded
the *Hornbook* as the beginning reading text, not only in New
England but in the schools of all the colonies except those
under the control of the Church of England.   For the next

In Adam's Fall
We sinned all.

Thy Life to mend,
This Book attend.

The Cat doth play,
And after slay.

A Dog will bite
A Thief at Night.

An Eagle' flight
Is out of sight.

The idle Fool
Is whipt at School

A page of the Illustrated Alphabet.

Praise to GOD for learning to Read.

THE Praises of my Tongue
I offer to the LORD,
That I was taught and learnt so young
To read his holy Word.

2 That I was brought to know
The Danger I was in,
By Nature and by Practice too
A wretched slave to Sin:

3 That I was led to see
I can do nothing well;
And whether shall a Sinner flee
To save himself from Hell.

A page of the Reading Matter.

FIG. 7. TWO SPECIMEN PAGES FROM THE NEW ENGLAND PRIMER

century and a quarter it was the chief school and reading book in use among the Dissenters and Lutherans in America. Such spelling as was taught was taught from it also. Being religious in the nature of its contents it was used both in the school and the church, the schoolmasters drilled the children in the reading matter and the catechism in the schools, and the people recited the catechism yearly in the churches. Every home possessed copies of it, and it was for sale at all bookstores, even in the smaller places, for a century and a half. It was reprinted throughout the colonies under different names, but the public preferred the title *New England Primer* to any other. Its total sales have been estimated to have been at least three million copies. It was used in the Boston dame schools as late as 1806, and in the country districts still later, but was gradually discarded for newer types of secular readers. Compared with the primers and first readers of to-day it seems poor and crude, but probably no modern textbook will ever exercise the influence over children and adults which was exercised by this little religious reader, $3\frac{1}{4}$ by $4\frac{1}{2}$ inches in size, and but 88 pages thick. It has been said of it that "it taught millions to read, and not one to sin." The *Psalter*, the *Testament*, and the *Bible* were its natural continuation, and constituted the main advanced reading books in the colonies before about 1750.

Other texts. A textbook was seldom used in teaching arithmetic by the colonial schoolmasters. The study itself was common, but not universal. It was not until the beginning of our national period that arithmetic was anywhere made a required subject of instruction. The subject was regarded as one of much difficulty, and one in which few teachers were competent to give instruction, or few pupils competent to understand. To possess a reputation as an "arithmeticker" was an important recommendation for a teacher, while for a pupil to be able to do sums in arithmetic was a matter of much pride to parents. Teacher's contracts frequently required that the teacher should

— do his faithful, honest, and true endeavor to teach the children or servants of those who have subscribed the reading and writing of English, and also arithmetick, if they desire it; as much as they are capable to learn and he capable to teach them within the compas of this year.

The teacher might or might not possess an arithmetic of his own, but the instruction to pupils was dictated and copied instruction. Each pupil made his own written book of rules and solved problems, and most pupils never saw a printed arithmetic. It was not until about the middle of the eighteenth century that printed arithmetics came into use, and then only in the larger towns.

Writing, similarly, was taught by dictation and practice, and the art of the "scrivener," as the writing master was called, was very elaborate and involved much drill and many flourishes. The difficulty of mastering the art, its lack of practical value to most children, the high cost of paper, and the necessity usually for special lessons, all alike tended to make writing a much less commonly known art than reading.

For the Latin grammar schools the great American text-book, for more than a century, was *Cheever's Accidence,* prepared by perhaps the most famous of all early American schoolmasters, Ezekiel Cheever. The book was prepared while Mr. Cheever was in charge of the Latin grammar school at New Haven (1641–1650), and was published prior to 1650. For more than a hundred years this was the text-book of the Latin grammar schools of all New England, and it was also extensively used as a text wherever Latin was taught in the other American colonies.

The teachers. The best teachers during the earlier colonial period were the teachers in the Latin grammar schools of New England. They were usually well-educated men, strict in the faith, and capable as teachers. A few attained a fame which has made them remembered to the present time. Among these Ezekiel Cheever (1614–1708), mentioned above, a graduate of Cambridge, in England, who came to America at the age of twenty-three, and who served

for seventy years as a teacher in New England and for
thirty-eight years as head of the Boston Latin School; and
Elijah Corlett (1611–1687), for forty-three years head of the
Cambridge Latin School, were the most famous. Of these,
Cotton Mather wrote, at the time of the death of Cheever:

> Tis CORLETS pains, & CHEEVER'S, we must own,
> That thou, *New England*, art not *Scythia* grown.

Many of the early teachers in the reading schools were
men of some learning, but the meager pay in time turned
the instruction in these schools over to college students and
local or itinerant schoolmasters in winter, and to women in
summer, and eventually the dame school supplanted the
town elementary school. Girls were usually admitted to
the summer, but not to the winter school, and they were
taught only reading, writing, and religion. The teachers
in the middle-colonies parochial schools were usually good,
carefully selected by their churches, sound in the faith, and
rendered service which for the time was reasonably satisfactory. This was especially true of the teachers in the
schools of the Anglican Church "Society for the Propagation of the Gospel in Foreign Parts," which operated in many
towns and cities in the English colonies between 1702 and
1782. The poorest teachers were to be found in the private
schools, many of them being itinerant teachers. Others
were of the so-called "indentured white servants" class —
poor men or criminals sent over from England and sold for a
certain number of years of labor, usually four or five, to pay
for their passage. These were let out by their purchasers
to conduct a school, the proceeds of which went to their
owners. The advertisement shows such a teacher for sale.

To Be DISPOSED of,

A Likely Servant Mans Time for 4 Years
who is very well Qualified for a Clerk or to teach
a School, he Reads, Writes, underſtands Arithmetick and
Accompts very well, Enquire of the Printer hereof.

Licensing of teachers. The licensing of teachers was carefully looked after in so far as religious faith was concerned, though private teachers usually were unlicensed. Where this was done locally, as in New England, the minister usually examined the candidate thoroughly to see that he was "sound in the faith." Little else mattered. In the parochial schools to the southward, where there was a connection with a home church in continental Europe, the license to teach not infrequently came, in theory at least, from a church synod or bishop in the home land. A modicum of learning was of course assumed on the part of the applicant, but this was not especially inquired into. The great consideration was that the teacher should adhere closely to the tenets of the particular church, and should abstain from attendance upon the services of any other church. For example, the Bishop of London issued the license to teach in schools under the direction of the English Church in the colonies. To hold such a license the applicant must conform to the Church liturgy, must have received the Sacrament in some Anglican church within a year, and for attending any other form of worship was usually subject to imprisonment and disbarment from teaching. Such conditions illustrate the intense religious bitterness of the times, and the dominance of the religious motive in all instruction. Had there not been churches to recruit for, and a feeling of the deep importance of church membership, there would have been little need for schools. It was the one compelling motive of the time for maintaining them.

Character of the early school instruction. Viewed from any modern standpoint the colonial schools attained to but a low degree of efficiency. The dominance of such an intense religious motive in itself precluded any liberal attitude in the instruction. In addition, the school hours were long, and most of the time was wasted as the result of an almost complete lack of any teaching equipment, books, and supplies, and of poor methods of teaching. The schoolhouses were of logs with a rough puncheon floor, and with seats and a rough board desk running around the walls. Paper, greased with lard, often took the place of glass in the windows. There were no blackboards or maps. Slates were not used until about 1820, and pencils and steel pens did not come into use until much later. Paper was expensive and not particularly good in quality, and hence used but sparingly. Sometimes birch bark was used for ciphering, and often the figures were traced in sand. The pens were goose quills, and one

FIG. 8. A TYPICAL EARLY SCHOOLROOM
INTERIOR

of the prerequisites for a schoolmaster was the ability to make and repair quill pens. The ink was home-made, and often poor.

The discipline in all classes of schools was severe. Even boys in college were still whipped, while in the lower schools little else than hard punishments were the rule. Whipping-posts were sometimes set up in the schoolroom, or in the yard or street outside. Pictures of schools of the time, especially European schools, usually show the schoolmaster with a bundle of switches near at hand. The ability to impose some sort of order on a poorly taught and, in consequence, an unruly school, was another of the prerequisites for a schoolmaster.

The greatest waste of time came from the individual methods of instruction uni-

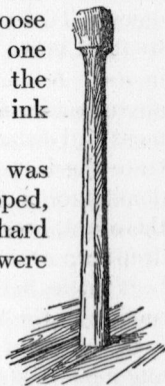

FIG. 9. A SCHOOL
WHIPPING-POST

Drawn from a picture of a five-foot whipping-post which once stood in the floor of a school-house at Sunderland, Massachusetts. Now in the Deerfield museum.

versally followed in teaching. Children came forward to the
teacher's desk and recited individually to the master or
dame, and so wasteful was the process that children might
attend school for years and get only a mere start in reading
and writing. Hearing lessons, assigning new tasks, setting
copies, making quill pens, dictating sums, and keeping order
completely absorbed the teacher's time.

IV. CHANGE IN CHARACTER AFTER ABOUT 1750

The period of establishment. The seventeenth century
was essentially a period of transplanting, during which little or no attempt at adaptation or change was made. The
customs of the mother countries in manners, morals, dress,
religious observances, education, and classes in society were
all carefully transplanted. In most of the colonies the
early settlements were near the coast. This was particularly the case in New England, where the danger from In-
dian massacres had been greater than farther south. King
Philip's War (1675–78) had cost the New England colonists
half a million dollars — a large sum for that time — and
had almost exhausted the people. Twelve out of the ninety
existing towns had been destroyed, and forty others had witnessed fire and massacre. A number of towns were so poor
they could not pay their colony taxes, and the maintenance
of schools, either by tuition or tax, became exceedingly
difficult.

The general result, though, of the war was such a punishment of the Indians that the colonists felt free thereafter
to form settlements inland, and a marked expansion of New
England took place. The same was true of the central
colonies, new settlements now being founded farther and
farther inland. These new towns in the wilderness, owing
their foundation to an entirely different cause than the
original towns, and being founded by younger people who
had never known European religious zeal or oppression, at
once gave evidence of less interest in religion and learning
than had been the case with the towns nearer the coast.

Even in these earlier coast towns, the second and third generation then in control began to turn from religion and agriculture to shipping and commerce, and with the rise of trade new interests began slowly to displace the dominant religious concern of the early colonists.

Waning of the old religious interest.   As early as 1647 Rhode Island had enacted the first law providing for freedom of religious worship ever enacted by an English-speaking people, and two years later Maryland enacted a similar law.   Though the Maryland law was later overthrown, and a rigid Church-of-England rule established there, these laws were indicative of the new spirit arising in the New World.   The witchcraft persecutions at Salem and elsewhere in New England did much to weaken the hold of the ministry on the people there.   By the beginning of the eighteenth century a change in attitude toward the old problem of personal salvation and church attendance became evident.   New settlements amid frontier conditions, where hard work rather than long sermons and religious disputations were the need; the gradual rise of a civil as opposed to a religious form of town government; the increase of new interests in trade and shipping, and inter-colony commerce; the beginnings of the breakdown of the old aristocratic traditions and customs, originally transplanted from Europe; the rising individualism in both Europe and America; — these all helped to weaken the hold on the people of the old religious doctrines.   The importation of many "indentured white servants," who for a time were virtually slaves, and the deportation from England of many paupers and criminals from the English jails, most of whom went to the central and southern colonies, likewise tended not only to reduce the literacy and religious zeal of the colonies, but also to develop a class of "poor whites" who later deeply influenced educational progress in the States in which they settled.

By 1750 the change in religious thinking had become quite marked.   Especially was the change evidenced in the dying

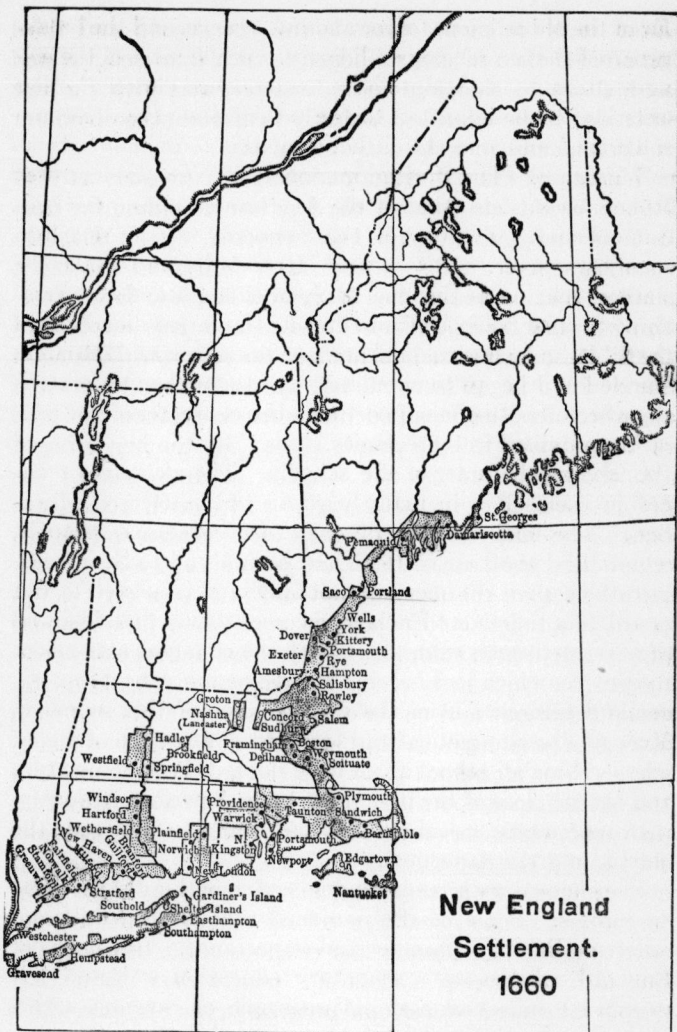

New England
Settlement.
1660

St. Georges
Pemaquid
Damariscotta
Saco Portland
Wells
York
Dover Kittery
Portsmouth
Exeter Rye
Amesbury Hampton
Salisbury
Rowley
Groton Salem
Nashua Concord Sudbury
(Lancaster)
Hadley Framingham
Westfield Brookfield Dedham Weymouth
Springfield Scituate
Plymouth
Windsor Providence Sandwich
Hartford Warwick Taunton
Wethersfield Barnstable
New Haven Plainfield Portsmouth
Guilford Norwich Kingston
Stamford New London Newport Edgartown
Greenwich Gardiner's Island Nantucket
Stratford Shelter Island
Southold Easthampton
Westchester Southampton
Hempstead
Gravesend

FIG. 10. HOW THE EARLY NEW ENGLAND TOWNS WERE LOCATED
From L. K. Mathews's *The Expansion of New England*, p. 35.

out of the old religious fervor and intolerance, and the breaking up of the old religious solidarity. While most of the colonies continued to maintain an "established church," other sects had to be admitted to the colony and given freedom of worship, and, once admitted, they were found not to be so bad after all. The Puritan monopoly of New England was broken, as was also that of the Anglican church in the central colonies. The day of the monopoly of any sect in a colony was over. New secular interests began to take the place of religion as the chief topic of thought and conversation. Secular books began to dispute the earlier monopoly of the Bible, and a few colonial newspapers (seven by 1750) were founded and began to circulate. All these changes materially affected both the support and the character of the education provided in the colonies.

Changing character of the schools. These changes man-ifested themselves in many ways in the matter of education. The maintenance of the Latin grammar schools, required by the Law of 1647, had been found to be increasingly difficult of enforcement, not only in Massachusetts, but in all the other New England colonies which had followed the Massachusetts example. With the changing attitude of the people, which had become clearly manifest by 1750, the demand for relief from the maintenance of this school in favor of a more practical and less aristocratic type of higher school, if higher school at all were needed, became marked, and by the close of the period the more American Academy, with its more practical studies, had begun to supersede the old Latin grammar school.

The elementary schools experienced something of the same difficulties. Some of the parochial schools died out, and others declined in character and importance. In Church of England colonies all elementary education was now left to private initiative and philanthropic or religious effort. In the southern colonies the classes in society made common tax-supported schools impossible. In New England the eighteenth century was a continual struggle on the one hand to prevent the town school from dying out, and on the other to establish in its place a series of scattered and inferior district schools, while tuition fees and taxation for support became harder and harder to obtain. Among other changes of importance the reading school and the writing school now became definitely united in all smaller places and in the rural districts to form the American elementary school of the 3-Rs, while the dame school was definitely adopted as the beginners' school. Both these changes were measures of economy, as well as distinctively American adaptations.

New textbooks, containing less of the gloomily religious than the *New England Primer*, and secular rather than religious matter, appeared and began to be used in the schools. Dilworth's *A New Guide to the English Tongue*, first published in England in 1740, began to be used in the American colonies by 1750. This contained words for spelling and a number of fables, and was the first of a line of some half-dozen so-called spelling books which finally culminated in the first distinctively American textbook — Noah Webster's blue-backed *Spelling Book*, first published at Hartford, in 1783.

Disintegration of the New England town. One of the most fundamental changes which now took place among New England people, and one which vitally modified future educational administration in almost all our American States, was the breakdown of the unity of the old New England town and the rise of the school district as the unit for school maintenance in its stead. It came about in this way.

Originally each New England settlement was a unit, and the irregular area included — twenty to forty square miles, a little smaller than a western township — was called a town. At the center, and usually facing on the town common, were the Meeting-House and the town school, and later the town hall. All citizens were required by law to live within one half-mile of the Meeting-House, to attend the town meetings, and to send their children to the town school. In the town meeting, at first held in the churches, all matters relating to the interests of the town were discussed, taxes were levied, and town by-laws were enacted. In time these towns, originally founded as religious republics, became centers for the discussion of all forms of public questions, and schools for training the people in the principles of government and parliamentary procedure. In them the people learned how to safeguard their own interests.

By the close of the seventeenth century, as has been stated, many of the forces which at first required a compact form of settlement had begun to lose their hold. New settlements arose within the towns, miles away from the meeting- and schoolhouses. To attend church or town meeting in winter was not always easy, and for children to attend the town school was impossible. The old laws as to place of residence accordingly had to be repealed or ignored, and as a result church en-

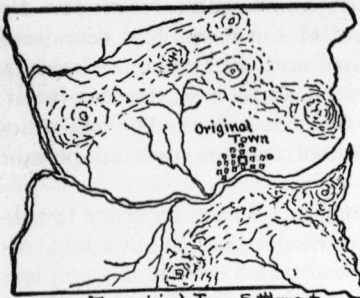

1642 - The original Town Settlement.

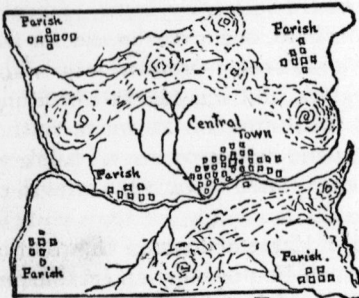

1710. Parishes within the Town

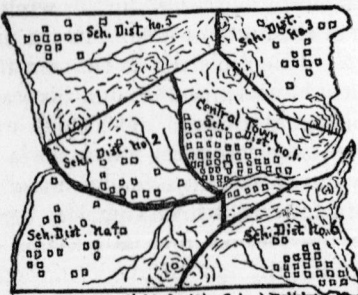

1760 - Town divided into School Districts.

FIG. 11. SHOWING THE EVOLUTION OF THE DISTRICT SYSTEM IN MASSACHUSETTS

thusiasm, town as opposed to individual interests, and zeal for education alike declined. New towns also arose farther inland, which soon broke up into divisions or districts. By 1725 the population of most of the towns had been scattered over much of the town's area, and small settlements, cut off from that of the central town by hills, streams, forest, or mere distance, had been formed. Due to the difficulties of communication, these little settlements tended to become isolated and independent.

The rise of the district system. As the tendency to subdivide the town became marked, these subdivisions demanded and obtained local rights. The first demand was for a minister of their own, or at least for separate services. As a result parishes were created within the town, and each parish, with its parish officers, became a new center for the rise of democracy and the assertion of parish rights. The town was next divided into road districts for the repair and maintenance of roads, and then into districts for recruiting the militia, and for assessing and collecting taxes. All these decentralizing tendencies contributed toward the growth of a district consciousness and the breakdown of town government. The establishment of dame schools in the district parishes in the summer, which had become an established institution in New England by 1700, and the presence of private tuition-schools taught by a master in the winter, naturally provided more convenient schooling than the distant town school afforded. This latter, too, had usually been supported in part at least by a tuition fee or a tax (rate bill) on the parents of children attending. The result was a serious crippling of the central town school, which the laws required must be maintained. The towns finally found it necessary to meet the competition by making the town school entirely free, but to do this the general taxation of all property had to be resorted to.

This was the opportunity of the parishes, and the price they demanded for consent to a general town tax for schools was the division of the central town school. Either the school must be moved about, and taught proportionately in each parish, or separate schools must be established and maintained in each. The result, at first, was the moving town school, which became established in New England by about 1725, the school being held in each parish and at the center of the town a number of weeks each year proportional to the amount of taxes for education paid by each. The next step was to give back to each parish, or school district as it now came to be called, the money it had paid and let it maintain its own school. This came about during the latter part of the eighteenth century, and the right to elect school trustees, levy district school taxes, and select a teacher alone were needed to complete the establishment of the full district system. These were legally granted in all the New England States shortly after the close of the Revolutionary War. From New England the district system in time spread over nearly all of the United States.

Rise of the civil or state school. As has been stated earlier, the school everywhere in America arose as a child of the Church. In the colonies where the parochial-school conception of education became the prevailing type, the school remained under church control until after the founding of our national government. In New England, however, and the New England evolution in time became the prevailing American practice, the school passed through a very interesting development during colonial times from a church into a state school.

As we have seen, each little New England town was originally established as a religious republic, with the Church in complete control. The governing authorities for church and civil affairs were much the same. When acting as church officers they were known as Elders and Deacons; when acting as civil or town officers they were known as Selectmen. The State, as represented in the colony legislature or the town meeting, was clearly the servant of the Church, and existed in large part for religious ends. It was the State acting as the servant of the Church which enacted the

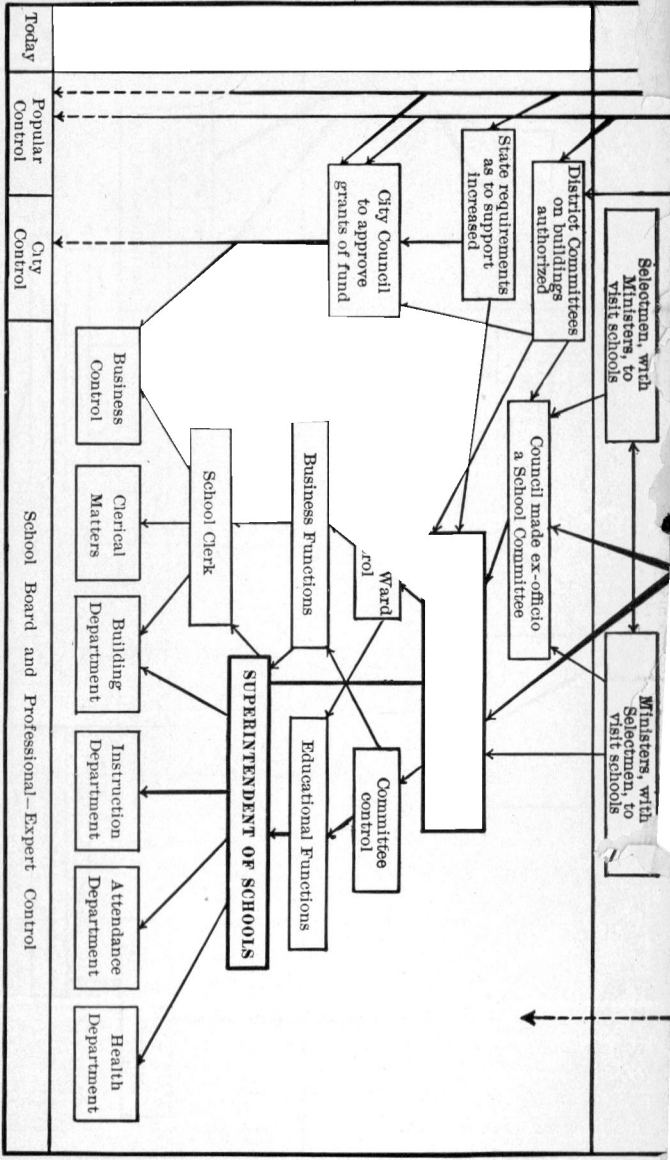

Fig. 12. CHART SHOWING THE EVOLUTION OF THE MODERN STATE SCHOOL, WITH ITS COMPLICATED ADMINISTRATION, OUT OF THE LITTLE RELIGIOUS SCHOOL OF THE EARLY NEW ENGLAND TOWN

Today	Popular Control	City Control	School Board and Professional–Expert Control

Selectmen, with Ministers, to visit schools

District Committees on buildings authorized

State requirements as to support increased

City Council to approve grants of fund

Council made ex-officio a School Committee

Ministers, with Selectmen, to visit schools

Business Control

Clerical Matters

School Clerk

Business Functions

Ward rol

Building Department

Instruction Department

Attendance Department

Health Department

SUPERINTENDENT OF SCHOOLS

Educational Functions

Committee control

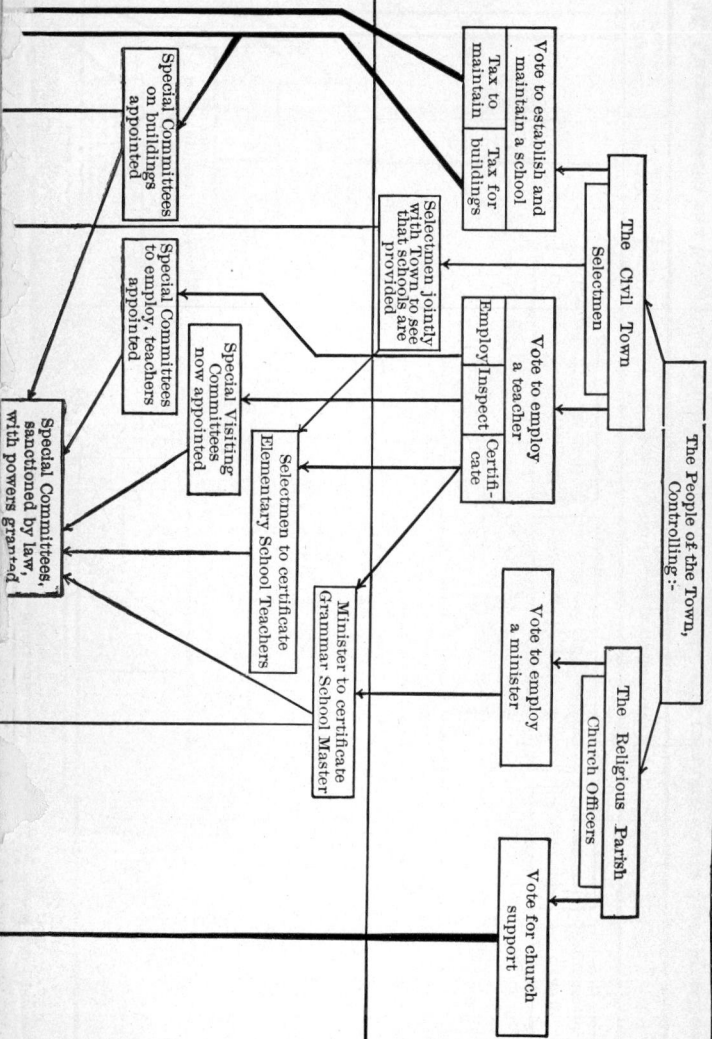

The People of the Town, Controlling:—

The Civil Town — Selectmen

Vote to establish and maintain a school

Tax to maintain | Tax for buildings

Selectmen jointly with Town to see that schools are provided

Special Committees on buildings appointed

Vote to employ a teacher

Employ | Inspect | Certificate

Special Committees to employ teachers appointed

Selectmen to certificate Elementary School Teachers

Special Visiting Committees now appointed

Minister to certificate Grammar School Master

Special Committees, sanctioned by law, with powers granted

The Religious Parish — Church Officers

Vote to employ a minister

Vote for church support

laws of 1642 and 1647, requiring the towns to maintain schools for religious purposes. Now, so close was the connection between the religious town which controlled church affairs, and the civil town which looked after roads, fences, taxes, and defense — the constituency of both being one and the same, and the meetings of both being held at first in the Meeting-House — that when the schools were established the colony legislature placed them under the civil, as involving taxes and being a public service, rather than under the religious town. The interests of one were the interests of both, and, being the same in constituency and territorial boundaries, there seemed no occasion for friction or fear. From this religious beginning the civil school, and the civil school town and township, with all our elaborate school administrative machinery, were later evolved.

The erection of a town hall, separate from the meeting-house, was the first step in the process. School affairs were now discussed at the town hall, instead of in the church. Town taxes, instead of church taxes, were voted for buildings and maintenance. The minister continued to certificate the grammar-school master until the close of the colonial period, but the power to certificate the elementary-school teachers passed to the town authorities early in the eighteenth century. By the close of this century all that the minister, as the surviving representative of church control, had left to him was the right to accompany the town authorities in the visitation of the schools. Thus gradually but certainly did the earlier religious school pass out from under the control of the Church and become a state school. When our national government and the different state governments were established, the States were ready to accept, in principle at least, the theory gradually worked out in New England that schools are state institutions and should be under the control of the State.

European traditions no longer satisfy. The changes in the character and in the administration of the schools alike reflect the spirit of the times, which was one of rising individualism in both Europe and America. By 1750 it is clearly evident that European traditions and ways and manners and social customs and types of schools were no longer completely satisfactory. There is clearly manifest a desire to modify all these various forces so as to adapt them better to purely American needs. There is also a tendency, strongly marked in the South, to discard schools for all but a few as being unnecessary under new-world conditions. The growing exasperation with the mother country for her foolish colonial policy tended to emphasize this feeling of independence, while Braddock's defeat, after his insulting boastfulness, had a great effect in giving the people of all the colonies a new confidence in their ability to care for themselves.

The evolution of the public or state school in New England from the original religious school; the formation generally of the American common school; the rise of the district system; the introduction of new types of textbooks; the decline of the Latin grammar schools; the rise of the essentially American Academy; the establishment of two new colleges (Pennsylvania, 1749; Kings, 1754), which from the first placed themselves in sympathy with the more practical studies; and the abandonment by Yale in 1767 and Harvard in 1773 of the practice of listing the students in the Catalogue according to the rank and social standing of their parents; — all these were clear indications that the end of the colonial period marked the abandonment of the transplanting of English educational ideas and schools and types of instruction. Instead, the beginnings of the evolution of distinctively American types of schools, better adapted to American needs, are clearly evident. This evolution was checked by the war which closed the period of colonial dependence, and something like half a century of our national life passed before we note again the rise of a distinctively American educational consciousness and the development of distinctively American schools once more begins.

QUESTIONS FOR DISCUSSION

1. State the change in the importance of education which resulted from the Protestant Reformation in Europe.
2. Explain what is meant by "the Puritan Church appealed to what was then its servant, the State," etc.
3. State the important contributions of Calvinism to our new-world life.
4. Explain the significance of the prelude to the Massachusetts Law of 1647, which begins by stating that it had been "one chief point of that old deluder, Satan," etc.
5. Do the fundamental principles stated by Mr. Martin as underlying the Massachusetts Laws of 1642 and 1647 still hold true?
6. Explain why a parochial-school system in colonial times was certain to be less effective than the Massachusetts state system.
7. Explain how climate and crop differences between Massachusetts and Virginia in themselves would have tended to develop different governmental and educational attitudes, even had there been no difference in religion.
8. What explanation can you give for the great indifference to education of the English Church during the entire colonial period?
9. Explain the origin of the American school of the 3-Rs.
10. Explain the establishment in the New England wilderness of the Latin grammar school as the important school of the early colonial period.
11. Were the conditions demanded for a teacher's license perfectly legitimate for the time? Compare these conditions with conditions demanded of teachers for licensing to-day.
12. What explanation can you give for the general prevalence of the individual instead of the class method of instruction during colonial times?
13. Explain how the seventeenth century was essentially a period of transplanting, or, as Eggleston states it, a period of the "transit of civilization."
14. Why did the rising individualism of later colonial times tend to weaken the religious zeal of earlier times?
15. Explain the stages of development of the Massachusetts district-school system.
16. Explain the development of the civil state school out of the religious town school.
17. Show how the moving school was merely a first step in the creation of district schools.
18. Why should the South have tended to discard schools altogether, except for the few?

TOPICS FOR INVESTIGATION AND REPORT

Intended for brief reading and quite brief written or class report.

1. Indebtedness to England for our early educational traditions and practices. (Brown, E. E.; Eggleston.)
2. The early New England Latin grammar schools, and their work. (Brown, E. E.; Barnard; Small.)
3. The work of Ezekiel Cheever and Elijah Corlett as types of grammar-school masters. (Barnard; Brown, E. E.)
4. Early parochial schools in the central colonies. (Murray; Wickersham — See Bibl. to Chap. IV.)
5. Dutch schools in colonial New Amsterdam. (Fitzpatrick.)
6. The schools of the "Society for the Propagation of the Gospel." (Kemp; Monroe; Palmer [Chap. III.].)
7. The apprenticeship system in the colonies. (Heatwole; Knight; Seybolt.)
8. The moving school in Massachusetts. (Updegraff.)
9. The New England Primer. (Ford; Johnson).
10. The teaching of arithmetic in colonial times. (Monroe, W. S.)
11. The religious aim in early New England education. (Brown, E. E. & S. W.)

SELECTED REFERENCES

The most important references are indicated by a *.

Barnard, Henry. "Ezekiel Cheever"; in Barnard's *American Journal of Education*, vol. 1, pp. 297–314.

An interesting sketch of the life and work of this famous New England schoolmaster, with notes on the early free grammar school of New England.

Boone, R. G. *Education in the United States.* 402 pp. D. Appleton & Co., New York, 1889.

Chapters I and II form good supplemental reading for this chapter.

*Brown, Elmer E. *The Making of our Middle Schools.* 547 pp. Longmans, Green & Co., New York, 1903.

A standard history of the rise of the Latin grammar school and the later high schools. The first seven chapters bear particularly on the subject-matter of this chapter.

Brown, S. W. *The Secularization of American Education.* 160 pp. Teachers College Contributions to Education, No. 49, New York, 1912.

Chapters I and II contain many extracts from old records relating to the religious aim of education, and to the instruction of orphans and dependents.

Dexter, E. G. *A History of Education in the United States.* 656 pp. The Macmillan Co., New York, 1904.

A collection of facts rather than an interpretation. The first five chapters deal with the period covered by this chapter.

*Eggleston, Edw. *The Transit of Civilization.* 344 pp. D. Appleton & Co., New York, 1901.

A very interesting description of the transfer of English civilization to America in the seventeenth century. Chapter V, on the transfer of educational traditions, is specially important.

*Fitzpatrick, E. A. *The Educational Views and Influence of De Witt Clinton.* 156 pp. Teachers College Contributions to Education, No. 44, New York, 1911.

Part I is a very interesting study of educational conditions in New York State during the later colonial period.

*Ford, Paul L. *The New England Primer.* Dodd, Mead & Co., New York, 1899.

A reprint, with an historical introduction, of the earliest known edition of this famous book.

Heatwole, C. J. *A History of Education in Virginia.* 382 pp. The Macmillan Co., New York, 1916.

The first four chapters give a good general account of educational efforts in Virginia, and the English attitude expressed there.

Jackson, G. L. *The Development of School Support in Colonial Massachusetts.* 95 pp. Teachers College Contributions to Education, No. 25, New York, 1909.

A study of the different methods employed in supporting schools, and the evolution of the town-supported school.

*Johnson, Clifton. *Old-Time Schools and School Books.* 381 pp. 234 Ills. The Macmillan Co., New York, 1904.

A very interesting collection of pictures and bits of historical information, woven together into fourteen chapters descriptive of old schools and school books.

Kemp, W. W. *The Support of Schools in Colonial New York by the Society for the Propagation of the Gospel in Foreign Parts.* 279 pp. Teachers College Contributions to Education, No. 56, New York, 1913.

A very full and detailed study of the work of this Society in the different parts of the colony.

Kilpatrick, Wm. H. *The Dutch Schools of New Netherlands and Colonial New York.* 239 pp. United States Bureau of Education, Bulletin No. 12, Washington, D.C., 1912.

An excellent detailed study of Dutch education, with good descriptions of the schools and school work.

*Knight, Edgar W. *Public School Education in North Carolina.* 384 pp. Houghton Mifflin Co., Boston, 1916.

Chapter II contains a very good brief account of the apprentice system in the State during the colonial period.

*Martin, Geo. H. *The Evolution of the Massachusetts Public School System.* 284 pp. D. Appleton & Co., New York, 1894.

A standard interpretative history of the rise of the Massachusetts schools. Chapters I and II deal with the early period represented by this chapter, and Chapter III with the decline in school spirit and the rise of the district system and the Academy.

*Monroe, Paul. *Cyclopedia of Education.* The Macmillan Co., New York, 1911–13.

> The following articles are specially important.
> 1. "Colonial Period in American Education," vol. II, pp. 115–122.
>   Very good on the period covered by this chapter.
> 2. "Society for the Propagation of the Gospel in Foreign Parts," vol. V, pp. 254–56.
>   Good on the charity-school work of the Church of England in the colonies.
> 3. The historical portion of the different articles on the school systems of the American States, as Connecticut, Massachusetts, New York, Pennsylvania, Virginia, etc.

*Monroe, W. S. *Development of Arithmetic as a School Subject.* 170 pp. United States Bureau of Education, Bulletin No. 10, Washington, 1917.

> Contains an interesting introduction on the teaching of arithmetic in colonial times.

Murray, David. *History of Education in New Jersey.* 344 pp. United States Bureau of Education, Circular of Information No. 1, Washington, 1899.

> Chapter VIII very good on colonial schools in New Jersey.

Seybolt, R. F. *Apprenticeship and Apprenticeship Education in Colonial New York and New England.* 121 pp. Teachers College Contributions to Education, No. 85, New York, 1917.

> An interesting study of old records relating to apprenticeship education.

Small, W. H. "The New England Grammar School," 1635–1700; in *School Review,* vol. X, pp. 513–31. (Sept., 1902.)

> A description of the founding of the early grammar schools, with interesting extracts from the records.

*Small, W. H. *Early New England Schools.* 401 pp. Ginn & Co., Boston, 1914.

> A very interesting collection of source extracts, copied from the early records, and classified into chapters describing all phases of early school life.

Suzzallo, Henry. *The Rise of Local School Supervision in Massachusetts, 1635–1827.* 154 pp. Teachers College Contributions to Education, No. 3, New York, 1906.

> A study of the evolution of the School Committee and its powers out of the town meeting.

Updegraff, H. *The Origin of the Moving School in Massachusetts.* 186 pp. Teachers College Contributions to Education, No. 17, New York, 1908.

> A very readable account of colonial education in Massachusetts, and of how the district school evolved out of the town school.

CHAPTER III

EARLY NATIONAL AND STATE ATTITUDES
(1775–1825)

I. The National Government and Education

Effect of the war on education. The effect of the War for Independence, on all types of schools, was disastrous. The growing troubles with the mother country had, for more than a decade previous to the opening of hostilities, tended to concentrate attention on other matters than schooling. Political discussion and agitation had largely monopolized the thinking of the time.

With the outbreak of the war education everywhere suffered seriously. Most of the rural and parochial schools closed, or continued a more or less intermittent existence. In some of the cities and towns, the private and charity schools continued to operate, but in others they were closed entirely. Usually the charity schools closed first, the private pay schools being able to keep open longest. In New York City, then the second largest city in the country, practically all schools closed with British occupancy and remained closed until after the end of the war. The Latin grammar schools and academies often closed from lack of pupils, while the colleges were almost deserted. Harvard and Kings, in particular, suffered grievously, and sacrificed much for the cause of liberty. The war engrossed the energies and the resources of the peoples of the different colonies, and schools, never very securely placed in the affections of the people, outside of New England, were allowed to fall into decay or entirely disappear. The period of the Revolution and the period of reorganization which followed, up to the beginning of our national government (1775–1789), were together a time of rapid decline in educational advantages and increasing illiteracy among the people. Meager as had been the opportunities for schooling before 1775, the opportunities by 1790, except in a few cities and in the New England districts, had shrunk almost to the vanishing point.

The close of the war found the country both impoverished and exhausted. All the colonies had made heavy sacrifices, many had been overrun by hostile armies, and the debt of the Union and of the States was so great that many thought it could never be paid. The thirteen States, individually and collectively, with only 3,380,000 people, had incurred an indebtedness of $75,000,000 for the prosecution of the conflict. Commerce was dead, the government of the Confederation was impotent, petty insurrections were common, the States were quarreling continually with one another over all kinds of trivial matters, England still remained more or less hostile, and foreign complications began to appear. It seemed as if the colonies, having united to obtain political liberty, might now lose it through quarreling among themselves. The period from the surrender of Cornwallis at Yorktown, in 1781, to the adoption of the Constitution and the inauguration of the new government, in 1789, was a very critical period in American history. That during such a crucial period, and for some years following, but little or no attention was anywhere given to the question of education was only natural.

The Constitution does not mention education. The new Constitution for the Union, as framed by the Constitutional Convention, nowhere contains any mention of any form of education, and a search of the debates of the Convention reveals that only once was anything relating to education brought before that body. Even then it was but a question, answered by the chairman, and related to the power under the new Constitution to establish a national university at the seat of government. The chair ruled that the new government would have such power. Were the Constitution to be reframed to-day there is little doubt but that education would occupy a prominent place in it.

It is not surprising, however, when we consider the time, the men, and the existing conditions, that the founders of our Republic did not deem the subject of public education important enough to warrant consideration in the Convention or inclusion in the document. Education almost everywhere was still a private matter, and quite generally under the control of the Church. The New England colonies had formed a notable exception to the common practice, both in this country and abroad.

Everywhere in Catholic countries education as an affair of the State had not been thought of. In France elementary education had been left to the Brothers of the Christian Schools, and secondary education to the Jesuits. In 1792 the Brothers of the Christian Schools, after over a century of effort, had but 121 teaching communities in all France, about 1000 teaching brothers, and approximately 36,000 pupils enrolled, out of an estimated total population of 26,000,000, or about 1 child in each 150 of the population. In England education had, since the days of Elizabeth, been considered as "no business of the State," and the great nineteenth-century agitation for state schools had not as yet been started. Even in Scotland, where schools were opened generally in the church parishes following the Reformation there, and had continued to be well maintained, they were church and not state schools. Only in the larger German Protestant States had education been declared a state function and subject to state supervision, but even in these States the schools were still partially under church control, through the pastors of the churches being appointed school inspectors and superintendents for the State.

Even the theory of education, aside from that relating to instruction in Latin secondary schools and colleges, had not been thought out and formulated at the time the Constitution was framed. Pestalozzi had not as yet done his great work in Switzerland, or written out his ideas as to the nature of elementary education. Herbart was a small child at the time, and Froebel a mere infant in arms. Herbert Spencer

was not born for more than a quarter of a century afterward.

Again, it must be remembered that the Constitutional
Convention embraced in its membership the foremost men
of colonial times.   Practically every one of them was a product of the old aristocratic and private type of tuition training, and probably few had any particular sympathy with
the attempts at general education made by the charity-
school type of instruction provided by the churches, or with
the indifferent type of teachers found in most of the pay
schools before 1775.   The Convention, too, it must be remembered, had weighty problems of State to find a solution
for, serious differences between the States to reconcile, and
important compromises to work out and make effective.   Its
great task was to establish a stable government for the new
States, and in doing this all minor problems were left to the
future for solution.   One of these was education in all its
forms, and accordingly no mention of education occurs in
the document.

By the tenth amendment to the Constitution, ratified in
1791, which provided that "powers not delegated to the
United States by the Constitution, nor prohibited by it to
the States, are reserved to the States respectively, or to
the people," the control of schools and education passed,
as one of the unmentioned powers thus reserved, to the
people of the different States to handle in any manner which
they saw fit.

How the Constitution helped solve the religious question.
A reference to Figure 2 (page 14) will show that this Na-
tion was settled by a large number of different religious
sects, and this number was further increased with time.
While the colonies were predominantly Protestant, these
Protestant sects differed greatly among themselves, and
between them there was often as bitter rivalry as between
Protestants and Catholics.   This was almost as true of their
schools as of their churches.   At the beginning of the War of
Independence the Anglican (Episcopal) faith had been de-

clared "the established religion" of the seven English colonies, and the Congregational was the established religion in three of the New England colonies, while but three colonies had declared for religious freedom and refused to give a state preference to any religion. Catholics in particular were under the ban, they not being allowed to vote or hold religious services except in Pennsylvania and Maryland.

This religious problem had to be met by the Constitutional Convention, and it handled it in the only way it could have been intelligently handled in a nation composed of so many different religious sects as was ours. The solution worked out was both revolutionary and wholesome. It simply incorporated into the Constitution provisions which guaranteed the free exercise of their religious faith to all, and forbade the establishment by Congress of any state religion, or the requirement of any religious test or oath as a prerequisite for holding any office under the control of the Federal Government. We thus took a stand for religious freedom at a time when the hatreds of the Reformation still burned fiercely, and when tolerance in religious matters was as yet but little known.

Importance of the solution arrived at. The far-reaching importance for our future national life of these sane provisions, and especially their importance for the future of public education, can hardly be overestimated. This action led to the early abandonment of state religions, religious tests, and public taxation for religion in the old States, and to the prohibition of these in the new. It also laid the foundations upon which our systems of free, common, public, tax-supported, non-sectarian schools have since been built up. How we ever could have erected a common public school system on a religious basis, with the many religious sects among us, it is impossible to conceive. Instead, we should have had a series of feeble, jealous, antagonistic, and utterly inefficient church school systems, confined chiefly to elementary education, and each largely intent on teaching

its peculiar church doctrines and struggling for an increasing
share of public funds.

How much we as a people owe the Fathers of our Republic for this most intelligent provision few who have not
thought carefully on the matter can appreciate. To it we
must trace not only the almost inestimable blessing of religious liberty, which we have for so long enjoyed, but also
the final establishment of our common, free, public school
systems. It still required a half century of struggle with
the churches to break their strangle hold on the schools and
to create really public schools, but the beginning of the
emancipation of education from church domination goes
back to this wise provision inserted in our National Constitution.

The new motive for education. Up to near the time of
the outbreak of the War for Independence there had been
but one real motive for maintaining schools — the religious.
To be sure, this had clearly begun to wane by 1750, but it
still continued to be the dominant motive. The Declaration of Independence had asserted that "all men are created
equal," that "they are endowed by their Creator with certain inalienable rights," and that "to secure these rights
Governments are instituted among men, deriving their just
powers from the consent of the governed." The long struggle
for independence, with its sacrifice and hardships, had tended
to clinch firmly this belief among the colonists, and the new
Constitution, with its extension of the right to vote for
national officers to a largely increased number of male citizens, had carried the theory expressed in the Declaration
of Independence over into practice. By 1830 most States
had abolished property qualifications for voting, and general
manhood suffrage was a concrete reality. These new political beliefs tended to create a new political motive for education, which was destined to grow in importance and in time
entirely supersede the old religious motive.

At first those responsible for the government in the States
and the Nation were too busy with problems of organization,

finance, and order to think much of other things, but soon after a partial measure of these had been established we find the leading statesmen of the time beginning to express themselves as to the need for general education in a government such as ours. Jefferson, writing to James Madison from Paris, as early as 1787, had said:

Above all things, I hope the education of the common people will be attended to; convinced that on this good sense we may rely with the most security for the preservation of a due degree of liberty.

Writing from Monticello to Colonel Yancey, after his retirement from the presidency, in 1816, Jefferson again said:

If a nation expects to be ignorant and free in a state of civilization it expects what never was and never will be. . . . There is no safe deposit [for the functions of government], but with the people themselves; nor can they be safe with them without information.

In his Farewell Address to the American people, written in 1796, Washington said:

Promote then, as an object of primary importance, institutions for the general diffusion of knowledge. In proportion as the structure of a government gives force to public opinion, it is essential that public opinion should be enlightened.

John Jay, first Chief Justice of the United States, in a letter to his friend, Dr. Benjamin Rush, wrote:

I consider knowledge to be the soul of a Republic, and as the weak and the wicked are generally in alliance, as much care should be taken to diminish the number of the former as of the latter. Education is the way to do this, and nothing should be left undone to afford all ranks of people the means of obtaining a proper degree of it at a cheap and easy rate.

James Madison, fourth president of the United States, wrote:

A satisfactory plan for primary education is certainly a vital desideratum in our republics.

A popular government without popular information or the means of acquiring it is but a prologue to a farce or a tragedy, or, perhaps, both. Knowledge will forever govern ignorance; and a people who mean to be their own governors must arm themselves with the power which knowledge gives.

John Adams, with true New England thoroughness, expressed the new motive for education still more forcibly when he wrote:

The instruction of the people in every kind of knowledge that can be of use to them in the practice of their moral duties as men, citizens, and Christians, and of their political and civil duties as members of society and freemen, ought to be the care of the public, and of all who have any share in the conduct of its affairs, in a manner that never yet has been practiced in any age or nation. The education here intended is not merely that of the children of the rich and noble, but of every rank and class of people, down to the lowest and the poorest. It is not too much to say that schools for the education of all should be placed at convenient distances and maintained at the public expense. The revenues of the State would be applied infinitely better, more charitably, wisely, usefully, and therefore politically in this way than even in maintaining the poor. This would be the best way of preventing the existence of the poor. . . .

Laws for the liberal education of youth, especially of the lower classes of people, are so extremely wise and useful that, to a humane and generous mind, no expense for this purpose would be thought extravagant.

Having founded, as Lincoln so well said later at Gettysburg, "on this continent a new Nation, conceived in liberty, and dedicated to the proposition that all men are created equal," and having built a constitutional form of government based on that equality, it in time became evident to those who thought at all on the question that that liberty and political equality could not be preserved without the general education of all. A new motive for education was thus created and gradually formulated, and the nature of school instruction came in time to be colored through and through by this new political motive. The necessary schools, however, did not come at once. On the contrary, the struggle to establish that general education required the best efforts of those interested in the highest welfare of the Republic for more than a half-century to come.

Beginnings of national aid for education. By cessions made by the original States, the new National Government was given title to all the lands lying between the Alleghenies and the Mississippi River. This it was agreed was to constitute a great National Domain, from which future States might be carved. The Revolutionary War had hardly ceased before a stream of soldiers and other immigrants began to pour into this new territory. These people demanded to be permitted to purchase the land, but before it could be sold it must be surveyed. Accordingly Congress adopted a rectangular form of land survey, under which the new territory was laid out into "Congressional Townships," six miles square. Each township was in turn subdivided into sections one mile square, and into quarter sections, and a regular system of numbering for each was begun. In adopting the

6	5	4	3	2	1
7	8	9	10	11	12
18	17	**16**	15	14	13
19	20	21	22	23	24
30	29	28	27	26	25
31	32	33	34	35	36

Fig. 13. A Congressional Township

Showing numbering and location of Section 16.

Ordinance for the government of that part of the territory lying north of the Ohio, in 1787, Congress provided that "Religion, morality, and knowledge being necessary to good government and the happiness of mankind, schools and the means of education shall be forever encouraged" in the States to be formed from this territory. This provision, and the ultimate settlement of the territory largely by people of New England stock, settled the future attitude as to public education of the States eventually erected therefrom.

When the first State came to be admitted, Ohio, in 1802, the question arose as to the right of the new State to tax the public lands of the United States. By way of settling this question amicably Congress offered to the new State that if it would agree not to tax the lands of the United States, and the same when sold for five years after sale (the purchase price usually being paid in five annual installments), the United States would in turn give to the new State the sixteenth section of land in every township for the maintenance of schools within the township.   The offer was accepted, and was continued in the case of every new State admitted thereafter, except Texas, which owned its own land when admitted, and West Virginia and Maine, which were carved from original States.   With the admission of California, in 1850, the grant was raised to two sections in each township, the sixteenth and the thirty-sixth, and all States since admitted have received two sections in each township for schools.   In the admission of Utah, Arizona, and New Mexico, due to the low value of much of the land, four sections were granted to each of these States.   To these section grants some other lands were later added, — saline lands, swamp lands, and lands for internal improvements, and these constitute the National Land Grants for the endowment of public education, and form the basis of the permanent school funds in all the States west of the Alleghenies.   In all, the national government has given to the States for common schools, in these section and other grants, a total of approximately 132,000,000 acres of public lands.   This, at the traditional government price of $1.25 an acre, would constitute a gift for the endowment of common school education in the different States of approximately $165,000,000.   As a matter of fact, due to the better care taken of their lands by the newer Western States, and the higher prices for more recent sales, these grants will produce at least half a billion dollars for educational endowment.

These gifts by Congress to the new States of national lands for the endowment of public education, though begun in large part as a land-selling proposition, helped greatly in the early days to create a sentiment for state schools, stimulated the older States to set aside lands and moneys to create state school funds of their own, and did much to enable the new States to found state school systems instead of copying the parochial or charity schools of the older States to the east.

II. What the States were doing

Education having been left to the States as an unmentioned power by the tenth amendment to the Federal Constitution, we next turn to the different States to see what action was taken by them in the matter of education during the early years of our national history. In doing so we need to examine both the state constitutions which they framed, and their early educational legislation.

The early state constitutions. During the period from the adoption of the Declaration of Independence to the close of the eighteenth century (1776–1800), all the States, except Rhode Island and Connecticut, which considered their colonial charters as satisfactory, formulated and adopted new state constitutions. A number of the States also amended or revised their constitutions one or more times during this period. Three new States also were admitted before 1800 — Vermont, Kentucky, and Tennessee. Some idea of the importance attached to general education by the early States may be gained by an examination of these early state constitutions.

Of these, the state constitutions of New Hampshire, New Jersey, Delaware, Maryland, Virginia, and South Carolina, all framed in 1776; New York, framed in 1777; South Carolina, revised in 1778 and again in 1790; Kentucky, framed in 1792, and revised in 1799; and Tennessee, framed in 1796 — all were equally silent on the matter of schools and education. New Hampshire and Delaware, in later revisions, included a brief section on the subject. Maryland amended its constitution four times, before 1864, without including any mention of education. Of the sixteen States forming the Union in 1800, nine had by that time made no mention of education in any of their constitutions.

The constitutions of the seven States which had made some mention fall into three classes. The first, represented by Delaware and the first Georgia constitution, merely briefly direct the establishment of schools; the second, represented by Massachusetts, New Hampshire, and Vermont, have good sections directing the encouragement of learning and virtue and the protection and encouragement of school societies; while the third, represented by North Carolina and the first Pennsylvania and Vermont constitutions, direct the establishment of schools where tuition shall be cheap. In its second constitution Pennsylvania went over completely to the maintenance of a pauper-school system. A few extracts will illustrate these early state constitutional provisions.

Delaware made no mention of education in its first (1776) constitution, but in its second (1792) very briefly directed the Legislature, when it saw fit, to provide schools, as may be seen from the following section:

Art. VIII, Sec. 12. The Legislature shall, as soon as conveniently may be, provide by law for . . . establishing schools, and promoting arts and sciences.

Georgia had given somewhat similar directions as to schools in 1777, but in 1798 withdrew these directions and substituted a section relating only to the promotion of arts and sciences in seminaries of learning, and directed the Legislature to protect the endowment funds of such.

Massachusetts and New Hampshire, in almost identical words, gave the most complete directions of any States as to the encouragement of learning and private school societies, and the establishment of schools, and Massachusetts included a long article making detailed provisions for the protection and maintenance of Harvard College. Of the eight other colleges in the colonies at the beginning of the War of Independence, no other State made any constitutional mention regarding them. The Massachusetts and New Hampshire provisions for the encouragement of learning are so excellent, and so much ahead of the general conception of the time, that the Massachusetts provision, which was later copied by New Hampshire, is worth quoting in full.

Chap. V, Sec. 2. Wisdom and knowledge, as well as virtue, diffused generally among the body of the people, being necessary for the preservation of their rights and liberties; and as these depend on spreading the opportunities and advantages of education in the various parts of the country, and among the different orders of the people, it shall be the duty of the legislatures and magistrates, in all future periods of this Commonwealth, to cherish the interests of literature and the sciences, and all seminaries of them; especially the university at Cambridge, public schools, and grammar schools in the towns; to encourage private societies and public institutions, by rewards and immunities, for the promotion of agriculture, arts, sciences, commerce, trades, manufactures, and a natural history of the country; to countenance and inculcate the principles of humanity and general benevolence, public and private charity, industry and frugality, honesty and punctuality in their dealings; sincerity, good humor, and all social affections and generous sentiments among the people.

Vermont, in its first constitution (1777), directed the establishment of schools in each town "with such salaries to the masters, paid by the town" as would "enable them to instruct youth at low prices," and also directed the establishment of a grammar school in each county, and a university for the State. North Carolina, in its constitution of the preceding year, had inserted a similar provision for low-priced instruction, and for the creation of a state university. In a supplemental section Vermont also directed the encouragement of learning and private school societies, somewhat after the Massachusetts example. In the revision of 1787, all was omitted from the Vermont constitution except the supplemental section.

Pennsylvania, in its constitution of 1776, directed the establishment of a school in each county, "with such salaries to the masters, paid by the public, as may enable them to instruct youth at low prices"; directed the encouragement of learning in one or more universities; and then added a supplemental section, as had Vermont, directing the en-

couragement of learning and school societies. In the revision of 1790 all this was abandoned for the following
brief and indefinite directions for the establishment of a
pauper-school system:

Sec. 1. The legislature shall, as soon as conveniently may be,
provide, by law, for the establishment of schools throughout the
State, in such manner that the poor may be taught *gratis*.

Sec. 2. The arts and sciences shall be promoted in one or more
seminaries of learning.

These constitutional provisions represent the mandates relating to public education which seven early States thought
desirable or necessary. Compared with a modern Western
State constitution the mention of education made in them
seems very hesitating and feeble. As in the earlier period
of American education, it was Calvinistic New England
which provided the best constitutional provisions for learning. On the other hand, it was the old Anglican Church
colonies and the new States of Kentucky and Tennessee
which were silent on the subject.

The early state school laws. Turning next to the early
state laws regarding schools, we find in them a still better
index as to state interest in and effort for general education.
Examining the legislation relating to the establishment of
public schools which was enacted before 1820, and omitting
legislation relating to colleges and academies, we find that
the sixteen States in the Union before 1800 classify themselves into three main groups, as follows:

1. The good-school-conditions group.

Vermont	Connecticut
New Hampshire	New York
Massachusetts	
(including Maine)	

2. The pauper-parochial-school group.

Pennsylvania	Maryland
New Jersey	Virginia
Delaware	Georgia

3. The no-action group.

Rhode Island   Kentucky
North Carolina   Tennessee
South Carolina

The good-school-conditions group.   It is the four New
England States, settled originally by Calvinistic Puritans,
and the State of New York, which by 1810 had become virtually a westward extension of New England by reason of
the settlement of all central New York by New England
people (see Fig. 14), which early made the best provisions
for schools.   Beside supporting the three colony colleges,
Dartmouth, Harvard, and Yale, and maintaining grammar
schools and academies, the laws made, for the time, good
provisions for elementary education.   Summarized briefly
by States the laws enacted provided as follows:

Vermont. First general state school law in 1782.   District system authorized.   Support of schools by district tax or rate bill on
parents optional.   State aid granted.   1797 — Districts failing to
provide schools to receive no state assistance.   Reading, writing,
and arithmetic to be taught in all schools.   1810 — Town school
tax obligatory, and gradually increased from 1 per cent to 3 per
cent by 1826.   1825 — State school fund created.   1827 — New
school law required towns to build school buildings; required
certificates of teachers; made the beginnings of school supervision;
and added spelling, grammar, history, geography, and good behavior to the list of required school subjects.

New Hampshire. First general state school law in 1789.   Town
tax required, and rate fixed; teachers' certificates required; English schools and Latin schools required in the larger towns.   1791
— Town taxes for schools increased.   1821 — State school fund
created.   1827 — Poor children to be provided with schoolbooks
free.

Massachusetts. First general state school law in 1789.   This
legalized the practices in education of the past hundred and fifty
years, and changed them into state requirements.   A six-months
elementary school required in every town, and twelve-months if
having 100 families.   Also a six-months grammar school required
of every town having 150 families, and twelve-months if 200 families.   All teachers to be certificated, and all grammar school

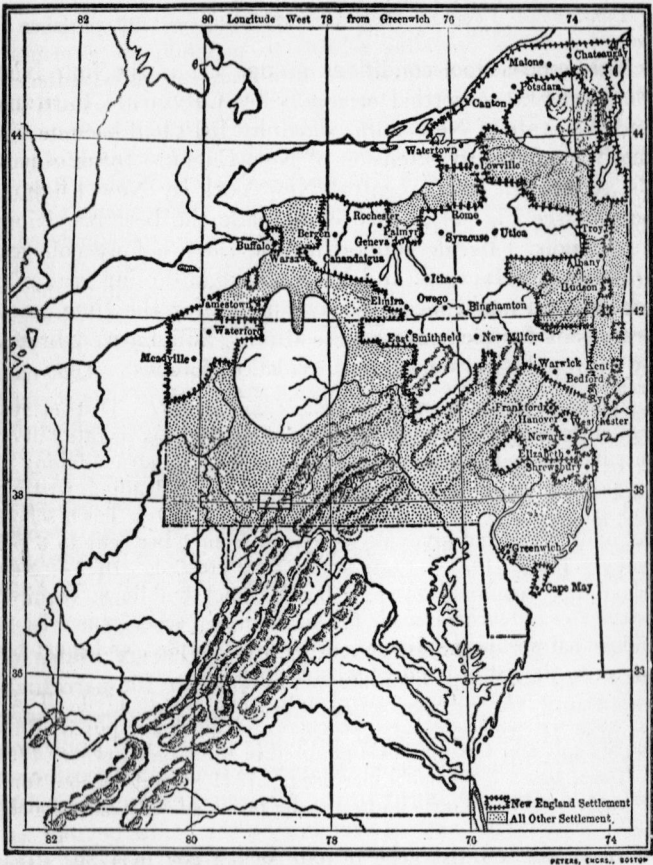

FIG. 14. SHOWING THE WESTWARD EXPANSION OF NEW ENGLAND INTO
NEW YORK, NEW JERSEY, AND PENNSYLVANIA, BY 1810

From L. K. Mathews's *The Expansion of New England;* Houghton Mifflin Co., Boston,
1909. By permission.

teachers to be college graduates or certificated by the minister as skilled in Latin. These laws also applied to Maine, which was a part of Massachusetts until 1820.

Connecticut. Laws of 1700 and 1712 required all parishes or school societies operating schools to maintain an elementary school for from six to eleven months a year, varying with the size of the parish. Law of 1714 required inspection of schools and teachers. These laws continued in force by the new State. A permanent school fund had been created in 1750 by the sale of some Connecticut lands, and in 1795, on the sale of the Western Reserve in Ohio for $1,200,000. This was added to the permanent school fund. 1798 — School visitors and overseers ordered appointed.

New York. Little of an educational nature had been done in this State before the Revolution, except in the matter of church charity schools. In 1795 a law, valid for five years, was enacted which distributed $100,000 a year to the counties for schools. By 1798 there were 1352 schools in 16 of the 23 counties, and 59,660 children were enrolled. On the expiration of the law, in 1800, it could not be reënacted. By 1812, when the first permanent school law was enacted, New England immigration into the State had counterbalanced the private-parochial-charity-school attitude of New York City. The Massachusetts district system was instituted, local taxation required, state aid distributed on the basis of school census, and the first State Superintendent of Schools provided for. In 1814 teachers were ordered examined. By 1820 New York schools probably the best of any State in the Union.

The pauper-parochial-school group.

The six States of this group are the old middle colonies, where the parochial-school and the pauper-school attitudes, described under Chapter II, had been most prominent, and one Southern State. The idea had become so fixed in these middle colonies that education belonged to the Church and to charitable organizations that any interference by the State, beyond assisting in the maintenance of pauper schools, came in time to be bitterly resented. Briefly summarized, by States, the legislation enacted provided as follows:

Pennsylvania. The constitution of 1776 had directed the establishment of a school in each county, where youths should be taught at low prices, but the constitution of 1790 had directed instead the establishment, at the convenience of the legislature, of a series of pauper schools. The first law was in 1802, and this provided only for the education of the pauper children in each county. In 1824 a better law was enacted, but its acceptance was optional, and in 1826 it was repealed and the pauper-school law of 1802 continued. The first free-school law dates from 1834. Even this was optional, and was at first accepted by but little more than half of the school districts in the State.

Delaware. In 1796 a state school fund was created from the proceeds of tavern and marriage licenses. This accumulated unused until 1817, when $1000 a year was appropriated from the income to each of the three counties for the instruction of the children of the poor in reading, writing, and arithmetic. In 1821 aid was extended to Sunday Schools. In 1821 a so-called free-school law was enacted, by which the State duplicated amounts raised by subscription or contribution, but by 1833 only 133 districts in the State were operating under the law. The schools of Wilmington date from 1821. In 1843 an educational convention adopted a resolution opposing taxation for free schools. First real school law in 1861.

Maryland. No constitutional mention until 1864. Many academies chartered, and lotteries much used for their aid between 1801 and 1817. 1812 — School fund begun by a tax on banks. 1816 — First property tax to aid schools for the poor. 1826 — First general school law, but acceptance optional with the counties; too advanced and never in operation, except in Baltimore. No school system until after the Civil War.

Virginia. The efforts of Jefferson to establish a complete school system for the State failed. 1796 — Optional school law, but little done under it. 1810 — Permanent school fund started. 1818 — Law providing for a charity school system enacted. By 1843 estimated that half the indigent children in the State were receiving sixty days schooling. 1846 — Better school law enacted, but optional, and only nine counties ever used it. 1870 — First real school law.

New Jersey. This State might also be classed in the no-action group. Nothing was done until 1816, when a state school fund was begun. In 1820 permission to levy a local tax for schools was granted. In 1828 a report showed that one third of the children of the State were growing up without a chance for any education. Largely in consequence of this the first general school law was enacted, in 1829, but the next year this was repealed, as a result of bitter opposition from the private and church-school interests, and the State followed Pennsylvania's example and went over to the pauper-school idea of state action. In 1830 and 1831 laws limited state educational effort to aiding schools for the education of the children of the poor. In 1838 the beginnings of a state public school system were made, and in 1844 state aid was limited to public schools. First constitutional mention of education in 1844.

Georgia. In 1817 a fund of $250,000 was created for free schools. Schools for poor children were opened in Savannah in 1818, and Augusta in 1821. 1822 — Income of fund appropriated to pay tuition of poor children. 1837 — Free school system established, but law repealed in 1840. 1858 — Word "poor" eliminated from law. Real state school system dates from after Civil War.

The no-action group. This group contains the religious-freedom state of Rhode Island, two of the States which were for long imbued with the Anglican "no-business-of-the-State" attitude, and the two new States of Tennessee and Kentucky, settled largely by "poor whites" and others from the Carolinas and Virginia. Examining the legislation, or rather lack of legislation in these States, we find the following:

Rhode Island. First constitutional mention in 1842. The first school law for the colony was enacted in 1800, at the instance of a group of citizens of Providence. Schools were ordered established in every town in the State for instruction in reading, writing, and arithmetic, and some state aid was given. Providence and other towns established schools, and so great was the opposition to the law that it was repealed in 1803. In 1825 Newport was permitted to start schools for its poor children. It was not until 1828 that a permissive state school law was enacted, and by 1831 there were only 323 public schools and 375 public teachers in the State.

North Carolina. A School Society for the education of females was chartered in 1811. In 1816 legislature appointed a commission to report a school law. 1817 — Good plan reported, but legislature would not approve. 1824 — Another commission appointed. 1825 — Reported a bill for a pauper-school system, which also was not approved. 1825 — Permanent state school fund begun. 1839 — First bill creating an elementary school system.

South Carolina. In 1811 Charleston permitted to organize charity schools. 1836 — Report made recommending a state system of charity schools; not adopted. 1854 — Charleston petitioned to be permitted to make its schools free; granted in 1856. State school system dates from after the Civil War.

Kentucky. First provision for aid for common schools in 1821, but legislature diverted funds. 1830 — First general school law; dead letter, largely through lack of any interest in schools. 1853 — School in each county for first time.

Tennessee. First school law in 1830, establishing the district system, and schools open to all.

State attitudes summarized. Figure 15 sets forth graphically the state attitudes toward education which have just

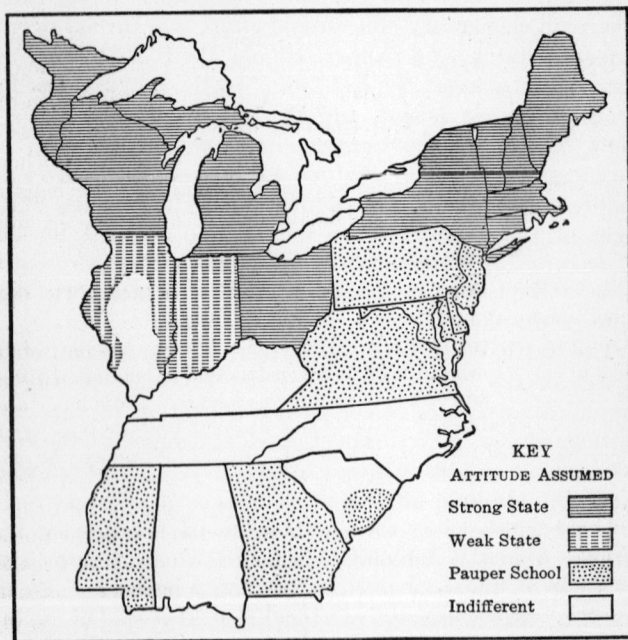

Fig. 15. EARLY ATTITUDE ASSUMED TOWARD PUBLIC EDUCATION BY THE ORIGINAL STATES, AND THE STATES LATER CARVED FROM THE CEDED NATIONAL DOMAIN

been summarized.   From this map it will be seen, even
better than from the descriptions of constitutional enact-
ments and early legislation, what an important part religion played, with us, in the establishment of a public school
attitude.   It was the Calvinistic-Puritan States of New
England which most deeply believed in education as a necessity for salvation, and they so established the school idea
among their people that this belief in schools persisted after
the religious motive for education had died out.   Spreading
westward, they carried their belief in education into the new
States in which they settled.   In the middle colonies, where
the parochial school idea and the plan of apprenticing and
educating orphans and paupers dominated, we see States
where all elementary educational effort was turned over to
private, church, and pauper schools, the State aiding only
the last, or at most the last two.   In the religious-freedom
State of Rhode Island, and the old Anglican colonies of
New Jersey and the Carolinas, we see the English "no-
business-of-the-State" attitude for a time reflected in the
indifference of the State to education.   The four new States
west of these southern colonies — Kentucky, Tennessee,
Mississippi, and Alabama — in large part reflected the attitude of the States to the eastward from which their early
immigrants came.

The North-West-Territory States.   The settlement of the
States of the North-West Territory is an interesting ex-
emplification of the influence on education of the early
settlements we have so far studied, and much of the early
educational history of these States is to be understood when
viewed in the light of their settlement.

Immediately after the close of the Revolutionary War
settlers from the different States of the new Union began
to move to the new territory to the westward.   To the
north, a great movement of New England people began into
central New York and northern Pennsylvania, and from
then until 1810, when the tide of immigration turned farther
westward, the history of these two regions is in large part

the history of the westward expansion of New England.   By 1810 more than one half of New York, one fourth of Pennsylvania, portions of New Jersey, and the Western Reserve in Ohio (see map, Fig. 14) had been settled by New England people.   In New York they counterbalanced the earlier predominance of the Anglicans, helped materially in securing the first permanent school law for the State, in 1812, and in carrying the State for free schools in the referenda of 1849 and 1850.   They also helped to counteract the German Lutheran parochial element in the battle for free schools in Pennsylvania, in 1834 and 1835.

After 1810 the tide of migration of New England people set in strong to the new States to the west of New York, following the northern route, and by 1850 one half of the settled portions of the old North-West Territory had been populated by New England stock, while many settlements had been founded beyond the Mississippi River.   The history of these migrations often repeated the old story of the Puritan migrations to New England.   Congregations, with their ministers, frequently migrated to the West in a body. A new Granville, or Plymouth, or Norwalk, or Greenwich in the wilderness was a child of the old town of that name in New England.   An almost ceaseless train of wagons poured westward, and the frontier was soon pushed out to and beyond the Mississippi.   Wherever the New Englander went he invariably took his New England institutions with him.   Congregational churches were established, new Yales and Dartmouths founded, common schools and the Massachusetts district system were introduced, and the town form of government and the town meeting were organized in the new Congressional townships — a ready-made unit which the New Englander found easily adaptable to his ideas of town government.

Into these new States and territories to the westward came also other settlers, along the southern route, with different political, religious, and educational training.   Those from Pennsylvania came from where town government was

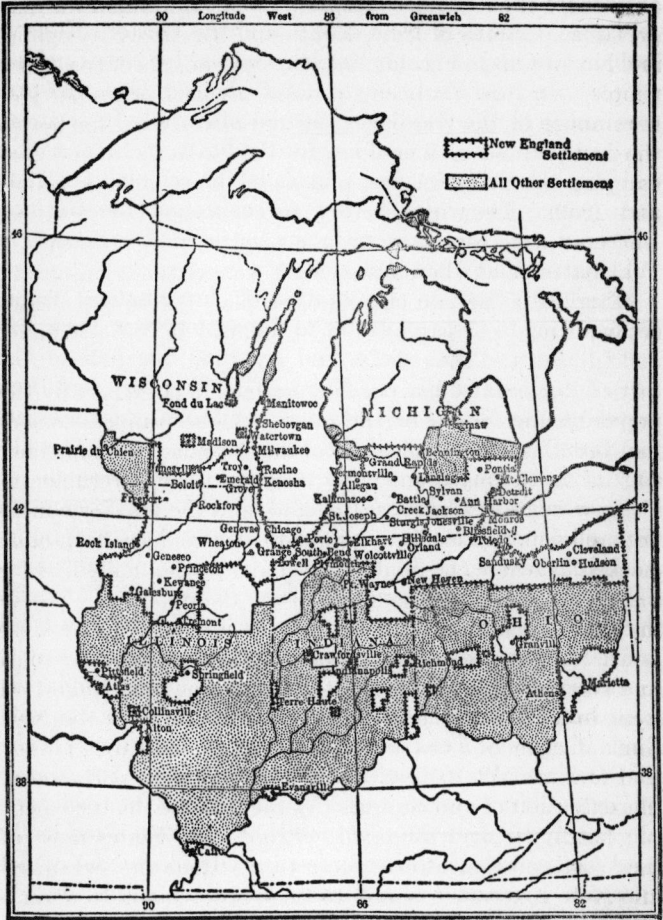

Fig. 16. Showing the Westward Expansion of New England into the Old North-West Territory by 1840

From L. K. Mathews's *The Expansion of New England;* Houghton Mifflin Co., Boston, 1909. By permission.

weak, where public free schools had not been developed, and where the charity conception of education had for long prevailed. Settlers from Kentucky, Tennessee, Virginia, and North Carolina, commonly the descendants of the "poor whites" who had not been able to secure land or property or to establish themselves there, also moved westward and north-ward and settled in the river valleys of the southern and cen-tral portions of Ohio, Indiana, and Illinois. These people came from States where slavery and plantation life prevailed, where religion, especially for the poor, was by no means a vital matter, and where free schools were virtually unknown.

Mingling of the two classes of people. These two classes of people met and struggled for supremacy in Ohio, Indiana, and Illinois, and the political, religious, and educational his-tory of these States has been determined in large part by the preponderance of one or the other of these people. Where the New England people were in the ascendancy, as in Ohio, and also in Michigan and early Wisconsin, the governmental forms were most like New England, and the zeal for educa-tion, religion, and local governmental control have been most marked. Where the Southern element predominated, as for a time in Illinois, the result has been the opposite. Where the two mingled on somewhat even terms, as in Indiana, we find a compromise between them. The opening of Missouri to slavery, in 1820, deflected the tide of southern migration from Indiana and Illinois to that State, and gave the New England element a chance to extend its influence over almost all the North-West-Territory States. The importance of this extension of and conquest by the New England element can hardly be overestimated. From these States most of the West and Southwest was in turn settled and organized into state governments, and to these new regions New Eng-land educational ideas in time were spread.

Educational attitudes in the North-West States. The effect of the predominance or mingling of these two classes is clearly shown in the early state attitudes toward educa-tion, as stated in the constitutions and laws.

The Ohio constitutional provision of 1802 is noteworthy for its strong stand for the encouragement of learning and the interdiction of pauper schools in the State, and as reflecting the influence of the national land grants and the national attitude regarding religious freedom. It reads:

Art. VIII, 25. That no law shall be passed to prevent the poor in the several counties and townships within the State from an equal participation in the schools, academies, colleges, and universities within this State, which are endowed, in whole or in part, from the revenues arising from the donations made by the United States for the support of schools and colleges; and the doors of said schools, academies, and universities shall be open for the reception of scholars, students, and teachers of every grade, without distinction, or preference whatever, contrary to the intent for which said donations were made.

In 1821 a permissive school law was enacted, and in 1825 a new school law laid the foundations of a state system, based on the Massachusetts district system, county taxation, and the certification of teachers.

The Indiana constitution of 1816 threw safeguards about the national land grants for schools, and was the first to issue a comprehensive mandate to the legislature ordering the establishment of a complete free state system of schools. This latter reads:

Art IX, Sec. 2. It shall be the duty of the general assembly, as soon as circumstances will permit, to provide by law for a general system of education, ascending in regular gradations from township schools to a State university, wherein tuition shall be gratis and equally open to all.

So evenly balanced were the Northern and Southern elements in Indiana, however, that this mandate of the constitution was difficult to carry out, and, despite legislation which will be described in Chapter IV, the real beginning of a state school system in Indiana dates from 1851.

Illinois shows the Southern element in control. Neither the constitution of 1818 nor the one of 1848 made any men-

tion of education. A good school law, said to have been
the best outside of New England, was enacted in 1825, but
was nullified two years later by legislation which provided
that no man could be taxed for schools without his written
consent, and which permitted the maintenance of schools
in part by tuition fees. It was not until 1841, and after the
New England people had become a majority, that this
nullifying legislation of 1827 could be repealed.

Michigan was not admitted as a State until 1835, but the
territorial legislature, in 1827, adopted a good school law,
modeled on the Massachusetts legislation. In 1829 the
property of non-residents was made subject to taxation
for schools — at that time rather advanced legislation.
The first state constitution, of 1835, provided for the appointment of the first permanent State Superintendent of
Public Instruction in any State, and ordered:

Sec. 3. The legislature shall provide for a system of common
schools, by which a school shall be kept up and supported in each
school district at least three months in every year; and any school
district neglecting to keep up and support such school may be
deprived of its equal proportion of the interest of the public (school)
fund.

Wisconsin was a part of Michigan until 1836, and the
Michigan legislation applied to Wisconsin territory. In
1840 the first Wisconsin school law provided for the Massachusetts district school system, a school census, and district taxation for schools, and when the State was admitted,
in 1848, the New England traditions as to education had
become so firmly fixed, and the new forces working for popular education in the State had begun to have such an influence, that the school code of 1849 was quite modern in
character.

No real educational consciousness before about 1820.
Regardless of the national land grants for education made
to the new States, the provisions of the different state constitutions, the beginnings made here and there in the few
cities of the time, and the early state laws, we can hardly

be said, as a people, to have developed an educational consciousness, outside of New England and New York, before
about 1820, and in some of the States, especially in the
South, a state educational consciousness was not awakened
until very much later.   Even in New England there was a
steady decline in education, as the district system became
more and more firmly fixed, during the first fifty years of
our national history.

There were many reasons in our national life for this lack
of interest in education among the masses of our people.
The simple agricultural life of the time, the homogeneity
of the people, the absence of cities, the isolation and independence of the villages, the lack of full manhood suffrage
in a number of the States, the want of any economic demand
for education, and the fact that no important political question calling for settlement at the polls had as yet arisen,
made the need for schools and learning seem a relatively
minor one.   There were but six cities of 8000 inhabitants
or over in the country as late as 1810, and even in these life
was far simpler than in a small Western village to-day.
There was little need for book learning among the masses
of the people to enable them to transact the ordinary business of life.   A person who could read and write and cipher
in that time was an educated man, while the absence of
these arts was not by any means a matter of reproach.

The country, too, was still very poor.   The Revolutionary
War debt still hung in part over the Nation, and the demand
for money and labor for all kinds of internal improvements
was very large.   The country had few industries, and its
foreign trade was badly hampered by European nations.
France gave us trouble for a decade, while England made it
evident that, though we had gained our political independence, we should have to fight again if we were to win our
commercial freedom.   Ways and means of strengthening
the existing government and holding the Union together,
rather than plans which could bear fruit only in the future,
occupied the attention of the leaders of the time.   "The

Constitution," as John Quincy Adams expressed it, "was extorted from the grinding necessities of a reluctant people" to escape anarchy and the ultimate entire loss of independence, and many had grave doubts as to the permanence of the Union. It was not until after the close of the War of 1812 that belief in the stability of the Union and in the capacity of the people to govern themselves became the belief of the many rather than the very few, and plans for education and national development began to obtain a serious hearing.

When we had finally settled our political and commercial future by the War of 1812–14, and had built up a national consciousness on a democratic basis in the years immediately following, and the Nation at last possessed the energy, the money, and the interest for doing so, we then turned our energies toward the creation of a democratic system of public schools. In the meantime, education, outside of New England and in part even there, was left largely to private individuals, churches, incorporated school societies, and such state schools for the children of the poor as might have been provided by private or state funds, or the two combined.

The real interest in advanced education. In so far as we may be said to have possessed a real interest in education during the first half-century of our national existence, it was manifested in the establishment and endowment of academies and colleges rather than in the creation of schools for the people. The colonial Latin grammar school had been almost entirely an English institution, and never well suited to American needs. As democratic consciousness began to arise, the demand came for a more practical institution, less exclusive and less aristocratic in character, and better adapted in its instruction to the needs of a frontier society. Arising about the middle of the eighteenth century, a number of so-called Academies had been founded before the new National Government took shape. While essentially private institutions, arising from a church foun-

dation, or more commonly a local subscription or endowment, it became customary for towns, counties, and States
to assist in their maintenance, thus making them semi-
public institutions.   Their management, though, usually
remained in private hands, or under boards or associations.
After the beginning of our national life a number of the
States founded and endowed a state system of academies.
Massachusetts, in 1797, granted land endowments to approved academies.   Georgia, in 1783, created a system of
county academies for the State.   New York extended state
aid to its academies, in 1813, having put them under state
inspection as early as 1787.   Maryland chartered many
academies between 1801 and 1817, and authorized many
lotteries to provide them with funds, as did also North Carolina.   Ohio, Kentucky, and Indiana, among Western States,
also provided for county systems of academies.

Character of the academy training.   The study of Latin
and a little Greek had constituted the curriculum of the old
Latin grammar school, and its purpose had been almost exclusively to prepare boys for admission to the colony colleges.   In true English style, Latin was made the language
of the classroom, and even attempted for the playground as
well.   As a concession, reading, writing, and arithmetic were
sometimes taught.   The new academies, while retaining the
study of Latin, and usually Greek, though now taught
through the medium of English, added a number of new
studies adapted to the needs of a new society.   English
grammar was introduced and soon rose to a place of great
importance, as did also oratory and declamation.   Arithmetic, algebra, geometry, geography, and astronomy were in
time added, and surveying, rhetoric (including some literature), natural and moral philosophy, and Roman antiqui-
ties were frequently taught.   Girls were admitted rather
freely to the new academies, whereas the grammar schools
had been exclusively for boys.   For better instruction a
"female department" was frequently organized.   The academies, beside offering a fair type of higher training before

the days of high schools, also became training schools for teachers, and before the rise of the normal schools were the chief source of supply for the better grade of elementary teachers. These institutions rendered an important service during the first half of the nineteenth century, but were in time displaced by the publicly supported and publicly controlled American high school, the first of which dates from 1821. This evolution we shall describe more in detail in a later chapter.

FIG. 17. A PENNSYLVANIA ACADEMY

York Academy, York, Pennsylvania, founded by the Protestant Episcopal Church, in 1787.

The colleges of the time. Some interest also was taken in college education during this early national period. College attendance, however, was small, as the country was still new and the people were poor. As late as 1815 Harvard graduated a class of but 66; Yale of 69; Princeton of 40; Williams of 40; Pennsylvania of 15; and the University of South Carolina of 37. After the organization of the Union the nine old colonial colleges were reorganized, and an attempt was made to bring them into closer harmony with the ideas and needs of the people and the governments of the States. Dartmouth, Kings (now rechristened Columbia), and Pennsylvania were for a time changed into state institutions, and an unsuccessful attempt was made to make a state university for Virginia out of William and Mary. Between 1790 and 1825 there was much discussion as to the desirability of founding a national university at the seat of government, and Washington in his will (1799) left, for that time, a considerable sum to the Nation to inaugurate the new undertaking. Nothing ever came of it, however. Before 1825 six States — Virginia, North Carolina, South

Carolina, Georgia, Indiana, and Michigan — had laid the foundations of future state universities. The National Government had also granted to each new Western State two entire townships of land to help endow a university in each, — a stimulus which eventually led to the establishment of a state university in every Western State.

QUESTIONS FOR DISCUSSION

1. Why does education not make much progress during periods of warfare or intense political agitation?
2. Contrast conditions as regards education in 1789 and to-day.
3. Explain how the religious-freedom attitude of the national constitution conferred an inestimable boon on the States in the matter of public schools.
4. Explain the change from the religious to the political motive for maintaining schools.
5. Does the quotation from Washington evidence as clear a conception of educational needs in a democracy as those from Jefferson?
6. What conception of education had John Jay in mind?
7. After the leaders of the time had come to see the need for the education of the masses, why did it take so long to obtain the establishment of state school systems?
8. Try to picture what might have been the educational conditions and development in this country: (a) Had the New England element had small families and remained in New England; (b) Had New England been settled by Anglicans, and no Calvinistic Puritans had ever come to North America; (c) Had the Puritans settled in Virginia, as they started out to do.
9. Explain why we were so slow in developing an educational consciousness.
10. Explain why the academy and the college naturally awakened a much deeper interest before 1820 than did common schools.
11. Explain why Oratory and Declamation naturally played such a prominent part in the work of the early academies and colleges.
12. Explain the great popularity of the academy, as compared with the older Latin grammar school.
13. Explain the larger interest in secondary and advanced education during the first quarter of a century of our national history.
14. How might the educational history of the North-West-Territory States have been different had the Nation never made the Louisiana purchase?
15. Explain the more liberal provisions of the Ohio constitution.

TOPICS FOR INVESTIGATION AND REPORT

1. The National land grants for education, and their influence. (Cubberley & Elliott; Monroe.)
2. The rise and early influence of the Academy. (E. E. Brown.)
3. Early state constitutional provisions. (Cubberley & Elliott.)
4. The early American colleges and the nature of their work. (Dexter.)
5. The westward expansion of New England. (Mathews.)

SELECTED REFERENCES

Cubberley, E. P. and Elliott, E. C. *State and County School Administration; Source Book.* 728 pp. The Macmillan Co., New York, 1915.

Chapter I reproduces all constitutional provisions before 1800, and Chapter II gives all the important sources relating to the national land grants to the States.

Dexter, E. G. *History of Education in the United States.* 656 pp. The Macmillan Co., New York, 1904.

Contains a good brief summary of the work of the early colleges.

Martin, G. H. *The Evolution of the Massachusetts Public School System.* 284 pp. D. Appleton & Co., New York, 1894.

*Mathews, Lois K. *The Expansion of New England.* 301 pp. Houghton Mifflin Co., Boston, 1909.

Chapters VI–VIII are excellent on the great migrations to the westward, and the planting of new commonwealths in the wilderness.

Monroe, Paul. *Cyclopedia of Education.* The Macmillan Co., New York, 1911–13.

The following article is especially important:
"National Government and Education"; vol. ii, pp. 372–82.

CHAPTER IV

INFLUENCES TENDING TO AWAKEN AN EDUCATIONAL CONSCIOUSNESS

I. PHILANTHROPIC INFLUENCES

A half-century of transition. The first half-century of our national life may be regarded as a period of transition from the church-control idea of education over to the idea of education under the control of and supported by the State. It required time to make this change in thinking. Up to the period of the beginnings of our national development education had almost everywhere been regarded as an affair of the Church, somewhat akin to baptism, marriage, the administration of the sacraments, and the burial of the dead. Even in New England, which formed an exception, the evolution of the civic school from the church school was not yet complete. A number of new forces — philanthropic, political, social, economic — now combined to produce conditions which made state rather than church control and support of education seem both desirable and feasible. The rise of a new national government based on the two new principles of political equality and religious freedom, together with the rise of new economic conditions which made some education for all seem necessary for economic as well as for political ends, changed this age-old situation.

The church charity school had become, as we have seen, a familiar institution before the Revolution. The English "Society for the Propagation of the Gospel in Foreign Parts," which maintained schools in connection with the Anglican churches in the Anglican colonies, and provided an excellent grade of charity-school master, withdrew at the close of the Revolutionary War from work in this country. The different churches after the war continued their efforts to maintain their church charity schools, though there was for a time a decrease in both their numbers and their effectiveness. In the meantime the demand for education grew rather rapidly, and the task soon became too big for the churches to handle. For long the churches made an effort to keep up, as they were loath to relinquish in any way their former hold on the training of the young. The churches, however, were not interested in the problem except in the old way, and this was not what the new democracy wanted. The result was that, with the coming of nationality and the slow but gradual growth of a national consciousness, national pride, national needs, and the gradual development of national resources in the shape of taxable property, — all alike combined to make secular instead of religious schools seem both desirable and possible to a constantly increasing number of citizens. This change in attitude was facilitated by the work of a number of semi-private philanthropic agencies, the most important of which were: (1) the Sunday School Movement; (2) the growth of City School Societies; (3) the Lancastrian Movement; and (4) the coming of the Infant-School Societies. These will be described briefly, and their influence in awakening an educational consciousness pointed out.

1. The Sunday School Movement

Secular schools before the religious. One of the earliest of these philanthropic movements designed to afford a minimum of education for the children of the poor was the so-called Sunday School Movement. This originated in England shortly after the middle of the seventeenth century, but amounted to little until 1780, when a publisher by the name of Robert Raikes, of Gloucester, gathered together the children in the pin factories of that city and paid four women a shilling each to spend their Sundays in instructing these poor working children "in reading, and the Church catechism." In 1783 Raikes published a description of the plan and its results, and soon the idea spread to many parts of England. So successful did the plan prove that in 1785 there was organized "The Society for promoting Sunday Schools throughout the British Dominions." The historian Green has declared that "the Sunday Schools established by Mr. Raikes were the beginnings of popular education" in England.

Raikes's idea was soon brought to the United States. In 1786 a Sunday School after the Raikes plan was organized in Hanover County, Virginia, at the house of one Thomas Crenghaw, and in 1787 a Sunday School for African children was organized at Charleston, South Carolina. In 1791 "The First Day, or Sunday School Society," was organized at Philadelphia, for the establishment of Sunday Schools in that city. In 1793 Katy Ferguson's "School for the Poor" was opened in New York, and this was followed by an organization of New York women for the extension of secular instruction among the poor. In 1797 Samuel Slater's Factory School was opened at Pawtucket, Rhode Island. These schools, being open to all instead of only to the poor and lowly, had a small but an increasing influence in leveling class distinctions, and in making a common day school seem possible. (The movement for secular instruction on Sundays, though, soon met in America with the opposition of the churches, and before long they took over the idea, superseded private initiative and control, and changed the character of the instruction from a day of secular work to an hour or so of religious teaching.)

Though there had been some Sunday instruction earlier at a few places in New England, the introduction of the Sunday School from England, in 1786, marks the real beginning of the religious Sunday School in America. After the churches had once caught the idea of a common religious school on Sundays for the instruction of any one, a number of societies were formed to carry on and extend the work. The most important of the earlier foundations were:

1808. The Evangelical Society of Philadelphia.
1816. The Female Union for the Promotion of Sabbath Schools (New York).

1816. The New York Sunday School Union.
1816. The Boston Society for the Moral and Religious Instruction of the Poor.
1817. The Philadelphia Sunday and Adult School Union.
1824. The American Sunday School Union.

2. The City School Societies

Before 1825 a number of subscription societies, many of which were able to effect financial connections with the city or the State, were formed in the few cities of the time to develop schools "for the education of such poor children as do not belong to, or are not provided for by any religious society." These societies were usually organized by philanthropic citizens, willing to contribute something yearly to provide some little education for a few of the many children in the city having no opportunities for any instruction.

Early New York City societies. One of the first of these societies was "The Manumission Society," organized in New York in 1785, for the purpose of "mitigating the evils of slavery, to defend the rights of the blacks, and especially to give them the elements of an education." Alexander Hamilton and John Jay were among its organizers. A free school for colored pupils was opened, in 1787. This grew and prospered and was aided from time to time by the city, and in 1801 by the State, and finally, in 1834, all its schools were merged with those of the "Public School Society" of the city. In 1801 the first free school for poor white children "whose parents belong to no religious society, and who, from some cause or other, cannot be admitted into any of the charity schools of the city," was opened. This was provided by the "Association of Women Friends for the Relief of the Poor," which engaged "a widow woman of good education and morals as instructor" at £30 per year. This Association also prospered, and received some city or state aid up to 1824. By 1823 it was providing free elementary education for 750 children. Its schools also were later merged with those of the "Public School Society."

"The Public School Society." Perhaps the most famous of all the early subscription societies for the maintenance of schools for the poor was the "New York Free School Society," which later changed its name to that of "The Public School Society of New York." This was organized in 1805 under the leadership of De Witt Clinton, then mayor of the city, he heading the subscription list with a promise of $200 a year for support. On May 14, 1806, the following advertisement appeared in the daily papers:

FREE SCHOOL

The Trustees of the Society for establishing a Free School in the city of New York, for the education of such poor children as do not belong to, or are not provided for by any religious Society, having engaged a Teacher, and procured a School House for the accommodation of a School, have now the pleasure of announcing that it is proposed to receive scholars of the descriptions alluded to without delay; applications may be made to, &c.

This Society was chartered by the legislature "to provide schooling for all children who are the proper objects of a

FIG. 18. THE FIRST SCHOOLHOUSE BUILT BY THE FREE SCHOOL SOCIETY IN NEW YORK CITY

Built in 1809, in Tryon Row. Cost, without site, $13,000.

gratuitous education." It organized free public education
in the city, secured funds, built schoolhouses, provided and
trained teachers, and ably supplemented the work of the
private and church schools. By its energy and its persist-
ence it secured for itself a large share of public confidence,
and aroused a constantly increasing interest in the cause of
popular education. In 1853, after it had educated over
600,000 children and trained over 1200 teachers, this Society,
its work done, surrendered its charter and turned over its
buildings and equipment to the public school department
of the city, which had been created by the legislature in
1842.

School Societies elsewhere. The "Benevolent Society.
of the City of Baltimore for the Education of the Female
Poor," founded in 1799, and the "Male Free Society of
Baltimore," organized a little later, were two of these early
school societies, though neither became so famous as the
Public School Society of New York. From the *Annual
Report of the Baltimore Male Free Society*, for 1822, we read:

It is truly gratifying to the Trustees to witness the increasing
interest taken in the education of the poor, — to see the talents,
the zeal, and the means now employed to give instruction to indigent youth. . . . To the liberality of the citizens of Baltimore, they
(the poor boys) are indebted for the ample means of instruction
which they now enjoy.

The schools of the city of Washington were started by
subscription, in 1804, and for some time were in part supported by subscriptions from public-spirited citizens.
Thomas Jefferson's name appears in the first subscription
list as giving $200, and he was elected a member of the first
governing board. This was composed of seven citizens appointed by the city council, and six elected from among the
subscribers. The chief sources of support of the schools,
which up to 1844 remained pauper schools, were subscriptions lotteries, a tax on slaves and dogs, certain license fees,
and a small appropriation ($1500) each year from the city
council. This society did an important work in accustoming

the people of the capital city to the provision of some form of free education.

In 1800 "The Philadelphia Society for the Free Instruction of Indigent Boys" was formed, which a little later changed to "The Philadelphia Society for the Establishment and Support of Charity Schools." This organization opened the first schools in Philadelphia for children regardless of religious affiliation, and for thirty-seven years rendered a useful service there. In 1814 "The Society for the Promotion of a Rational System of Education" was organized in Philadelphia, and four years later the public sentiment awakened by a combination of the work of this Society and the coming of the Lancastrian system of instruction enabled the city to secure a special law permitting Philadelphia to organize a system of city schools for the education of the children of its poor. Other educational societies which rendered useful service include the "Mechanics and Manufacturers Association," of Providence, Rhode Island, organized in 1789; "The Albany Lancastrian School Society," organized in 1826, for the education of the poor of the city in monitorial schools; and the school societies organized in Savannah, in 1818, and Augusta, in 1821, "to afford education to the children of indigent parents." Both these Georgia societies received some support from state funds.

Another type of free school, of which a number came to exist, resulted through establishments by will. Of these the gift of John Kidd, a wealthy baker of Cincinnati, who died in 1818 and bequeathed $1000 per year "for the education of poor children and youths of Cincinnati," is an example. Another bequest was made to the same city and for the same purpose, in 1824, by a citizen named Thomas Hughes.

The formation of these school societies, the subscriptions made by the leading men of the cities, the bequests for education, and the grants of some city and state aid to these societies, all of which in time became somewhat common, indicate a slowly rising interest in providing schools for the education of all. This rising interest in education was

greatly stimulated by the introduction from England of a
new and what for the time seemed a wonderful system for
the organization of education, which we next describe.

3. The Lancastrian monitorial system of instruction

Origin of the idea. In 1797 Dr. Andrew Bell published in
England an account of an experiment in education by means
of monitors, which he had made some years earlier in an
orphan asylum in Madras, India. About the same time a
young English schoolmaster, by the name of Joseph Lancaster, was led independently to a similar discovery of the
advantages of using monitors by reason of his needing assistance in his school and being too poor to pay for additional
teachers. The idea attracted attention from the first, and
was spread rapidly over England, in part by reason of a
bitter church quarrel between the followers of the two men
as to which was entitled to credit for originating the system.
The plans of the two men were much the same. Bell's
system was taken up and his claims supported by the Church-
of-England educational organizations, while Lancaster's
was supported by the Dissenters. It was the Lancastrian
plan which was brought to this country, Church-of-England
ideas not being in much favor after the Revolution. The
plan was so cheap, and so effective in teaching reading and
the fundamentals of religion, that it soon provided England
with a sort of a substitute for a national system of schools.

Once introduced into the United States, where the first
school was opened in New York City, in 1806, the system
quickly spread from Massachusetts to Georgia, and as far
west as Cincinnati, Louisville, and Detroit. In 1826 Maryland instituted a state system of Lancastrian schools, with
a Superintendent of Public Instruction, but in 1828 abandoned the idea and discontinued the office. A state Lancastrian system for North Carolina was proposed in 1832,
but failed of adoption by the legislature. In 1829 Mexico
organized higher Lancastrian schools for the Mexican State
of Texas. In 1818 Lancaster himself came to America, and

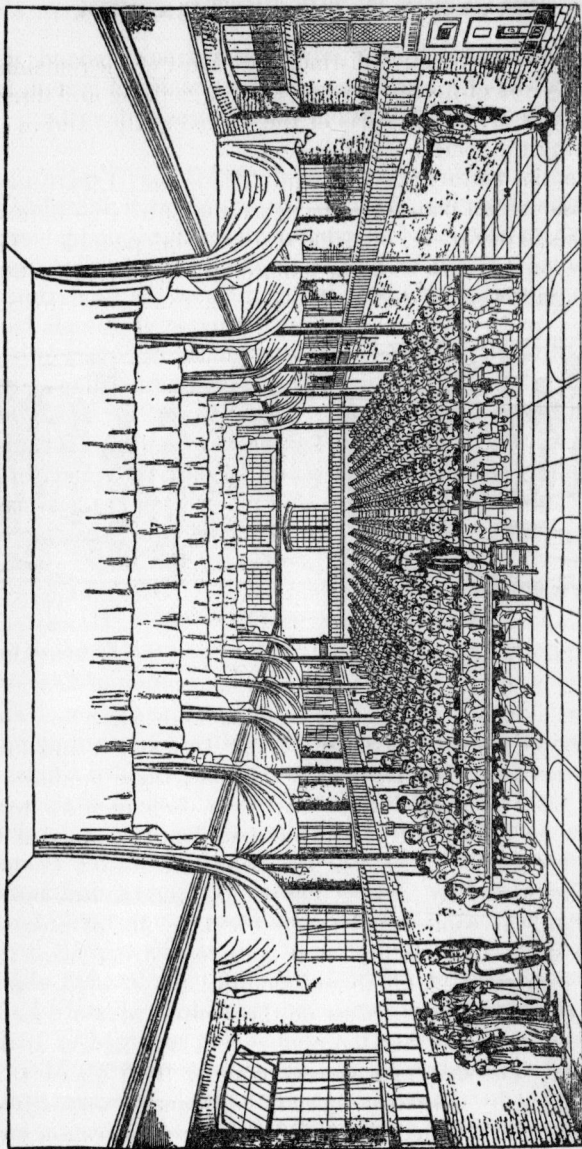

FIG. 19. A LANCASTRIAN SCHOOL IN OPERATION

This shows 365 pupils seated

was received with much distinction. Most of the remaining twenty years of his life were spent in organizing and directing schools in various parts of the United States, and in expounding the merits of his system.

Essential features of the plan. The essential features of the Lancastrian plan were the collection of a large number of pupils in one room, from 200 to 1000 being possible. The picture on page 91 shows a monitorial school seating 365. The pupils were sorted and seated in rows, and to each

FIG. 20. MONITORS TEACHING READING

Three draughts of ten each, with their toes to the semicircles painted on the floor, are being taught by monitors from lessons suspended on the wall.

row was assigned a clever boy who was known as a monitor. A common number for each monitor to instruct and look after was ten. The teacher first taught these monitors a lesson from a printed card, and then each monitor took his row to a "station" about the wall and proceeded to teach the other boys what he had just learned.

At first used only for teaching reading and the catechism, the plan was soon extended to the teaching of writing, simple sums, and spelling, and later to instruction in the higher branches. A number of monitorial high schools were organized in different cities of the United States, and it was even proposed that the plan should be adopted in the colleges. The system was very popular from about 1810 to 1830, but by 1840 its popularity had waned. In many of the now rapidly rising cities the first free schools established

were Lancastrian schools. The first free schools in Philadelphia (1818) were an outgrowth of Lancastrian influence,
as was also the case in many other Pennsylvania cities, —
Lancaster, Columbia, Harrisburg, Pittsburg, Milton, Erie,
New Castle, and Greencastle being among the number.
Baltimore began a Lancastrian school six years before the
organization of public schools was permitted there by law.

Such schools were naturally highly organized, the organization being largely mechanical. The *Manuals of Instruc-*

FIG. 21. MONITOR INSPECTING WRITTEN WORK AT SIGNAL, "SHOW
SLATES"

tion gave complete directions for the organization and management of monitorial schools, the details of recitation work,
use of the apparatus, order, and classification being minutely
laid down. By carefully studying and following these any
person could soon learn to become a successful teacher in
a monitorial school. The schools, mechanical as they now
seem, were a great improvement over the individual method
upon which colonial schoolmasters had wasted so much of
their own and their pupils' time. In place of their idleness,
inattention, and disorder, Lancaster introduced activity,
emulation, order, and a kind of military discipline which was
of much value to the type of children attending these schools.
Lancaster's biographer, Salmon, has written of the system
that so thoroughly was the instruction worked out that the

teacher had only to organize, oversee, reward, punish, and inspire:

When a child was admitted a monitor assigned him his class; while he remained, a monitor taught him (with nine other pupils); when he was absent, one monitor ascertained the fact, and another found out the reason; a monitor examined him periodically, and, when he made progress, a monitor promoted him; a monitor ruled the writing paper; a monitor had charge of slates and books; and a monitor-general looked after all the other monitors. Every monitor wore a leather ticket, gilded and lettered, "Monitor of the First Class," "Reading Monitor of the Second Class," etc.

Value of the system in awakening interest. The Lancastrian system of instruction, coming at the time it did, exerted a very important influence in awakening a public interest in and a sentiment for free schools. It did much toward making people see the advantages of a common school system, and become willing to contribute to the support of the same. Under the plans previously in use education had been a slow and an expensive process, because it had to be carried on by the individual method of instruction, and in quite small groups. Under this new plan it was now possible for one teacher to instruct 300, 400, 500, or more pupils in a single room, and to do it with much better results in both learning and discipline than the old type of schoolmaster had achieved. It is not strange that the new plan aroused widespread enthusiasm in many discerning men, and for almost a quarter of a century was advocated as the best system of education then known. Two quotations will illustrate what leading men of the time thought of it. De Witt Clinton, for twenty-one years president of the New York "Free School Society," and later governor of the State, wrote, in 1809:

When I perceive that many boys in our school have been taught to read and write in two months, who did not before know the alphabet, and that even one has accomplished it in three weeks — when I view all the bearings and tendencies of this system — when I contemplate the habits of order which it forms, the spirit of

JOSEPH LANCASTER
(1778–1838)

emulation which it excites, the rapid improvement which it pro-
duces, the purity of morals which it inculcates — when I behold
the extraordinary union of celerity in instruction and economy of
expense — and when I perceive one great assembly of a thousand
children, under the eye of a single teacher, marching with unex-
ampled rapidity and with perfect discipline to the goal of knowledge, I confess that I recognize in Lancaster the benefactor of the
human race. I consider his system as creating a new era in education, as a blessing sent down from heaven to redeem the poor and
distressed of this world from the power and dominion of ignorance.

In a message to the legislature of Connecticut, a State
then fairly well supplied with schools of the Massachusetts
district type, Governor Wolcott said, in 1825:

If funds can be obtained to defray the expenses of the necessary
preparations, I have no doubt that schools on the Lancastrian
model ought, as soon as possible, to be established in several parts
of this state. Wherever from 200 to 1000 children can be con-
vened within a suitable distance, this mode of instruction in every
branch of reading, speaking, penmanship, arithmetic, and bookkeeping, will be found much more efficient, direct, and economical
than the practices now generally pursued in our primary schools.

Value in preparing the way for taxation for education.
One of the main difficulties up to this time had been the cost
of education among people who were relatively poor, and
unwilling to spend money for anything for which they did
not clearly see the need. The private tutor as a means for
education was out of the question for any except the well-
to-do. The churches had their hands more than full in supporting schools, largely by tuition fees, for the children of
those of their members able to contribute something toward
their education, with a few free places for their deserving
poor. So long as the time-honored individual method of instruction, with its accompanying waste of time and disorder, continued to be the prevailing method, only a small
number of pupils could be placed under the control of a
single teacher. The expense for this made general education
almost prohibitive.

All at once, comparatively, a new system had been introduced which not only improved but tremendously cheapened education. In 1822 it cost but $1.22 per pupil per year to give instruction in New York City, though by 1844 the per-capita cost, due largely to the decreasing size of the classes, had risen to $2.70, and by 1852 to $5.83. In Philadelphia, in 1817, the expense was $3, as against $12 in the private and church schools. One finds many notices in the newspapers of the time as to the value and low cost of the new system. The following note, from *The Recorder* of Boston, for August 21, 1816, is typical:

A school on the Lancastrian plan has been recently established in Chillicothe, Ohio. The progress of the children is much more rapid than in the common schools; their exercises highly conducive to health; their lessons calculated to promote the purest morality; their books furnished; and the expenses no more than $2.50 by the quarter.

These sums are very low compared with present-day costs, or costs of even a decade ago.

The Lancastrian schools materially hastened the adoption of the free school system in all the Northern States by gradually accustoming people to bearing the necessary taxation which free schools entail. They also made the common school common and much talked of, and awakened thought and provoked discussion on the question of public education. They likewise dignified the work of the teacher by showing the necessity for teacher training. The Lancastrian Model Schools, first established in 1818, were the precursors of our normal schools.

4. The Infant-School Societies

Origin of the Infant-School idea. A curious condition in this country was that in some of the cities where public schools had been established, by one agency or another, no provision had been made for beginners. These were supposed to obtain the elements of reading at home, or in the dame schools. In Boston, for example, where public schools were maintained by the city, no children could be received into the schools who had not learned to read and write. This made the common age of admission somewhere near eight years. The same was in part true of Hartford, New York, Philadelphia, Baltimore, and other cities. When the monitorial schools were established they tended to restrict their membership in a similar manner, though not always able to do so.

In 1816 there came to this country, also from England, a valuable supplement to education as then known in the form of the so-called Infant-School idea. It had originated at New Lanark, in Scotland, in 1799, where a manufacturer by the name of Robert Owen had established a school for the children in his town and factories. The factory children were poor children of the town who had been bound out to him at five, six, and seven years of age, for a period of nine years. They worked as apprentices and helpers twelve to thirteen hours a day in the factories, and at early manhood were turned free to join the ignorant mass of the population. Owen sought to remedy this situation by opening a school which took the children at three years of age, and by amusements and instruction tried to give them moral, physical, and intellectual training. The idea, in the hands of his teachers, worked well; but in the hands of others elsewhere it was soon formalized, and book learning was made a prominent feature of the Infant Schools.

Infant Schools in the Eastern cities. In this formalized state the idea reached Boston, in 1816, and for the next two years an agitation was carried on for the establishment of Infant or Primary Schools. In 1818 the city appropriated $5000 for the purpose of organizing such schools to supplement the public school system, and appointed a supplemental school committee of three citizens in each of the then twelve wards to organize and direct the so-called primary schools. These schools were to admit children at four years of age, were to be taught by women, were to be open all the year round, and were to prepare the children for

admission to the city schools, which by that time had come
to be known as English grammar schools.   Separate schools
were established, separate school buildings were erected,
and a new set of teachers was employed.   The management of the primary schools remained separate from that
of the grammar schools until 1854, when the two were combined under one city School Committee.   Providence, similarly, established primary schools in 1828 for children between the ages of four
and eight, to supple-
ment the work of the
public schools, there
called writing schools.
For New England the
establishment of pri-
mary schools virtually
took over the dame
school instruction as a
public function, and add-
ed the primary grades
to the previously exist-
ing school. We have here
the origin of the divi-
sion, often still retained
at least in name in the
Eastern States, of the
"primary grades" and
the "grammar grades"
of our elementary school.

FIG. 22. "MODEL" SCHOOL BUILDING OF
THE PUBLIC SCHOOL SOCIETY

Erected in 1843. Cost (with site), $17,000. A typi-
cal New York school building, after 1830. The Infant or Primary school was on the first floor, the
second floor contained the girls' school, and the third
floor the boys' school. Each floor had one large room
seating 252 children; the primary schoolroom could be
divided into two rooms by folding doors, so as to
segregate the infant class. This building was for long
regarded as the perfection of the builder's art, and
its picture was printed for years on the cover of the
Society's *Annual Reports*.

An "Infant-School So-
ciety" was organized in
New York in 1827.   The first Infant School was established
under the direction of the Public School Society as the
"Junior Department" of School No. 8, with a woman teacher
in charge, and using monitorial methods.   A second school
was established the next year.   In 1830 the name was
changed from Infant School to Primary Department, and

where possible these departments were combined with the existing schools. In 1832 it was decided to organize ten primary schools, under women teachers, for children from four to ten years of age, and after the Boston plan of instruction. This abandoned the monitorial plan of instruction for the new Pestalozzian form, described in Chapter IX, which was deemed better suited to the needs of the smaller

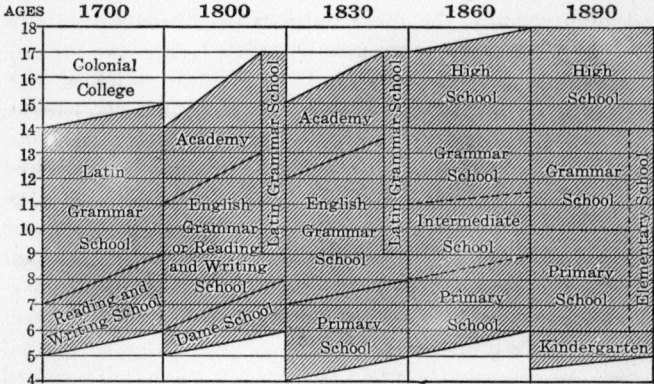

FIG. 23. EVOLUTION OF THE ESSENTIAL FEATURES OF THE AMERICAN PUBLIC SCHOOL SYSTEM

children. By 1844 fifty-six Primary Departments had been organized in connection with the upper schools of the city.

In Philadelphia there were three Infant-School Societies founded in 1827–28, and such schools were at once established there. By 1830 the directors of the school system had been permitted by the legislature of the State to expend public money for such schools, and thirty such, under women teachers, were in operation in the city by 1837.

Primary education organized. The Infant-School idea was soon somewhat generally adopted by the Eastern cities, and changed somewhat to make of it an American primary school. Where children had not been previously admitted to the schools without knowing how to read, as in Boston, they supplemented the work of the public schools by adding a new school beneath. Where the reverse had been the case, as in New York City, the organization of Infant Schools as Junior Departments enabled the existing schools to advance their work. Everywhere it resulted, eventually, in the organization of primary and grammar school departments, often with intermediate departments in between, and, with the somewhat contemporaneous evolution of the first high schools, the main outlines of the American free public school system were now complete.

Unlike the monitorial schools, the infant schools were based on the idea of small-group work, and were usually conducted in harmony with the new psychological conceptions of instruction which had by that time been worked out by Pestalozzi in Switzerland, and introduced into the Infant Schools of England. The Infant-School idea came at an opportune time, as the defects of the mechanical Lancastrian instruction were becoming evident and its popularity was waning. It gave a new and a somewhat deeper philosophical interpretation of the educational process, created a stronger demand than had before been known for trained teachers, established a preference for women teachers for primary work, and tended to give a new dignity to teaching and school work by revealing something of a psychological basis for the instruction of little children. It also contributed its share toward the awakening of a sentiment for intelligently directed public education.

These four important educational movements — the secular Sunday School, the semi-public city School Societies, the Lancastrian plan for instruction, and the Infant-School idea — all arising in philanthropy, came as successive educational ideas to America during the first half of the nineteenth century, supplemented one another, and together accustomed a new generation to the idea of a common school for all.

II. Social, Political, and Economic Influences

It is hardly probable, however, that these philanthropic efforts alone, valuable as they were, could have resulted in the great battle for tax-supported schools, at as early a date as this took place, had they not been supplemented by a number of other movements of a social, political, and economic character which in themselves materially changed the nature and direction of our national life. The more important of these will be described briefly.

1. The growth of the cities

Growth of city population. At the time of the inauguration of our national government nearly every one lived on the farm or in some little village. The first forty years of our national life were essentially an agricultural and a pioneer period. Even as late as 1820 there were but thirteen cities of 8000 inhabitants or over in the whole of the twenty-three States at that time comprising the Union, and these thirteen cities contained but 4.9 per cent of the total population of the Nation. Under such conditions education was largely a rural affair and, except in the more settled portions of the country, was almost certain to be generally neglected for the more important duties of cutting down the forests, draining the swamps, establishing farms and homes, and providing food and shelter for family and stock. Every child was then an asset, and was put to work at as early an age as possible. Few could be spared to go to school. It was a time of hard work, with few comforts and pleasures, and with but little need for the school of books.

After about 1825 these conditions began to change. By 1820 many little villages were springing up, and these frequently proved the nuclei for future cities. In New England many of these places were in the vicinity of some waterfall, where cheap power made manufacturing on a large scale possible. Lowell, Massachusetts, which in 1820 did not exist and in 1840 had a population of over twenty thousand people, collected there largely to work in the mills, is a good illustration. Other cities, such as Cincinnati and Detroit, grew because of their advantageous situation as exchange and wholesale centers. With the revival of trade and commerce after the second war with Great Britain the cities grew rapidly both in number and size, as may be seen from the following table.

GROWTH OF CITY POPULATION, 1790–1860

| Year | Number of cities having a population of | | | | | Percentage of total population in cities |
	8000 or over	8000 to 20,000	20,000 to 75,000	75,000 to 250,000	250,000 or over	
1780	5	4	1			2.7
1790	6	4	2			3.3
1800	6	1	5			4.0
1810	11	6	3	2		4.9
1820	13	7	4	2		4.9
1830	26	19	4	3		6.7
1840	44	28	11	4	1	8.5
1850	85	56	21	6	2	12.5
1860	141	96	35	7	3	16.1

The rise of the new cities and the rapid growth of the older ones materially changed the nature of the educational problem, by producing an entirely new set of social and educational conditions for the people of the Central and Northern States to solve. The South, with its plantation life, negro slavery, and absence of manufacturing was largely unaffected by these changed conditions until well after the close of the Civil War. In consequence the educational awakening there did not come for nearly half a century after it came in the North.

2. The rise of manufacturing

The beginnings in our country. During the colonial period manufacturing was still in the home or village stage of development. Almost all articles of use and wear were made by the family in the home. Wagons and furniture were made in the villages, and the traveling shoemaker came around from time to time to make up shoes for all the family. In 1787 the first American factory is said to have been started, at Beverly, Massachusetts. In 1791 the first cotton spinning-mill was set up on the falls of the Pawtucket River, in Rhode Island, and the beginnings of New England's supremacy in the cotton-spinning industry were made. By 1804 there were four cotton-mills in operation, and by 1807, fifteen.

Up to 1807, though, the development of our country was almost wholly agricultural. This had meant a scattered and an isolated population, with few common ideas, common interests, or common needs. Nearly all the manufactured articles not made in the homes or the villages were made in Great Britain. The Embargo of 1807, laid by Congress on American shipping, cut off articles of English manufacture and soon led to the rise of many "infant industries." Many of the legislative acts of the next five years had to do with the granting of charters and privileges to various kinds of manufactories. The War of 1812, the troubles with Napoleon, and the general westward movement of the population, all tended for a time to build up manufacturing faster than agriculture. At the end of the struggle with Napoleon (1815) this country, due to the lack of any adequate protective tariff, was for a time flooded with manufactured articles from Europe. As a result, the "infant industries" were paralyzed, and an era of hard times set in which continued to about 1820. This condition was in time corrected by the protective tariff, and following its enactment a great industrial development took place.

The industrial transformation. The three decades from 1820 to 1850 were characterized by a rapid development of manufacturing and a rapid growth of cities, in which most of the new manufacturing plants were established. The introduction of the steamboat (1809) and the steam railroad (1826), together with the digging of many canals (the famous Erie Canal was opened in 1825), opened up the possibility of doing business on a scale before unthought of, and led to a great demand for manufactured articles and labor-saving machinery of every sort.   The first steam railroad, three miles long, was built in 1826, and by 1850, 9021 miles had been constructed in the United States.   One could now travel by rail from Maine to North Carolina, to Buffalo on Lake Erie, and from the western end of Lake Erie to Cincinnati or Chicago.   By 1860 steam railways had been built westward into Iowa, Missouri, and Arkansas, and thirty thousand miles of rails were carrying agricultural products from the interior and manufactured products from the seaboard cities back to the interior.   The invention of the telegraph (first line, 1844) also tremendously increased the possibilities of doing business on a large scale.

The inventive genius of our people was now called into play, and Yankee ingenuity manifested itself in every direction.   After 1825 the threshing machine began to supplant the flail and the roller; after 1826 edge tools began to be made in this country; and shortly after this time the Fairbanks platform scale, the mower, the reaper, and the lock-stitch sewing machine were invented.   Kerosene lamps were devised, improved cook-stoves were put on the market, and the friction match superseded the flint.   The coal measures west of the Alleghenies were opened, and anthracite in the East was put to use.   The great work of steam had begun, the chimneys of factories were rising over the land, and the steam engine was applied to both boat and train, to running the power loom and the printing-press, and to the steam hammer for working iron and steel.   Between 1820 and 1850 industrial methods in America were revolutionized.

How manufacturing changed the position of the city.   In the cities in the coast States north of Maryland, but particularly in those of New York and New England, manufacturing developed very rapidly.   Cotton-spinning in particular became a New England industry, as did also the weaving of wool, while Pennsylvania became the center of the iron

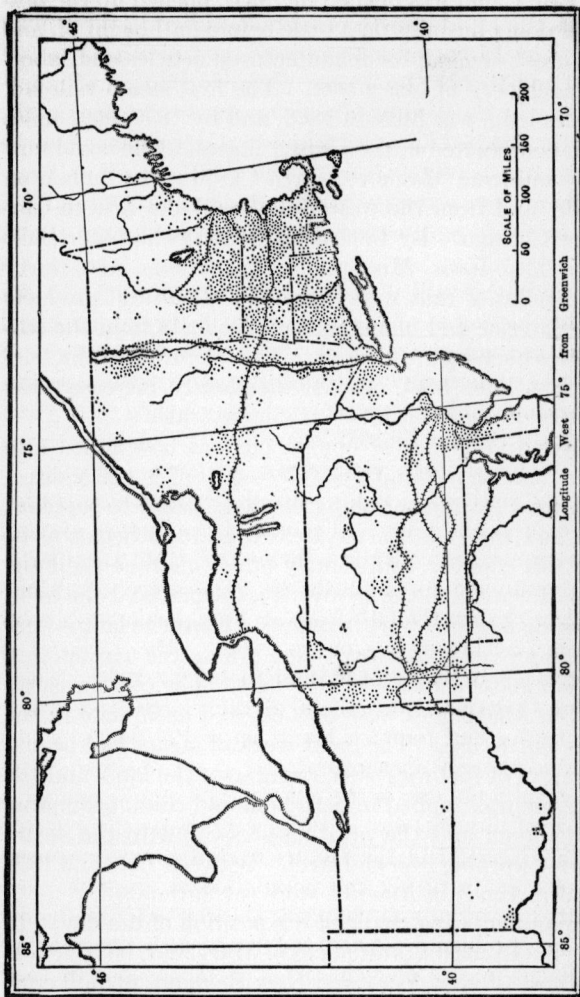

Fig. 24. Distribution of Industrial Plants in the United States in 1833.
From W. E. Dodd's *Expansion and Conflict*; Houghton Mifflin Co., 1915. Reproduced by permission.

manufacturing industries. The cotton-spinning industry illustrates the rapid growth of manufacturing in the United States. The 15 cotton-mills of 1807 had increased to 801 by 1831, and to 1240 by 1840. The distribution of industrial plants in the United States by 1833, pictured in the map on the preceeding page, shows the development in the Northern and Eastern cities. The South owed its prosperity chiefly to cotton-growing and shipping, and did not develop factories and workshops until a much more recent period.

Now the development of this new type of factory work meant the beginnings of the breakdown of the old home and village industries, the start of the cityward movement of the rural population, and the concentration of manufacturing in large establishments, employing many hands to perform continuously certain limited phases of the manufacturing process. This in time was certain to mean a change in educational methods. It also called for the concentration of both capital and labor. The rise of the factory system, business on a large scale, and cheap and rapid transportation, all combined to diminish the importance of agriculture and to change the city from an unimportant to a very important position in our national life. The 13 cities of 1820 increased to 44 by 1840, and to 141 by 1860. There were four times as many cities in the North, too, where manufacturing had found a home, as in the South, which remained essentially agricultural.

New social problems in the cities. The many changes in the nature of industry and of village and home life, effected by the development of the factory system and the concentration of manufacturing and population in the cities, also contributed materially in changing the character of the old educational problem. When the cities were as yet but little villages in size and character, homogeneous in their populations, and the many social and moral problems incident to the congestion of peoples of mixed character had not as yet arisen, the church and charity and private school solution of the educational problem was reasonably satisfactory. As the cities now rapidly increased in size, became more city-like in character, drew to them diverse elements previously largely unknown, and were required by state laws to extend the right of suffrage to all their citizens, the need for a new type of educational organization began slowly but clearly to manifest itself to an increasing number of citizens. The church, charity, and private school system completely broke down under the new strain. School Societies and Educational Associations, organized for propaganda, now arose in the cities; grants of city or state funds for the partial support of both church and society schools were demanded and obtained; and numbers of charity organizations began to be established in the different cities to enable them to handle better the new problems of pauperism, intemperance, and juvenile delinquency which arose.

In 1833 it was estimated that one eighth of the total population of New York City was composed of public paupers or criminals, while the city had one saloon for every eighty men, women, and children in the total population. Other cities presented somewhat similar conditions. Child labor and woman labor, for long hours and for very low wages, became very common. The powerful restraining influences of the old home, with its strict moral code and religious atmosphere, seriously weakened. Idle and uneducated children, with little or no home control, appeared in numbers on the streets, and the prevalence of juvenile crime and juvenile arrests began to turn attention to education as a possible remedy. The disintegrating effects of the new city life on the family, and its demoralizing effect upon the children, made a deep impression upon those possessed of humanitarian impulses, as it did also on many of the parents of the children concerned. We soon find these two very dissimilar groups of people — the humanitarians on the one hand and the new city laboring classes on the other — uniting in a propaganda for tax-supported schools.

3. *The extension of the suffrage*

Breaking the rule of a class. As was stated in the preceding chapter, the Constitution of the United States, though framed by the ablest men of the time, was framed by men who represented the old aristocratic conception of education and government. The same was true of the conventions which framed practically all the early state constitutions. The early leaders in our government — Washington, Madison, Hancock, Adams, Hamilton, Jay — had been of this older aristocratic class. The Federalist Party, a party which rendered very conspicuous service in welding the States into a strong and enduring Union, had nevertheless represented this older privileged group, and by 1817 had done its work and been broken up. The early period of our national life was thus characterized by the rule of a class — a very well educated and a very capable class, to be sure — but a class elected by a ballot based on property qualifications and belonging to the older type of political and social thinking.

Notwithstanding the statements of the Declaration of Independence, the change came but slowly. Up to 1815 but four States had granted the right to vote to all male citizens, regardless of property holdings or other somewhat similar restrictions. After 1815 a democratic movement, which sought to abolish all class rule and all political inequalities, arose and rapidly gained strength. In this the new States to the westward, with their absence of old estates or large fortunes, and where men were judged more on their merits than in an older society, were the leaders. As will be seen from the map, every new State admitted east of the Mississippi River, except Ohio (admitted in 1802), where the New England element predominated, and Louisiana (1812), provided for full manhood suffrage at the time of their admission to statehood. Five additional Eastern States had extended the same full voting privileges to their citizens by 1845, while the old requirements had been materially modified in most of the other Northern States. Writing on the influence of the West, Professor Turner says:

The frontier States that came into the Union in the first quarter of a century of its existence came in with democratic suffrage provisions, and had reactive effects of the highest importance upon

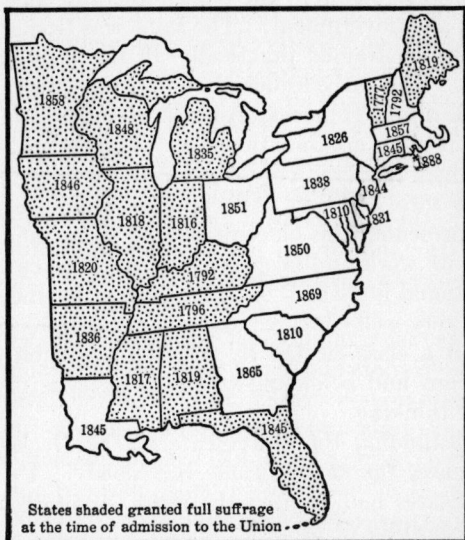

FIG. 25. DATES OF THE GRANTING OF FULL MANHOOD SUFFRAGE

Some of the older States granted almost full manhood suffrage at an earlier date, retaining a few minor restrictions until the date given on the map.

the older States whose people were being attracted there. An extension of the suffrage became essential. It was western New York that forced an extension of the suffrage in the constitutional convention of that State in 1821; and it was western Virginia that compelled the tide-water region to put in a more liberal provision in the constitution of 1830, and to give the frontier region a more nearly proportional representation with the tide-water aristocracy.

Significance of the election of Jackson.   The struggle for the overthrow of the old class government came to a head in 1828, when Andrew Jackson was elected President.   From Washington down to John Quincy Adams the Presidents had been drawn from the old aristocratic class, and the educated and propertied classes of Massachusetts, New York, and Virginia had largely furnished the leaders for the Nation.   Jackson, on the other hand, represented the frontier, and was everywhere regarded as "a man of the people."   His election was a reaction against trained leadership in governmental affairs.   The period when the people were to follow men of education and good breeding was now for a time largely past.   The people had become impatient of the old claims as to the superiority of any class, and the demand for equal suffrage and for full participation in the functions of government now became too insistent to be disregarded longer.

This impatience and distrust expressed itself also with reference to governors and legislatures, and a popular demand for changes here now arose.   In place of the former plan of electing a governor and allowing him to appoint most of the other officials, a long list of elected officials now appeared. The people demanded and usually obtained the right to vote for every possible officer, and short terms in office became the rule.   Legislatures, too, instead of being allowed to meet when and for as long as they pleased, were now closely limited as to length of session, and allowed to meet only at stated times. [This democratic movement for the leveling of all distinctions between white men became very marked after 1820, and the final result was full manhood suffrage in all the States.] This gave the farmer in the West and the new working classes in the cities a preponderating influence in the affairs of government.   Jackson represented both these elements, and was elected by an electoral vote of 178 to 83 over John Quincy Adams, in 1828, and by a vote of 219 to 49 over Henry Clay, in 1832.

Educational significance of the extension of the suffrage.

The educational significance of the extension of full manhood suffrage to all was enormous and far reaching. Up to the time of the separation of Church and State, education had not been conceived of as a function with which the State was specially concerned. Since the right to vote was closely limited by religious or property qualifications, or both, there was no particular reason why the State should assume the rôle of schoolmaster. Such citizens as were qualified by faith or property holdings to vote or hold office were amply able to pay for the education of their children privately. It was not necessary, either, for more than a small percentage of the people to be educated. The small educated class conducted the affairs of Church and State; the great majority formed "the hewers of wood and the drawers of water" for society.

With the extension of the suffrage to all classes of the population, poor as well as rich, laborer as well as employer, there came to thinking men, often for the first time, a realization that general education had become a fundamental necessity for the State, and that the general education of all in the elements of knowledge and civic virtue must now assume that importance in the minds of the leaders of the State that the education of a few for the service of the Church and of the many for simple church membership had once held in the minds of ecclesiastics.

This new conception is well expressed in the preamble to the first (optional) school law enacted in Illinois (1825), which declares:

To enjoy our rights and liberties, we must understand them; their security and protection ought to be the first object of a free people; and it is a well-established fact that no nation has ever continued long in the enjoyment of civil and political freedom, which was not both virtuous and enlightened; and believing that the advancement of literature always has been, and ever will be the means of developing more fully the rights of man, that the mind of every citizen in a republic is the common property of society, and constitutes the basis of its strength and happiness; it is therefore considered the peculiar duty of a free government, like ours, to encourage and extend the improvement and cultivation of the intellectual energies of the whole.

4. New public demands for schools

Utterances of public men. Governors now began to recommend to their legislatures the establishment of tax-supported schools, and public men began to urge state action and state control. De Witt Clinton, for nine years governor of New York, in a message to the legislature, in 1826, defending the schools established, said:

> The first duty of government, and the surest evidence of good government, is the encouragement of education. A general diffusion of knowledge is a precursor and protector of republican institutions, and in it we must confide as the conservative power that will watch over our liberties and guard them against fraud, intrigue, corruption, and violence. I consider the system of our common schools as the palladium of our freedom, for no reasonable apprehension can be entertained of its subversion as long as the great body of the people are enlightened by education.

Again in his message of 1827, he added:

> The great bulwark of republican government is the cultivation of education; for the right of suffrage cannot be exercised in a salutary manner without intelligence.

In an address delivered before the Pennsylvania legislature, in 1835, defending the Free School Law of 1834, which it was then proposed to repeal, Thaddeus Stevens declared:

> If an elective Republic is to endure for any length of time, every elector must have sufficient information not only to accumulate wealth and take care of his pecuniary concerns, but to direct wisely the legislature, the ambassadors, and the Executive of the Nation — for some part of all these things, some agency in approving or disapproving of them, falls to every freeman. If, then, the permanency of our Government depends upon such knowledge, it is the duty of Government to see that the means of information be diffused to every citizen. This is a sufficient answer to those who deem education a private and not a public duty.

DE WITT CLINTON
(1769–1828)

First President of the Free School Society
Mayor of the City of New York
Governor of the State of New York

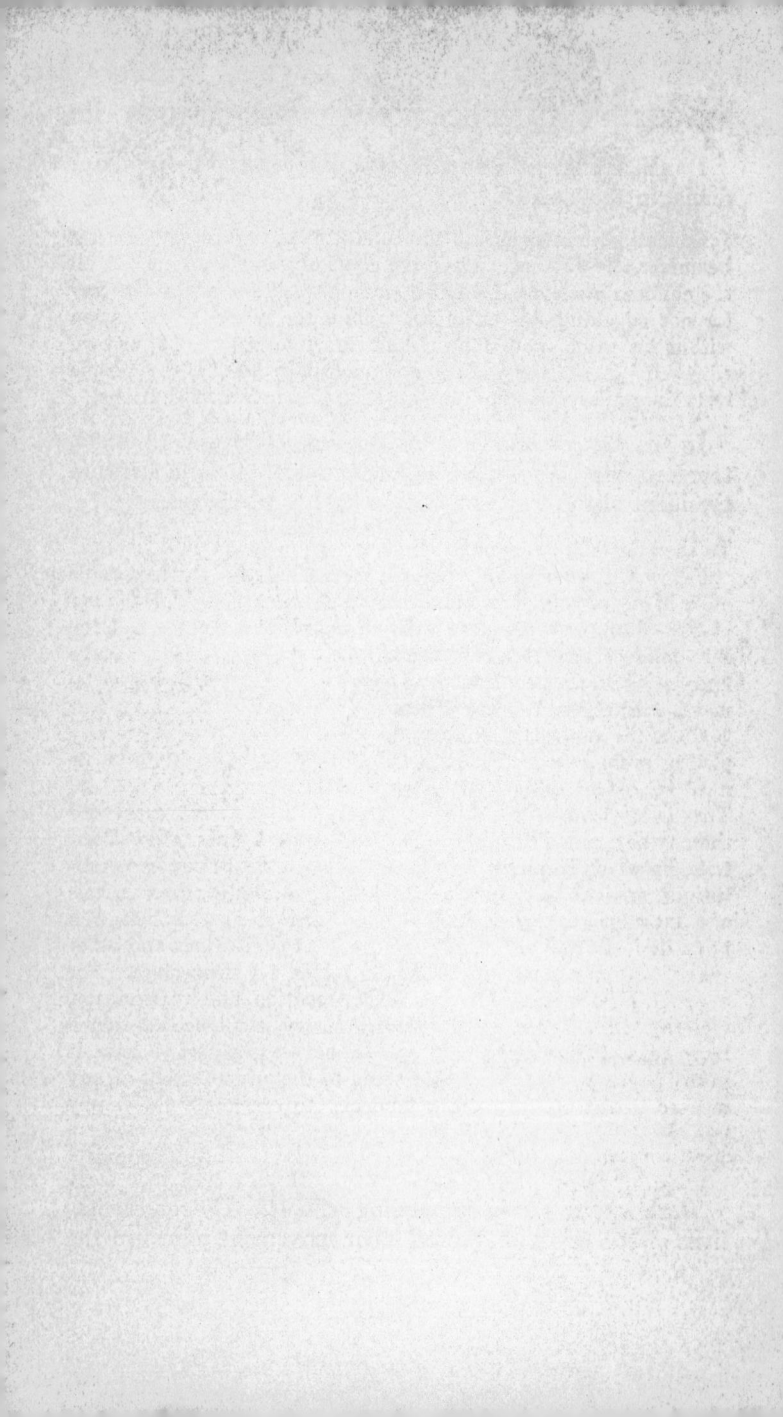

Daniel Webster, in an address delivered at Madison, Indiana, in 1837, said:

Education, to accomplish the ends of good government, should be universally diffused. Open the doors of the schoolhouses to all the children in the land. Let no man have the excuse of poverty for not educating his offspring. Place the means of education within his reach, and if he remain in ignorance, be it his own reproach. . . . On the diffusion of education among the people rests the preservation and perpetuation of our free institutions.

In the *Sangamon (Illinois) Journal*, of March 15, 1832, there appeared an interesting communication from a future president of the United States, a part of which read:

To the People of Sangamo(n) County:

Fellow Citizens: Having become a candidate for the honorable office of one of your Representatives in the next General Assembly of this State, in accordance with an established custom and the principles of true republicanism, it becomes my duty to make known to you, the people whom I propose to represent — my sentiments with regard to local affairs. . . .

Upon the subject of education, not presuming to dictate any plan or system respecting it, I can only say that I view it as the most important subject which we as a people can be engaged in. That every man may receive at least a moderate education, and thereby be enabled to read the histories of his own and other countries, by which he may duly appreciate the value of our free institutions, appears to be an object of vital importance, even on this account alone, to say nothing of the advantages and satisfaction to be derived from all being able to read the Scriptures and other works, both of a religious and moral nature, for themselves. For my part, I desire to see the time when education, and by its means, morality, sobriety, enterprise, and industry, shall become much more general than at present, and should be gratified to have it in my power to contribute something to the advancement of any measure which might have a tendency to accelerate the happy period.

A. LINCOLN

Workingmen join in demanding schools. The representatives of the newly organized labor movement joined in the

demands for schools and education, urging the free education of their children as a natural right.   In 1829 the workingmen of Philadelphia asked each candidate for the legislature for a formal declaration of the attitude he would
assume toward the provision of "an equal and a general system of education" for the State.   In 1830 the Workingmen's
Committee of Philadelphia submitted a detailed report, after
five months spent in investigating educational conditions
in Pennsylvania, vigorously condemning the lack of provision for education in the State, and the utterly inadequate
provision where any was made.   Seth Luther, in an address
on "The Education of Workingmen," delivered in 1832,
declared that "a large body of human beings are ruined by
a neglect of education, rendered miserable in the extreme,
and incapable of self-government."   Stephen Simpson, in
his *A Manual for Workingmen*, published in 1831, declared
that "it is to education, therefore, that we must mainly look
for redress of that perverted system of society, which dooms
the producer to ignorance, to toil, and to penury, to moral
degradation, physical want, and social barbarism."

With the invention of the steam printing-press the first
modern newspapers at a cheap price appeared.   These
usually espoused progressive measures, and tremendously
influenced public sentiment.   Those not closely connected
with church or private-school interests usually favored public tax-supported schools.   The *Delaware Free Press*, for
example, in 1835, declared a part of its mission to be:

> To awaken the attention of Working People to the importance
> of coöperation in order to attain the rank and station in society
> to which they are justly entitled by virtue of their industry, *but
> from which they are excluded by want of a system of Equal Republican
> Education.*

In 1837 the Providence (Rhode Island) Association of
Mechanics and Manufacturers petitioned the city council
for an improvement of the schools of the city, in particular
asking for more schools, smaller classes, and better salaries

for the teachers, and affirming that "no subject can be of more importance to the inhabitants of this city than the education of the rising generation."

At first various substitutes for state support and control were tried. School Societies, as we have seen, were chartered. Religious and benevolent schools were subsidized. Numerous lotteries for the support of schools were authorized by law. Grants of public land for their endowment were made. State support only of pauper schools was tried. Freedom of taxation to schools and educational societies was granted. Finally, all these makeshifts failing to meet the needs of the time, they were gradually discarded as unsatisfactory and insufficient, and the battle for free, tax-supported, non-sectarian, and publicly controlled and directed schools, to serve the needs of society and the State, was begun.

QUESTIONS FOR DISCUSSION

1. Explain why the development of a national consciousness was practically necessary before an educational consciousness could be awakened.
2. Show how the many philanthropic societies for the education of the children of the poor came in as a natural transition from Church to State education.
3. Show the importance of the School Societies in accustoming people to the idea of free and general education.
4. Show how the Lancastrian system formed the necessary bridge between private philanthropy in education and tax-supported State schools.
5. Why were the highly mechanical features of the Lancastrian organization so advantageous in its day, whereas we of to-day would regard them as such a disadvantage?
6. Account for the Lancastrian system's great superiority over the methods of colonial schoolmasters.
7. Explain how the Lancastrian schools dignified the work of the teacher by revealing the need for teacher training.
8. What were two of the important contributions of the Infant-School idea to American education?
9. Why are schools and education much more needed in a country experiencing a city and manufacturing development than in a country experiencing an agricultural development?

10. Show how the development of cities caused the old forms of education to break down, and made evident the need for a new type of education.
11. Show how each extension of the suffrage necessitates an extension of educational opportunities and advantages.
12. Show how the utterances of public men on education, quoted in this chapter, evidence a much clearer conception of the need for public education than do those quoted in the preceding chapter, with the possible exception of the quotation from John Adams.

TOPICS FOR INVESTIGATION AND REPORT

1. Work of the New York Public School Society.
2. Educational services of De Witt Clinton.
3. Organization and work of the Lancastrian schools.
4. The workingmen's movement of 1825–40.

SELECTED REFERENCES

*Barnard, Henry, Editor. *The American Journal of Education.* 31 vols. Consult *Analytical Index* to; 128 pp. Published by United States Bureau of Education, Washington, 1892.

Binns, H. B. *A Century of Education, 1808–1908.* 330 pp. J. M. Dent & Co., London, 1908.

A centenary history of the British and Foreign School Society, which promoted Lancastrian schools. Chapter I contains a sketch of Lancaster.

Boese, Thomas. *Public Education in the City of New York.* 288 pp. Harper & Bros., New York, 1869.

A history of the development, taken from the official records. An important work, though now out of print, but listed because still found in many libraries.

Bogart, E. L. *The Economic History of the United States.* 522 pp. Longmans, Green & Co., New York, 1908.

Contains good chapters (X–XII) on the introduction and growth of the factory system.

*Carleton, F. T. *Education and Social Progress.* 320 pp. The Macmillan Co., New York, 1908.

Chapters I and II deal with epochs in American educational progress, and point out the relation between educational advance and industrial progress.

*Dodd, W. E. *Expansion and Conflict.* 329 pp. Houghton Mifflin Co., Boston, 1915.

Chapter I is good on the significance of the election of Jackson, and Chapter XI gives a very good brief general sketch of American culture between about 1830 and 1860.

Ellis, Chas. C. *Lancastrian Schools in Philadelphia.* 88 pp. University of Pennsylvania Thesis, 1907.

A good study of Lancastrian schools in Philadelphia.

*Fitzpatrick, E. A. *The Educational Views and Influence of De Witt Clinton.* 156 pp. Teachers College Contributions to Education, No. 44. New York, 1911.

A study of educational conditions in New York at the time, Clinton's educational views, and his influence.

Knight, Edgar W. *Public School Education in North Carolina.* 384 pp. Houghton Mifflin Co., Boston, 1916.

An excellent example of a brief history of education in a State. Chapters 6, 7, and 8 are good on the establishment of the permanent school fund, the awakening of educational sentiment, and the beginnings of public education.

Manuals of the Lancastrian System. ca. 90 pp. Various dates, 1805–1850.

Various forms of these are found in libraries. Some are of the British and Foreign School Society, and others of the New York School Society, of various dates. Any one will usually outline the system of instruction employed in the Lancastrian schools.

*McManis, J. T. "The public school society of New York City"; in *Educational Review*, vol. 29, pp. 303–11. (March, 1905.)

A brief but sympathetic sketch of the work of this Society.

*Monroe, Paul. *Cyclopedia of Education.* The Macmillan Co., New York, 1911–13.

The following articles are particularly important:
1. "Joseph Lancaster," III, pp. 621–22.
   A brief biography.
2. "Monitorial System," IV, pp. 296–99.
   A brief description of the rise and spread of the idea.
3. "New York City," IV, pp. 451–53.
   Sketches briefly the history of early education in.

*Palmer, A. E. *The New York Public School.* 440 pp. The Macmillan Co., New York, 1905.

The first sixteen chapters describe the work of the Public School Society in some detail, and contain much important data.

*Reigart, J. F. *The Lancastrian System of Instruction in the Schools of New York City.* 105 pp. Teachers College Contributions to Education, No. 81, New York, 1916.

An excellent study of the introduction of the system, and the methods of instruction employed in the schools.

*Salmon, David. *Joseph Lancaster.* 76 pp. Longmans, Green & Co., London, 1904.

The standard biography of Lancaster.

*Simons, A. M. *Social Forces in American History.* 325 pp. The Macmillan Co., New York, 1911.

Very simple and well-written chapters on the birth of the factory system (XIII), changing interests of the people (XIV), condition of the workers (XVI), and the first labor movement (XVII).

CHAPTER V

THE BATTLE FOR FREE STATE SCHOOLS

I. ALIGNMENT OF INTERESTS, AND PROPAGANDA

Stages in the development of a public school sentiment.
Speaking broadly and of the Nation as a whole, and always
excepting certain regions in New England, where the free-
school idea had become thoroughly established, a study of
the history of educational development in the older States
to the North and East reveals, as we have so far partially
pointed out, approximately the following stages in the development of a public school sentiment and the establishment of a state school system:

1. An attempt to solve the problem through private benevolence
   or church charity, often aided by small grants of public funds.
2. Aid granted to private or semi-private schools or school societies, in the form of small money grants, license taxes, permission to organize lotteries, or land endowments, to enable such
   schools or societies to extend their instruction or to reduce
   their tuition rates, or both.
3. Permission granted generally, or to special districts request-
   ing it, to form a tax district and organize schools — at first
   often only for pauper children, but later for others.
4. Laws requiring the education of the indigent poor.
5. Laws requiring a certain local effort for the maintenance of
   schools, in return for state aid received, with permission to
   supplement these sums with tuition fees.
6. Elimination of the tuition fees, thus establishing free schools.
7. Elimination of the pauper-school idea and of aid to sectarian
   schools, thus establishing the American common school.

Something like half a century of agitation and conflict,
again speaking broadly and of the Nation as a whole, was
required to produce the succession of changes indicated
above, but by 1850 it may be said that the question of

providing a common-school education for all children at public expense had been settled, in principle at least, in every Northern State. In some of the Southern States, as well, quite a respectable beginning looking toward the creation of state school systems had been made before the coming of the Civil War for a time put an end to all educational development there.

The alignment of interests. The second quarter of the nineteenth century may be said to have witnessed the battle for tax-supported, publicly controlled and directed, and non-sectarian common schools. In 1825 such schools were the distant hope of statesmen and reformers; in 1850 they were becoming an actuality in almost every Northern State. The twenty-five years intervening marked a period of public agitation and educational propaganda; of many hard legislative fights; of a struggle to secure desired legislation, and then to hold what had been secured; of many bitter contests with church and private-school interests, which felt that their "vested rights" were being taken from them; and of occasional referenda in which the people were asked, at the next election, to advise the legislature as to what to do. Excepting the battle for the abolition of slavery, perhaps no question has ever been before the American people for settlement which caused so much feeling or aroused such bitter antagonisms. Old friends and business associates parted company over the question, lodges were forced to taboo the subject to avoid disruption, ministers and their congregations often quarreled over the question of free schools, and politicians avoided the issue. The friends of free schools were at first commonly regarded as fanatics, dangerous to the State, and the opponents of free schools were considered by them as old-time conservatives or as selfish members of society.

Naturally such a bitter discussion of a public question forced an alignment of the people for or against publicly supported and controlled schools, and this alignment of interests may be roughly stated to have been about as follows:

I. For public schools.
    Men considered as:
1. "Citizens of the Republic."
2. Philanthropists and humanitarians.
3. Public men of large vision.
4. City residents.
5. The intelligent workingmen in the cities.
6. Non-taxpayers.
7. Calvinists.
8. "New-England men."

II. Lukewarm, or against public schools.
    Men considered as:
1. Belonging to the old aristocratic class.
2. The conservatives of society.
3. Politicians of small vision.
4. Residents of rural districts.
5. The ignorant, narrow-minded, and penurious.
6. Taxpayers.
7. Lutherans, Reformed-Church, Mennonites, and Quakers.
8. Southern men.
9. Proprietors of private schools.
10. The non-English-speaking classes.

It was, of course, not possible to so classify all persons, as a man might belong to two or more of the above classes. An example of such would be a Lutheran and a non-taxpaying workingman in a city, or a Calvinist and a heavy taxpayer. In all such cases there would be a conflict of interests with the stronger one prevailing, but, in a general way, the above classification of the alignment of interests is approximately correct.

Arguments for and against free schools. Both sides to the controversy advanced many arguments for and against state tax-supported schools, the more important on each side being the following:

I. Arguments for public tax-supported schools.
1. That education tends to prevent pauperism and crime.
2. That education tends to reduce poverty and distress.
3. That education increases production, and eliminates wrong ideas as to the distribution of wealth.

4. That a common state school, equally open to all, would prevent that class differentiation so dangerous in a Republic.

5. That the old church and private school education had proved utterly inadequate to meet the needs of a changed society.

6. That a system of religious schools is impossible in such a mixed nation as our own.

7. That the pauper-school idea is against the best interests of society, inimical to public welfare, and a constant offense to the poor, many of whom will not send their children because of the stigma attached to such schools.

8. That education as to one's civic duties is a necessity for the intelligent exercise of suffrage, and for the preservation of republican institutions.

9. That the increase of foreign immigration (which became quite noticeable after 1825, and attained large proportions after 1845) is a menace to our free institutions, and that these new elements can be best assimilated in a system of publicly supported and publicly directed common schools.

10. That the free and general education of all children at public expense is the natural right of all children in a Republic.

11. That the social, moral, political, and industrial benefits to be derived from the general education of all compensate many times over for its cost.

12. That a State which has the right to hang has the right to educate.

13. That the taking over of education by the State is not based on considerations of economy, but is the exercise of the State's inherent right to self-preservation and improvement.

14. That only a system of state-controlled schools can be free to teach whatever the welfare of the State may demand.

II. *Arguments against public tax-supported schools.*

1. Impractical, visionary, and "too advanced" legislation.

2. Will make education too common, and will educate people out of their proper position in society.

3. Would not benefit the masses, who are already as well cared for as they deserve.

4. Would tend to break down long-established and very desirable social barriers.

5. Would injure private and parochial schools, in which much money had been put and "vested rights" established.

6. Fear of the churches that state schools might injure their church progress and welfare.

7. Fear of the non-English speaking classes that state schools might supplant instruction in their languages.

8. The "conscientious objector" claimed that the State had no right to interfere between a parent and his child in the matter of education.

9. That those having no children to be educated should not be taxed for schools.

10. That taking a man's property to educate his neighbor's child is no more defensible than taking a man's plow to plow his neighbor's field.

11. That the State may be justified in taxing to defend the liberties of a people, but not to support their benevolences.

12. That the industrious would be taxed to educate the indolent.

13. That taxes would be so increased that no State could long meet such a lavish drain on its resources.

14. That there was priestcraft in the scheme, the purpose being first to establish a State School, and then a State Church.

The work of propaganda. To meet the arguments of the objectors, to change the opinions of a thinking few into the common opinion of the many, to overcome prejudice, and to awaken the public conscience to the public need for free and common schools in such a democratic society as ours, was the work of a generation. With many of the older citizens no progress could be made; the effective work everywhere had to be done with the younger men of the time. It was the work of many years to convince the masses of the people that the scheme of state schools was not only practicable, but also the best and most economical means for giving their children the benefits of an education; to convince propertied citizens that taxation for education was in the interests of both public and private welfare; to convince legislators that it was safe to vote for free-school bills; and to overcome the opposition due to apathy, religious jealousies, and private interests. In time, though, the desirability of common, free, tax-supported, non-sectarian, state-controlled schools became evident to a majority of the citizens in the different American States, and as it did the American State School, free and equally open to all, was finally evolved and took its place as the most important institution in our national life working for the perpetuation of our free democracy and the advancement of the public welfare.

For this work of propaganda hundreds of School Societies and Educational Associations were organized; many conventions were held, and resolutions favoring state schools were adopted; many "Letters" and "Addresses to the Public" were written and published; public-spirited citizens traveled over the country, making addresses to the people explaining the advantages of free state schools; many public-spirited men gave the best years of their lives to the state-school propaganda; and many governors sent communications on the subject to legislatures not yet convinced as to the desirability of state action. At each meeting of the legislatures for years a deluge of resolutions, memorials, and petitions for and against free schools met the members.

Propaganda societies. One of the earliest of these propaganda societies for state schools was the "Pennsylvania Society for the Promotion of Public Economy," organized in 1817. Ten years later a branch of this Society became the "Pennsylvania Society for the Promotion of Public Schools." This Society for many years kept up a vigorous campaign for a state free-school law. Another early society of importance was the "Hartford Society for the Improvement of Common Schools," founded in 1827. Another was the "Western Academic Institute and Board of Education," formed in 1829, at Cincinnati, largely by New England people, for propaganda work in the State of Ohio. Another was the Boston "Society for the Diffusion of Useful Knowledge," organized in 1829, with the promotion of public education as one of its objects. In 1830 the "American Institute of Instruction" was organized at Boston, and in 1838 this Association offered a prize of $500 for the best essay on "A System of Education best adapted to the Common Schools of our Country." A number of societies for propaganda were organized in New York State between 1830 and 1840. In New Jersey the "Society of Teachers and Friends of Education" held conventions, drew up memorials and petitions, and its members visited all parts of the State advocating general education at public expense, and especially the elimination of pauper-school education. Much valuable work was done by associations of teachers in Pennsylvania, between 1838 and 1852. In 1839 a national convention was held in Philadelphia to discuss the needs of education in the United States. In 1850 an important education convention was held in Harrisburg, the proceedings of which were printed and widely circulated. In 1838 a convention of the "Friends of Education" was held at Trenton, and a committee was appointed to prepare an "Address" to the people of the State. The result was a new school law which instituted a partial state school system, and secured an increase in the state appropriation for schools from $20,000 to $30,000 yearly.

The decades of the thirties and the forties witnessed the formation of a large number of these educational associations, organized to build up a sentiment for public education. They were founded not only in the older States of the East, but also in such widely scattered States as Georgia, Florida, and Tennessee. In 1829 the "Western Academic Institute and Board of Education" was formed at Cincinnati, such men as Samuel Lewis, Lyman Beecher, and Professor Calvin E. Stowe being prominent in its organization. For more than a decade this association and its successor, the

"Western Literary Institute and College of Professional Teachers" (1832) made Cincinnati the center of educational propaganda in the then West. It raised money, employed an agent to visit the schools of the State, diffused information as to education, tried to elevate the character of the teachers of the State, and repeatedly sent delegations to the legislature to ask for action. It sent Professor Stowe to Europe to investigate education there, and on his return induced the legislature (1837) to print 10,000 copies of his *Report on Elementary Education in Europe* for distribution. This *Report* was also reprinted afterward by the legislatures of Pennsylvania, Michigan, Massachusetts, North Carolina, and Virginia. In 1836 it called a state convention of the "Friends of Education," in 1837 induced the legislature to create the office of Superintendent of Common Schools, and in 1838 the culmination of its efforts came in what has been frequently called "the great school law of Ohio."

In 1834 over half the counties of Illinois sent delegates to an "Illinois Educational Convention" at Vandalia, which appointed a committee of seven to draft a memorial to the legislature and outline a plan for common schools and an "Address" to the people of the State. In 1844 a convention of "Friends of Education," held at Peoria, demanded of the legislature the appointment of a State Superintendent of Schools and the levying of a state school tax. In 1845 the Democratic Convention of Wilkinson County, Kentucky, adopted elaborate resolutions in favor of the establishment of free public schools, and instructed its delegates to the state convention to press the matter. In 1847 a number of "State Common School Conventions" were held in Indiana to build up sentiment for taxation for schools. These are but examples of the work of the numerous propaganda societies, formed in increasing numbers between 1825 and 1850.

Support from associations of workingmen. Workingmen, too, through their newly formed organizations, also took a prominent part in the propaganda for the establishment

of public tax-supported schools.   Among the many resolutions adopted by these wage-earners the following are
typical:

At a General Meeting of Mechanics and Workingmen
held in New York City, in 1829, it was:

Resolved, that next to life and liberty, we consider education the
greatest blessing bestowed upon mankind.

Resolved, that the public funds should be appropriated (to a
reasonable extent) to the purpose of education upon a regular
system that shall insure the opportunity to every individual of
obtaining a competent education before he shall have arrived at
the age of maturity.

At a meeting of workingmen held in Philadelphia, in
1829, it was declared that:

No system of education, which a freeman can accept, has yet
been established for the poor; whilst thousands of dollars of the
public money has been appropriated for building colleges and
academies for the rich.

Each candidate for the state legislature was formally asked
to declare his attitude toward "an equal and general system
of Education."   In 1830 they adopted a long *Report* on the
conditions of education in Pennsylvania, demanded schools,
and declared that there could be "no real liberty in a republic without a wide diffusion of real intelligence."

In 1830 the Workingmen's Party of Philadelphia included,
as the first plank in its platform:

Resolved, that the time has arrived when it becomes the para-
mount duty of every friend to the happiness and freedom of man
to promote a system of education that shall embrace equally all
the children of the state, of every rank and condition.

In 1830 an Association of Workingmen was formed at
New Castle, Delaware, and in their constitution they provided:

Let us unite at the polls and give our votes to no candidate who
is not pledged to support a rational system of education to be paid
for out of the public funds.

At a Boston meeting of "Workingmen, Mechanics, and others friendly to their interests," in 1830, it was:

Resolved, that the establishment of a liberal system of education, attainable by all, should be among the first efforts of every law-giver who desires the continuance of our national independence.

In 1830 the "Farmers', Mechanics', and Workingmen's" Party of New York State, in convention at Salina, included as one of the planks in its platform the following:

Resolved, that a scheme of education, more universal in its effects, is practicable, so that no child in the republick, however poor, should grow up without an opportunity to acquire at least a competent English education; and that the system should be adapted to the conditions of the poor both in the city and country.

In 1835 the workingmen of the city of Washington enumerated as one of their demands the establishment of "a universal system of education," and in 1836 the "General Trades Union" of Cincinnati, in an "Appeal to the Working-men of the West," urged that they try to elevate their condition by directing their efforts toward obtaining "a national system of education."

Recommendations of governors. A number of the early governors were public men of large vision, who saw the desirability of the State establishing a general system of education years before either the legislature or the people had clearly sensed the need. In Delaware, for example, almost every year from 1822 to 1829 succeeding governors urged the legislature to establish a genuine system of education, as provided for in the state constitution (p. 62). The people, however, were unwilling to tax themselves for schools, and only the city of Wilmington made any real headway in providing them. In Pennsylvania, in 1825, the governor made a strong plea for a system of education, and again in 1828 the legislature was urged to establish a public school system, but the first free school law dates from 1834. The messages of the New York governors, especially the two Clintons, form famous documents in favor of free tax-supported schools.   In 1826, 1827, 1828, 1829, 1835, and 1836 New York governors urged the State's duty, and held that the establishment of a good system of public instruction was an evidence of good government.   In Connecticut (1825, 1828), Massachusetts (1826, 1837), and Maine (1831) governors recommended an improvement in the schools, and a dependence upon a wide diffusion of education for the happiness and security of the State.

After 1825, and especially through the decade of the thirties, governors generally began to give emphasis to education in their messages.   In the new Western States the messages often were clear and emphatic, and the arguments for education strong.   While usually at the time not influencing a legislature to action, these messages were influential in effecting a change in the attitude of the people toward the question of tax-supported schools.

II. Phases of the Battle for State-Supported Schools

The problem which confronted those interested in establishing state-controlled schools was not exactly the same in any two States, though the battle in many States possessed common elements, and hence was somewhat similar in character.   Instead of tracing the struggle in detail in each of the different States, it will be much more profitable for our purposes to pick out the main strategic points in the contest, and then illustrate the conflict for these by describing conditions in one or two States where the controversy was most severe or most typical.   The seven strategic points in the struggle for free, tax-supported, non-sectarian, state-controlled schools were:

1. The battle for tax support.
2. The battle to eliminate the pauper-school idea.
3. The battle to make the schools entirely free.
4. The battle to establish state supervision.
5 The battle to eliminate sectarianism.

6. The battle to extend the system upward.

7. Addition of the state university to crown the system.

In this and the two following chapters we shall consider each of these, in order.

1. The battle for tax support

Early support and endowment funds. In New England, land endowments, local taxes, direct local appropriations, license taxes, and rate bills (that is, a per-capita tax levied on the parents of the children attending school) had long been common. Land endowments began early in the New England colonies, while rate bills date back to the earliest times and long remained a favorite means of raising money for school support. These means were adopted in the different States after the beginning of our national period, and to them were added a variety of license taxes, while occupational taxes, lotteries, and bank taxes also were employed to raise money for schools. A few examples of these may be cited:

Connecticut, in 1774, turned over all proceeds of liquor licenses to the towns where collected, to be used for schools. New Orleans, in 1826, licensed two theaters on condition that they each pay $3000 annually for the support of schools in the city. New York, in 1799, authorized four state lotteries to raise $100,000 for schools, a similar amount again in 1801, and numerous other lotteries before 1810. Congress passed fourteen joint resolutions, between 1812 and 1836, authorizing lotteries to help support the schools of the city of Washington. Bank taxes were a favorite source of income for schools, between about 1825 and 1860, banks being chartered on condition that they would pay over each year for schools a certain sum or percentage of their earnings. These all represent what is known as indirect taxation, and were valuable in accustoming the people to the idea of public schools without appearing to tax them for their support.

The National Land Grants, begun in the case of Ohio in-

1802 (p. 59), soon stimulated a new interest in schools. Each State admitted after Ohio also received the sixteenth section for the support of common schools, and two townships of land for the endowment of a state university. The new Western States, following the lead of Ohio (p. 60), dedicated these section lands and funds to free common schools. The sixteen older States, however, did not share in these grants, so most of them now set about building up a permanent school fund of their own, though at first without any very clear idea as to how the income from the fund was to be used. Connecticut and New York both had set aside lands, before 1800, to create such a fund, Connecticut's fund dating back to 1750. Delaware, in 1796, devoted the income from marriage and tavern licenses to the same purpose, but made no use of the fund for twenty years. Connecticut, in 1795, sold its "Western Reserve" in Ohio for $1,200,000, and added this to its school fund. New York, in 1805, similarly added the proceeds of the sale of half a million acres of state lands, though the fund then formally created accumulated unused until 1812. Tennessee began to build up a permanent state school fund in 1806; Virginia in 1810; South Carolina in 1811; Maryland in 1812; New Jersey in 1816; Georgia in 1817; Maine, New Hampshire, Kentucky, and Louisiana in 1821; Vermont and North Carolina in 1825; Pennsylvania in 1831; and Massachusetts in 1834. These were established as permanent state funds, the annual income only to be used, in some way to be determined later, for the support of some form of schools. Some of these funds, as has just been stated, accumulated for years before any use was made of the income (New York for twelve; Delaware for twenty; New Jersey for thirteen), while the income in other of the States was for a time used exclusively for the support of pauper schools. New Jersey, Pennsylvania, Delaware, Maryland, Virginia, and Georgia all for a time belonged to this latter class. These permanent funds also represented a form of indirect taxation, and formed important accumulations of capital, the income of which later went for school support and to that extent relieved taxation.

The beginnings of school taxation. The early idea, which seems for a time to have been generally entertained, that the income from land grants, license fees, and these permanent endowment funds would in time entirely support the necessary schools, was gradually abandoned as it was seen how little in yearly income these funds and lands really produced, and how rapidly the population of the States was increasing. By 1825 it may be said to have been clearly recognized by thinking men that the only safe reliance of a system of state schools lay in the general and direct taxation of all property for their support. "The wealth of the State must educate the children of the State" became a watchword, and the battle for direct, local, county, and state taxation for education was clearly on by 1825 to 1830 in all the Northern States, except the four in New England where the principle of taxation for education had for long been established. Now for the first time direct taxation for schools was likely to be felt by the taxpayer, and the fight for and against the imposition of such taxation was on in earnest. The course of the struggle and the results were somewhat different in the different States, but, in a general way, the progress of the conflict was somewhat as follows:

1. Permission granted to communities so desiring to organize a school taxing district, and to tax for school support the property of those consenting and residing therein.
2. Taxation of all property in the taxing district permitted.
3. State aid to such districts, at first from the income from permanent endowment funds, and later from the proceeds of a small state appropriation or a state or county tax.
4. Compulsory local taxation to supplement the state or county grant.

Types of early permissive legislation. In the older States, always excepting the four Calvinistic New England States, the beginnings of this permissive legislation were usually obtained by the cities. With their pressing new social problems they could not afford to wait for the rural sections of their States. Accordingly they sought and obtained permissive city school-tax legislation, and proceeded to organize their schools independently, incorporating them later into the general state organization. Thus Providence began schools in 1800, and Newport in 1825, whereas the first Rhode Island general law was not enacted until 1828; the "Free School Society" of New York City was chartered by the legislature in 1805, and the first permanent state school law dates from 1812; Philadelphia was permitted to organize schools by special legislation in 1812 and 1818, while the first general school law for Pennsylvania dates from 1834; Baltimore secured a special law in 1825, a year ahead of the first Maryland general school legislation; and Mobile was given special permission to organize schools in 1826, though the first general state school law in Alabama dates from 1854.

As other examples typical of early permissive state legislation may be mentioned the Maryland law of 1816, giving permission to the voters of Caroline County to decide whether they would support a school by subscription or taxation; the New Jersey law of 1820, which permitted any county in the State to levy a county tax for the education of the children of the poor; the Missouri law of 1824, which permitted a district tax for schools, on written demand of two thirds of the voters of the district, to maintain a school the length of time each year the majority of the parents should decide; the Illinois optional tax law of 1825, nullified in 1827 by providing that the voters might decide to raise only half the cost of the school by taxation, and that no man could be taxed for schools unless he filed his consent in writing; the Rhode Island law of 1828, giving the towns permission to levy a tax for schools, if they saw fit; the optional district tax laws of 1830 in Kentucky, 1834 in Pennsylvania, and 1840 in Iowa; the Mississippi optional tax law of 1846, which permitted a district tax only after a majority of the heads of families in the district had filed their consent in writing; and the Indiana optional county tax law of 1848. Many of these early laws proved to be dead letters, except in the few cities of the time and in a few very progressive communities, partly because it was made too difficult to initiate and too easy to prevent action, and partly because they were too far ahead of public sentiment to be carried into force.

The struggle to secure such legislation, weak and ineffective as it seems to us to-day, was often hard and long. "Campaigns of education" had to be prepared for and carried through. Many thought that tax-supported schools would be dangerous for the State, harmful to individual good, and thoroughly undemocratic. Many did not see the need for schools at all, and many more were in the frame of mind of the practical New England farmer who declared that "the Bible and figgers is all I want my boys to know." Often those in favor of taxation were bitterly assailed, and even at times threatened with personal violence. Henry Barnard, who rendered such useful service in awakening Connecticut and Rhode Island, between 1837 and 1845, to the need for better schools, tells us that a member of the Rhode Island legislature told him that a bill providing a small state tax for schools, which he was then advocating, even if passed by the legislature could not be enforced in Rhode Island at the point of the bayonet. A Rhode Island farmer threatened to shoot him if he ever caught him on his property advocating "such heresy as the partial confiscation of one man's property to educate another man's child." A member of the Indiana legislature, of 1837, declared that when he died he wanted engraved on his tombstone, "Here lies an enemy to free schools."

Growth of a public school sentiment illustrated by taxation in Ohio. The progress of the struggle to secure taxation for the maintenance of public schools differed somewhat in detail in the different States, but Ohio and Indiana offer us good illustrative examples — the first of a slow but peaceful settlement of the question, the other of a settle-

ment only after vigorous fighting.   The history in Ohio
may be summarized as follows:

1802. State admitted to the Union.
1806, 1816. Organization of schools permitted.   Only means of
    support rents of school section lands and rate-bills.
1821. All property of residents of district made taxable for
    schools.
1825. Building of schoolhouses permitted; site must be donated.
1825. A county school tax of one half mill required to be levied.
1827. State permanent school fund created.
1827. Building repairs limited to $300, and two thirds vote re-
    quired to authorize this expenditure.
1829. Special organization and tax law enacted for Cincinnati.
1831. Non-resident property-holders also made liable for district
    school taxes.
1834. Each parent sending a child to school must provide his
    quota of wood.
1836. County tax increased to one and one half mills.
1838. Purchase of a school site permitted.   Majority vote for
    repairs reduced to one half.
1838. First state school tax of one half mill levied.
1853. Rate-bill abolished, and schools made free.

Some of the older States and a number of the newer States
have had a somewhat similar history of a slow but gradual
education of the people to the acceptance of the burdens of
school support.

The battle for taxation illustrated by Indiana.   Ohio was
predominantly New England in stock (see map, p. 73),
but Indiana represented a more mixed type of population.
The New England element dominated the northern part of
the State, and was prominent along the eastern edge and
down the Ohio, especially near Cincinnati.   The Southern
element was in the majority in the southern and central
portion of the State.   Between these two elements there
was a conflict for a generation over the question of tax-
supported schools.   Even more was it a battle between
the charity and pauper-school conception of education of the
Southern element, and the strong-state conception of the
New England Yankee.

Though admitted in 1816, with a constitution making careful provision for a complete state system of schools (see p. 75), the first general school law was not enacted until 1824. This merely authorized schools where wanted, and permitted their support by a district tax or by the rate-bill. Nothing more was done until 1836. In this year two laws were enacted which provided a form of compulsory township taxation for schools. The first gave back to each township one fourth of its state poll taxes, and the second gave back five per cent of the general state taxes collected therein, with the provision that these moneys should be used to help maintain schools in the townships. This was regarded as an entering wedge to state taxation for a system of public education, and was so bitterly opposed that it became the chief election issue in 1837. The opponents of tax-supported schools carried the day, and the legislature then elected met and promptly repealed the law.

Nothing more was done until 1848. In 1847 a "State Common School Convention" was held, and a bill was prepared which provided for a personal poll tax of 25 cents, a state tax of .6 of a mill, and a similar township tax for schools. This was presented to the legislature of 1848, with a demand for action. The legislature, however, was cautious and undecided, and voted to obtain first a referendum on the subject at the elections of 1848. This was done, with the result shown on the map on the following page. The New England element in the population came out strong for tax-supported schools, the Southern element opposing. Though 66 per cent of the counties and 56 per cent of the population favored tax-supported schools, the legislature of 1849 was still afraid to act. Finally an optional law, providing for a 25-cent poll tax, a general county tax of 1 mill, and an insurance premium tax was enacted, with permission to levy additional taxes locally. The law, however, was not to apply to any county until accepted by the voters thereof, and a new referendum on the law was ordered for 1849. The vote in 1849 was not essentially different from that of 1848. Two counties that had favored the tax in 1848 by very small margins now fell below, while four counties reversed themselves

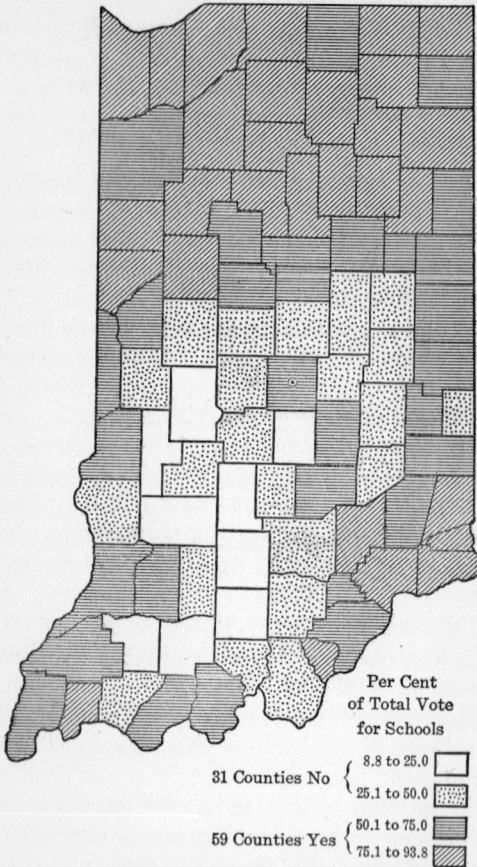

Per Cent
of Total Vote
for Schools

31 Counties No { 8.8 to 25.0 / 25.1 to 50.0

59 Counties Yes { 50.1 to 75.0 / 75.1 to 93.8

FIG. 26. THE INDIANA REFERENDUM OF 1848

Thirty-four per cent of the counties and forty-four per cent of the electors voted No.

the other way. The map for the referendum of 1848 is essentially true also for the referendum of 1849. The two referenda gave the following results:

	1848	1849
Total vote on the question	140,410	142,391
Vote for tax-supported schools	78,523	79,079
Vote against tax-supported schools	61,887	63,312
Majority for tax-supported schools	16,636	15,767
Voters favoring tax-supported schools	56%	55%
Voters opposing tax-supported schools	44%	45%
Counties favoring tax-supported schools	66%	68%
Counties opposing tax-supported schools	34%	32%

The new constitution of 1851 settled the matter, despite much opposition, by providing for a state tax-supported school system, and in 1852 the first general state school tax (of 1 mill) was levied on all property in the State. This ended the main battle in Indiana.

The struggle to prevent misappropriation as illustrated by Kentucky. At approximately the same time as the struggle in Indiana a conflict was also taking place in Kentucky which was illustrative of early political standards regarding education and educational funds. The Kentucky Act of 1830 had provided for schools and local taxation, but so great was the indifference of the people to education and their unwillingness to bear taxation that the law remained practically a dead letter. In 1837 the State received $1,433,754 as a virtual gift from the National Government in the distribution of the so-called Surplus Revenue, and $850,000 of this was put into a state school fund and invested in state internal improvement bonds. At that time an investigation showed that one half the children of school age in the State had never been to school, and that one third of the adult population could not read or write.

In 1840 the State refused to pay the interest on the school fund bonds, and in 1845 the legislature ordered the bonds destroyed and repudiated the state's debt to the school fund. Now began a battle to change conditions, led by the Reverend Robert J. Breckinridge, a descendant of a Scotch Covenanter who had come to Kentucky from Pennsylvania, and who became State Superintendent of Common Schools in 1847. He first obtained from the legislature of 1848 a new bond for the confiscated school funds for $1,225,768, thus adding all unpaid interest to the principal of the bond. The next year he secured legislation permitting the people to vote at the fall elections for a two-mill state school tax, stumped the State for the measure, and carried the proposal by a majority of 36,882. In the constitutional convention of 1850 he not only secured the first constitutional mention of education and made provision for a state system of schools, but also had the debt to the state school fund recognized at $1,326,770, and the fund declared inviolable. In the legislature of 1850, against the determined opposition of the governor, he secured further legislation making the interest on the school fund due to the schools a first charge on any moneys in the state treasury. This closed the fight of ten years to force the State to be honest with and support education in the State. Similar fights, involving school lands or funds, took place in some of the other States, though not always so successfully as in Kentucky.

State support fixed the state system. With the beginnings of state aid in any substantial sums, either from the income from permanent endowment funds, state appropriations, or direct state taxation, the State became, for the first time, in a position to enforce quite definite requirements in many matters. Communities which would not meet the State's requirements would receive no state funds.

One of the first requirements to be thus enforced was that communities or districts receiving state aid must also levy a local tax for schools. Commonly the requirement was a duplication of state aid. Generally speaking, and recognizing exceptions in a few States, this represents the beginnings of compulsory local taxation for education. As early as 1797 Vermont had required the towns to support their schools on penalty of forfeiting their share of state aid. New York in 1812, Delaware in 1829, and New Jersey in 1846 required a duplication of all state aid received. Wisconsin, in its first constitution of 1848, required a local tax for schools equal to one half the state aid received. The

next step in state control was to add still other requirements, as a prerequisite to receiving state aid.   One of the
first of such was that a certain length of school term, commonly three months, must be provided in each school district.   Another was the provision of free heat, and later on
free school books and supplies.

When the duplication-of-state-aid-received stage had
been reached, compulsory local taxation for education had
been established, and the great central battle for the creation of a state school system had been won.   The right to
tax for support, and to compel local taxation, was the key
to the whole state system of education.   From this point
on the process of evolving an adequate system of school
support in any State has been merely the further education
of public opinion to see new educational needs.   The process generally has been characterized by a gradual increase
in the amount of the required school tax, the addition of
new forms of or units for taxation, and a broadening of the
scope and purpose of taxation for education.   The development has followed different lines in different States, and
probably no two States to-day stand at exactly the same
place in the evolution of a system of school support.   So
vital is school finance, however, that the position of any
state school system to-day is in large part determined by
how successful the State has been in evolving an adequate
system of public school support.

2. The battle to eliminate the pauper-school idea

The pauper-school idea.   The home of the pauper-school
idea in America, as will be remembered from the map
given on page 70, was the old Central and Southern States.
New Jersey, Pennsylvania, Delaware, Maryland, Virginia,
and Georgia were the chief representatives, though the idea
had friends among certain classes of the population in other
of the older States.   The new and democratic West would
not tolerate it.   The pauper-school conception was a direct
inheritance from English rule, belonged to a society based on

classes, and was wholly out of place in a Republic founded on the doctrine that "all men are created equal, and endowed by their Creator with certain inalienable rights." Still more, it was a very dangerous conception of education for a democratic form of government to tolerate or to foster. Its friends were found among the old aristocratic or conservative classes, the heavy taxpayers, the supporters of church schools, and the proprietors of private schools. Citizens who had caught the spirit of the new Republic, public men of large vision, intelligent workingmen, and men of the New England type of thinking were opposed on principle to a plan which drew such invidious distinctions between the future citizens of the State. To educate part of our children in church or private pay schools, they said, and to segregate those too poor to pay tuition and educate them at public expense in pauper schools, often with the brand of pauper made very evident to them, was certain to create classes in society which in time would prove a serious danger to our democratic institutions.

Large numbers of those for whom the pauper schools were intended would not brand themselves as paupers by sending their children to the schools, and others who accepted the advantages offered, for the sake of their children, despised the system. Concerning the system "The Philadelphia Society for the Establishment and Support of Charity Schools" in an "Address to the Public," in 1818, said:

In the United States the benevolence of the inhabitants has led to the establishment of Charity Schools, which, though affording individual advantages, are not likely to be followed by the political benefits kindly contemplated by their founders. In the country a parent will raise children in ignorance rather than place them in charity schools. It is only in large cities that charity schools succeed to any extent. These dispositions may be improved to the best advantage, by the Legislature, in place of Charity Schools, establishing Public Schools for the education of all children, the offspring of the rich and the poor alike.

The battle for the elimination of the pauper-school idea was fought out in the North in the States of Pennsylvania and New Jersey, and the struggle in these two States we shall now briefly describe.

The Pennsylvania legislation. In Pennsylvania we find the pauper-school idea fully developed. The constitution of 1790 (p. 64) had provided for a state system of pauper schools, but nothing was done to carry even this constitutional direction into effect until 1802. A pauper-school law was then enacted, directing the overseers of the poor to notify such parents as they deemed sufficiently indigent that, if they would declare themselves to be paupers, their children might be sent to some specified private or pay school and be given free education. The expense for this was assessed against the education poor-fund, which was levied and collected in the same manner as were road taxes or taxes for poor relief. No provision was made for the establishment of public schools, even for the children of the poor, nor was any standard set for the education to be provided in the schools to which they were sent. No other general provision for elementary education was made in the State until 1834.

With the growth of the cities, and the rise of their special problems, something more than this very inadequate provision for schooling became necessary. "The Philadelphia Society for the Establishment and Support of Charity Schools" had long been urging a better system, and in 1814 "The Society for the Promotion of a Rational System of Education" was organized in Philadelphia for the purpose of educational propaganda. Bills were prepared and pushed, and in 1818 Philadelphia was permitted, by special law, to organize as "the first school district" in the State of Pennsylvania, and to provide, with its own funds, a system of Lancastrian schools for the education of the children of its poor. In 1821 the counties of Dauphin (Harrisburg), Allegheny (Pittsburg), Cumberland (Carlisle), and Lancaster (Lancaster) were also exempted from the state pauper-school law, and allowed to organize schools for the education of the children of their poor.

That this plan for the education of the children of the poor reached but few children in the State not otherwise provided for was shown by a *Report* made to the legislature, in 1829. At that time but 31 of the 51 counties of the State reported children as being educated under the poor-law act, and these showed that the number of poor children being paid for had been only:

4940, in 1825;	9014, in 1827;
7943, in 1826;	4477, in 1828.

There were at that time estimated to be 400,000 children in the State between the ages of 5 and 15, not over 150,000 of whom were attending any kind of school. In 1833, the last year of the pauper-school system, the number educated had increased to 17,467 for the State, and at an expense of $48,466.25 to the counties, or an average yearly expense per pupil of $2.10. No wonder the heavy taxpayers regarded favorably such an inexpensive plan for public education.

In 1824 an optional free-school law was enacted which permitted the organization of public schools, but provided that no child could attend school at public expense longer than three years. Even this was repealed in 1826, and the old pauper-school law was reinstated.

The Law of 1834. In 1827 "The Pennsylvania Society for the Promotion of Public Schools" began an educational propaganda, which did much to bring about the Free-School Act of 1834. In an "Address to the Public" it declared its objects to be the promotion of public education throughout the State of Pennsylvania, and the "Address" closed with these words:

This Society is at present composed of about 250 members, and a correspondence has been commenced with 125 members, who reside in every district in the State. It is intended to direct the continued attention of the public to the importance of the subject; to collect and diffuse all information which may be deemed valuable; and to persevere in their labors until they shall be crowned with success.

Memorials were presented to the legislature year after year, governors were interested, "Addresses to the Public" were prepared, and a vigorous propaganda was kept up until the Free-School Law of 1834 was the result.

This law, though, was optional. It created every ward, township, and borough in the State a school district, a total of 987 being created for the State. Each school district

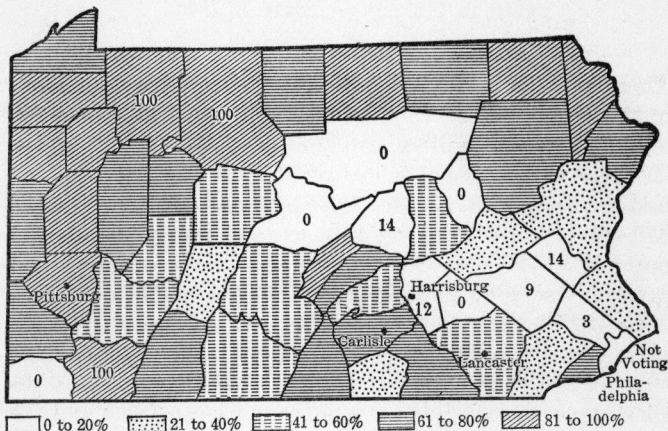

FIG. 27. THE PENNSYLVANIA SCHOOL ELECTIONS OF 1835

Showing the percentage of school districts in each county organizing under and accepting the School Law of 1834. Percentage of district accepting indicated on the map for a few of the counties.

was ordered to vote that autumn on the acceptance or rejection of the law. Those accepting the law were to organize under its provisions, while those rejecting the law were to continue under the educational provisions of the old Pauper-School Act.

The results of the school elections of 1834 are shown, by counties, on the above map. Of the total of 987 districts created, 502, in 46 of the then 52 counties (Philadelphia County not voting), or 52 per cent of the whole number, voted to accept the new law and organize under it; 264 dis-

tricts, in 31 counties, or 27 per cent of the whole, voted definitely to reject the law; and 221 districts, in 46 counties, or
21 per cent of the whole, refused to take any action either
way.   In 3 counties, indicated on the map, every district accepted the law, and in 5 counties, also indicated, every district rejected or refused to act on the law.   A study of this
map, in comparison with the map given on page 73, shows
once more the influence of the New England element settled
along the northern border of the State.   The democratic
West, with its Scotch-Irish Presbyterian population, is also
in evidence.   It was the predominantly German counties,
located in the east-central portion of the State, which were
strongest in their opposition to the new law.   One reason
for this was that the new law provided for English schools;
another was the objection of the thrifty Germans to taxation; and another was the fear that the new state schools
might injure their German parochial schools.

The final victory over the pauper-school forces.   The real
fight for free *versus* pauper schools was yet to come.   Legislators who had voted for the law were bitterly assailed,
and, though it was but an optional law, the question of its
repeal and the reinstatement of the old Pauper-School Law
became the burning issue of the campaign in the autumn of
1834.   Many legislators who had favored the law were de-
feated for reëlection.   Others, seeing defeat, refused to run.
Petitions for the repeal of the law, and remonstrances against
its repeal, flooded the legislature.   Some 32,000 persons
petitioned for a repeal of the law, 66 of whom signed by
making their mark, and "not more than five names in a
hundred," reported a legislative committee which inves-
tigated the matter, "were signed in English script."   It was
from among the Germans that the strongest opposition to
the law came.   This same committee further reported that
so many of the names were "so illegibly written as to afford
the strongest evidence of the deplorable disregard so long
paid by the Legislature to the constitutional injunction to
establish a general system of education."

The Senate at once repealed the law, but the House, largely under the leadership of a Vermonter by the name of Thaddeus Stevens, refused to reconsider, and finally forced the Senate to accept an amended and a still stronger bill. This defeat finally settled, in principle at least, the pauper-school question in Pennsylvania, though it was not until 1873 that the last district in the State accepted the new system. The law provided for state aid, state supervision of schools, and county and local taxation, but districts refusing to accept the new system could receive no portion of the new funds. During the first year a three and one-half months' free school was provided. By 1836 the new free-school law had been accepted by 75 per cent of the districts in the State, by 1838 by 84 per cent, and by 1847 by 88 per cent. In 1848 the legislature ordered free schools in all districts, but, not attaching a compulsory feature to the enactment beyond the forfeiting of any state aid, it was twenty-five years longer before the last district gave in and accepted the law. In 1849 a four months' free school was made necessary to receive any state aid.

Eliminating the pauper school idea in New Jersey. No constitutional mention of education was made in New Jersey until 1844, and no educational legislation was passed until 1816. In that year a permanent state school fund was begun, and in 1820 the first permission to levy taxes "for the education of such poor children as are paupers" was granted. In 1828 an extensive investigation showed that one third of the children of the State were without educational opportunities, and as a result of this investigation the first general school law for the State was enacted, in 1829. This provided for district schools, school trustees and visitation, licensed teachers, local taxation, and made a state appropriation of $20,000 a year to help establish the system. The next year, however, this law was repealed and the old pauper-school plan reëstablished, largely due to the pressure of church and private-school interests. In 1830 and 1831 the state appropriation was made divisible among private and parochial schools, as well as the public pauper schools, and the use of all public money was limited "to the education of the children of the poor."

Between 1828 and 1838 a number of conventions of friends of free public schools were held in the State, and much work in the nature of propaganda was done. At a convention in 1838 a committee was appointed to prepare an "Address to the People of New Jersey" on the educational needs of the State, and speakers were sent over the State to talk to the people on the subject. That "every free State must provide for the education of all its children" was held to be axiomatic. The pauper-school idea was vigorously condemned. Concerning this the "Address" said:

We utterly repudiate as unworthy, not of freemen only, but of men, the narrow notion that there is to be an education for the poor as such. Has God provided for the poor a coarser earth, a thinner air, a paler sky? Does not the glorious sun pour down his golden flood as cheerily on the poor man's hovel as upon the rich man's palace? Have not the cotter's children as keen a sense of all the freshness, verdure, fragrance, melody, and beauty of luxuriant nature as the pale sons of kings? Or is it on the mind that God has stamped the imprint of a baser birth, so that the poor man's child knows with an inborn certainty tnat his lot is to crawl, not climb? It is not so. God has not done it. Man cannot do it. Mind is immortal. Mind is imperial. It bears no mark of high or low, of rich or poor. It asks but freedom. It requires but light.

The campaign against the pauper school had just been fought to a conclusion in Pennsylvania, and the result of the appeal in New Jersey was such a popular manifestation in favor of free schools that the legislature of 1838 instituted a partial state school system. The pauper-school laws were repealed, and the best features of the short-lived Law of 1829 were reënacted. In 1844 a new state constitution limited the income of the permanent state school fund exclusively to the support of public schools.

With the pauper-school idea eliminated from Pennsylvania

and New Jersey, the North was through with it. The wisdom of its elimination soon became evident, and we hear little more of it among Northern people. The democratic West never tolerated it. It continued some time longer in Maryland, Virginia, and Georgia, and at places for a time in other Southern States, but finally disappeared in the South as well in the educational reorganizations which took place following the close of the Civil War.

3. The battle to make the schools entirely free

The schools not yet free. The rate-bill, as we have previously stated, was an old institution, also brought over from England, as the term "rate" signifies. It was, as we have said, a charge levied upon the parent to supplement the school revenues and prolong the school term, and was assessed in proportion to the number of children sent by each parent to the school. In some States, as for example Massachusetts and Connecticut, its use went back to colonial times; in others it was added as the cost for education increased, and it was seen that the income from permanent funds and authorized taxation was not sufficient to maintain the school the necessary length of time. The deficiency in revenue was charged against the parents sending children to school, *pro rata*, and collected as ordinary tax-bills. The charge was small, but it was sufficient to keep many poor children away from the schools.

This is well illustrated by the case of New York City, where The Public School Society, finding its funds inadequate to meet its growing responsibilities, attempted, in 1826, to raise additional funds by adding the rate-bill for those who could afford to pay. The rates were moderate, as may be seen from the following schedule of charges:

Per quarter

For the Alphabet, Spelling, and Writing on Slates, as far as the
   3d Class, inclusive $0.25
Continuance of above, with Reading and Arithmetical Tables,
   or the 4th, 5th, and 6th Classes........................... 0.50

Continuance of last, with Writing on Paper, Arithmetic, and
    Definitions, or the 7th, 8th, and 9th Classes.............. **1.00**
The preceding, with Grammar, Geography, with the use of Maps
    and Globes, Bookkeeping, History, Composition, Mensuration,
    Astronomy, etc.. **2.00**
No additional charge for Needlework, nor for Fuel, Books, or
    Stationery.

Two days before the system went into effect there were
3457 pupils in the schools of the Society, six months later
there were but 2999, while the number taking the $2 per
quarter studies dropped from 137 to 13. The amount received from fees in 1826 was $4426, but by 1831 this had
fallen to $1366. What to do was obvious, and, securing ad-
ditional funds, the schools were made absolutely free again
in 1832.

The rising cities, with their new social problems, could
not and would not tolerate the rate-bill system, and one by
one they secured special laws from legislatures which enabled them to organize a city school system, separate from
city council control, and under a local "board of education." One of the provisions of these special laws nearly
always was the right to levy a city tax for schools sufficient
to provide free education for the children of the city.

In New York State, to illustrate, we find special legislation, which provided free schools for the city, enacted as
follows:

1832. New York City.	1848. Syracuse.
1838. Buffalo.	1849. Troy.
1841. Hudson.	1850. Auburn.
1841. Rochester.	1853. Oswego.
1843. Brooklyn.	1853. Utica.
1843. Williamsburg.	

The State of New York did not provide for free schools
generally until 1867. In other States, it might be added,
that the schools in Providence, Baltimore, Charleston,
Mobile, New Orleans, Louisville, Cincinnati, Chicago, and
Detroit were free for about a quarter-century before the
coming of free state schools.

The fight against the rate-bill in New York. The attempt to abolish the rate-bill and make the schools wholly free was most vigorously contested in New York State, and the contest there is most easily described. From 1828 to 1868, this tax on the parents produced an average annual sum of $410,-685.66, or about one half of the sum paid all the teachers of the State for salary. While the wealthy districts were securing special legislation and taxing themselves to provide free schools for their children, the poorer and less populous districts were left to struggle to maintain their schools the four months each year necessary to secure state aid. Finally, after much agitation, and a number of appeals to the legislature to assume the rate-bill charges in the form of general state taxation, and thus make the schools entirely free, the legislature, in 1849, referred the matter back to the people to be voted on at the elections that autumn. The legislature was to be thus advised by the people as to what action it should take. The result was a state-wide campaign for free, public, tax-supported schools, as against partially free, rate-bill schools.

The result of the 1849 election was a vote of 249,872 in favor of making "the property of the State educate the children of the State," and 91,952 against it. This only seemed to stir the opponents of free schools to renewed action, and they induced the next legislature to resubmit the question for another vote, in the autumn of 1850.

The result of the referendum of 1850 is shown on the next map. The opponents of tax-supported schools now mustered their full strength, doubling their vote in 1849, while the majority for free schools was materially cut down. The interesting thing shown on this map was the clear and unmistakable voice of the cities. They would not tolerate the rate-bill, and, despite their larger property interests, they favored tax-supported free schools. The rural districts, on the other hand, strange to say, opposed the idea.

We have here clearly set forth a growing conflict between city and rural interests, in matters of education, which continued to become more acute with time. The cities demanded educational progress and were determined to have it, regardless of cost. If it could be had by general legisla-

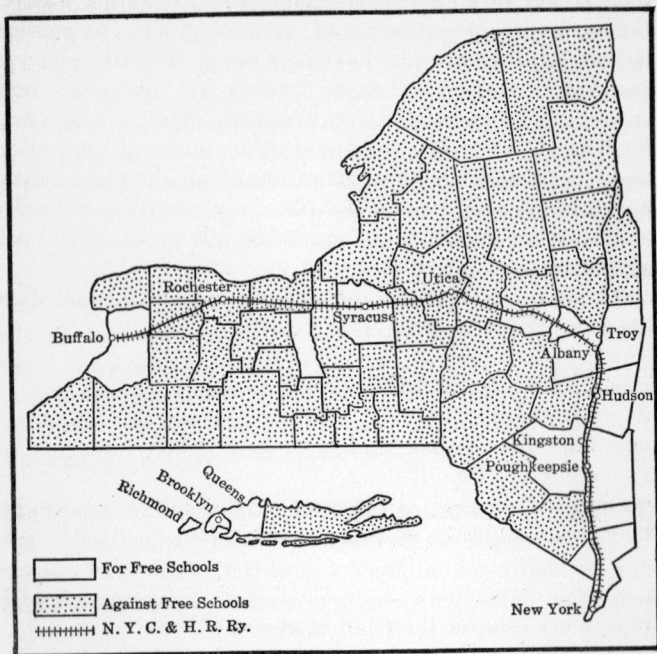

FIG. 28. THE NEW YORK REFERENDUM OF 1850

Total vote: For free schools, 17 counties and 209,346 voters; against free schools, 42 counties and 184,308 voters.

tion, in which the whole State shared, well and good; if not, then special laws and special taxing privileges would be sought and obtained. The result of this attitude, clearly shown in the New York referendum of 1850, was that the substantial progress in almost every phase of public education during the second half of the nineteenth century was made by the cities of our country, while the rural districts lagged far behind.

The rate-bill in other States. These two referenda virtually settled the question in New York, though for a time a compromise was adopted. The state appropriation for schools was very materially increased, the rate-bill was retained, and the organization of "union districts" to provide free schools by local taxation where people desired them was authorized. Many of these "union free districts" now arose in the more progressive communities of the State, and finally, in 1867, after rural and other forms of opposition had largely subsided, and after almost all the older States had abandoned the plan, the New York legislature finally abolished the rate-bill and made the schools of New York entirely free.

The dates for the abolition of the rate-bill in the other older Northern States were:

1834. Pennsylvania.	1867. New York.
1852. Indiana.	1868. Connecticut.
1853. Ohio.	1868. Rhode Island.
1855. Illinois.	1869. Michigan.
1864. Vermont.	1871. New Jersey.

The New York fight of 1849 and 1850 was the pivotal fight; in the other States it was abandoned by legislative act, and without a serious contest. In the Southern States free education came with the educational reorganizations following the close of the Civil War.

Other school charges. Another per-capita tax usually levied on parents, in the early days of public education, was the fuel or wood tax. Unless each parent had hauled, or paid some one to do so, his proper "quota of wood" to the schoolhouse during the summer, it was assessed against him as was the rate-bill. This was vexatious, because small, and often hard to collect. Finally State after State abandoned the charge and assessed it, with other necessary expenses, against the property of the school district, thus making wood or coal a public charge.

The provision of textbooks has been another charge gradually assumed by cities and States. The earliest provision

of free textbooks, as in the case of free schooling, was made
by the cities. The earliest city to provide free textbooks
was probably Philadelphia, in 1818. New Hampshire ordered free textbooks for indigent children as early as 1827.
Jersey City began to provide free textbooks in 1830, and
Newark in 1838. Charleston, South Carolina, began in
1856; and Elizabeth and Hoboken, New Jersey, some time
before 1860. Massachusetts gave permission to furnish
free textbooks in 1873, and made them obligatory in 1884.
Maine followed in 1889, and New Hampshire in 1890. Many
other States have since ordered free textbooks provided
for their schools.

Free school supplies — pens, ink, paper, pencils — have
also been shifted gradually from an individual charge to
general taxation, and, within recent years, as we shall see
in later chapters, many new charges have been assumed
by the public as in the interests of better school education.

QUESTIONS FOR DISCUSSION

1. Explain the theory of "vested rights" as applied to private and
   parochial schools.
2. How do you explain the intense bitterness developed over the transition from Church to State education?
3. Take each of the leading arguments advanced for tax-supported state
   schools and show its validity, viewed from a modern standpoint.
4. Take each of the leading arguments advanced against tax-supported
   state schools and show its weakness, viewed from a modern standpoint.
5. Does every great advance in provisions for human welfare require a
   period of education and propaganda? Illustrate.
6. Explain why the legislatures were so unwilling to follow their governors in the matter of establishing schools.
7. What items have gone into the building up of the permanent state
   school fund in your State? What are its present total and per-capita
   income values?
8. What is the size of the permanent state school fund in your State,
   how is its income apportioned, and what percentage of the total cost
   per pupil each year does it pay?
9. What has been the history of the development of school taxation in
   your State?

10. Explain just what is meant by "the wealth of the State must educate the children of the State."
11. Show how, with the beginnings of state support, general state requirements could be enforced for the first time.
12. Show how the retention of the pauper-school idea would have been dangerous to the life of the Republic.
13. Why were the cities more anxious to escape from the operation of the pauper-school law than were the towns and rural districts?
14. Why were the pauper-school and rate-bill so hard to eliminate?
15. Enumerate the items furnished free, in your State, in addition to tuition.

TOPICS FOR INVESTIGATION AND REPORT

1. Thaddeus Stevens and the Pennsylvania school law of 1834. (Monroe; Stevens; Wickersham.)
2. Caleb Mills and the Indiana awakening. (Barnard; Boone.)
3. A comparison of educational development in Ohio and Indiana before 1850. (Boone; Miller; Orth; Rawles.)
4. The fight for free schools in New Jersey. (Murray.)
5. Use of the lottery for school endowment and support.
6. History of the Connecticut state school fund.
7. History of the New York state school fund.
8. Work of the western Academic and Literary Institutes.

SELECTED REFERENCES

Barnard, Henry, Editor. *The American Journal of Education*, 31 vols. Consult *Analytical Index* to; 128 pp. Published by United States Bureau of Education, Washington, 1892.

Boone, R. G. *Education in the United States.* 402 pp. D. Appleton & Co., New York, 1889.

Chapter VI forms good supplemental reading on the formation of permanent school funds.

*Boone, R. G. *History of Education in Indiana.* 454 pp. D. Appleton & Co., New York, 1892.

Chapters VIII and IX give very good descriptions of the awakening, the enactment of the law of 1848, and the referendum of 1349.

*Fairlie, John A. *Centralization of Administration in New York State.* Columbia University Studies in History, Economics, and Public Law, vol XI, No. 3, New York, 1898.

Chapter II describes briefly the centralizing tendencies in educational administration in New York State.

Mayo, Rev. A. D. "Original Establishment of State School Funds"; in *Report of the United States Commissioner of Education*, 1874–95, vol. II, pp. 1505–11.

A brief descriptive article.

*Miller, E. A. *History of Educational Legislation in Ohio, 1803–1850.* 280 pp. University of Chicago Press, 1918.

A good digest of educational legislation and progress.

*Monroe, Paul. *Cyclopedia of Education.* The Macmillan Co., New York, 1911–13. 5 vols.

The following articles form good supplemental references:
1. "District of Columbia"; vol. ii, pp. 342–45.
2. "Philadelphia, City of"; vol. iv, pp. 666–67.
3. "School Funds"; vol. v, pp. 269–73.
4. The historical portions of the articles on state school systems, such as Indiana, New York, Ohio, Pennsylvania, etc.

Murray, David. *History of Education in New Jersey.* 344 pp. United States Bureau of Education, Circular of Information, No. 1, Washington, 1899.

Chapter III describes the struggle to establish free schools in New Jersey.

*Orth, S. P. *Centralization of Administration in Ohio;* Columbia University, Studies in History, Economics, and Public Law, vol. xvi, No. 3, New York, 1903.

Chapter II gives a good sketch of the centralization in educational affairs, and the development of taxation for education.

*Randall, S. S. *The Common School System of the State of New York.* 94 pp. Troy, New York, 1851.

An old classic, now out of print, but still found in many libraries. Pages 72–79 describe the battle to abolish the rate-bill in New York.

*Rawles, W. A. *Centralizing Tendencies in the Administration of Indiana.* Columbia University Studies in History, Economics, and Public Law, vol. xvii, No. 1, New York, 1903.

Pages 26 to 141 very good on the development of educational administration in Indiana.

*Stevens, Thaddeus. "Speech in defense of the Pennsylvania Free School System"; in *Report of the United States Commissioner of Education,* 1898–99, vol. i, pp. 516–24.

Historical note, and the speech made in the Pennsylvania House of Representatives, in 1835, in opposition to the attempt to repeal the Law of 1834.

*Wickersham, J. P. *A History of Education in Pennsylvania.* 683 pp. Lancaster, Pa., 1886.

A very valuable volume, now somewhat rare. Chapters XIII, XV, and XVI very good on pauper education and the fight to establish free schools.

CHAPTER VI

THE BATTLE TO CONTROL THE SYSTEM

II. Phases of the Battle for State-Supported Schools — *continued*

4. *The battle to establish school supervision*

Local nature of all early schools. The history of our educational evolution as so far described must have clearly revealed to the reader how completely local the evolution of schools has been with us. Everywhere development has been from the community outward and upward, and not from the State downward. At first the schools were those of individual teachers, churches, philanthropic societies, towns, or districts, organized and maintained without any thought of connection or state relationship. Even in Massachusetts and Connecticut the local nature of the education provided was one of its marked characteristics.

After the New England towns, in response to the demand for greater local rights and local control of affairs, had split their town governments up into fragments, known at first as parishes and later as school districts, as described in Chapter II, and after the Massachusetts district school system thus evolved had been confirmed in the new state laws (1789) it spread to other States, and soon became the almost universal unit for school organization and control. The reasons for its early popularity are not hard to find. ‖It was well suited to the primitive needs and conditions of our early national life. Among a sparse and hard-working rural population, between whom intercourse was limited and intercommunication difficult, and with whom the support of schools by taxation was as yet an unsettled question, it answered a very real need. The simplicity and democracy of the system was one of its chief merits. Communities or neighborhoods which wanted schools and were willing to pay for them could easily meet and organize a school district, vote to levy a school tax on their own property, employ a teacher, and organize and maintain a school. On the other hand, communities which did not desire schools or were unwilling to tax themselves for them could do without them, and let the free-school idea alone. The first state laws generally, as we have pointed out in Chapter V, were permissive in nature and not mandatory, and under these permissive laws the progressive communities of each State gradually organized a series of local schools. These have since been brought together into township, county, and state organizations to form the state systems which we know to-day.

The schools thus established would naturally retain their local character so long as their support was entirely local. Schools might even be ordered established, as in the case of the town schools of Massachusetts and Connecticut, or the pauper schools of Pennsylvania, and, so long as the State contributed nothing to their maintenance, their organization, management, and control would almost of necessity be left to local initiative. The more progressive communities would obey the law and provide schools supported largely or wholly by taxation; the unwilling communities would either ignore the law or provide schools dependent upon tuition fees and rate-bills.

Beginnings of state control. The great battle for state schools, which we have briefly described in the preceding chapter, was not only for taxation to stimulate their development where none existed, but was also indirectly a battle for some form of state control of the local systems which had already grown up. The establishment of permanent state school funds by the older States, to supplement any other aid which might be granted, also tended toward the establishment of some form of state supervision and control of the local school systems. Under the early permissive laws all state aid for schools might of course be rejected, and frequently was, and usually large option and power of initiative had at first to be left to the local units, but the State, once any aid from permanent state endowment funds or any form of state taxation was accepted by a community school system, was now in position to make and enforce demands in return for the state aid granted.   In return for the state aid accepted the local school authorities must now make reports as to attendance, length of term, kind of teacher, and income and expenses, and must comply with the requirements of the state school laws as to district meetings, levying of local taxes to supplement the state aid, subjects to be taught, certificate for the teacher, and other similar matters. The acceptance of state aid inevitably meant a small but a gradually increasing state control. The first step was the establishment of some form of state aid; the next was the imposing of conditions necessary to secure this state aid.

State oversight and control, however, does not exercise itself, and it soon became evident that the States must elect or appoint some officer to represent the State and enforce the observance of its demands. It would be primarily his duty to see that the laws relating to schools were carried out, that statistics as to existing conditions were collected and printed, and that communities were properly advised as to their duties and the legislature as to the needs of the State. We find now the creation of a series of school officers to represent the State, the enactment of new laws extending control, and a struggle to integrate, subordinate, and reduce to some semblance of a state school system the hundreds of community school systems which had grown up.   The communities were usually very willing to accept the state aid offered, but many of them resented bitterly any attempt to curb their power to do as they pleased, or to force them to make reports and meet general state requirements.

The first state school officers. The first American State to create a state officer to exercise supervision over its schools was New York, in 1812. It will be remembered that this State had enacted an experimental school law, and made an annual state grant for schools, from 1795 to 1800. Then, unable to reënact the law, the system was allowed to lapse and was not reëstablished until the New England element gained control, in 1812. In enacting the new law providing for state aid for schools the first State Superintendent of Common Schools in the United States was created. So far as is known this was a distinctively American creation, uninfluenced by the practice in any other land. It was to be the duty of this officer to look after the establishment and maintenance of the schools throughout the State. By his vigorous work in behalf of schools the first appointee, Gideon Hawley, gave such offense to the politicians of the time that he was removed from office, in 1821, and the legislature then abolished the position and designated the Secretary of State to act, *ex officio*, as Superintendent. This condition continued until 1854, when New York again created the separate office of Superintendent of Public Instruction. Maryland created the office in 1826, but two years later abolished it and did not re-create it until 1864. Illinois directed its Secretary of State to act, *ex officio*, as Superintendent of Schools in 1825, as did also Vermont in 1827, Louisiana in 1833, Pennsylvania in 1834, and Tennessee in 1835. Illinois did not create a real State Superintendent of Schools, though, until 1854, Vermont until 1845, Louisiana until 1847, Pennsylvania until 1857, or Tennessee until 1867.

The first States to create separate school officials who have been continued to the present time were Michigan and Kentucky, both in 1837. Influenced by Cousin's *Report* (Chapter IX) on the organization of schools in Prussia, the leaders in the Michigan constitutional convention of 1835 — Pierce and Crary — insisted on the title of Superintendent of Public Instruction and on constitutional provisions which would insure, from an administrative point of view, a state school system rather than a series of local systems of schools. Kentucky, on the other hand, evolved, as had New York, a purely American-type official, known as Superintendent of Common Schools. The Michigan title in time came to be the one commonly used, though few States in adopting it have been aware of its Prussian origin. Other States followed these, creating a state school officer under one of a number of titles, and in some States, such as Connecticut, Ohio, Iowa, and Missouri, the office was created, abolished, and re-created one or more times before it became permanently established. Often quite a legislative struggle took place to secure the establishment of the office, and later on to prevent its abolition.

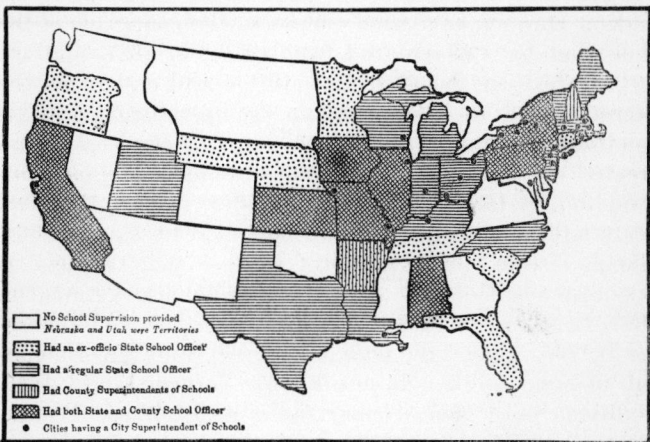

FIG. 29. STATUS OF SCHOOL SUPERVISION IN THE UNITED STATES BY 1861

For a list of the 28 City Superintendencies established up to 1870, see Cubberley's *Public School Administration*, p. 58. For the history of the state educational office in each State see Cubberley and Elliott, *State and County School Administration, Source Book*, pp. 283–87.

By 1850 there were *ex-officio* state school officers in nine, and regular school officers in seven, of the then thirty-one States, and by 1861 there were *ex-officio* officers in nine and regular officers in nineteen of the then thirty-four States, as well as one of each in two of the organized Territories. The above map shows the growth of supervisory oversight by 1861 — forty-nine years from the time the first American

state school officer was created. The map also shows the
ten of the thirty-four States which had, by 1861, also created
the office of County Superintendent of Schools, as well as
the twenty-five cities which had, by 1861, created the office
of City Superintendent of Schools. Only three more cities
— Albany, Washington, and Kansas City — were added
before 1870, making a total of twenty-eight, but since that
date the number of city superintendents has increased to
something like fourteen hundred to-day.

Early duties; selection by election. The office of State
Superintendent of Common Schools, Superintendent of
Free Schools, Superintendent of Education, Superintendent
of Public Instruction, or Commissioner of Education —
terms which are significant of the educational evolution
through which we have passed — was thus evolved with us
to represent the State in its dealings with the local school
systems to which it now proposed to extend some financial
aid. At the time the office arose there were few of our
present-day problems to be solved, and the early functions
attached to the office were almost exclusively clerical, statistical, and exhortatory. These early functions have become
crystallized in the laws and have formed the traditions of
the office. Even more have they formed the traditions of
the office of County Superintendent of Schools. To collect,
tabulate, and edit the school statistics as to attendance,
teachers, term, and finances demanded by the law; to advise as to the law; to apportion the state aid to the school
districts; to visit the different counties and advise the local
school authorities; to exhort the people to found and improve
their schools; and to advise the legislature as to the condition and needs of the schools, — these constituted the chief
duties of these early officials. With time, and with the
gradual change in the popular conception as to the place and
purpose of public education, so many new duties have been
added to the office that it has now come to be conceived of
in an entirely new light.

The creation of these new state officials came just at the

time when the rising democratic consciousness and distrust
of legislatures and governors had reached its height, and
when the belief in the ability of the people to select all their
public servants had reached, with the general attainment
of full manhood suffrage, a maximum.   The appointed city
school superintendent had not as yet arisen to point the
way to a better method of selection, — there were but ten
such in the United States by 1850, — the analogy to a state
auditor or a county clerk seemed clear, the expert functions
which now ought to characterize the office had not developed, and nomination and election by the people seemed the
perfectly natural method to follow.   In consequence, almost everywhere these new state and county officials were
placed in the elective column, instead of being appointed
to office.   Even in the cities the elective method was at
first tried, though all cities have now discarded it as a
means for selecting a city superintendent of schools.   In
the earlier period, when the duties of these new officials
were far simpler than they now are, and when almost no
professional functions had arisen, the elective method of
choosing a person to fill these educational offices naturally
gave much better results than it does to-day.   Only in New
England was a better method followed from the first.

Curbing the district system.   One of the chief duties of
these early state school officials, aside from the collection
of statistics and exhorting the people to establish and maintain schools, was that of trying to institute some control
over the local school communities, and the introduction
of some uniformity into school practices.   By the time the
States began to create state and county school officers, the
Massachusetts district system, the origin of which we described in Chapter II, had overrun the country.   The first
school law enacted by Massachusetts (1789) recognized and
legalized the district system of school organization and control, as it had evolved in the State during the preceding
hundred years.   In 1800 the districts were given full local
power to tax for schools; in 1817 full power was given them

to contract and to sue and be sued; and in 1827 the full culmination of the district system was attained by laws which
authorized the districts to select district school trustees,
and gave to these trustees the power to choose the textbooks
and employ and certificate their teachers.

Maine, Vermont, New Hampshire, Rhode Island, and
Connecticut also accepted the district system early. It
spread to New York in 1812, and was carried by New England people in their great migration toward the West and
South. Ohio definitely accepted the district system of
organization in 1821, Illinois in 1825, Tennessee in 1830,
Indiana in 1833, Michigan in 1837, Kentucky and Iowa in
1838, North Carolina in 1839, and Virginia in its optional
law of 1846. Once established amid pioneer people it became firmly rooted, and has since been changed only after
much effort, though almost all the conditions which gave
rise to it have since passed away.

In most of the States the system soon ran rampant. The
district meeting became a forensic center in which questions the most remote and personal animosities of long
standing were fought out. Petty local interests and a "dog-
in-the-manger spirit" too often prevailed, to the great detri-
ment of the schools. District jealousies prevented needed
development. An exaggerated idea of district rights, district importance, and district perfection became common.
District independence was often carried to a great extreme.
In Massachusetts, for example, Horace Mann found that in
two thirds of the towns teachers were allowed to begin teaching without any examination or certification, and frequently
were paid without either; that the trustees refused generally
to require uniform textbooks, or to furnish them to poor
children, as required by the law; and that one third of the
children of school age in the State were absent from school
in the winter and two fifths in the summer, without the
trustees concerning themselves in any way about the situation. In Ohio the trustees "forbade the teaching of any
branches except reading, writing, and arithmetic," and in

1840 the early laws requiring schools in the English language were repealed, and the districts were permitted to authorize schools in the German language. In Indiana the system went to such an extreme as almost to destroy the schools. In 1836 and 1837 laws were passed which permitted householders to make individual contracts with teachers to teach their children, and in 1841 the requirement of any form of a teacher's certificate was made optional with the district trustees. In many States school district trustees were allowed to determine what subjects should be taught and how, and the people determined who should teach and how long a term of school should be maintained.

To enforce reports giving statistics as to the schools, to enforce local taxation to supplement the state aid, to enforce the requirement of some form of a teacher's certificate, to see that the school subjects required in the law were taught in the schools, and that the schools were maintained at least the length of time demanded by the State, were among the early functions of these state, county, and township school superintendents. All these were important as establishing some form of state control over the school districts, and marked the beginnings of their integration into a series of county and state school systems.

Creating supervision in Massachusetts. The struggle to subordinate and control the district system is well illustrated by the history of Massachusetts. Once foremost in general education, a great decline had set in after the coming of statehood, and this decline continued steadily up to about 1826. The decline in the importance of its schools was closely paralleled by the growth in importance of the district system of school control. The growth of manufacturing, the social changes in the cities, and the philanthropic and humanitarian movements we have described in Chapter IV, all tended in Massachusetts, as elsewhere, to awaken an educational consciousness and a demand for educational reform. As early as 1821 a young Harvard graduate and teacher, by the name of James G. Carter

(1795–1845), had published a series of *Letters . . . on the Free Schools of New England*. In these letters the glaring defects of the district system and the decline in importance of the schools were pointed out. Deeply impressed with conditions, he soon became a leader in educational propaganda and educational reform.

The first result of the agitation he started was the law of 1826, whereby each town (township) was required to appoint a Town School Committee (School Board) to exercise general supervision over all the district schools in the town, select the textbooks, and examine and certificate all the teachers employed. This law met with bitter opposition from many districts, it being regarded as an infringement of district "rights." In 1834 the state school fund was created, and to share in its income all towns were required to raise a town tax of one dollar per child and to make statistical reports as required. In 1837 came the culmination of Mr. Carter's labors, when he secured passage of a bill creating the first real State Board of Education in the United States. Instead of following the practice of the time, and creating an elected State Superintendent of Schools, Mr. Carter, much more wisely, provided for a small appointed State Board of Education which in turn was to select a Secretary, who was to act in the capacity of a state school officer and report to the Board, and through it to the legislature and the people. Neither the Board nor the Secretary were given any powers of compulsion, their work being to investigate conditions, report facts, expose defects, and make recommendations as to action to the legislature. The permanence and influence of the Board thus depended very largely on the character of the Secretary it selected.

The new Secretary and his problems. A prominent Brown University graduate and lawyer in the State Senate, by the name of Horace Mann (1796–1859), who as president of the Senate had been of much assistance in securing passage of the bill creating the State Board of Education, was finally induced by the Governor and the Board to accept the position of Secretary. He entered on his duties in June, 1837. The choice proved to be a particularly fortunate one, as Mr. Mann possessed the characteristics needed for such an office — enthusiasm, courage, vision, lofty ideals, and practical legislative experience. Few State Superintendents of Public Education since his time have risen to a higher conception of the importance of their office, and his career forms a worthy study for any one interested in educational leadership. He gave up a promising career in the law and in politics to accept the office at a beggarly salary that often left him without money for his dinner, but, once he had made up his mind to do so, he entered upon the work with all the energy he possessed. To a friend he wrote:

My law books are for sale. My office is to let. The bar is no longer my forum. I have abandoned jurisprudence and betaken myself to the larger sphere of mind and morals.

On the day he accepted the office he wrote in his diary:

Henceforth so long as I hold this office I devote myself to the supremest welfare of mankind upon earth. . . . I have faith in the improvability of the race — in their accelerating improvability. This effort may do, apparently, but little. But mere beginning a good cause is never little. If we can get this vast wheel into any perceptible motion, we shall have accomplished much.

The problems which Mr. Mann faced, growing out of bad legislation in the past and the resulting state of affairs, are thus stated by Hinsdale:

1. The whole State needed to be thoroughly aroused to the importance and value of public instruction.
2. The public schools needed to be democratized; that is, the time had more than come when they should be restored to the people of the State, high as well as low, in the good old sense of the name.
3. The public necessities demanded an expansion of public education in respect to kinds of schools and range of instruction.
4. The legal school organization and machinery, as existing,

were not in harmony with the new social conditions. Moreover, current methods of administration were loose and unbusinesslike.

5. The available school funds were quite insufficient for maintaining good schools, and called loudly for augmentation.

6. The schools were, to a great extent, antiquated and outgrown in respect to the quantity and quality of the instruction that they furnished, as well as in methods of teaching, management, discipline, and supervision.

The work of Horace Mann. Mr. Mann now began a most memorable work of educating public opinion, and soon became the acknowledged leader in school organization in the United States. State after State called upon him for advice and counsel, while his twelve annual *Reports* to the State Board of Education will always remain memorable documents. Public men of all classes — lawyers, clergymen, college professors, literary men, teachers — were laid under tribute and sent forth over the State explaining to the people the need for a reawakening of educational interest in Massachusetts. Every year Mr. Mann organized a "campaign." It resembled somewhat the recent national campaign to explain to our people the meaning and moral significance of our participation in the World War in Europe. So successful was he, and so ripe was the time for such a movement, that he not only started a great common school revival in Massachusetts which led to the regeneration of the schools there, but one which was felt and which influenced development in every Northern State.

His controversy with the Boston schoolmasters, whose sensibilities he had wounded by his praise of European schools, attracted much attention, made a deep impression on the public mind, and did much to fix Mr. Mann's place in educational history. His controversy with the religious societies marked the beginning of the struggle in the United States for non-sectarian schools. Everywhere he preached the doctrine of liberal taxation for public education, with the result that during the twelve years of his secretaryship the appropriations for public education were more than

HORACE MANN
(1796–1859)
(From a painting in the Westfield, Massachusetts, Normal School)

HENRY BARNARD
(1811–1900)
From a picture taken about 1890

doubled, salaries of teachers greatly increased, and a full month added to the length of the school term. He organized the first three state normal schools in America, and some of the earliest teachers' institutes. He labored continually at the improvement of teaching method, and especially worked for the introduction of Pestalozzian reforms and the substitution of the word-method in teaching reading for the slow, wasteful, and unintelligent alphabet method. He edited the *Massachusetts Common School Journal*, wrote a careful report on schoolhouse hygiene, introduced school libraries throughout the State, and stimulated the development of the high school. In his hands the printed "school returns," first required by the law of 1826, became "powerful instruments in educating the public." His vigorous condemnation of the district system, to which he devoted his fourth *Report*, contributed to its ultimate abandonment. The Massachusetts Law of 1789, which legalized it, he repeatedly stated to have been "the most unfortunate law on the subject of common schools ever enacted in the State," and he declared that "no substantial and general progress can be made so long as the district system exists." So entrenched was the system "behind statutory rights and immemorial usage" that it required thirty years longer to free the State from its inimical influence.

His twelve carefully written *Reports* on the condition of education in Massachusetts and elsewhere, with his intelligent discussion of the aims and purposes of public education, occupy a commanding place in the history of American education, while he will always be regarded as perhaps the greatest of the "founders" of our American system of free public schools. No one did more than he to establish in the minds of the American people the conception that education should be universal, non-sectarian, and free, and that its aim should be social efficiency, civic virtue, and character, rather than mere learning or the advancement of sectarian ends. Under his practical leadership an unorganized and heterogeneous series of community school systems was reduced to organization and welded together into a state school system, and the people of Massachusetts were effectively recalled to their ancient belief in and duty toward the education of the people.

Henry Barnard in Connecticut and Rhode Island. Almost equally important, though of a somewhat different character, was the work of Henry Barnard in Connecticut and Rhode Island. A graduate of Yale, and also educated for the law, he turned aside to teach and became deeply interested in education. The years 1835–37 he spent in Europe studying schools, particularly the work of Pestalozzi's disciples. On his return to America he was elected a member of the Connecticut legislature, and at once formulated and secured passage of the Connecticut law (1839) providing for a State Board of Commissioners for Common Schools, with a Secretary, after the Massachusetts plan. Mr. Barnard was then elected as its first Secretary, and reluctantly gave up the law and accepted the position at the munificent salary of $3 a day and expenses. Until the legislature abolished both the Board and the position, in 1842, he rendered for Connecticut a service scarcely less important than the better-known reforms which Horace Mann was at that time carrying on in Massachusetts.

It will be remembered that Connecticut had established a state school fund as early as 1750, and on the sale of the Western Reserve for $1,200,000, in 1795, had added this sum to the fund. The fund experienced excellent management, and by the time of the creation of the State Board had reached nearly $2,000,000 in value, producing a yearly income large enough to pay a substantial portion of the then cost of maintaining the schools. This had made the people negligent as to taxation, and this, combined with the growing strength of the district system, led to a decline in interest in education in Connecticut similar to that which had taken place in Massachusetts. The schools were poor, private schools were increasing, the people objected to taxation, the teachers were without training or professional interest, the pauper-school idea began to be advocated, and a general decline in educational affairs had set in. An investigation, made in 1838, showed that not one half of the children of the State were attending school. From probably the best schools of any State at the end of the colonial period, the Connecticut schools had fallen to a very inferior position.

It was the work of Barnard to recall Connecticut to her ancient duty. He visited and inspected the schools, and made many public addresses. In 1839 he organized the first teachers' institute in America which met for more than a few days (his was for six weeks, with daily instruction in classes), and he used this new instrument extensively to awaken the teachers of the State to proper conceptions of their work. He established the *Connecticut Common School Journal* to disseminate his ideas. He also organized school libraries, and urged the establishment of evening schools. He strove to improve the physical condition of the schools by writing much on schoolhouse construction. He studied the "school returns," and used the statistical data to arouse interest. In 1842, through the animus of a governor who objected to the "useless expense," and the "dangerous innovation" of union schools to provide advanced education, the Board was abolished, the laws repealed, and Mr. Barnard was legislated out of office.

In 1843 he was called to Rhode Island to examine and report upon the existing schools, and from 1845 to 1849 acted as State Commissioner of Public Schools there, where he rendered a service similar to that previously rendered in Connecticut. In addition he organized a series of town libraries throughout the State. For his teachers' institutes he devised a traveling model school, to give demonstration lessons in the art of teaching. From 1851 to 1855 he was again in Connecticut, as principal of the newly established state normal school and *ex-officio* Secretary of the Connecticut State Board of Education. He now rewrote the school laws, increased taxation for schools, checked the power of

the districts, there known as "school societies," and laid
the foundations of a state system of schools.

Barnard as the scholar of the " awakening."   In 1855
he began the editing of his famous *American Journal of
Education*, a vast encyclopædia of educational information
which finally reached thirty-one volumes.   In this venture
he sunk his entire private fortune, and in his old age was a
poor man.   The collection still remains a great storehouse
of educational information and biography, covering almost
every phase of the history of education from the earliest
times down to 1870.   It gave to American educators, who
had so long been isolated and who had been slowly evolving
a thoroughly native school system out of the English inheritance, a needed conception of historical development in
other lands and a useful knowledge of recent development
and practice in other lands and nations.   From 1858 to 1860
he served as president of the University of Wisconsin, and
from 1867 to 1870 as the first United States Commissioner
of Education.   He published much, was distinctively the
scholar of the great public school awakening of the second
quarter of the nineteenth century, and was closely associated with the most progressive movements in American
education for approximately forty years.   Mann and Barnard stand out as the two conspicuous leaders during the
formative period of American education.   Mann in particular pointed the way to many subsequent reforms in the
administration of public education, while to Barnard we owe
a special debt as our first great educational scholar.

The " awakening " elsewhere; the leaders.   The work
of Mann and Barnard had its influence throughout all the
Northern States, and encouraged the friends of education
everywhere.   Almost contemporaneous with them were
leaders in other States who helped fight through the battles
of state establishment and state organization and control,
among the more prominent of whom should be mentioned
Calvin Stowe, Samuel Lewis, and Samuel Galloway in
Ohio; Caleb Mills in Indiana; Ninian W. Edwards in Illi-

CALEB MILLS
(1806–1879)
President of Wabash College
Author of six *Messages* "by one of the people"

REV. CALVIN E. STOWE
(1802–1886)
Professor in Lane Theological Seminary, Cincinnati
Author of *Report on Elem. Educ. in Europe* (1837)

TWO LEADERS IN THE COMMON SCHOOL AWAKENING IN INDIANA AND OHIO

SAMUEL GALLOWAY
(1811–1872)
Ex-officio State Superintendent of
Common Schools, 1844–1851

REV. SAMUEL LEWIS
(1799–1854)
First State Superintendent of
Common Schools, 1837–1840

TWO EARLY OHIO STATE SCHOOL SUPERINTENDENTS

nois; John D. Pierce and Isaac E. Crary in Michigan; Robert
J. Breckinridge in Kentucky; Calvin H. Wiley in North Carolina; and John Swett in California.

It is not perhaps without its significance, as showing the
enduring influence of the Calvinistic educational traditions,
that of these Stowe was a graduate of Bowdoin College in
Maine, and that the Stowe family goes back to 1634, in
Roxbury, Massachusetts; that Lewis was born in Massachusetts, was descended from one of the first colonists in
Plymouth, and floated down the Ohio with his parents to
Cincinnati in the great westward migration of New England people; that Galloway was of Scotch-Irish ancestry, and
was educated among New England people in Ohio; that
Mills was born in New Hampshire, and had been graduated
from Dartmouth; that Pierce was born in New Hampshire,
educated in Massachusetts, and had been graduated from
Brown; that Crary was of Puritan ancestry, born and educated in Connecticut, and a graduate of Trinity College;
that Breckinridge was a descendant of a Scotch Covenanter
who fled to America, at the time of the restoration of the
Stuarts in England, and settled in Pennsylvania; that Wiley
was of early Scotch-Irish Presbyterian stock ; and that Swett
was born and educated in New Hampshire, taught school
in Massachusetts in the days of Horace Mann, and was
descended from a family of that name which landed at
Massachusetts Bay in 1642.

5. The battle to eliminate sectarianism

The secularization of American education. The Church,
it will be remembered, was with us from the earliest colonial
times in possession of the education of the young. Not
only were the earliest schools controlled by the Church and
dominated by the religious motive, but the right of the
Church to dictate the teaching in the schools was clearly
recognized by the State. Still more, the State looked to
the Church to provide the necessary education, and assisted
it in doing so by donations of land and money. The min-

ister, as a town official, naturally examined the teachers and the instruction in the schools. After the establishment of our National Government this relationship for a time continued. New York and the New England States specifically set aside lands to help both church and school. When Connecticut sold its Western Reserve, in 1795, and added the sum to the Connecticut school fund, it was stated to be for the aid of "schools and the gospel." In the sales of the first national lands in Ohio (1,500,000 acres to The Ohio Company, in 1787; and 1,000,000 acres in the Symmes Purchase, near Cincinnati, in 1788), section 16 in each township was reserved and given as an endowment for schools, and section 29 "for the purposes of religion." After about 1800 these land endowments for religion ceased, but grants of state aid for religious schools continued for nearly a half-century longer. Then it became common for a town or city to build a schoolhouse from city taxation, and let it out rent-free to any responsible person who would conduct a tuition school in it, with a few free places for selected poor children. Still later, with the rise of the state schools, it became quite common to take over church and private schools and aid them on the same basis as the new state schools.

In colonial times, too, and for some decades into our national period, the warmest advocates of the establishment of schools were those who had in view the needs of the Church. Then gradually the emphasis shifted, as we have shown in Chapter III, to the needs of the State, and a new class of advocates of public education now arose. Still later the emphasis has been shifted to industrial and civic and national needs, and the religious aim has been almost completely eliminated. This change is known as the secularization of American education. It also required many a bitter struggle, and was accomplished in the different States but slowly. The two great factors which served to produce this change have been:

1. The conviction that the life of the Republic demands an educated and intelligent citizenship, and hence the general

education of all in common schools controlled by the State; and

2. The great diversity of religious beliefs among our people, which has forced tolerance and religious freedom through a consideration of the rights of minorities.

The secularization of education with us must not be regarded either as a deliberate or a wanton violation of the rights of the Church, but rather as an unavoidable incident connected with the coming to self-consciousness and self-government of a great people.

So long as there was little intercommunication and migration, and the people of a community remained fairly homogeneous, it was perfectly natural that the common religious faith of the people should enter into the instruction of the school.   When the schools were purely local and voluntary this was not a serious objection.   With the rise of state support, and the widening of the units for maintenance and control from the lone community or district to the town, the county, and the State, the situation changed. With the coming of foreign immigration, which began to be marked after about 1825, and the intermingling of peoples of different faiths in the rapidly evolving cities, religious uniformity ceased to exist.   Majority rule now for a time followed, but this was soon forced to give way to the still more important governmental principle of religious freedom.   As necessity gradually compelled the State to provide education for its children, sectarian differences made it increasingly evident that the education provided must be non-sectarian in character.   As Brown (S. W.) has so well stated it:

Differences of religious belief and a sound regard on the part of the State for individual freedom in religious matters, coupled with the necessity for centralization and uniformity, rather than hostility to religion as such, lie at the bottom of the movement toward the secular school.

Gradual nature of the change.   The change to non-sectarian schools came very gradually, and it is hard to assign a date for its beginning. The chart between pages 44 and 45, showing the process of evolving the civic out of the earlier religious schools, discloses a gradual fading out of religious influence and control during the eighteenth century, and the gradual assumption of state control early in the nineteenth century. The change began early in our national history — in a way it was but a sequel to the waning religious interest which characterized the last fifty years of the colonial period — but it was not until the decade of the forties that the question became at all acute. At first it was largely a matter of change in the character of instruction, marked by a decreasing emphasis on the religious element and an increasing emphasis on secular material.

Cc *Stands for* Camel, who lives in the east;

Dd *Stands for* Drunkard, a worse looking beast.

FIG. 30. THE ALPHABET

From *The Columbian Primer*, 1802. A small, 84-page, modernized and secularized imitation of the *New England Primer*. Each letter was illustrated; the illustrations for C and D are here reproduced.

The use of the English Dilworth's *A New Guide to the English Tongue*, after about 1760; the publication of Noah Webster's *American Spelling Book*, a combined speller and reader, in 1783; and the *Columbian Primer* and the *Franklin Primer*, in 1802; soon broke the almost exclusive hold of the *New England Primer*, with its Shorter Catechism, on the schools. By 1806 the *Primer* had been discarded in the dame schools of Boston, as well as in the lower schools in most other cities, though it continued to be used in the rural districts until near the beginning of the second quarter of the nineteenth century. Other American textbooks, more literary and less religious in character, also helped along the process of change. Some of the more prominent of these were Caleb Bingham's *American Preceptor* (1794) and *Columbian Orator* (1806), Lindley Murray's *Grammar* (1795), and the *Franklin Primer* (1802). Readings from these new books now took the place of readings from the Bible.

The Lancastrian schools also gave but little attention to religious instruction as such, though having religious exercises, and these, it will be remembered, became for a time exceedingly popular throughout the country. The most significant single fact, and one clearly expressive of the process which had for long been under way, was the Massachusetts Act of 1827 which declared that School Committees should "never direct to be used or purchased in any of the town schools any school books which were calculated to favor the tenets of any particular sect of Christians." This Act merely registered what the slow operation of public opinion had already decided. In 1833 Massachusetts gave up taxing for church support, as had Connecticut in 1818.

The fight in Massachusetts. The educational awakening in Massachusetts, brought on by the work of Carter and Mann, was to many a rude awakening. Among other things, it revealed that the old school of the Puritans had gradually been replaced by a new and purely American type of school, with instruction adapted to democratic and national rather than religious ends. Mr. Mann stood strongly for such a conception of public education, and being a Unitarian, and the new State Board of Education being almost entirely liberal in religion, an attack was launched against them, and for the first time in our history the cry was raised that "The public schools are Godless schools." Those who believed in the old system of religious instruction, those who bore the Board or its Secretary personal ill-will, and those who desired to break down the Board's authority and stop the development of the public schools, united their forces in this first big attack against secular education. Horace Mann was the first prominent educator in America to meet and answer the religious onslaught.

A violent attack was opened in both the pulpit and the press. It was claimed that the Board was trying to eliminate the Bible from the schools, to abolish correction, and to "make the schools a counterpoise to religious instruction at home and in Sabbath schools." The local right to demand religious instruction was insisted upon. Even as conservative a journal as the *Princeton Review* declared:

> The people of each school district have the right to make the schools as religious as they please; and if they cannot agree they have the right severally of withdrawing their proper proportion of the public stock of funds.

Mr. Mann felt that a great public issue had been raised which should be answered carefully and fully. In three public letters and in one of his *Reports* he answered the criticisms and pointed out the errors in the argument. The Bible, he said, was an invaluable book for forming the character of children, and should be read without comment in the schools, but it was not necessary to teach it there. He showed that most of the towns had given up the teaching of the Catechism before the establishment of the Board of Education. He contended that any attempt to decide what creed or doctrine should be taught would mean the ruin of the schools.

The attack culminated in the attempts of the religious forces to abolish the State Board of Education, in the legislatures of 1840 and 1841, which failed dismally. Most of the orthodox people of the State took Mr. Mann's side, and Governor Briggs, in one of his messages, commended his stand by inserting the following:

> Justice to a faithful public officer leads me to say that the indefatigable and accomplished Secretary of the Board of Education has performed services in the cause of common schools which will earn him the lasting gratitude of the generation to which he belongs.

The attempt to divide the school funds. As was stated earlier, in the beginning it was common to aid church schools on the same basis as the state schools, and sometimes, in the beginnings of state aid, the money was distributed among existing schools without at first establishing any public schools. In many Eastern cities church schools at first shared in the public funds. In Pennsylvania church and

private schools were aided from poor-law funds up to 1834.
In New Jersey the first general school law of 1829 had been
repealed a year later through the united efforts of church
and private school interests, who fought the development
of state schools, and in 1830 and 1831 new laws had permitted all private and parochial schools to share in the small
state appropriation for education.

After the beginning of the forties, when the Roman Catholic influence came in strongly with the increase in Irish
immigration to the United States, a new factor was introduced and the problem, which had previously been a Protestant problem, took on a somewhat different aspect.
Largely through the demands of the Catholics one of the
most interesting fights in the whole process of secularizing
American education was precipitated in the City of New
York.

It will be remembered that the Public School Society,
founded in 1805, had become the greatest single educational
organization in the city, and had received state money,
after 1807, to assist it in its work.   In 1820 the Bethel
Baptist Church was admitted to a share in the state appropriation.   To this the Public School Society objected, and
the legislature in 1825 turned over the quota of New York
City to the city council, to divide as it thought best. The
council cut off the Baptist schools, three of which were by
that time running, and refused to grant public money to
any religious society.   In 1828 the Public School Society
was permitted to levy a local tax to supplement its resources,
it being estimated that at that time there were 10,000 children in the city with no opportunities for education.   The
Society was regarded as a non-denominational organization,
though chartered to teach "the sublime truths of religion
and morality contained in the Holy Scriptures" in its
schools.

In 1831 the Catholic Orphan Asylum applied to the city
council for a grant of funds, which was allowed.   The
Methodists at once applied for a similar grant, and were

refused. The religious question now became more and more
prominent, though without any progress being made toward
its settlement. By 1840 the Massachusetts conflict was on,
and in that year Governor Seward, of New York, urged the
establishment of schools in the cities of the State in which
the teachers should be of the same language and religion as
the foreign patrons. This dangerous proposal encouraged
the Catholics, and they immediately applied to the New
York City council for a division of the city school fund, and,
on being refused, carried their demand to the legislature of
the State. A Hebrew and a Scotch Presbyterian Church
also applied for their share, and supported the Catholics in
their demands. On the other hand the Methodists, Epis-
copalians, Baptists, Dutch Reformed, and Reformed Presbyterians united with the Public School Society in opposing
all such divison of the funds.

The legislature deferred action until 1842, and then did
the unexpected thing. The heated discussion of the question in the city and in the legislature had made it evident
that, while it might not be desirable to continue to give
funds to a privately organized corporation, to divide them
among the quarreling and envious religious sects would be
much worse. The result was that the legislature created for
the city a City Board of Education, to establish real public
schools, and stopped the debate on the question of aid to
religious schools by enacting that no portion of the school
funds was in the future to be given to any school in which
"any religious sectarian doctrine or tenet should be taught,
inculcated, or practiced." Thus the real public school system of New York City was evolved out of this attempt to
/divide the public funds among the churches. The Public
School Society continued for a time, but its work was now
done, and in 1853 it surrendered its buildings and property
to the City Board of Education and disbanded.

The contest in other States. As early as 1830, Lowell,
Massachusetts, had granted aid to the Irish Catholic
parochial schools in the city, and in 1835 had taken over

two such schools and maintained them as public schools. In 1853 the representatives of the Roman Catholic Church made a demand on the state legislature for a division of the school fund of the State. To settle the question once for all a constitutional amendment was submitted by the legislature to the people, providing that all state and town moneys raised or appropriated for education must be expended only on regularly organized and conducted public schools, and that no religious sect should ever share in such funds. This measure failed of adoption at the election of 1853 by a vote of 65,111 for and 65,512 against, but was re-proposed and adopted in 1855. This settled the question in Massachusetts, as Mann had tried to settle it earlier, and as New Hampshire had settled it in its constitution of 1792 and Connecticut in its constitution of 1818.

Other States now faced similar demands, but no demand for a share in or a division of the public school funds, after 1840, was successful. The demand everywhere met with intense opposition, and with the coming of enormous numbers of Irish Catholics after 1846, and German Lutherans after 1848, the question of the preservation as unified state school systems of the schools just established now became a burning one. Petitions deluged the legislatures, and these were met by counter-petitions. Mass meetings on both sides of the question were held. Candidates for office were forced to declare themselves. Anti-Catholic riots occurred in a number of cities. The Native American Party was formed, in 1841, "to prevent the union of Church and State," and to "keep the Bible in the schools." In 1841 the Whig Party, in New York, inserted a plank in its platform against sectarian schools. In 1855 the national council of the Know-Nothing Party, meeting in Philadelphia, in its platform favored public schools and the use of the Bible therein, but opposed sectarian schools. This party carried the elections that year in Massachusetts, New Hampshire, Connecticut, Rhode Island, Maryland, and Kentucky.

To settle the question in a final manner legislatures now

began to propose constitutional amendments to the people of their several States which forbade a division or a diversion of the funds, and these were almost uniformly adopted at the first election after being proposed.   The States, with the date of adoption of such a constitutional prohibition, are:

States amending constitution		Adopted when admitted	
New Jersey	1844	Wisconsin	1848
Michigan	1850	Oregon	1857
Ohio	1851	Kansas	1859
Indiana	1851	Nevada	1864
Massachusetts	1855	Nebraska	1867
Iowa	1857	West Virginia	1872
Mississippi	1868	Colorado	1876
South Carolina	1868	North Dakota	1889
Arkansas	1868	South Dakota	1889
Illinois	1870	Montana	1889
Pennsylvania	1872	Washington	1889
Alabama	1875	Idaho	1890
Missouri	1875	Wyoming	1890
North Carolina	1876	Utah	1896
Texas	1876	Oklahoma	1907
Minnesota	1877	New Mexico	1912
Georgia	1877	Arizona	1912
California	1879		
Louisiana	1879		
Florida	1885		
Delaware	1897		

In 1875 President Grant, in his message to Congress, urged the submission of an amendment to the Federal Constitution making it the duty of the States to support free public schools, free from religious teaching, and forbidding the diversion of school funds to church or sectarian purposes.   In a later message he renewed the recommendation, but Congress took no action because it considered such action unnecessary.   That the people had thoroughly decided that the school funds must be kept intact and the system of free public schools preserved may be inferred from the fact that no State admitted to the Union after

1858, excepting West Virginia, failed to insert such a provision in its first state constitution. Hence the question may be regarded as a settled one in our American States. Our people mean to keep the public school system united as one state school system, well realizing that any attempt to divide the schools among the different religious denominations (The *World Almanac* for 1917 lists 49 different denominations and 171 different sects in the United States) could only lead to inefficiency and educational chaos.

QUESTIONS FOR DISCUSSION

1. Explain why with us schools naturally developed from the community outward.
2. Why did state organization and compulsion eventually become necessary?
3. Do state support and state control always go together?
4. State your explanation for the older States beginning to establish permanent school funds, often before they had established a state system of schools.
5. What was the reason the local school communities so resented state control, when anxious to accept state funds?
6. Compare the duties of the chief state school officer in your state to-day with those described for the early state officials.
7. Explain how the different titles for the chief state school officer, given on page 160, are "significant of the educational development through which we have passed."
8. Explain how the district system naturally became what it did.
9. Show the gradual transition from church control of education, through state aid of church schools, to secularized state schools.
10. Show why secularized state schools were the only possible solution for the United States.
11. Show that the quotation from Brown, on page 173, represents the statesman-like manner in which we have handled the question.
12. Show that secularization would naturally take place in the textbooks and the instruction before manifesting itself in the laws.
13. What would be the effect on education if every one followed the declaration of the writer in the *Princeton Review* (p. 176)? Would the attempt of the Catholics to divide the school funds have resulted in the same thing?
14. What would have been the probable result had the New York legislature followed Governor Seward's recommendation?
15. Would a good system of high schools ever have been possible had we divided the school funds among the churches?

TOPICS FOR INVESTIGATION AND REPORT

1. The work of Horace Mann.
2. The work of Henry Barnard.
3. The work of James G. Carter. (Barnard.)
4. The messages of Caleb Mills. (Boone; Tuttle.)
5. Barnard's Rhode Island school survey report. (Wells.)
6. The work of Lewis and Stowe in Ohio. (Barnard.)
7. The work of Pierce and Crary in Michigan. (Hoyt-Ford.)
8. The work of Breckinridge in Kentucky. (Barnard.)
9. The work of Calvin Wiley in North Carolina. (Barnard; Knight.)
10. The work of John Swett in California.

SELECTED REFERENCES

Barnard, Henry, Editor. *The American Journal of Education.* 31 vols. Consult *Analytical Index* to; 128 pp. Published by United States Bureau of Education, Washington, 1892.

Barnard, Henry. *American Teachers and Educators.* 526 pp. C. W. Bardeen, Syracuse, New York.

A reprint of articles found in different volumes of the *American Journal of Education.* Contains biographies with portraits of Carter, Lewis, Mann, Peirce, Stowe, and others.

Barnard, Henry. Memorial Addresses on; in *Proceedings of the National Education Association,* 1901, pp. 390–439.

1. Influence in establishing normal schools — Lyte.
2. Influence on schools in West — Dougherty.
3. Home Life and Work in Connecticut and Rhode Island — Keyes.
4. As an educational critic — Parker.
5. His relation to the establishment of the office of United States Commissioner of Education, with historical reviews — Harris.

*Boese, Thos. *Public Education in the City of New York.* 288 pp. Harper & Bros., New York, 1869.

An important work, compiled from the documents. Still found in many libraries.

Boone, R. G. *Education in the United States.* 402 pp. D. Appleton & Co., New York. 1889.

Chapter VII forms good supplemental reading on the establishment of state and local school supervision.

*Brown, S. W. *The Secularization of American Education.* 160 pp. Teachers College Contributions to Education, No. 49. New York, 1912.

A standard work on the subject. Chapters IX and X form especially good supplemental reading for this chapter.

Harris, Wm. T. "Horace Mann"; in *Educational Review,* vol. XII, pp. 105–19. (Sept., 1896.) Same in *Proceedings of the National Education Association,* 1896, pp. 52–63; and in *Report of the United States Commissioner of Education,* 1895–96, part I, pp. 887–97.

*Hinsdale, B. A. *Horace Mann, and the Common School Revival in the United States.* 326 pp. Chas. Scribner's Sons, New York, 1898.

A very good and a very readable sketch of the work and influence of Mann.

Hoyt, C. O., and Ford, R. C. *John D. Pierce.* 162 pp. Ypsilanti, Michigan, 1905.

A study of education in the Northwest, and of the founding of the Michigan school system.

*Martin, Geo. H. "Horace Mann and the Educational Revival in Massachusetts"; in *Educational Review*, vol. 5, pp. 434–50. (May, 1893.)

A good brief sketch.

*Martin, Geo. H. *The Evolution of the Massachusetts Public School System.* 284 pp. D. Appleton & Co., New York, 1894.

Chapter IV describes the work of Horace Mann and the revival in Massachusetts.

*Monroe, Paul. *Cyclopedia of Education.* The Macmillan Co., New York, 1911–13. 5 volumes.

The following articles form good supplemental references:
1. "Barnard, Henry"; vol. I, pp. 324–25.
2. "Bible in the Schools"; vol. I, pp. 370–77.
3. "Mann, Horace"; vol. IV, pp. 118–20.
4. The historical portion of the articles on state school systems, such as Indiana, New York, etc.
5. "Superintendent of Schools," vol. V, pp. 463–64.

*Monroe, W. S. *The Educational Labors of Henry Barnard.* 32 pp. C. W. Bardeen, Syracuse, New York, 1893.

A good brief sketch, with bibliography of his writings.

*Tuttle, Jos. F. Caleb Mills and Indiana Common Schools; in Barnard's *American Journal of Education*, vol. 31, pp. 135–44.

A sketch of his life and work, and an outline of his six messages to the people regarding education.

Wells, Guy F. "The First School Survey"; in *Educational Review*, vol. 50, pp. 166–74. (Sept., 1915.)

On Barnard's 1845 *Rhode Island Report.*

Winship, A. E. *Great American Educators.* 252 pp. Werner School Book Co., Chicago, 1900.

Good short biographical articles on Mann and Barnard, as well as Mary Lyon, David Page, and others.

"Henry Barnard: His Labors in Connecticut and Rhode Island"; in Barnard's *American Journal of Education*, vol. 1, pp. 659–738.

A detailed statement of his work, reproducing many documents.

CHAPTER VII

THE BATTLE TO EXTEND THE SYSTEM

III. Phases of the Battle for State-Supported Schools — *continued*

6. *The battle to establish the American high school*

The elementary or common schools which we have seen had been established in the different States, by 1850, supplied an elementary or common-school education to the children of the masses of the people, and the primary schools which, as we have also seen, were added, after about 1820, carried this education downward to the needs of the beginners. In the rural schools the American school of the 3-Rs provided for all the children, from the little ones up, so long as they could advantageously partake of its instruction. Education in advance of this common school training was in semi-private institutions — the academies and colleges — in which a tuition fee was charged. The next struggle came in the attempt to extend the system upward so as to provide to pupils, free of charge, a more complete education than the common schools afforded.

The transition Academy. About the middle of the eighteenth century a tendency manifested itself, in Europe as well as in America, to establish higher schools offering a more practical curriculum than the old Latin schools had provided. In America it became particularly evident, after the coming of nationality, that the old Latin grammar-school type of instruction, with its limited curriculum and exclusively college-preparatory ends, was wholly inadequate for the needs of the youth of the land. The result was the gradual dying out of the Latin school and the evolution of the tuition Academy, previously referred to briefly at the close of Chapter III.

Franklin's Academy at Philadelphia, which began instruction in 1751 with three organized departments — the Latin School, the English School, and the Mathematical School — and which later evolved into the University of Pennsylvania, was probably the first American academy.   Others claim the honor of earlier establishment, but this is the first the foundation of which is perfectly clear.   The first academies in Massachusetts were the Dummer Academy, in South Byfield, founded in 1761, and opened for instruction in 1763; and the Phillips Academy at Andover, founded in 1778, and opened for instruction in 1780.   The academy movement spread rapidly during the first half of the nineteenth century.   By 1800 there were 17 academies in Massachusetts, 36 by 1820, and 403 by 1850. By 1830 there were, according to Hinsdale,   950   incorporated academies in the United States, and many unincorporated ones, and by 1850,

FIG. 31. A TYPICAL NEW ENGLAND ACADEMY

Pittsfield Academy, New Hampshire, where John Swett went to school.

according to Inglis, there were, of all kinds, 1007 academies in New England, 1636 in the Middle Atlantic States, 2640 in the Southern States, 753 in the Upper Mississippi Valley States, and a total reported for the entire United States of 6085, with 12,260 teachers employed and 263,096 pupils enrolled.   The movement gained a firm hold everywhere east of the Missouri River, the States incorporating the largest number being New York with 887, Pennsylvania with 524, Massachusetts with 403, Kentucky with 330, Virginia with 317, North Carolina with 272, and Tennessee with 264.   Some States, as Kentucky and Indiana, provided for a system of county academies, while many States extended to them some form of state aid. In New York State they found a warm advocate in Governor De Witt Clinton, who urged (1827) that they be located at the county towns of the State to give a practical scientific education suited to the wants of farmers, merchants, and mechanics, and also to train teachers for the schools of the State. The greatest period of their development was from 1820 to 1830, though they continued to dominate secondary education until 1850, and were very prominent until after the Civil War.

Characteristic features. The most characteristic features of these academies were their semi-public control, their broadened curriculum and religious purpose, and the extension of their instruction to girls. The Latin Grammar School was essentially a town free school, maintained by the towns for the higher education of certain of their male children. It was aristocratic in type, and belonged to the early period of class education. With the decline in zeal for education, after 1750, these tax-supported higher schools largely died out, and in their place private energy and benevolence came to be depended upon to supply the needed higher education. Many of the earlier foundations were from estates left by will for the purpose by some public-spirited citizen, and others were organized by private subscriptions, or as private stock companies. A few others were organized along denominational lines, and were under ecclesiastical control. Practically all charged a tuition fee, and most of them had dormitories and boarding halls. The board of trustees was usually a local private corporation, usually reported to the state school authorities, and often was constituted as a self-perpetuating body. Many of these academies became semi-state institutions through the state aid extended to them.

One of the main purposes expressed in the endowment or creation of the academies was the establishment of courses which should cover a number of subjects having value aside from mere preparation for college, particularly subjects of a modern nature, useful in preparing youths for the changed conditions of society and government and business. The study of real things rather than words about things, and useful things rather than subjects merely preparatory to college, became prominent features of the new courses of study. The new emphasis given to the study of English, mathematics, and book-science is noticeable. New subjects appeared in proportion as the academies increased in numbers and importance. Of 149 new subjects for study appearing in the academies of New York, between 1787 and 1870, 23 appeared before 1826, 100 between 1826 and 1840, and 26 after 1840. Between 1825 and 1828 one half of the new subjects appeared. This also was the maximum period of development of the academies. Among the most commonly found new subjects were algebra, astronomy, botany, chemistry, general history, United States history, English literature, surveying, intellectual philosophy, declamation, debating, etc.

Not being bound up with the colleges, as the earlier Latin grammar schools had largely been, the academies became primarily independent institutions, taking pupils who had completed the English education of the common school and giving them an advanced education in modern languages, the sciences, mathematics, history, and the more useful subjects of the time, with a view to "rounding out" their studies and preparing them for business life and the rising professions. They thus built upon, instead of running parallel to the common school course, as the old Latin grammar school had done (see Fig. 23, p. 99), and hence clearly mark a transition from the aristocratic and somewhat exclusive college-preparatory Latin grammar school of colonial times to the more democratic high school of to-day. The academies also served a very useful purpose in supplying to the lower schools the best-educated teachers of the time. Governor Clinton strongly urged their extension because of their teacher-training value. They offered no instruction in pedagogy, except in rare instances, but because of their advanced instruction in subjects related to

the work of the common school they served as the fore-
runners of the normal schools.

In religious matters, too, the academies also represent
such a transition. They were nearly always pervaded by a
genuine religious spirit, but were usually kept free from the
doctrines of any particular church. The foundation grant
of one of the earliest, the Phillips Academy, at Andover,
Massachusetts, states well this broader religious purpose.
The aim of the Academy was to be

to lay the foundation of a public free school or ACADEMY for
the purposes of instructing Youth, not only in English and Latin
Grammar, Writing, Arithmetic, and those Sciences wherein they
are commonly taught; but more especially to learn them the
GREAT END AND REAL BUSINESS OF LIVING . . . it is
again declared that the *first* and *principle* object of this Institution
is the promotion of TRUE PIETY and VIRTUE; the *second*, instruction in the English, Latin, and Greek Languages, together
with Writing, Arithmetic, Music, and the Art of Speaking; the
third, practical Geometry, Logic, and Geography; and the *fourth*,
such other liberal Arts and Sciences or Languages, as opportunity
and ability may hereafter admit, and as the TRUSTEES shall
direct.

Though this breathes a deep religious spirit it does not evidence a narrow denominationalism, and this was a characteristic of the academies. They bridged over the transition from the ecclesiasticism of the Latin grammar schools
of colonial times to the secularized high school of the present.

The old Latin grammar school, too, had been maintained
exclusively for boys. Girls had been excluded as "Im-
proper & inconsistent wth such a Grammar Schoole as y[e] law
injoines, and is y[e] Designe of this Settlem[t]." The new academies soon reversed this situation. Almost from the first
they began to be established for girls as well as boys, and
in time many became co-educational. In New York State
alone 32 academies were incorporated between 1819 and
1853 with the prefix "Female" to their title. In this respect, also, these institutions formed a transition to the mod-

ern co-educational high school.   The higher education of women in the United States clearly dates from the establishment of the academies.   Troy (New York) Seminary, founded by Emma Willard, in 1821, and Mt. Holyoke (Massachusetts) Seminary, founded by Mary Lyon, in 1836, though not the first institutions for girls, were nevertheless important pioneers in the higher education of women.

The demand for higher schools.   The different movements tending toward the building up of free public school systems in the cities and States, which we have described in the two preceding chapters, and which became clearly defined in the Northern States after 1825, came just at the time when the Academy had reached its maximum development.   The settlement of the question of general taxation for education, the elimination of the rate-bill by the cities and later by the States, the establishment of the American common school as the result of a long native evolution (Fig. 23, p. 99), and the complete establishment of public control over the entire elementary-school system, all tended to bring the semi-private tuition academy into question. Many asked why not extend the public school system upward to provide the necessary higher education for all in one common state-supported school.   The existence of a number of colleges, basing their entrance requirements on the completion of the classical course of the academy, and the establishment of a few embryo state universities in the new States of the West and the South, naturally raised the further question of why there should be a gap in the public school system.   The increase of wealth in the cities tended to increase the number who passed through the elementary course and could profit by more extended education; the academies had popularized the idea of more advanced education; while the new manufacturing and commercial activities of the time called for more training than the elementary schools afforded, and of a different type from that demanded for entrance by the small colleges of the time.

The demand for an upward extension of the public school, which would provide academy instruction for the poor as well as the rich, and in one common public higher school, now made itself felt. As the colonial Latin grammar school had represented the educational needs of a society based on classes, and the academies had represented a transition period and marked the growth of a middle class, so the rising democracy of the second quarter of the nineteenth century now demanded and obtained the democratic high school, supported by the public and equally open to all, to meet the educational needs of a new society built on the basis of a new and aggressive democracy. Where, too, the academy had represented in a way a missionary effort — that of a few providing something for the good of the people — the high school on the other hand represented a coöperative effort on the part of the people to provide something for themselves.

FIG. 32. THE FIRST HIGH SCHOOL IN THE UNITED STATES

Established at Boston in 1821.

The first American high school. The first high school in the United States was established in Boston, in 1821. For three years it was known as the "English Classical School," but in 1824 the school appears in the records as the "English High School." The name seems to be Scotch in origin, having been suggested by the description of the High School at Edinburgh, by Professor Griscom, in an article in the North American Review, then published in Boston, in January, 1824. In 1826 Boston also opened the first high school for girls, but abolished it in 1828, due to its great popularity, and instead extended the course of study for girls in the elementary schools.

The matter of establishing an English high school was

first considered in 1820, and a committee was appointed to consider the matter further. This committee reported, in January, 1821, among other things, that:

The mode of education now adopted, and the branches of knowledge that are taught at our English grammar [elementary] schools are not sufficiently extensive nor otherwise calculated to bring the powers of the mind into operation nor to qualify a youth to fill usefully and respectably many of the stations, both public and private, in which he may be placed. A parent who wishes to give a child an education that shall fit him for active life, and shall serve as a foundation for eminence in his profession, whether mercantile or mechanical, is under the necessity of giving him a different education from any which our public schools can now furnish. Hence many children are separated from their parents and sent to private academies in the vicinity, to acquire that instruction which cannot be obtained at the public seminaries.

The report recommended the establishment of a new type of higher school. The report was approved; the course of study as recommended was adopted; and the school was opened in May, 1821, as a three-year high school. Boys to be admitted were required to be at least twelve years of age, instead of nine, as in the Latin grammar school (see Fig. 42, p. 226), and to "be well acquainted with reading, writing, English grammar in all its branches, and arithmetic as far as simple proportion." Three years later English literature and geography were added. The teachers were required to have been educated at some university. No other language than English was to be taught; English, declamation, science, mathematics and its applications, history, and logic were the principal studies. The course of instruction was definitely built upon that of the English reading and writing and grammar schools, instead of paralleling these. It was in consequence clearly American in nature and purpose, rejecting entirely the English parallel-class-education idea of the Latin grammar school. The aim of the school, too, as stated in the report of the committee, was quite practical. This aim was restated in the

Regulations of the School Committee for the school, adopted in 1833, which read:

It was instituted in 1821, with the design of furnishing the young men of the city who are not intended for a collegiate course of study, and who have enjoyed the usual advantages of the other public schools, with the means of completing a good English education to fit them for active life or qualify them for eminence in private or public station.

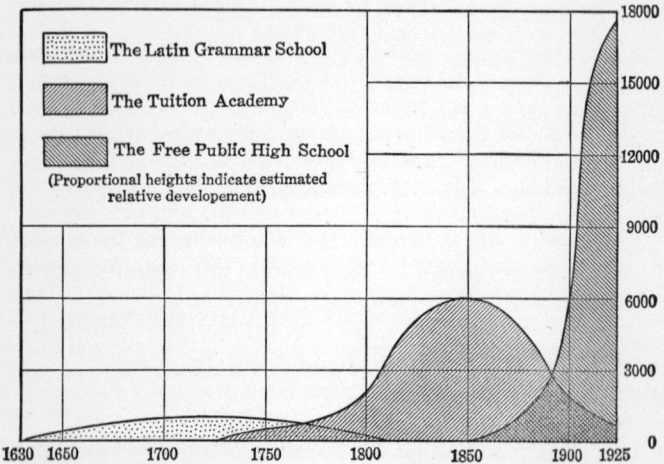

FIG. 33. THE DEVELOPMENT OF SECONDARY SCHOOLS IN THE UNITED STATES

The transitional character of the Academy is well shown in this diagram.

Josiah Quincy, who was mayor of Boston at the time of the establishment of the school, gives further corroborative evidence, in his *Municipal History of the Town and City of Boston*, as to the purpose in establishing the new high school. He says:

In 1820 an English Classical School was established, having for its object to enable the mercantile and mechanical classes to obtain an education adapted for those children, whom their parents wished to qualify for active life, and thus relieve them from the necessity of incurring the expense incident to private academies.

The free public high school thus arose, to provide at public expense what the public schools had failed to provide, and had been provided privately. The history of many an extension of public education since that day has had a similar origin.

This same conception of the aim and purpose of the new high school is well expressed in the *First Annual Report of the High School Society* of New York City, which opened a public high school there in 1825. This document reads:

It should never be forgotten, that the grand object of this institution is to prepare the boys for such advancement, and such pursuits in life, as they are destined to after leaving it. All who enter the school do not intend to remain for the same period of time — and many who leave it expect to enter immediately upon the active business of life. It is very plain that these circumstances must require corresponding classifications of scholars and of studies.

Some pursuits are nevertheless common to all. All the scholars in this department attend to Spelling, Writing, Arithmetic, Geography, Elocution, Composition, Drawing, Philosophy, Natural History, and Book-Keeping. Philosophy and Natural History are taught chiefly by lectures and by questions; and these branches, together with Elocution and Composition, are severally attended to one day in every week.

The Massachusetts Law of 1827. Though Portland, Maine, established a high school in 1821; Worcester, Massachusetts, in 1824; and New Bedford, Haverhill, and Salem, Massachusetts, in 1827; copying the Boston idea, the real beginning of the American high school as a distinct institution dates from the Massachusetts Law of 1827, enacted through the influence of James G. Carter. This law formed the basis of all subsequent legislation in Massachusetts, and deeply influenced development in other States. The law is significant in that it required a high school in every town having 500 families or over, in which should be taught United States history, bookkeeping, algebra, geometry, and surveying, while in every town having 4000 inhabitants or over, instruction in Greek, Latin, history, rhetoric, and logic must be added. A heavy penalty was attached for failure to comply with the law. In 1835 the law was amended so as to permit any smaller town to form a high school as well.

This Boston and Massachusetts legislation clearly initiated the public high school movement in the United States. It was there that the new type of higher school was founded, there that its curriculum was outlined, there that its standards were established, and there that it developed earliest and best. With two or three exceptions the high schools of the United States, says Inglis,

owe the basis of their aim, theory, and practice to the high school first created and earliest developed in Massachusetts. As in most other educational matters, Massachusetts led the way in the older Latin grammar school education and in the newer type of secondary education — the public high school. It is all the more to her glory that no direct influence from other countries has been traced in regard to the high school system. The American high school was an institution peculiarly adapted to the needs and wants of the American people, and is an everlasting tribute to the democracy of Massachusetts and America.

Among the early high schools established before 1850, the dates of which seem certain, may be mentioned the following:

1821. Boston, Mass.
      Portland, Me.
1824. Worcester, Mass.
1825. New York City.
1826. Boston H. S. for Girls (abold.
         1828).
1827. New Bedford, Mass. (abold.
         1829).
      Salem, Mass.
      Haverhill, Mass.
1829. Burlington, Vt.
1830. Fitchburg, Mass.
1831. Lowell, Mass.
1835. Augusta, Me.
      Brunswick, Me.
      Medford, Mass.
1837. Pittston, Me.
      Harrisburg, Pa.

1838. Philadelphia, Pa.
      Cambridge, Mass.
      Taunton, Mass.
1839. Buffalo, N.Y.
1841. Springfield, Mass.
1842. Binghampton, N.Y.
1843. New Orleans, La.
      Providence, R.I.
1844. Detroit, Mich.
1845. Chelsea, Mass.
1846. Cleveland, Ohio.
1847. Cincinnati, Ohio.
      Hartford, Conn.
1849. Toledo, Ohio.
      Lynn, Mass.
      Lawrence, Mass.
      Lancaster, Pa.

MARY LYON
(1797-1849)
Founder of Mt. Holyoke College
for Girls

JAMES G. CARTER
(1795-1849)
Teacher, Legislator, Publicist
"Father of the Massachusets School System"

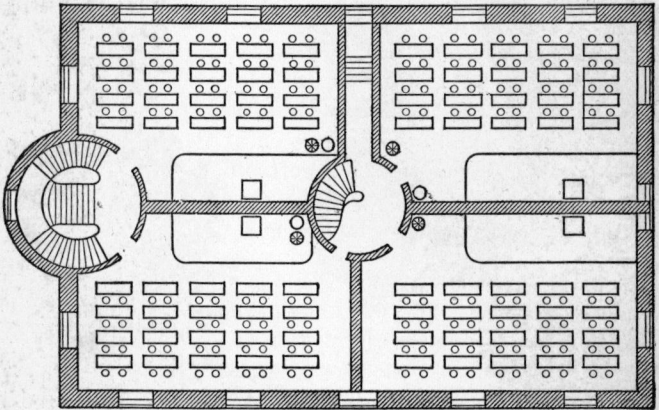

FIG. 34. THE FIRST HIGH SCHOOL AT PROVIDENCE, RHODE ISLAND

Established by city ordinance in 1838. In 1843 a superintendent of schools was employed, this building dedicated, and the high school opened, with the superintendent acting as its principal. The floor plan shows how completely it was a teacher-and-textbook high school. Almost all high school buildings erected before 1860 were of this type.

The struggle to establish and maintain high schools.   The development of the American high school, even in its home, was slow.   Up to 1840 not much more than a dozen high schools had been established in Massachusetts, and not more than an equal number in the other States.   The Academy was the dominant institution, the district system for common schools stood in the way of any higher development, the cost of maintenance was a factor, and the same opposition to an extension of taxation to include high schools was manifested as was earlier shown toward the establishment of common schools.   The early state legislation, as had been the case with the common schools, was nearly always permissive and not mandatory.   Massachusetts forms a notable exception in this regard.   The support for the schools had to come practically entirely from increased local taxation, and this made the struggle to establish and maintain high schools in any State for a long time a series of local struggles.   Years of propaganda and patient effort were required, and, after the establishment of a high school in a community, constant watchfulness was necessary to prevent its abandonment.   Many of the early schools ran for a time, then were discontinued for a period, and later were reëstablished.   In an address given at the dedication of a new building at Norwich, Connecticut, in 1856, one of the founders of the school thus describes these early struggles to establish and maintain high schools:

. . . The lower schools up to the grade of the grammar school were well sustained.   Men were to be found in all our communities who had been themselves educated up to that point, and understood, practically, the importance of such schools, in sufficient numbers to control popular sentiment, and secure for them ample appropriations and steady support.   But the studies of the high school, Algebra, Geometry, Chemistry, Natural Philosophy, Ancient History, Latin, Greek, French and German, were a perfect *terra incognita* to the great mass of the people.   While the High School was a new thing and while a few enlightened citizens had the control of it, in numerous instances it was carried to a high state of perfection. But after a time the burden of taxation would begin to be felt. Men would discuss the high salaries paid to the accomplished teachers which such schools demand, and would ask, "To what purpose is this waste?" Demagogues, keen-scented as wolves, would snuff the prey. "What do we want of a High School to teach rich men's children?" they would shout. "It is a shame to tax the poor man to pay a man $1800 to teach the children to make x's and pot-hooks and gabble parley-vous." The work would go bravely on; and on election day, amid great excitement, a new school committee would be chosen, in favor of retrenchment and popular rights. In a single day the fruit of years of labor would be destroyed.

The struggle to establish and maintain high schools in Massachusetts and New York preceded the development in most other States, because there the common school had been established earlier. In consequence, the struggle to extend and complete the public school system came there earlier also. The development was likewise more peaceful there, and came more rapidly. In Massachusetts this was in large part a result of the educational awakening started by James G. Carter and Horace Mann. In New York it was due to the early support of Governor De Witt Clinton, and the later encouragement and state aid which came from the Regents of the University of the State of New York. Maine, Vermont, and New Hampshire were like Massachusetts in spirit, and followed closely its example. In Rhode Island and New Jersey, due to old conditions, and in Connecticut, due to the great decline in education there after 1800, the high school developed much more slowly, and it was not until after 1865 that any marked development took place in these States. The democratic West soon adopted the idea, and established high schools as soon as cities developed and the needs of the population warranted. In the South the main high school development dates from relatively recent times.

Establishing the high school by court decisions. In many States, legislation providing for the establishment of high

schools was more difficult to secure than in New England
and New York, and often when secured was afterward attacked in the courts.   In most of the States shown on the
map in Figure 35, west of New England and New York, the
constitutionality of the establishment of the high school
or of taxation therefor was at some time attacked in the
courts and decided in favor of the schools.

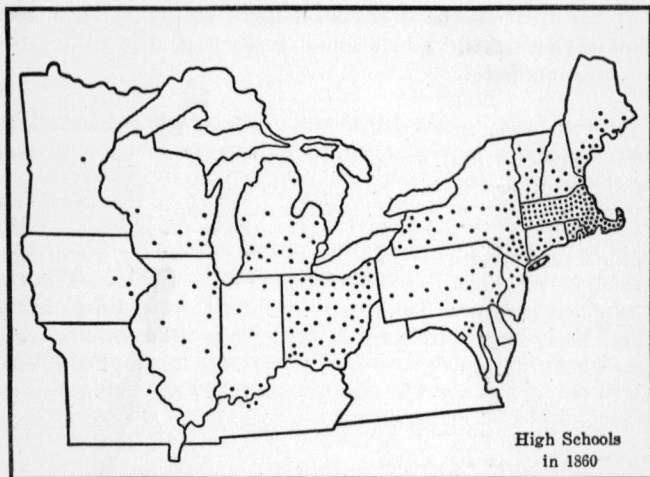

High Schools
in 1860

FIG. 35. HIGH SCHOOLS IN THE UNITED STATES BY 1860

Based on the table given in the *Report of the United States Commissioner of Education*,
1904, vol. II, pp. 1782–1989.   This table is only approximately correct, as exact information
is difficult to obtain.   This table gives 321 high schools by 1860, and all but 35 of these were
in the States shown on the above map.   There were two schools in California and three in
Texas, and the remainder not shown were in the Southern States.   On the 321 high schools
reported, over half (167) were in the three States of Massachusetts (78), New York (41),
and Ohio (48).   Compare the distribution of high schools shown on this map with the distribution of New England people shown on the map on page 73.

One of the clearest cases of this came in Michigan, in
1872, and the verdict of the Supreme Court of that State
was so positive that it influenced all subsequent decisions
in other States.   The case is commonly known as the Kalamazoo case.   The city of Kalamazoo, in 1872, voted to es-

tablish a high school and employ a superintendent of schools, and levied additional school taxes to cover the expense. A citizen by the name of Stuart brought suit to prevent the collection of the additional taxes. The case was carried to the Supreme Court of the State, and the decision was written by Chief Justice Cooley. After stating the case in hand, the contention of the plaintiff that high schools were not comprehended under the heading "common schools," and that the district board should supervise the schools, and after reviewing the educational history of the State, the court concluded:

If these facts do not demonstrate clearly and conclusively a general state policy, beginning in 1817 and continuing until after the adoption of the present state constitution, in the direction of free schools in which education, and at their option the elements of classical education, might be brought within the reach of all the children of the State, then, as it seems to us, nothing can demonstrate it. We might follow the subject further and show that the subsequent legislation has all concurred with this policy, but it would be a waste of time and labor. We content ourselves with the statement that neither in our state policy, in our constitution, nor in our laws, do we find the primary school districts restricted in the branches of knowledge which their officers may cause to be taught, or the grade of instruction that may be given, if their voters consent in regular form to bear the expense and raise the taxes for the purpose.

Having reached this conclusion, we shall spend no time upon the objection that the district in question had no authority to appoint a superintendent of schools, and that the duties of the superintendency should be performed by the district board. We think the power to make the appointment was incident to the full control which by law the board had over the schools of the district, and that the board and the people of the district have been wisely left by the legislature to follow their own judgment in the premises.

In almost all the Upper Mississippi Valley States this decision has deeply influenced development. In more than one State a Supreme Court decision which established the high school has been clearly based on this Michigan decision.

It ranks, therefore, along with the Massachusetts law of 1827 as one of the important milestones in the establishment of the American public high school.

Gradually the high school has been accepted as a part of the state common school system by all our States, and the funds and taxation originally provided for the common schools have been extended to cover the high school as well. The new States of the West have based their legislation on what the Eastern and Central States earlier fought out, though often the Western States have provided separate and additional support for their high schools. California is perhaps our best example of such separate support.

7. The state university crowns the system

The earlier colleges — Harvard, William and Mary, Yale — had been created by the religious-state governments of the earlier colonial period, and continued to retain some state connections for a time after the coming of nationality. As it early became evident that a democracy demands intelligence on the part of its citizens, that the leaders of democracy are not likely to be too highly educated, and that the character of collegiate instruction must ultimately influence national development, efforts were accordingly made to change the old colleges or create new ones, the final outcome of which was the creation of state universities in all the new and in most of the older States. The evolution of the state university, as the crowning head of the free public school system of the State, represents the last phase which we shall trace of the struggle of democracy to create a system of schools suited to its peculiar needs.

The colonial colleges. The close of the colonial period found the colonies possessed of nine colleges. These, with the dates of their foundation, the colony founding them, and the religious denomination they chiefly represented were:

1636. Harvard College	Massachusetts	Puritan
1693. William and Mary	Virginia	Anglican

1701.	Yale College	Connecticut	Congregational
1746.	Princeton	New Jersey	Presbyterian
1753–55.	Academy and College	Pennsylvania	Non-denominational
1754.	King's College (Columbia)	New York	Anglican
1764.	Brown	Rhode Island	Baptist
1766.	Rutgers	New Jersey	Reformed Dutch
1769.	Dartmouth	New Hampshire	Congregational

The religious purpose had been dominant in the founding of each institution, though there was a gradual shading-off in strict denominational control and insistence upon religious conformity in the foundations after 1750. Still the prime purpose in the founding of each was to train up a learned and godly body of ministers, the earlier congregations, at least, "dreading to leave an illiterate ministry to the churches when our present ministers shall lie in the dust." In a pamphlet, published in 1754, President Clap of Yale declared that "Colleges are *Societies of Ministers*, for training up Persons for the Work of the *Ministry*," and that "The great design of founding this School (Yale), was to Educate Ministers in our *own Way*." In the advertisement published in the New York papers announcing the opening of King's College, in 1754, it was stated that:

IV. The chief Thing that is aimed at in this College, is, to teach and engage the Children *to know God in Jesus Christ*, and to love and serve him in all *Sobriety*, *Godliness*, and *Richness* of Life, with a perfect Heart and a Willing Mind: and to train them up in all Virtuous Habits, and all such useful Knowledge as may render them creditable to their Families and Friends, Ornaments to their Country, and useful to the Public Weal in their generation.

These colonial institutions were all small. For the first fifty years of Harvard's history the attendance at the college seldom exceeded twenty, and the President did all the teaching. The first assistant teacher (tutor) was not appointed until 1699, and the first professor not until 1721, when a professorship of divinity was endowed. By 1800 the instruction was conducted by the President and three professors — divinity, mathematics, and "Oriental languages" — assisted by a few tutors who received only class fees, and the graduating classes seldom exceeded forty. The course was four years in length, and all students studied the same subjects. The first three years were given largely to the so-called "Oriental languages" — Hebrew, Greek, and Latin. In addition, Freshmen studied arithmetic; Sophomores, algebra, geometry, and trigonometry; and Juniors, natural (book) science; and all were given much training in oratory, and some general history was added. The Senior year was given mainly to ethics, philosophy, and Christian evidences. The instruction in the eight other older colleges, before 1800, was not materially different.

National interest in higher education. One of Washington's most cherished ideas, and one warmly advocated by many leading citizens of the time, was that the new government should found a National University at the seat of the Federal Government,

> where the youth from all parts of the United States might receive the polish of erudition in the arts, sciences, and belles-lettres . . . and where, during . . . the juvenal period of life, when friendships are formed, and habits established, that stick by one, the youth or young men from different parts of the United States would be assembled together, and would by degrees discover that there was not that cause for those jealousies and prejudices which one part of the Union had imbibed against another part.

Washington repeatedly called the matter to the attention of Congress, as did Presidents Adams, Madison, Monroe, and the second Adams; a square of land was at one time set aside at the National Capital for the new institution and was officially designated as University Square; and Washington, in his will (1799), left a substantial sum to the Government of the United States, in trust, to start the endowment of the new university. For reasons hard to understand nothing ever came of the idea, and nothing is known to-day as to what became of the money which Washington left.

Immediately after the close of the Revolutionary War settlers began to move to the new territory along the Ohio, and when the sale of 1,500,000 acres of land in south central Ohio was made by Congress, in 1787, to "The Ohio Company," a New England organization, the company was granted section 16 for schools, section 29 for religion, and, upon its request, two whole townships (72 sections, — 46,080 acres) "for the purposes of a university." In 1803 the new State of Ohio was granted another township (36 sections) "for the purposes of establishing an academy in the district of Cincinnati," which district had also been settled by New England people. The former of these grants formed the original endowment of Ohio University, at Athens, and the latter the endowment of Miami University, at Oxford — the first state universities in the new West. The grant of two or more whole townships of land "for a seminary of learning," or "state university," begun by Congress as a land-selling proposition in the case of Ohio, was continued with the admission of each new State afterward, and these township grants for a seminary of learning formed the beginning of the state universities which were created in all the new Western and Southern States.

Growth of colleges by 1860. Fifteen additional colleges were founded before 1800, and it has been estimated that by that date the two dozen American colleges then existing did not have all told over one hundred professors and instructors, not less than one thousand nor more than two thousand students, or property worth over one million dollars. Their graduating classes were small (p. 80). No one of the twenty-four admitted women in any way to its privileges. After 1820, with the firmer establishment of the Nation, the awakening of a new national consciousness, the development of larger national wealth, and a court decision (p. 206) which safeguarded the endowments, interest in the founding of new colleges perceptibly quickened, as may be seen from the table on page 204, and between 1820 and 1880 came the great period of denominational effort. The map on page 205, shows the colleges established by 1860, from which it will be seen how large a part the denominational colleges played in the early history of higher education in the United States.   Up to about 1870 the provision of higher education, as had been the case earlier with the provision of secondary education by the academies, had been left largely to private effort. There were, to be sure, a few state universities before 1870, though usually these were not better than the denomina- tional colleges around them, and often they maintained a non-denominational character only by preserving a proper balance between the different denominations in the employ- ment of their faculties. Speak- ing generally, higher education

Before 1780	10
1780–89	7
1790–99	7
1800–09	9
1810–19	5
1820–29	22
1830–39	38
1840–49	42
1850–59	92
1860–69	73
1870–79	61
1880–89	74
1890–99	54
Total	494

COLLEGES FOUNDED UP TO 1900

(After a table by Dexter, corrected by U.S. Comr. Educ., data. Only approx- imately correct.)

in the United States before 1870 was provided very largely in the tuitional colleges of the different religious denomina- tions, rather than by the State. Of the 246 colleges founded by the close of the year 1860, as shown on the map, but 17 were state institutions, and but two or three others had any state connections.

The new national attitude toward the colleges. After the coming of nationality there gradually grew up a wide- spread dissatisfaction with the colleges as then conducted, because they were aristocratic in tendency, because they devoted themselves so exclusively to the needs of a class, and because they failed to answer the needs of the States in the matter of higher education. Due to their religious origin, and the common requirement that the president and trustees must be members of some particular denomination, they were naturally regarded as representing the interests of some one sect or faction within the State rather than the interests of the State itself. With the rise of the new demo- cratic spirit after about 1820 there came a demand, felt least

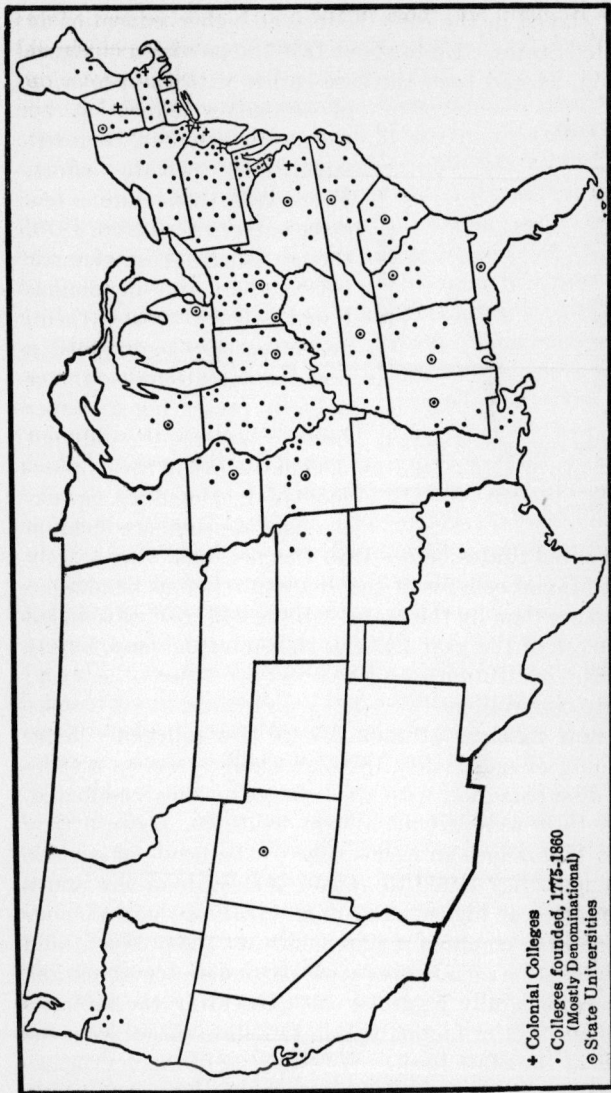

+ Colonial Colleges

• Colleges founded, 1775–1860
  (Mostly Denominational)

⊙ State Universities

FIG. 36. COLLEGES AND UNIVERSITIES ESTABLISHED BY 1860. Of the 246 colleges shown on the map, but 17 were state institutions, and but two or three others had any state connections.

Compiled from data given in the *Reports of the United States Commissioner of Education.*

in New England and most in the South and the new States in the West, for institutions of higher learning which should represent the State. It was argued that colleges were important instrumentalities for moulding the future, that the kind of education given in them must ultimately influence the welfare of the State, and that higher education cannot be regarded as a private matter. The type of education given in these higher institutions, it was argued, "will appear on the bench, at the bar, in the pulpit, and in the senate, and will unavoidably affect our civil and religious principles." For these reasons, as well as to crown our state school system and to provide higher educational advantages for its leaders, it was argued that the State should exercise control over the colleges.

This new national spirit manifested itself in a number of ways. In New York we see it in the reorganization of King's College, the rechristening of the institution as Columbia, and the placing of it under at least the nominal supervision of the governing educational body of the State. In Pennsylvania an attempt was made to bring the university into closer connection with the State, but this failed. In New Hampshire the legislature tried, in 1816, to transform Dartmouth College into a state institution. This act was contested in the courts, and the case was finally carried to the Supreme Court of the United States. There it was decided, in 1819, that the charter of a college was a contract, the obligation of which a legislature could not impair.

Effect of the Dartmouth College decision. The effect of this decision manifested itself in two different ways. On the one hand it guaranteed the perpetuity of endowments, and the great period of private and denominational effort (see table, p. 204) now followed. On the other hand, since the States could not change charters and transform old establishments, they began to turn to the creation of new state universities of their own. Virginia created its state university the same year as the Dartmouth case decision. The University of North Carolina, which had been established in 1789, and which began to give instruction in 1795, but which had never been under direct state control, was taken over by the State in 1821. The University of Vermont, originally chartered in 1791, was rechartered as a state university in 1838. The University of Indiana was established in 1820. Alabama provided for a state university in its first constitution, in 1819, and the institution opened for instruction in 1831. Michigan, in framing its first constitution preparatory to entering the Union, in 1835, made careful provisions for the safeguarding of the state university and for establishing it as an integral part of its state school system, as Indiana had done in 1816. Wisconsin provided for the creation of a state university in 1836, and embodied the idea in its first constitution when it entered the Union in 1848, and Missouri provided for a state university in 1839, Mississippi in 1844, Iowa in 1847, and Florida in 1856. The state university is to-day found in every "new" State and in some of the "original" States, and practically every new Western and Southern State followed the patterns set by Indiana, Michigan, and Wisconsin and made careful provision for the establishment and maintenance of a state university in its first state constitution.

There was thus quietly added another new section to the American educational ladder, and the free public school system was extended farther upward. Though the great period of state university foundation came after 1860, and the great period of state university expansion after 1885, the beginnings were clearly marked early in our national history. Of the sixteen States having state universities by 1860 (see Fig. 36), all except Florida had established them before 1850. For a long time small, poorly supported by the States, much like the church colleges about them in character and often inferior in quality, one by one the state universities have freed themselves alike from denominational restrictions on the one hand and political control on the other, and have set about rendering the service to the State which a state university ought to render. Michigan,

the first of our state universities to free itself, take its proper
place, and set an example for others to follow, opened in
1841 with two professors and six students.   In 1844 it was
a little institution of three professors, one tutor, one assistant, and one visiting lecturer, had but fifty-three students,
and offered but a single course of study, consisting chiefly
of Greek, Latin, mathematics, and intellectual and moral
science.   As late as 1852 it had but seventy-two students,
but by 1860, when it had largely freed itself from the incubus
of Baptist Latin, Congregational Greek, Methodist intellectual philosophy, Presbyterian astronomy, and Whig
mathematics, and its remarkable growth as a state university had begun, it enrolled five hundred and nineteen.

The rise of professional instruction.   The colonial colleges, as has been pointed out, were largely training schools
for the ministry, and this long continued to be their one
professional purpose.   It was largely because of this that so
many of the early leaders in education — Stowe, Pierce,
Hall, and Bateman, — among others — were men who had
been trained for the ministry.   It was not until 1812 that
theology was separated off in a school by itself at Princeton,
1819 at Harvard, and 1822 at Yale.

The first professional instruction to be added by the early
universities was medicine, a medical school being established
at Pennsylvania as early as 1765, King's in 1767, Harvard
in 1782, Dartmouth in 1798, the University of Maryland
department of medicine and the College of Physicians and
Surgeons at New York both being established in 1807, and
at Yale in 1813.   Out of the instruction in medicine came
chemistry, the mother of modern science instruction, the
first professors of this subject being at William and Mary in
1774, Princeton in 1795, Columbia in 1802, and Yale in 1803.
The first law school in the United States was a private one
conducted by a judge in his office, at Litchfield, Connecticut,
from 1784 to 1833, and to this many students went for
practical training.   The first permanent instruction in law
by a university came with the establishment of the law

faculty of the University of Maryland, in 1812, and the opening of a law school at Harvard in 1817, Yale in 1824, and the University of Virginia in 1826. The medical and law schools of colonial times were the offices of practicing physicians and lawyers. Of the 3000 physicians in practice in the United States at the close of the Revolution, but 51 had taken degrees in America, and less than 350 anywhere else. There were no lawyers holding degrees. The first technical school, the Rensselaer Polytechnic, was founded in 1824. The first college of dentistry was opened in Baltimore in 1839, and the second at Cincinnati in 1845. The first college of pharmacy was opened at Philadelphia in 1822. These subjects, now so common in our state universities, are all of relatively recent development.

College education for women. Another change in the nature of instruction, thoroughly indicative of the democracy of the West, was the opening of collegiate and professional instruction to women. In 1800 women could not enter any college in the United States. In 1821 Emma Willard had opened a seminary for girls at Troy, New York, and in 1837 Mt. Holyoke Seminary (later college) was opened by Mary Lyon in Massachusetts. These mark the beginnings of higher education for girls. By 1840 there were but seven institutions of all kinds for the higher education of women, but by 1860 the number had increased to sixty-one. Perhaps half of these later developed into colleges for women. After the Civil War, during which so many women filled places formerly held by men, and especially in teaching, the colleges began to open their doors somewhat generally to women students. To-day eighty per cent of the non-Catholic colleges are open to women, while many special colleges for them also exist.

Mt. Holyoke Seminary in Massachusetts (1837), Rockford Seminary in Illinois (1849), and Elmira College (1855) and Vassar College (1865), both in New York, were among the earliest of the larger women's colleges, while Oberlin College (1833) and Antioch College (1853), both in Ohio, and the state university of Iowa (1856), were among the first institutions to open their instruction equally to men and women.   Every State west of the Mississippi River, except Missouri, made its state university co-educational from its first opening, and of those east of the same river all but three have since followed the lead of Indiana (1868) and Michigan and Illinois (1870) in opening their doors freely to women students.   The democratic spirit of the people west of the Allegheny Mountains has demanded, as the price of support, equal advantages for both their male and female children.

The new land-grant colleges.   In 1850 Michigan petitioned Congress for a grant of public land to found a college of agriculture, and in 1858 renewed its petition.   In 1859 a bill passed Congress making a grant of 20,000 acres of public land to each State, for each Senator and Representative the State had in Congress, to endow a college of agriculture and mechanic arts.   This was the Fellenberg manual-labor-seminary idea in a new form, with the manual-labor-support of students omitted.   President Buchanan vetoed the bill because, among other reasons:

5. This bill will seriously interfere with existing colleges in the different States, in many of which agriculture is taught as a science and in all of which it ought to be so taught.   These institutions of learning have grown up with the growth of the country, under the fostering care of the States and the munificence of individuals, to meet the advancing demands for education.   They have proved great blessings to the people.   Many, indeed most, are poor, and sustain themselves with difficulty.   What the effect would be on these institutions by creating an indefinite number of rival colleges sustained by the endowment of the Federal Government it is not difficult to determine.

In 1862 a similar bill, except that the grant was increased from 20,000 to 30,000 acres for each Senator and Representative, and that military science and tactics was added as a third required study, was passed by Congress and signed by President Lincoln.   A total of 11,367,832 acres of public land was given to the States to endow institutions for the teaching of the new subjects — an area one half as large as the State of Indiana — and fifty-one States and Territories, counting Porto Rico, Alaska, and Hawaii, now receive money grants from the National Government to help carry on this work. Eighteen States added the land-grant to the endowment of their existing state universities and combined the two institutions, three of the original States (originally five) gave the grant to private institutions already established within the State, and the remainder established separate agricultural and mechanical colleges.

The financial returns from the land-grants were disappointing, but the educational returns have been very large. Probably no aid for education given by the National Government to the States has proved so fruitful as have these grants of land, and subsequently of money, for instruction in agriculture and the mechanic arts. New and vigorous colleges have been created (Cornell, Purdue, and the state universities of Ohio and Illinois are examples); small and feeble state universities have been awakened into new life (Vermont and Wisconsin are examples); agriculture and engineering have been developed as new learned professions; and the States have been stimulated to make larger and rapidly-increasing appropriations for their universities, until to-day the state universities largely overshadow all but the best endowed of the old denominational colleges. The far-reaching educational importance of the Morrill Act of 1862, so named for the Senator who framed and sponsored it, is not likely to be overestimated.

The American free public school system now established. By the close of the second quarter of the nineteenth century, certainly by 1860, we find the American public school system fully established, in principle at least, in all our Northern States. Much yet remained to be done to carry into full effect what had been established in principle, but everywhere democracy had won its fight, and the American public school, supported by general taxation, freed from the pauper-school taint, free and equally open to all, under the direction of representatives of the people, free from sectarian control, and complete from the primary school through the high school, and in the Western States through the university as well, may be considered as established permanently in American public policy.   The establishment of the free public high school and the state university represent the crowning achievements of those who struggled to found a state-supported educational system fitted to the needs of great democratic States.   Probably no other influences have done more to unify the American people, reconcile diverse points of view, eliminate state jealousies, set ideals for our people, and train leaders for the service of the States and of the Nation than the academies, high schools, and colleges scattered over our land.   They have educated but a small percentage of our people, to be sure, but they have trained most of the leaders who have guided our democracy since its birth.

QUESTIONS FOR DISCUSSION

1. Show how the American academy was a natural development in our national life.
2. Show how the American high school was a natural development after the academy.
3. Show the thoroughly democratic nature of the new high schools.
4. Show why the high school could be opposed by men who had accepted tax-supported elementary schools.   Why have we abandoned such reasoning now?
5. Explain the difference, and illustrate from the history of our educational development, between establishing a thing in principle and carrying it into full effect.
6. Show why it was natural that higher education should have been left largely to denominational effort before 1860.
7. Was the early argument as to the influence of higher education on the State a true argument?   Why?
8. What would have been the probable results had the Dartmouth College case been decided the other way?
9. Explain why it required so long to get the state universities started on their real development.

10. What would have been the effect educationally had we followed President Buchanan's reasoning?
11. Show how the opening of collegiate instruction to women was a phase of the new democratic movement.
12. Show how college education has been a unifying force in our national life.

SELECTED REFERENCES

Barnard, Henry, Editor. *The American Journal of Education.* 31 vols. Consult *Analytical Index* to; 128 pp. Published by United States Bureau of Education, Washington, 1892.

Bradford, Gamaliel. "Mary Lyon"; in *Atlantic Monthly*, vol. 122, pp. 785–95. (Dec., 1918.)

   An interesting and sympathetic sketch of her work.

*Brown, E. E. *The Making of Our Middle Schools.* 547 pp. Longmans Green & Co., New York, 1903.

   A standard history. Chapters IX to XII describe the academies, and chapters XIII and XIV the rise of the high schools.

Brown, E. E. "Historic Development of Secondary Schools in the United States"; in *School and Society*, vol. III, pp. 227–31. (Feb. 12, 1916.)

*Brown, E. E. *Origin of the American State Universities.* 45 pp. University of California Publications on Education, vol. 3, No. 1, University Press, Berkeley, California, 1903.

   A very good sketch of the early colonial colleges, and the rise of the demand for state control. Good bibliography.

Cubberley, E. P., and Elliott, E. C. *State and County School Administration; Source Book.* 728 pp. The Macmillan Co., New York, 1915.

   Chapter II gives full sources for the endowment of the state universities and the land-grant colleges.

Davis, C. O. *Public Secondary Education.* 270 pp. Rand McNally & Co., Chicago, 1917.

   Chapters VII to IX give a very good detailed account of the rise of the academy and the high school in Michigan.

*Dexter, E. G. *A History of Education in the United States.* 656 pp. The Macmillan Co., New York, 1904.

   Chapter VI on the growth of the academies is a brief statement, with good statistical data. Chapter XV is a detailed history of college development, and Chapter XVI of professional schools. Chapter XXI is a good history of the education of girls and women in both public schools and colleges.

Draper, A. S. "The Rise of High Schools"; in his *American Education*, pp. 147–56. Houghton Mifflin Co., Boston, 1909.

   An interesting general sketch of the rise and change in the character of the secondary school.

Hinsdale, B. A.   "Early Views and Plans relating to a National University"; in *Report of the United States Commissioner of Education*, 1892–93, vol. II, pp. 1293–1312.

A very good history of the idea, with extracts from documents.

*Inglis, A. J.   *The Rise of the High School in Massachusetts*.   166 pp. Teachers College Contributions to Education, No. 45, New York, 1911.

An interesting and excellent description of the rise and curriculum of the high school in this State.

*Inglis, A. J.   *Principles of Secondary Education*.   741 pp.   Houghton Mifflin Co., Boston, 1918.

Chapter V, pp. 161–202, on the development of secondary education in America, forms excellent supplemental reading on the evolution of the high school.

*Monroe, Paul.   *Cyclopedia of Education*.   The Macmillan Co., New York 1911–13.   5 vols.

The following articles form good supplemental references:
  1. "Academy"; vol. I, pp. 19–23.
  2. "High Schools in the United States"; vol. III, pp. 263–65.
  3. "Women, Higher Education of"; vol. V, pp. 795–810.
  4. Articles on the various colleges, and their founders.

*Taylor, Jas. M.   "College Education for Girls in America"; in *Educational Review*, vol. 44, pp. 217–33, 325–47.   (Oct. and Nov., 1912.)

A good brief historical article.

*Taylor, Jas. M.   *Before Vassar Opened*.   287 pp.   Houghton Mifflin Co., Boston, 1914.

A valuable contribution to the history of the higher education of women in America. The first two chapters contain the preceding article.

Ten Brook, A.   *American State Universities and the University of Michigan*. 410 pp.   Robert Clark & Co., Cincinnati, 1875.

A history of the origin and development of our state universities, as illustrated by the University of Michigan.   An old classic.

Thompson, Wm. O.   "The Small College; its work in the past"; in *Proceedings of the National Education Association*, 1900, pp. 61–67.

The work of the small denominational colleges.

*Thwing, Chas. F.   *A History of Higher Education in America*.   501 pp. D. Appleton & Co., New York, 1906.

A very important volume.   Contains detailed histories of the early colleges, traces the rise of the state universities, courses of study, education of women, etc.

*Thwing, Chas. F.   *A History of Education in the United States since the Civil War*.   348 pp.   Houghton Mifflin Co., Boston, 1910.

Chapters V on the "Course of Study," and VII on "Changes in Collegiate Conditions," contain interesting descriptions of the changes of the past half-century.

CHAPTER VIII

CHARACTER OF THE SCHOOLS ESTABLISHED

SLOWLY, as we have seen, and after a series of conflicts, we gradually evolved a series of purely native American school systems to replace our earlier English inheritance. These extended from the primary school through the American-created English grammar school and English high school. In a few Southern and Western States — notably Virginia, the Carolinas, Georgia, Indiana, and Michigan — an embryo state university was early added at the top. In this chapter we shall examine briefly the character of the early schools thus established, and shall seek to determine about what development had taken place in our city and state school systems before the outbreak of the Civil War for a time materially checked our educational progress.

I. EVOLUTION OF THE GRADED ELEMENTARY SCHOOL

The American school of the 3-Rs. Toward the close of Chapter II we traced the rise of a distinctively American consciousness after 1750, and the beginnings of the evolution of distinctively American-type schools. This movement was checked by the War for Independence, but after about 1820 came out again in full force. Even before that time we have many clear indications of the lines along which development was eventually to take place. As schools before that time existed in their best form in New England, and as New England people carried the public school idea with them wherever they went, we naturally turn first to New England to see what types of schools were established there after the coming of nationality.

From the first the teaching of reading and writing had been a common requirement in all the New England colonies, excepting Rhode Island, and some arithmetic, though often quite small in amount, also was gradually added. The necessities of the rural districts, where separate teachers for writing and ciphering were not possible, forced a combination of the teaching of these three subjects, thus forming the American school of the 3-Rs. The dame school covered the needs of the A-B-C-darians, and inducted the youngsters into the mysteries connected with the beginnings of learning to read, while the regular winter school conducted by men teachers, and the summer school by women teachers, continued the instruction in these three subjects as long as the boys and girls were able to profit by it. With the short winter term, the slow individual method of instruction, and the famous books by Dilworth in English and Arithmetic to fall back upon, the learning process was so long drawn out that these three subjects, with the spelling of words, filled up all the time that could be devoted to learning by most children. These arts, too, were sufficient for almost all the ordinary needs of life, as their possession, in the early period of our national history, served to distinguish the educated man or woman from the uneducated.

FIG. 37. A SUMMER SCHOOL

From Bolles's Spelling Book, 1831.

New textbooks change the character of the old instruction. Almost immediately after the close of the Revolutionary War a long series of native American schoolbooks began to appear. These not only replaced those of English origin previously used, but also materially expanded the course of instruction by reducing new subjects of study to textbook form.

The publication of Noah Webster's "blue-backed" *American Spelling Book*, in 1783, a combined speller and reader, marked an epoch in the teaching of spelling and reading. It was after the plan of Dilworth, but was thoroughly American in character and put up in better teaching form. It at once superseded the expiring *New England Primer* in most of the cities. Spelling and word analysis now became and long con-

tinued to be one of the most popular subjects in the schools, and inter-school "spelling matches" became a favorite social amusement of both the old and the young. So great was the sale of the book that the author was able to support his family during the twenty years (1807–1827) he was at work on his *Dictionary of the English Language* entirely from the royalties from the *Speller*, though the copyright returns to him were less than one cent a copy. At the time of his death (1843) the sales were still approximately a million copies a year, and during the

KNOWLEDGE and FAME are gain'd not by surprise;
He that would win, must LABOUR for the prize:
'Tis thus the youth, from lisping A, B, C,
Attains, at length, a Master's high degree.

FIG. 38. FRONTISPIECE TO NOAH WEBSTER'S "AMERICAN SPELLING BOOK"

This is from the 1827 Edition, reduced one third in size.

thirty-five-year period from 1855 to 1890, when the copyright was controlled by D. Appleton & Company, of New York, its sales still averaged 865,419 copies a year. In 1890 the American Book Company took over the copyright, and the book may still be obtained from them. This was the first distinctively American textbook, and the most popular of all our early schoolbooks. Its publication was followed by a long line of spellers and readers, the most famous of which were Webster's *The Little Reader's Assistant* (1790); *The Columbian Primer* (1802), a modernized and secularized imitation of the old *New England Primer* (see Fig. 30); the *Franklin Primer* (1802), "containing a new and uſeful ſelection of Moral Leſſons adorned with a great variety of elegant cuts calculated to ſtrike a laſting impreſſion on the Tender Minds of Children"; and Caleb Bingham's *American Preceptor* (1794) and *Columbian Orator* (1806). The *Preceptor* was a graded reader and soon replaced the Bible as an advanced reading book, while the *Orator* was one of the earliest of a long list of books containing selections from poetry and prose for reading and declamation. These books suited well the new democratic spirit of the times, and became very popular. Selections from English poetry and the patriotic orations of Revolutionary leaders predominated. Many were illustrated with cuts, showing how to bow, stand, make gestures suitable to different types of declamation, etc. The speeches of John Adams, Hancock, and in particular Patrick Henry's "Give me Liberty or give me Death" were soon being declaimed in the schoolhouses all over the land.

FIG. 39. MAKING THE PRELIMINARY BOW TO THE AUDIENCE

From Lovell's *The Young Speaker*, 1844.

The English Dilworth's *The Schoolmaster's Assistant*, "being a compendium of Arithmetic, both practical and theoretical, in five parts," which went through many American editions before 1800, did much to popularize the study of arithmetic. In 1788 Nicholas Pike's *Arithmetic*, the first American text, appeared. It was a voluminous work of five hundred and twelve pages. It was soon "uſed as a claſſical book in all the Newengland Univerſities," but was too advanced for the schools. A number of briefer American arithmetics soon appeared and, in 1821, with the publication of Warren Colburn's *First Lessons in Arith-*

metic on the Plan of Pestalozzi, another famous American textbook, one that must be ranked with Webster's *Speller*, appeared. Arithmetic, and especially mental arithmetic, now became one of the great subjects of the common schools.

These early books, together with a long list of imitators, firmly fixed reading, spelling, declamation, and arithmetic as the fundamental subjects for the evolving American common school.

New subjects of study appear. New subjects of study also began to appear. The English Dilworth's *A New Guide to the English Tongue* had made the beginnings of the teaching of English word usage, and in 1795 the first of a large number of editions of Lindley Murray's *Grammar* made its appearance. This was soon followed by an almost equally popular text by Caleb Bingham, known as *The Young Lady's Accidence* (1799). The title page of this book declared it to be "a ſhort and eaſy Introduction to English Grammar. Deſigned principally for the uſe of young Learners, more eſpecially thoſe of the FAIR SEX, though proper for either." These two books became very popular, were extensively used and imitated, and firmly fixed the new study of English Grammar as a common-school ſubject.

The publication of the Reverend Jedediah Morse's *Geography*, in 1784, and his *Elements of Geography*, in 1795, added another subject which also became very popular. In 1821 the first little booklet on United States history appeared, though some historical material had been included in the earlier readers under the subject of Geography. In 1822 Goodrich's *A History of the United States* was published, and this at once leaped into popular favor. One hundred and fifty thousand copies had been sold by 1832, when Noah Webster's *History of the United States* appeared to contest its popularity. Both these histories long continued popular as school texts, and the introduction of a study of the Constitution of the United States by Webster into his book marked the beginning of the study of Civics in our grammar schools.

The elementary-school subjects fixed. The publication of these new texts opened up entirely new possibilities of instruction in the evolving American common school. The teaching of the old subjects was greatly enriched and expanded, while the new subjects made possible more advanced instruction and the upward extension and lengthening of the common-school course. John Howland, founder of the Providence schools, writing to a friend in 1824, said that the instruction in Providence remained as prescribed in 1800 (p. 223), except that grammar and geography were soon introduced. Of these new subjects he said:

Up to this time I had never seen a grammar — a sorry confession for a school committeeman, some may think — but observing that *The Young Lady's Accidence* was in use in the Boston schools, I sent to the principal bookseller in that town, and purchased one hundred copies for the use of ours.

The introduction of grammar was quite an advance in the system of education, as it was not taught at all except in the better class of private schools. The same was true of geography, which had never been taught before. I sent to Boston and purchased as many as were wanted for our schools. Dr. Morse, of Charlestown, had published the first volume of his geography, and that was the work we adopted. Many thought it an unnecessary study, and some in private objected to it because it would take off their attention from arithmetic. But it met with no public opposition.

A race now began between arithmetic and the new subject of English grammar — a race unhappily too long continued — to see which subject should take the place of first importance in the school. Fact-geography and fact-history also became important older-pupil subjects. Sewing and knitting also became common subjects of instruction for the girls, and, as the culmination of such instruction, each girl made a "Sampler," of which the copy opposite is a good example. These were made on linen, though in the girls' "boarding-schools" elaborate work on silk was sometimes executed. The name "Sampler" came from the expected future use in showing the proper form of letters to be used in marking the household linen. Much attention also was paid to manners, morals, and good behavior. These represented the secularized successor of the old religious instruc-

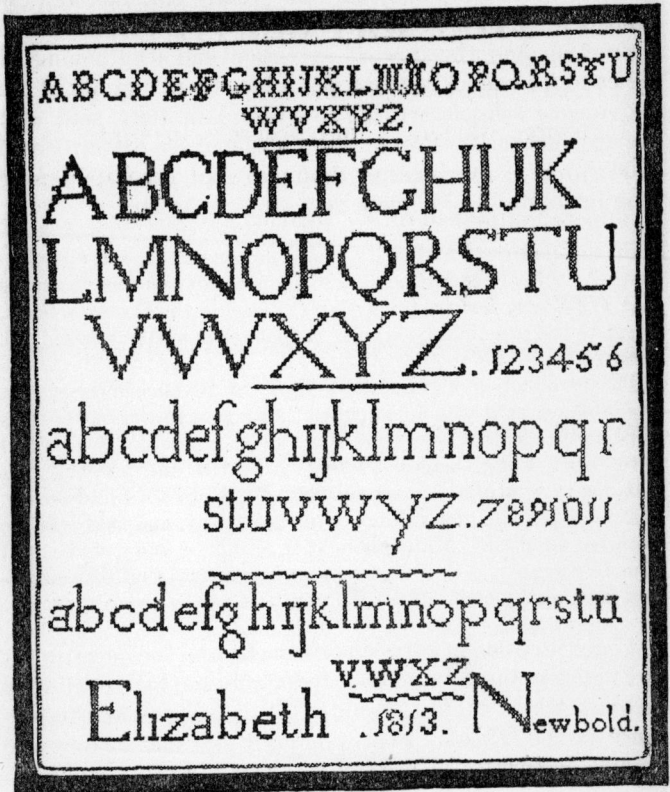

FIG. 40. A "SAMPLER"

A sampler worked on linen, in the possession of the author, which was made in a girls' school near Bristol, Pa., in 1813.

tion. It now became common to give to the children, at the end of the term, "Rewards of Merit" for good conduct, which read somewhat as follows:

The love of praise was planted to protect
And propagate the glories of the mind.

THIS MAY CERTIFY

THAT *Master Elijah Windsor*   by *his* good
behavior, diligence, and progress in study, is
entitled to the increased affection of *his* friends,
and the applause of *his* Instruct*ress.*

Matilda Dawson.

August 19th, 1823.

FIG. 41. A REWARD OF MERIT

By 1830, certainly, we have the full curriculum of our
elementary schools, as it was by 1860, clearly in use in our
better city systems. The subjects were these:

For the younger children	For the older children
Letters and syllables	Advanced Reading
Reading	Advanced Spelling
Writing	Penmanship
Spelling	Arithmetic
Numbers	Geography
Elementary Language	Grammar
Good Behavior	Manners and Morals
	United States History (?)

For the girls
Sewing and Darning

Legal aspect of this course of instruction. Many of the
early school laws enacted by the different States provided
for instruction in these subjects. Massachusetts, for example, which had required instruction in reading and writing
in the law of 1647, added orthography, good behavior, the
English language and grammar, and arithmetic to the re-

quired list in 1789, geography in 1826, and history of the United States in 1857. Vermont specified reading, writing, and arithmetic as required subjects in its law of 1797, and added spelling, geography, grammar, United States history, and good behavior in 1827. New England people, moving westward into the North-West Territory, carried these school requirements and the early textbooks with them, and the early schools set up in Ohio and Michigan were copies of those in the old home. Ohio, in its first school law of 1825, specified reading, writing, and arithmetic for all schools, and in 1831 permitted the cities and towns to organize instruction in other subjects. In 1848 geography and grammar were ordered added for all schools. Michigan, in the law of 1827, virtually adopted the Massachusetts plan for schools.

The Lancastrian schools, which were so prominent between about 1810 and 1830 in the cities and towns of the Middle Atlantic States, and to a degree spread to all parts of the then Nation, were organized to give instruction in:

Spelling   English Grammar
Reading   Geography
Writing   Religion
Arithmetic

Early city courses of study. The early courses of study adopted for the cities of the time reveal the same studies in the schools, as well as the beginnings of the classification of the pupils on the basis of the difficulty of the subjects. For example, the course of study and the textbooks adopted for the schools of Providence, Rhode Island, in 1800, reads:

The principal part of the Instruction will consist in Spelling, Accenting & Reading both Prose and Verse with propriety and accuracy, and a General Knowledge of English Grammar and Composition: Also writing a good hand according to the most approved Rules, and Arithmetic through all the previous Rules, and Vulgar and Decimal Fractions, including Tare and Tret, Fellowship, Exchange, Interest, &c.

The books to be used in carrying on the above Instruction are Alden's Spelling Book, 1st and 2nd part, the Young Ladies' Accidence, by Caleb Bingham, The American Preceptor, Morse, Geography, abridged, the Holy Bible in select portions, and such other Books as shall hereafter be adopted and appointed by the Committee. The Book for teaching Arithmetic shall be agreed on by the Masters.

The Scholars shall be put into separate Classes, according to their several improvements, each Sex by themselves.

This constituted the entire printed course of study for Providence in that day, and was typical of the time. Compared with the hundreds of printed pages of directions which we have to-day, the simplicity of such a course of study is evident. Though ungraded in character, the beginnings of a grading of schools is nevertheless evident. This was the so-called "common school." It presupposed that the children should have learned their letters and the beginnings of reading privately, or in some Dame School, before entering the public school. This requirement was common before the coming of Infant or Primary schools, about 1825.

In New York City the schools of the Free School Society were at first organized to cover only the work of the 3-Rs and religion. An abstract of "the employment and progressive improvement of the scholars for the last year," contained in the *Fourteenth Annual Report* of the Society, for 1819, shows that of the 1051 children then in the schools, 1044 were "known to attend public worship on the Sabbath," as required by the rules, and that the studies pursued by them were as follows:

297 Children have been taught to form letters in sand.
615 have been advanced from letters in sand, to monosyllabic reading on boards.
686 from reading on boards, to Murray's First Book.
335 from Murray's First Book, to writing on slates.
218 from writing on slates, to writing on paper.
341 to reading in the Bible.
277 to addition and subtraction.
153 to multiplication and division.
 60 to the compounds of the four first rules.
 20 to reduction.
 24 to the rule of three.

This shows the common American ungraded 3-Rs school, taking children from the very beginnings, and advancing them individually and by subjects, as their progress warranted.   Such schools were very common in the early period.

On August 2, 1822, a committee of the New York Society was appointed to consider and report "on the propriety of instructing some of the oldest, most orderly, and meritorious of our scholars in some of the higher branches of an English Education, say Grammar, Geography, History, Mathematics, &c."   This was done soon thereafter by changing the schools for a time to a pay basis, as described on page 147, and the price list there given shows that the subjects taught at that time were:

Alphabet	Grammar	Bookkeeping
Spelling	Geography	Mensuration
Writing	History	Astronomy
Reading	Composition	
Arithmetic	Needlework	

Boston offers another illustration, out of many that might be cited.   In 1789 the Town Meeting ordered three writing schools and three reading schools established in the town, for the instruction of children between the ages of seven and fourteen, who had previously learned to read, boys to be admitted all the year round, and girls only from April 20 to October 20 each year.   The subjects to be taught in these schools were:

The writing school	*The reading school*
Writing	Spelling
Arithmetic	Accentuation
	Reading of prose and verse
	English Grammar and Composition

By 1823 the study of geography had been added to the instruction in the reading schools, and a little later United States history also was added.   Each school building contained two rooms, and was divided between the two departments.   The upper room was occupied by the reading school, and the lower by the writing school.   The pupils were interchanged, thus attending two schools and **two** teachers each day. Children were admitted to these schools from the Primary Schools for beginners, first established (p. 97) in 1818.

The beginnings of school grading. In addition to the division of the schools horizontally into Primary Schools and English Grammar Schools, and the subdivision of the latter vertically into writing and reading schools, a beginning of classification and the grading of pupils had been made, by 1823, by the further subdivision of the reading school into four classes, as follows:

> Lowest class: Reading, spelling, accentuation.
> Second class: Same, and grammar memorized.
> Third class: Same, and grammar learned.
> Highest class: Same, and geography.

This made four classes for the seven-year course, with a three-year primary school beneath, divided into six classes, and clearly represents the beginnings of a graded system of schools. It is a ten-year elementary-school course, beginning at the age of four. In 1848 the reading or English grammar schools were further divided horizontally by putting a teacher in charge of each class, and in 1856 the same plan was extended downward to the primary schools. Figure 42 shows the organization of the Boston schools by 1823, as described in a volume, *The System of Education pursued at the Free Schools in Boston*, published that year.

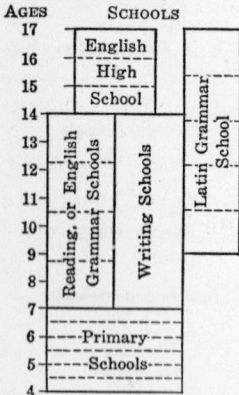

FIG. 42. THE BOSTON SCHOOL SYSTEM IN 1823

The dotted cross-lines indicate class divisions, though not under separate teachers.

One of the clearest cases of the evolution of the American ungraded common school into the American graded elementary school — clear because of

the presence of excellent records — is afforded by the city of
Providence, Rhode Island, the schools in which began in
1800. The evolution there can be best presented by the
use of a tabular statement taken from the courses of study
adopted, which shows the following:

1800	1820	1828
Common School (8–)	*Common Schools* (6–)	*Primary Schools* (4–7)
Reading	Reading	Reading
Spelling	Spelling	Spelling
Accentuation	Punctuation	
Writing	Writing	*Writing Schools* (7–)
Arithmetic	Arithmetic	Reading
Grammar	Grammar	Spelling
Composition		Writing
Geography		Arithmetic
Bible		Grammar
		Geography
		Bookkeeping
		Epistolary Composition

1838	1840	1848
Primary Schools (4–7)	*Primary Schools* (4–7)	*Primary Schools* (5–7½)
Reading	Reading	Reading
Spelling	Spelling	Spelling
		Arithmetic
		Music
Grammar or Writing School (7–)	*Grammar Schools* (7–14)	*Intermediate Schools* (7½–10)
Reading	Reading	Reading
Spelling	Spelling	Spelling
Writing	Writing	Writing
Arithmetic	Arithmetic	Arithmetic
Grammar	Grammar	Music
Geography	Geography	Geography
Bookkeeping	Bookkeeping	
Epistolary Composition	U.S. History	
	Composition	
	Practical Ethics	
	Constitution U.S.	

High School	*High School* (14–17)	*Grammar Schools* (10–14)
The branches of a good English education	List of 20 high-school subjects	Reading Writing Arithmetic Geography Grammar Composition U.S. History Declamation General History

High School (14–17)

Same as in 1840

This creation of schools of different grades took place largely as new buildings were needed and erected. With each additional building in the same district the children were put into better classified schools. This same division of schools for purposes of grading, as new building facilities were provided, took place generally over the United States, between 1820 and 1850, though with quite different results and nomenclature, as the following twenty-five selected cities will show. The numbers in parentheses indicate the number of years assigned to each school.

Portland, Me.	Primary, Intermediate, Grammar, High.
Fall River, Mass.	Primary, Intermediate, Grammar, High.
Lawrence, Mass.	Primary, Middle, High.
Worcester, Mass.	Subprimary, Primary, Intermediate-Primary, Secondary, Grammar (3), High.
Hartford, Conn.	Common Schools, enter High School at 12.
New Haven, Conn.	Common Schools, enter High School at 13.
Providence, R.I.	Primary (2½), Intermediate (2½), Grammar (4), High (4).
New York City	Primary (5), Grammar (6), College (4).
Kingston, N.Y.	Primary, Junior, Senior, Academic.
Oswego, N.Y.	Primary (3), Junior (3), Senior (3), High (3).
Rochester, N.Y.	Primary (2), Intermediate (2), Grammar (3), High (4).
Syracuse, N.Y.	Primary (3), Junior (3), Senior (3), High (3).
Troy, N.Y.	Primary (3), Intermediate (3), Grammar (3), High(4).
Harrisburg, Pa.	Primary (4), Secondary (4), High (4).

Philadelphia, Pa.	Primary, Secondary, Grammar, High.
Newark, N.J.	Primary (3), Grammar (3), High (4).
New Brunswick, N.J.	Primary (4), Grammar (4), High (3).
Cleveland, Ohio	Primary, Intermediate, Senior, High.
Dayton, Ohio	Primary (3), Secondary (2), Intermediate (3), High.
Toledo, Ohio	Primary (2), Secondary (2), Intermediate (2), Grammar (2), High (3).
Indianapolis, Ind.	Primary (4), Intermediate (4), High (4).
Louisville, Ky.	Primary (4), Intermediate (3), Grammar (3), High (4).
Springfield, Ill.	Primary, Secondary, Intermediate, Grammar, High.
Madison, Wis.	Primary (2), Intermediate (2), Grammar (2), Senior Grammar (2), High (2).
New Orleans, La.	Primary (2), Grammar, High.

The division of each school into classes. The first step in the evolution of the present class-grade organization of our schools was the division of the school system into schools of two or more different grades, such as Primary, Intermediate, Grammar, etc. The above table shows the results of such division for twenty-five of the larger cities of the time. This began early, and was accomplished generally in our cities by 1840 to 1845.

The next step in the evolution of the graded system was the division of each school into classes. This also began early, certainly by 1810, and was fully accomplished in the cities by 1840. It began by the employment of assistant teachers, known as "ushers," to help the "master," and the provision of small recitation rooms, off the main large room, for their use in hearing recitations. This step in the evolution of the graded system is well shown in the drawing of a Providence grammar-school building, given on p. 231, which is thoroughly typical of the period. Due to its later construction, however, the two schoolrooms in this building were smaller than was the case in earlier constructions. The New York school building of 1820, shown on page 87, was provided with 252 seats and three small recitation rooms. Boston buildings, in 1823, carried seats for approximately

300 pupils, and each room had a master and two ushers, but by 1848 the number had there been reduced to approximately 180 seats. Each grammar school in Providence contained two separate and distinct and duplicate schools, as was a common early practice. Each school was under

FIG. 43. AN "USHER" AND HIS CLASS

The usher, or assistant teacher, is here shown with a class in one of the small recitation rooms, off the large schoolroom. (From Pierpont's *The Young Reader*, Boston, 1831.)

the control of a master and one male or two female assistants. Each little group of teachers in charge of a room was independent of the other, there being no principal for the building. Only for janitor service, heating, and repairs was the building considered as one school.

The third and final step in the evolution of the graded system was to build schools with smaller classrooms, or to subdivide the larger rooms; change the separate and independent and duplicate school on each floor, which had been the common plan for so long, into parts of one school organization; sort and grade the pupils, and outline the instruction by years; and the class system was at hand. This process

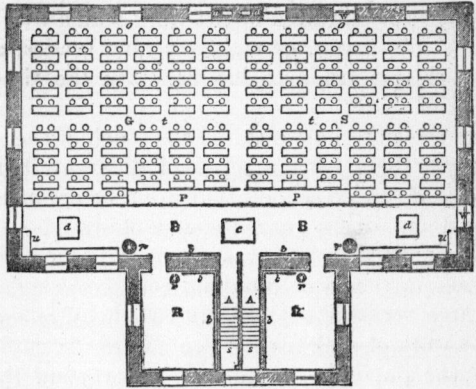

Fig. 44. Exterior and Interior of a Providence, Rhode Island
School

This was the typical grammar-school building of about 1840. Each floor seated 228 pupils, and was conducted as a separate school. Boys and girls were here seated on opposite sides of the central aisle, though the usual plan was to give one floor to each sex. In Boston the upper floor was used by the writing school, and the lower floor by the reading school. Two small recitation rooms are shown leading off the main room, for the use of the assistant teachers.

began in the decade of the thirties, and was largely accomplished in the cities by 1850. In the smaller places it came later, but usually was accomplished by or before 1870. In the rural districts class grading was not introduced until the last quarter of the nineteenth century.

The transition to the graded system a natural evolution.
The transition to the graded system came naturally and easily. For half a century the course of instruction in the evolving common or English grammar schools had been in the process of expansion, due in part to the preparation of better and longer textbooks, but largely through the addition of new subjects of study. The school term had been gradually lengthened, the years of school provided had been increased in number, the school course had been differentiated into various parts or schools, the master and his assistants had from the first divided up the work in each room on a rough age-and-grade classification basis, and the entire evolution, up to about 1830 to 1840, had prepared the way for a simple reorganization of the work which would divide the schools into seven, or eight, or nine grades, and give each teacher one grade to handle. By the time of the beginnings of state and city school supervision the school systems of the cities only awaited the touch of the organizer to transform them from a series of differentiated schools into a series of graded schools that could be organized into a unified system, with a graded course of study, and unified supervision over all. The waste in maintaining two duplicate schools in the same building, each covering the same two or three years of school work, when by re-sorting the pupils the work of each teacher could be made more specialized and the pupils better taught, was certain to become obvious as soon as school supervision by teachers began to supersede school organization by laymen.

As new buildings were erected with smaller classrooms, and as the large classrooms in old buildings were divided and the schools reorganized, the graded system, with a teacher in charge of each class, and a much smaller class at that (55 to 75 were common sizes at first), came in as a perfectly natural evolution and as a matter of course. There was no change in subject-matter, as that had become fixed long before. There was no material lengthening of the course, as a combined course of seven to nine years had become common before grading had been fully carried out. There was also no change in method or purpose, except as the coming, about this time, of some Pestalozzian ideas, described in the next chapter, tended to improve all method, and except as the elimination of sectarianism and the establishment of state-supported schools tended to give a clearer consciousness as to the citizenship-aim in instruction. Nor was there any general adoption of a new idea in organization from abroad. We merely evolved, as the result of something like a half-century of gradual educational development, the common and purely native American elementary school which we have known for so long. As shown in the last tabulation given, this varied from seven to nine years in length, with eight and nine years as the common numbers. The primary classes, in part due to the pressure of numbers, gradually ceased to take pupils earlier than five, and later earlier than six, outside of New England, and the present eight-year elementary school (nine in New England), with a teacher for each grade, was evolved. On top of this the English high school, also a purely native American creation, was superimposed, making a twelve or thirteen year course of public school instruction, which was tax-supported, state controlled, freed from sectarianism and the pauper taint, and equally open to all the children of the State. This evolution is shown somewhat roughly in Figure 23 (p. 99), and was fully accomplished by 1860 in all Northern States.

The high school fitted onto the graded system. In the process of this evolution the high school also was made thoroughly democratic. When the English high schools were first established they were everywhere built on top of the common or grammar-school course, the evolution of which we have just described. The Latin grammar schools, though, as shown in the case of Boston (Fig. 42), as well as the Classical Course in a few cities having both courses in one school, took pupils at an earlier age. In general this was confined to New England, though San Francisco, as late as the sixties, admitted pupils to its Latin high school at ten, and to its English high school at twelve. By 1860 this differentiation had been almost entirely abandoned as undemocratic and undesirable, and high-school courses had been based on the completion of the common-school course of study. This eliminated the last vestiges of the European class educational system with which we began, and put in its place the democratic educational ladder which has for so long characterized education in the United States.

By 1860 the English high school, now beginning to develop in all the States, had clearly begun to take over the work in English, modern languages, history, mathematics, and the physical sciences previously taught in the academies, and to offer, free from tuition, the subjects of study and courses of instruction which for so long had been found only in the tuition academies. Still more, the colleges were gradually forced to accept these new subjects as equal to the old Latin and Greek for admission, as is seen from the following table, giving where and when each new subject was first accepted for admission to the A.B. college course.

	Subject	Date	College first accepting
Old subjects	Latin	1640	Harvard
	Greek	1640	Harvard
	Arithmetic	1745	Yale
	Geography	1807	Harvard
	English Grammar	1819	Princeton
	Algebra	1820	Harvard
	Geometry	1844	Harvard
	Ancient History	1847	Harvard and Michigan
New subjects	Modern (U.S.) History	1869	Michigan
	Physical Geography	1870	Michigan and Harvard
	English Composition	1870	Princeton
	Physical Science	1872	Harvard
	English Literature	1874	Harvard
	Modern Languages	1875	Harvard

The colleges thus fitted their work onto that of the recently evolved English high school, and the American educational ladder was now complete. With the abolition of the rate-bill, which by 1860 had been done everywhere by the cities, and which still existed in the rural and town schools in but five of the then thirty-three States, this educational ladder was finally open to all American children as their educational birthright. The two requisites for the climb were money enough to obtain freedom from work in order to attend, and brains and perseverance enough to retain a place in the classes.

II. THE GREAT DAY OF THE DISTRICT SYSTEM

The second and third quarters of the nineteenth century marked the great day of the district system. By 1830 to 1835 it was everywhere in control, but after 1860 to 1865 its serious defects as a system of school administration had become evident in the cities, and were beginning to be apparent even in rural districts. Everywhere, by the latter dates, there was a ten-

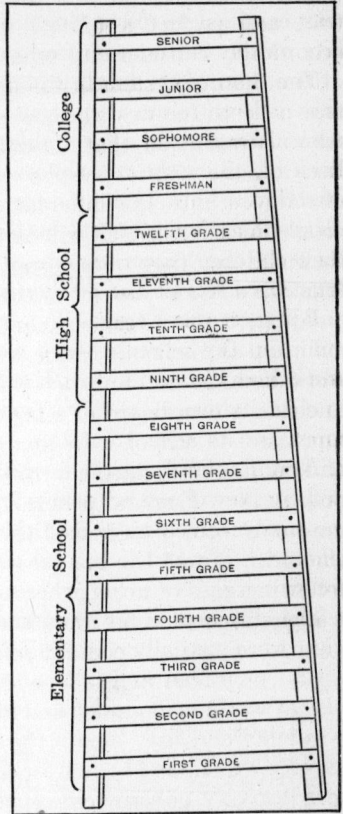

FIG. 45. THE AMERICAN EDUCATIONAL LADDER

Compare this with the figure on p. 268 and the democratic nature of the American school system will be apparent.

dency to limit the district powers, and later to abolish the system.

The cities were the first to curb and subordinate the district and perfect a unified school system, and we shall accordingly consider city school organization first.

The district system in the cities. In many of our cities, especially to the westward, no such unified system of school administration as that described for Providence existed. Instead, the district system of school administration was introduced into the different wards of the city. As the people in each ward felt willing to provide school facilities for their children they were permitted by law to call a meeting, organize a school district in the ward, vote to erect a school building, employ teachers, and vote to tax themselves to maintain the school. Some wards thus had public schools and others did not, but each ward so organizing was allowed to elect its own board of school trustees and to control and supervise its school. In many of our older cities outside of New England, particularly those which at first were settled by New England people, the first schools began under the same form of organization as the regular rural district schools. It was the one way to secure action in the progressive wards of unprogressive cities.

The different cities thus came to contain a number of what were virtually country school districts, each maintaining an ungraded and independent district school. As the city grew, these ungraded and independent schools increased in number and size. Later the situation became impossible, the city was unified by law for education as it had previously been for city government, a city board of education was created and given control of the scattered schools, and this board employed a new supervisory officer, now becoming known as a city superintendent of schools, to unify and supervise the schools. The early educational history of a number of our cities is the history of the formation of a number of such independent district schools in the different wards of the city, and their later unification into one city school system. It is from this that the old term "ward schools" has come down to us, as well as ward representation on the city school board and too frequently ward politics in the management of the schools as well.

Examples of city-district consolidations. The cities of Buffalo, Detroit, and Chicago illustrate this process very well.

The first schoolhouse in Buffalo was built privately, in 1806, and burned in 1813. In 1818 the first tax for a school in Buffalo was levied to rebuild this school. By 1832 six one-teacher school districts had been organized in the city, and by 1837 there were seven. The city by that time had something like 15,000 inhabitants. That year the first superintendent of city schools in the United States was appointed, to unify and supervise these seven schools. On the full establishment of the free-school system, in 1839, the number of districts was increased to fifteen, to supply deficiencies, and a school was ordered established in each, with a central school for instruction in the higher English branches.

The city of Detroit is another example, of a somewhat more extreme type. Here the dis-

FIG. 46. THE FIRST FREE PUBLIC SCHOOL IN DETROIT

A one-room school, opened in the Second Ward, in 1838.

trict system stood in the way of school organization, and had to be overthrown before any substantial progress could be made. Private and church schools had existed there since as early as 1816. The first public school, though, was not organized until the second ward took action, in 1838. Other wards not being willing to tax themselves for schools, little further progress was made until 1841. In that year an investigation showed that there were 27 schools of all kinds in the city, instructing a total of 714 pupils, and 1850 children of school age without any instruction whatever. Detroit was at that time a city of approximately 10,000 inhabitants. The result was a campaign for public schools, and a petition to amend the city charter to permit the organization of a city board of education to provide schools generally throughout the city. This was bitterly opposed, but the proposal carried at a city election and, in 1842, the legislature, following the best eastern practices of the time, abolished the district system in Detroit and provided for the organization of a unified system of schools for the city, under a city board of education.

Chicago is a third illustration of much the same type as Buffalo. A private school was opened there as early as 1816, but the first public school was not established until 1832. The town was incorporated in 1833, and in 1835 a special law for Chicago established the Massachusetts district system in the city. By 1837 there were 5 schools and 828 children, and by 1844 there were 8 teachers and 816 children, the enrollments of the 8 teachers being 97, 75, 130, 70, 131, 130, 110, and 75 children respectively. By 1853 there were 7 district schools, employing 34 teachers, and enrolling 3086 children, or an average of 91 children to the teacher. The schools at that time still were ungraded, and practically independent in methods, textbooks, and plan. They were also very insufficient in numbers, as they had been provided only in parts of the city where the demand for schools was strong enough to insure the voting of taxes. Thousands of children were being turned away because of lack of school facilities. In 1853 the city council appointed a city superintendent of schools to unify the work done in the districts. He at once graded and reorganized the instruction, and introduced uniform records and textbooks. In 1857 the legislature abolished the district system in the city, and created a city board of education to take charge of the schools. This established one city school system for the city. In 1861 the first graded course of study in Illinois was provided for the schools of Chicago.

Many other cities have had a similar educational administrative history, but practically everywhere the district system was early abolished, and to its early abolition and to the early unification of the school system the great educational progress of the cities during the past half-century is largely due.

Rural district management. As was stated at the beginning of Chapter VI, the district system was the natural system in the early days of state school organization and con-

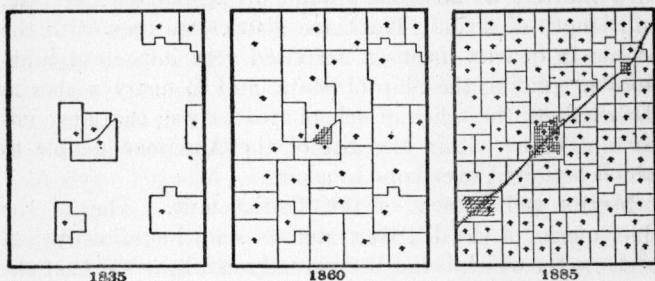

FIG. 47. HOW THE DISTRICT SYSTEM ORGANIZED A COUNTY

From Cubberley's *Rural Life and Education.*

trol. At a time when population was sparse, intercourse limited, communication difficult, supervision practically absent, and isolation the rule, the district system rendered its greatest service. It provided schools suited to the wants and needs of country people, and where and as fast as the people were willing to support them. The system was well adapted, too, to the earlier ideas as to the nature and purpose of education. Schools were then purely local affairs, and the imparting of a limited amount of information was almost their sole purpose. Knowledge then was power, and the schools were conducted on a knowledge basis, undisturbed by any ideas as to psychological procedure, social needs, or by the civic and economic problems of the present.

Each community lived largely for its own ends, and was largely a law unto itself. Freedom and liberty were conceived of, as expressed by one of our poets, as:

> The right of every freeborn man
> To do as he darned pleases.

Naturally, under such conditions, every little community felt itself competent to select and examine its teachers, adopt its own course of study, determine the methods of instruction, supervise and criticise the teacher, and determine all such matters as boarding-around arrangements, tax rate, and length of term. The three district trustees, with the people in district meeting, exercised very important functions in guiding the Ship of State, and to many a man in the districts the office of school trustee was the most important office within the gift of the American people to which he might ever hope to aspire.

Merits and defects of the district unit. One of the chief merits of the district system of school administration, and one for which it has been greatly extolled, was that the school district meeting served as a forensic center for the new democratic life of the time. The victory of Andrew Jackson was a victory for democracy which was felt even in remote rural districts. The school district has been and still is the smallest unit of local self-government in our political system, and the one small unit to which much power is still given. It corresponds to the parish in the management of church affairs, or to the early New England town meeting under the old régime. As a unit of local government it once doubtless did much to educate the people in civic spirit and patriotism, and trained them in the simple forms of parliamentary procedure. There they learned to speak and to defend their rights — real or imaginary — as well as to present their grievances and pay off old scores. At a time when general education at public expense hung in the balance, the district system doubtless did much toward awakening a conception of the need for and the benefits of popular education.

On the other hand, the system awakened an exaggerated idea as to district importance, an idea as to district perfection which rendered it impervious to criticism, a deep jealousy of larger and more prosperous districts, frequently a banding together to keep others from enjoying what the poorer ones could not enjoy, and usually persistent and bitter opposition to any attempt at reform.

Even by 1850 the tendency in the States had become marked to limit the powers of the district meeting, and to take away powers from the trustees and transfer them to the county and state superintendents which were then being created, or to determine the matter once for all by constitutional requirement or uniform state law. In most States the district meeting was shorn of such powers as the right to designate the teacher, select the textbooks, or make out the course of study, and the trustees were early shorn of their power to examine and certificate the teacher they selected. The length of term, the rate of tax that must be levied, and the subjects that must be taught were early specified in the laws. In about this form the district system has continued to the present, though a number of States have abandoned it for a better system of school administration. The earliest States to do so were Indiana, in 1852; Massachusetts, in 1882; New Hampshire, in 1885; Georgia, in 1887; Florida, in 1889; Maine and Ohio, in 1892; Vermont and Rhode Island, in 1904; and New Jersey, in 1894. Since 1900 a number of other States have taken similar action.

III. General Character of the Early Schools

Character of the early teachers. Our schools, like our clothing during this early period, were largely of the home-spun variety. Not only were the subjects of instruction those of the natively evolving American school, but our teachers and school officers were of the same native type.

The professional teacher and school officer had not as yet
appeared.   The first American state normal school opened
at Lexington, Massachusetts, in 1839, but as late as 1860
there were but twelve such state schools in the entire United
States, and these twelve were confined to nine Northern
States.   Teachers' institutes, first definitely organized by
Henry Barnard in Connecticut, in 1839, had been introduced

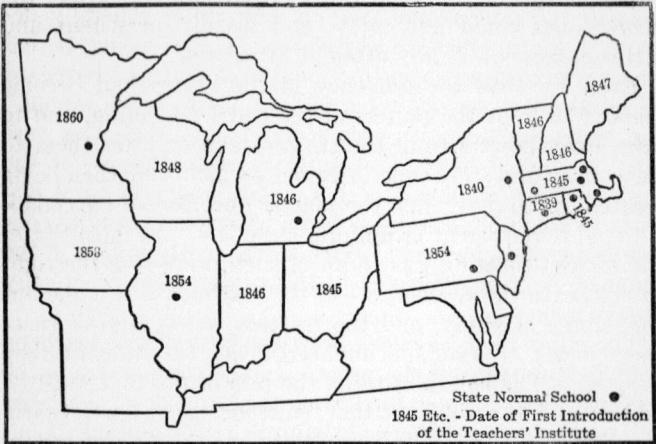

FIG. 48. TEACHER TRAINING IN THE UNITED STATES BY 1860

A few private training schools also existed, though less than half a dozen in all. Again
compare this development with the spread of New England people, as shown in the figure
on page 73.

into but fifteen other States by 1860, and these all in the
northeastern quarter of the United States.   But few books
of a professional nature, aside from the *School Journals*
which began to appear in the twenties and thirties (p. 260)
had as yet been published.   Samuel R. Hall's *Lectures on
Schoolkeeping*, published in 1829, was the first professional
book for teachers published in America, and David Page's
Theory and Practice of Teaching, first issued in 1847, was
one of the earliest, as well as one of the most successful of
all professional books.   Our best teachers were graduates

of the academies and the rising high schools, and the masters in the larger cities of the East were nearly always well-educated men, but the great mass of the teachers had little education beyond that of the schools they themselves taught. Terms were short, wages low and paid in part through "boarding-around" arrangements, and professional standards, outside a few cities, were almost completely absent. In place of the written examination in many subjects or the professional training now quite generally demanded for a teacher's certificate, in the earlier period teachers were given a short personal examination "in regard to moral character, learning, and ability to teach school." Not being satisfied with such requirements, the cities were early permitted to conduct separate examinations for the teachers they employed. It was customary in rural districts to hold both a summer and a winter term, and to contract separately for each. Women frequently taught in the summer, but the teachers in the winter were practically always men.

The cities then, as since, drew the best of the teachers, both in training and character. In the rural districts the teachers were men who worked on the farms or at day labor in the summer, and frequently left much to be desired. Contracts and rules of the time not infrequently required that the teacher conduct himself properly and "refrain from all spirituous liquors while engaged in this school, and not to enter the school house when intoxicated, nor to lose time through such intemperance." On the contrary, many schoolmasters of the time were excellent drill masters and kind of heart, and well merited George Arnold's description:

> He taught his scholars the rule of three,
>   Writing, and reading, and history too;
> He took the little ones up on his knee,
> For a kind old heart in his breast had he,
>   And the wants of the littlest child he knew.

The required studies were reading, writing, spelling, and arithmetic everywhere, with geography and grammar generally added by 1845. Composition, United States history, and simple bookkeeping were usually included for the town schools. These subjects the teacher obligated himself in his contract to teach "to all the youth of the district that may be placed under his care," and they constituted the instruction of the school and were taught by methods quite different from those now in use. Oral instruction, the word method in teaching reading, language lessons, instructions about realities, elementary science, geography built on the child's environment instead of the pages of a book, arithmetic by analysis instead of sums by rule, music, drawing, reasoning instead of memorizing, and teaching that comes from the full mind of the teacher rather than from the pages of a book — with all of which we are now so familiar — were hardly known in the forties in the best of our schools, or before 1860 outside of the more progressive cities. It was also made the duty of the teacher "to keep strict rules and good order," and the ability to discipline the school was an important part of the teacher's qualifications. There was little "soft pedagogy" in the management of either town or rural schools in the days before the Civil War.

The schoolhouses and their equipment. Up to the time Henry Barnard began to write on schoolhouse construction (about 1840), no one had given any particular attention to the subject. Schoolhouses were "home-made," and, outside of the few large cities, were largely built without plans or specifications. For one of the early schoolhouses built in Providence, Rhode Island, the entire contract consisted of a very rough pen-and-ink sketch, on a single sheet of paper, showing windows, rafters, steeple, and length and breadth, and across this the contractor had written:

For the confider one thoufan two hundred dollars erect & build finde the matearels & paintent the fame and lay the foundations build the chimney and compleated faid building fit for youse;

and signed his name. Many schoolhouses in the towns and rural districts were built in a similar manner until well after the close of the Civil War. In the rural districts "a weather-boarded box" or an old log schoolhouse, with two or three windows on each side, a few wooden benches, and an un-jacketed stove in the middle of the room, answered all needs. In the cities a very ornate school architecture came in after the building of high schools began, but few high-school buildings erected before 1860 contained any rooms beside class recitation

FIG. 49. ONE OF THE "WEATHER-BOARDED BOXES"

rooms, an office, and an assembly hall (see Fig. 34, p. 195). The instruction was still almost entirely book instruction, and little else than recitation rooms were needed. The school furniture consisted of long home-made benches in the rural schools, and double desks in the cities. The

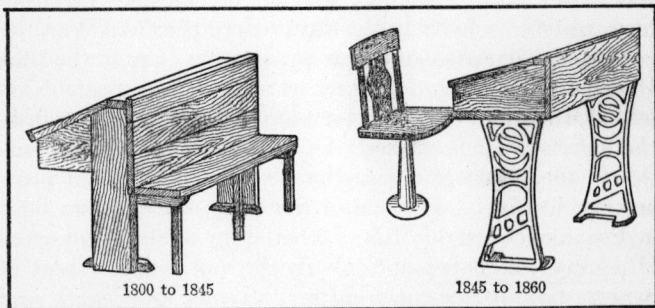

1800 to 1845   1845 to 1860

FIG. 50. SCHOOL DESKS BEFORE 1860

These represent the best types of city school furniture in general use at the time.

Quincy School, built in Boston in 1848, introduced a new type of school architecture in that the building contained a small classroom for each teacher — twelve in all, with seats for fifty-five pupils in each — an assembly room, a coat and cloak room off each classroom, and "a separate desk and chair for each pupil, this being the first grammar school-house," wrote the principal thirty years later, "here or elsewhere, so far as I know, into which this feature was introduced."

Blackboards were not in use until about 1820, and globes and maps were not common till later. The early geographies contained almost no maps, and the early histories few illustrations. Steel pens did not replace the use of quills until near the middle of the nineteenth century.

Purposes in instruction. The knowledge aim dominated all instruction. Knowledge was the important thing, as it was rather firmly believed that knowledge and virtue were somewhat synonymous terms. The fundamental subjects of the common-school course were drilled upon, and the trustees or the school committee, when they visited the school, examined the pupils as to their ability to read and spell, inspected the copybooks, and quizzed the pupils as to their knowledge of the rules of arithmetic and grammar, and the location of towns and rivers and capes. Competitive spelling and reading contests were common, to write a good and ornate hand was a matter of note, while the solving of arithmetical puzzles, parsing and diagramming of sentences, and locating geographical points were accomplishments which marked the higher stages of a common-school education. Arithmetic and English grammar became firmly fixed as the great subjects of the common-school course of study, and the momentum these two subjects accumulated in the early days of public education is as yet far from spent.

IV. The Civil War checks Development

Education in the Southern States. But little mention has so far been made of the school systems of the Southern States, for the reason that education there, as has already been stated, was much slower in getting under way than in the Northern States. In most of the Southern States, despite some promising beginnings, an educational system was not created until after the close of the Civil War. A brief digest of the important educational legislation enacted in the different States before the outbreak of the war will make this evident.

1. *The original States*

Delaware. State school fund created in 1796, but unused until 1817; then $1000 a year given to each county to educate pauper children in reading, writing, and arithmetic. In 1821 aid extended to Sunday Schools. First permissive free school law in 1821, and schools of Wilmington begun. People unwilling to tax themselves, and by 1833 only 133 school districts organized in the State. In 1843 an educational convention adopted a resolution opposing taxation for education, and little more was done until 1861, the date of the first law to really start the schools.

Maryland. Many academies chartered, and lottery much used before 1817. School fund begun by a bank tax, in 1812, and first property tax authorized, in 1816, to provide charity schools. Lottery to raise $50,000 a year for five years for such schools, between 1816 and 1821. First general school law in 1825, providing for State Superintendent and Lancastrian schools. Too advanced, never in operation, law repealed and superintendency abolished in 1827, and little more done. Virtually no school system outside of Baltimore by 1860. Real beginning of state school system dates from 1865.

Virginia. Optional school law in 1796, but little done under it. Literary Fund created in 1810. Second school law in 1818, provided for a charity school system, and $45,000 a year state aid for such. By 1843 estimated that one half the indigent children in the State were receiving sixty days schooling each year. Much educational agitation after 1837. Third school law in 1846, providing for school districts, taxation, and county school commissioners. Good law, but optional, and as only nine counties adopted it, the charity school law of 1818 virtually continued. The Civil War ended the old system; real beginning of state school system dates from 1870.

North Carolina. This State made a good beginning before the Civil War, and an excellent record during the war. State university opened in 1795. Many academies chartered, and lottery much used to aid them.   School law reported in 1817, but failed of passage.   Charity-school law reported in 1824, but also failed.   Lancastrian system proposed in 1832, and also failed.   Elementary school system created in 1839, and state superintendency in 1852.   Schools well under way after 1852.   From 1853 to 1865 history of school system almost a biography of the Scotch-Irish Superintendent, Calvin H. Wiley.   Temptation to use the $2,000,000 school fund for war needs resisted, and schools kept open during the war.   System abolished by reconstruction government in 1865.   Present system dates from 1868.   Wiley, in his last *Report*, well said:

> To the lasting credit of North Carolina, her public schools survived the terrible shock of the cruel war. . . . The common schools lived and discharged their useful mission through all the gloom and trials of the conflict, and when the last gun was fired, and veteran armies once hostile were meeting and embracing in peace upon our soil, the doors were still kept open, and they numbered their pupils by scores of thousands.

South Carolina. First law, in 1811, created virtually a charity school for Charleston.   Report in 1836 recommended charity schools for the State, but no action.   In 1854 Charleston asked to be permitted to provide free schools; granted in 1856.   Between 1790 and 1856 state constitution amended seven times, without including any mention of education.   Present state school system dates from 1868.

Georgia. The first state university chartered here in 1784, and opened in 1800.   In 1817 a fund created for free schools, and in 1822 income designated for tuition of poor children.   By 1820 thirty-one academies chartered, and academy fund permitted to be used to aid charity schools.   Free School Societies begun in Savannah in 1818, and Augusta in 1821, to provide charity schools.   In 1837 the academy fund turned over to the common-school fund, and a good free-school system established, but in 1840 law repealed and charity-school system reëstablished.   In 1858 word "poor" eliminated from school law, but by 1860 only one county had established a free-school system.   Present state school system dates from the Law of 1870.

2. New States, in order of admission

Kentucky. Admitted in 1792.   No general interest in education before 1820.   In 1821 first provision for aid to common schools and a fund created, but proved abortive, and legislature used the fund.

In 1830 first general law for schools, but proved a dead letter, due to lack of interest in education. In 1837 real interest began, and law provided for district organization, State Board of Education, and State Superintendent of Schools. At that time estimated that one half of the children of the State had never been to school, and one third of the adult population illiterate. Louisville schools date from 1819, were made free during 1829–30, and permanently after 1840. In 1848 the debt of the State to the school fund was acknowledged (see p. 138), in 1849 the first state school tax was levied, and the new constitution of 1850 made the first mention of education. By 1853 a school existed in each county for the first time. The Civil War interrupted the old system; present state system dates from 1870.

Tennessee. Admitted in 1796. In 1817 declared that "colleges and academies should form a complete system of education." First general school law, in 1830, provided for districts, trustees, and county commissioners, but no tax for maintenance. It also provided that no distinctions be made between rich and poor in schools. State school fund safeguarded in new constitution of 1834. In 1835 Secretary of State made *ex-officio* State Superintendent of Schools. Schools increased, but system lacked vigor before 1860. From 1860 to 1867 schools closed. Real beginnings of present state school system made by the Law of 1870.

Louisiana. Admitted in 1812. A University of Louisiana created in 1805, and a system of free schools in 1806, after the French model, but not put into effect. No mention of education in constitution of 1812, and nothing done toward a state system of free schools until new constitution of 1845. Law of 1847 began system, provided for state superintendent, and taxation. By 1851 estimated that one half the children of the State were attending public schools. The Civil War put an end to this system. Though the military government established schools in 1864, the present school system dates from 1877, when the withdrawal of Northern rule left the people free to inaugurate one of their own choice.

Mississippi. Admitted in 1817. Schools permitted in 1818. Literary Fund created in 1821, to be used in each county for education of selected poor in reading, writing, and arithmetic. In 1833 the fund was turned over to the counties, and the state system abandoned. Much agitation for schools from 1844, and new law of 1846 permitted schools, but no tax for without consent, each year, of majority of heads of families. This nullified the law.

Some special legislation to permit cities to organize schools. Present state system dates from 1868.

Alabama. Admitted in 1819. Constitutional mandate ineffective. School law for Mobile in 1826, and first general law for State in 1854. Latter provided for a state superintendent, county commissioners, a city superintendent for Mobile, and tuition schools, with aid from public funds to private teachers. The Civil War ended this system; real state system dates from 1875, when the people became free to adopt one in harmony with local wishes.

Missouri. Admitted in 1821. First public school in State organized at St. Louis, in 1838. First permissive law in 1839, but too advanced in nature, and little done under it. State university opened in 1844. Secretary of State made *ex-officio* state school officer in 1841, and state superintendency created in 1853. First high school in St. Louis in 1853. The Civil War interrupted the schools which had been created; present state school system dates from 1865.

Arkansas. Admitted in 1836. First general school law in 1843, providing for sale of 16th section lands, distribution of funds, and examination of teachers. In 1853 Secretary of State made *ex-officio* Superintendent of Schools. By 1854 estimated that 25 per cent of children of school age in some form of school. The Civil War ended this system; present state system dates from 1867.

Florida. Admitted in 1845. In 1849 schools authorized, and in 1850 county tax for schools permitted. By 1860 a sentiment favorable to education had developed, but little had been accomplished up to then. Real beginning of state school system dates from 1869, and real progress from about 1880.

Texas. The Mexican Government had organized Lancastrian tuition schools in the State in 1829. First constitution, in 1836, provided for state superintendent of schools. In 1840 each county given land endowments for schools, thus creating the county school funds. Entered the American Union, in 1845, and constitution provided for state schools. First law providing for their establishment in 1854, and first school established that year at San Antonio. The Civil War checked this development, and the present system dates from 1866.

The problem faced by the South. It will be seen from the above digest that, although the "common-school awakening" which took place in the Northern States after

Horace Mann began his work in Massachusetts (1837) was felt in some of the Southern States as well, and although some very commendable beginnings had been made in a few of these States before 1860, the establishment of state educational systems in the South was in reality the work of the period following the close of the Civil War. The coming of this conflict, evident for a decade before the storm broke, tended to postpone further educational development.

Following the close of the war the different Southern States started the work of building up state free public school systems with an energy which their depleted resources and lost school funds hardly warranted. This they did because they realized that the education of all classes of their people was the surest means for promoting the prosperity of the South. Robert E. Lee well expressed the best Southern feeling when he wrote, in 1866, to his friend Leyburn:

So greatly have those interests [educational] been disturbed at the South, and so much does its future condition depend upon the rising generation, that I consider the proper education of its youth one of the most important objects now to be attained, and one from which the greatest benefits may be expected. Nothing will compensate us for the depression of the standard of our moral and intellectual culture, and each State should take the most energetic measures to revive the schools and colleges, and, if possible, to increase the facilities for instruction and to elevate the standard of learning.

It was a tremendous undertaking, and called for much energy and pluck from a people whose property had been largely swept away and whose school funds had been largely lost. In addition, four millions of uneducated new citizens were added to the educational burden of the South as a result of the Civil War. The National Congress was repeatedly appealed to (1881–89) for assistance, and although a bill intended to aid the South passed the Senate three times, it each time failed of passage in the House. As a result the aid which would have been so useful and which ought to have been extended was denied. In consequence it required nearly a quarter of a century for the Southern States to get their school systems satisfactorily under way, and to take their proper educational position among the States of the Nation.

Development checked and changed in direction. The coming of the Civil War largely checked development at the North as well. The war itself absorbed the energies of our people, and it was a decade and a half after its close before any marked signs of expansion and development were evident, even in the North. The second quarter of the nineteenth century had been essentially a period of the establishment of the American free public school in the minds of the people and in the laws of the States. By 1850 the main lines for future development had been laid down, and the main battles had been won. The American people had definitely decided that they intended to establish and maintain a series of state systems of free, publicly controlled, tax-supported, non-sectarian common schools, and that these common-school systems should provide whatever educational advantages the needs of the States might seem to demand. Many minor points still remained to be decided, and many local struggles still remained to be fought out, but the main lines of future development had been firmly established.

After 1850 a number of additions to and extensions of the public-education idea began to be noted — evidences of a desire to extend the school systems and to make of them more useful instruments for state and national service. Evening schools, probably first begun in New York City, about 1833, began to be added by a number of cities to their school systems, and the first evening high school was opened in Cincinnati, in 1856. Music had been introduced into the schools of Boston in 1837, and Providence (see p. 227) before 1848, and was beginning to find favor here and there. Drawing first became an optional public school subject in Massachusetts in 1858, and was first taught regularly in Boston in 1860. In 1842 Massachusetts enacted the first child-labor law, and in 1852 the first compulsory school attendance law. School supervision was being extended, additional high schools were being created, the school term was being lengthened, increasing sums were being spent on the schools, and educational opportunity was being broadened. Taking into account all public and private schooling of whatever grade, the United States Bureau of Education estimated that each individual in our population received, during his lifetime, at the dates given, an average of the number of days and months (of 20 school days each) of schooling shown in the adjoining table. We had also, by 1860, made marked progress in opening up education of all grades to girls as well as boys, though in many places the girls were still taught in separate classrooms or schools.

Year	Total number of days	Total number of months
1800	82	4 m. 2 d.
1840	208	10 m. 8 d.
1850	450	22 m. 10 d.
1860	434	21 m. 14 d.
1870	582	29 m. 2 d.
1880	690	34 m. 10 d.
1890	770	38 m. 10 d.
1900	934	41 m. 14 d.
1910	1080	54 m. 0 d.
1916	1192	59 m. 12 d.

The coming of the Civil War for a time checked almost all material development at the North, and almost completely closed the schools in the South. Up to about 1880 at the North, and 1890 to 1895 at the South, further development and expansion came but slowly; expenses were kept down, school buildings were kept simple and along established lines, few new features were added to the curriculum, and few new school supervisory officers were employed. Then came the wonderful development in public education which has characterized the past twenty-five to thirty years.

In the meantime our educational system was being developed in another way. Up to 1835 certainly, and in most places for from one to two decades longer, all development was a purely native development. After about 1835 to 1840 we began to be touched by new influences from the outside, through new citizens and returning travelers who described for us the work of Pestalozzi and his disciples in Switzerland and the Pestalozzian organization of instruction in Holland and the German States. After 1860 we began seriously to introduce among our teachers a new method of instruction, based on the psychological foundations worked out by Pestalozzi and his successors. The period from about 1850 or 1860 to about 1880 or 1890 was the period of the introduction and organization of teaching method, when we made up in internal organization what we lacked in external development, and to this interesting addition to our educational ideas and practices we next turn.

QUESTIONS FOR DISCUSSION

1. Explain why declamation should have been so natural a subject to add to the school of the 3-Rs.
2. Show why English grammar, once introduced, would naturally become a popular subject of study.
3. Explain how the publication of the new textbooks on the new subjects "opened up entirely new possibilities in instruction."
4. Show how the spirit with which the introduction of new subjects at Providence was met, as described by Howland, was quite modern in character.
5. Was the Boston school system of 1823 a thoroughly democratic one, or not? Why?
6. Show how the absence of any professional supervision naturally tended to the independence of teachers and schools in the early period of our history.
7. Why should the new high schools have been fitted on to the grammar-school course, instead of beginning as the Latin grammar schools did at an earlier period?
8. What does the list of college entrance subjects given indicate as to the change in character of the colleges?
9. Why was it a natural condition to find the district system in the cities during their early history?
10. Show how city boards of education were a natural evolution out of city-council control of the early schools, and then how a city superintendent of schools came as a further natural evolution.
11. About what percentage of the school children of Buffalo could have been cared for in the seven public schools of 1837?
12. Picture the results in Chicago or Detroit or Buffalo to-day if the schools of the city were still managed under the district system.
13. Explain, historically, why so many cities in the older States have

special city boards of examination for teachers' credentials, instead of accepting the certificates issued by county or state authorities.

14. Show how natural it was that the knowledge aim should have dominated instruction during the 1830 to 1860 period.

15. Do you agree that the North should have aided the South in developing its schools after the close of the Civil War? Why?

16. Show how natural it was that the Civil War should have checked expansion and material development, and forced the schools to a development within.

TOPICS FOR INVESTIGATION AND REPORT

1. Early school buildings; plans and types. (Barnard.)
2. Early city courses of study. (Barnard.)
3. Subjects taught in the early high schools. (Barnard.)
4. Early standards for certificating teachers. (Barnard.)
5. History and character of the teachers' institutes. (Barnard.)
6. Educational opportunities for girls before 1850.
7. The Springfield Tests. (Riley.)
8. The Springfield and Norwich Tests compared. (Riley; Tirrell.)
9. Give the Springfield Tests to an equivalent school class to-day and compare results.
10. Character of the early instruction in reading, arithmetic, geography, or other subject before 1850.

SELECTED REFERENCES

Barnard, Henry, Editor. *The American Journal of Education.* 31 vols. Consult *Analytical Index* to; 128 pp. Published by United States Bureau of Education, Washington, 1892.

Fitzpatrick, E. A. *The Educational Views and Influences of De Witt Clinton.* 157 pp. Teachers College Contributions to Education, No. 44 New York, 1911.

Describes the schools of 1830.

Fitzpatrick, Frank A. "The Development of the Course of Study"; in *Educational Review*, vol. 49, pp. 1–19. (Jan., 1915.)

Takes Boston as a type and treats the subject historically.

Hedgepeth, V. W. B. "Spelling and Arithmetic in 1846 and Today"; in *School Review*, vol. 14, pp. 352–56. (May, 1906.)

The Springfield test at Goshen, Indiana. One of the many comparative studies.

*Johnson, Clifton. *Old-Time Schools and School Books.* 380 pp. The Macmillan Co., New York, 1904.

Chapter IV describes the district schools of the first half of the nineteenth century, and succeeding chapters the textbooks used. A valuable book.

Martin, G. H.   "Boston Schools 100 Years Ago"; in *New England Magazine*, vol. 26, pp. 628–42.   (July, 1902.)

A very general article.

McManis, John T.   "History in the Elementary Schools, 1825–1850"; in *Educational Bimonthly*, vol. 6, pp. 322–32.   (April, 1912.)

Historical.

*Monroe, W. S.   *Development of Arithmetic as a School Subject.*   170 pp. Bulletin No. 10, United States Bureau of Education, Washington, 1917.

An excellent collection of illustrative material on early arithmetic teaching.

*Murray, David.   *History of Education in New Jersey.*   344 pp.   Circular of Information No. 1, United States Bureau of Education, Washington, 1899.

Chapter VIII very good on the character of the schools during the colonial period and up to the middle of the nineteenth century.

Nelson, A. H.   "The Little Red Schoolhouse"; in *Educational Review*, vol. 23, pp. 304–17.   (April, 1902.)

Description of a rural school taught in Maine in the winter of 1858–59, which was characteristic of many rural school positions before 1870.

*Providence, Rhode Island.   *Centennial Report of the School Committee*, 1899–1900.   Providence, 1901.

Contains many valuable historical documents.

*Reeder, Rudolph R.   *The Historical Development of School Readers and Methods of Teaching Reading.*   Columbia University Contributions to Philosophy, Psychology, and Education, vol. VIII, No. 2.   The Macmillan Co., New York, 1900.

*Riley, J. L.   *The Springfield Tests, 1846–1906.*   51 pp.   Holden Patent Book Cover Co., Springfield, Mass., 1908.

A reprint of the results of the two examinations, showing the comparative results of the pupils in spelling, arithmetic, writing, and geography.

*Tirrell, Henry A.   "The Norwich Tests, 1862–1909"; in *School Review*, vol. 18, pp. 326–32.   (May, 1910.)

A comparative study, similar to the one at Springfield, and equally conclusive as to arithmetic, geography, history, and grammar.

CHAPTER IX

NEW IDEAS FROM ABROAD

I. ENGLISH ORIGINS AND EARLY INDEPENDENCE

Early influences largely English. As will have been seen from a study of the earlier chapters, the chief source from which our early educational ideas came was England. Throughout all the colonial period, and well into our national period also, we were English in our history, traditions, and development. Though the Dutch and Swedish parochial schools were introduced into New Amsterdam, though many French Huguenots settled along the Carolina coast, and though the German parochial school was firmly planted in Pennsylvania, these really influenced American development but little. The Dutch, Swedish, and French were rapidly absorbed and largely lost their identity after the English occupation, while the Germans became isolated and influenced development but little outside of eastern Pennsylvania. The great source of all our early educational traditions, types of schools, textbooks, and educational attitudes was England, and education was established and conducted here much after the fashion of the practices in the mother country. In New England it was the English Puritan with his Calvinistic viewpoint, and to the southward it was the Anglican churchman interpreting the Englishman's " no-business-of-the-State " attitude as to education.

The dame school, the tutor in the home, private and parochial pay schools, apprenticeship training, the pauper-school idea, the Latin grammar school, and the college — all were typical English institutions brought over by the early colonists and established here. For a century and a half the textbooks, and many of the teachers, were also imported from England. After the coming of nationality, the creation of distinctively American textbooks, and the evolution of more American-type schools, we still continued to draw our new educational ideas and creations from the old mother land. The Sunday School, the Charity School, the Church Society idea, the Lancastrian Monitorial Schools, and the Infant-School idea all came directly from England and were fitted into and onto the slowly evolving native American school. Even the Academy idea goes back in part to the Puritan academies of England.

Early French influences. After the French had extended aid to us in the War for Independence there was a tendency, for a time, to imitate French examples. The University of the State of New York, a governing body controlling all higher educational activities in the State, established in 1784 and organized in its permanent form in 1787, shows unmistakably the influence of the chief educational ideas of the French revolutionists. Jefferson was a great propagandist for French ideas, and tried, unsuccessfully, to secure the establishment of a complete system of public education for Virginia which would have embraced the best of French revolutionary conceptions. His proposed system comprehended the establishment of free elementary schools in every "hundred" (township), a number of secondary schools scattered throughout the State, and a state college (William and Mary) as the culmination of the State's educational system. Had he succeeded, a free education through college would have been provided for every worthy boy in Virginia, but his scheme was too far in advance of American educational ideas at the time to be accepted. He later (1819) secured the establishment of the University of Virginia, which to-day stands as a monument to his memory.

The College of New Orleans, created in 1805 with provision for academies for the counties, and the elementary school system organized for the State in 1806, were clearly modeled after Napoleon's law of 1802, organizing instruction throughout France. Only the college was ever put into operation. The early constitutional provisions regarding education in Indiana, providing for a system of free education "ascending in regular gradation from township schools to State University" (p. 75), probably owed their formulation to the influence in the constitutional convention of the French refugees then living in Vincennes. The founding of the University of Michigan, in 1817, with the absurd name of *Catholepistemiad*, and its whimsical organization, embodied the same French idea of a state organization of education extending from the elementary school to the university. We have comparatively little, though, that can be traced back to French sources, partly because we were so soon estranged from France by the unfriendly actions of Napoleon, and partly because France had, before the estrangement, done so little in education that we could imitate.

Our early isolation and independence. Up to the close of the first third of the nineteenth century we remained isolated and followed purely native lines of development, modified, as we have seen, by new ideas brought over from England and a few ideas as to organization from France. We were a young and a very independent nation, traveling but little, reading but little, and depending almost entirely upon our own ideas and resources. Schools were being evolved along purely native lines, and adapted to the needs of a new nation on a new continent which it was busily engaged in reducing to civilization.

Our teachers and schoolmasters were of the same native homespun variety, as were our early leaders as well. They were all alike innocent of such a thing as normal training, had read no professional literature, had attended few if any teachers' institutes, and knew little as to what even their neighbors, much less what peoples in other states and lands, were doing in the matter of organizing and directing schools. New ideas were spread by teachers moving about rather than by other means. As an evidence of this, it was almost twenty years after Warren Colburn's famous *Intellectual*

Arithmetic was published in Boston (1821) before it began to be used in New Jersey, "when those who had studied it in New England," according to Murray, "became teachers there." Yet this was the great book of its day, and shaped all subsequent teaching of the subject.

Educational journalism begins. It was not until the twenties that our educational literature began, and not until the decade between 1835 and 1845 that we really began to learn, for the first time, of what had been and was being done on the continent of Europe in the matter of organizing instruction. The earliest educational journals published in the United States were:

1. *The Academician*, New York, 1818–20. Twenty-five numbers, edited by Albert and John Picket.
2. *The American Journal of Education*, Boston, 1826–31. Five volumes, edited by William Russell.
3. *The American Annals of Education*, Boston, 1831–39. Nine volumes. A continuation of no. 2. Edited by Wm. C. Woodbridge.
4. *The Common School Assistant*, Albany, 1836–40. Five volumes, edited by J. Orville Taylor.
5. *The Common School Journal*, Boston, 1839–48. Ten volumes, edited by Horace Mann.
6. *The Connecticut Common School Journal*, Hartford, 1838–42. Four volumes, edited by Henry Barnard.
7. *The Rhode Island School Journal*, Providence, 1845–48. Three volumes, edited by Henry Barnard.
8. Barnard's *American Journal of Education*, Hartford, 1855–81. Thirty-one volumes, edited by Henry Barnard. A monumental work.

The circulation of these various journals was not large or extended, and for a time was confined almost altogether to New England, but they gradually reached the leaders of the time, and slowly but positively influenced public opinion. Their great service was that of spreading information as to what was being done, and in extending the work of propaganda for the maintenance of schools. With the beginnings of Barnard's *American Journal of Education*, in 1855, an

JEAN JACQUES ROUSSEAU
(1712-1778)

THOMAS JEFFERSON
(1743-1826)
Author of
The Declaration of American Independence
Of the Statute of Virginia for Religious Freedom
Father of the University of Virginia

educational journal was brought out which interpreted for American educators the best results of educational practice in all lands and times, and greatly extended the vision and enlarged the point of view of the American schoolman.

II. Work and Influence of Pestalozzi

The inspiration of Pestalozzi. One of the greatest books of the eighteenth century, the *Émile* of Jean-Jacques Rousseau, a French Swiss by birth then living in Paris, appeared in 1762. In this Rousseau vigorously attacked the formalism of the age in religion, manners, and education. The book described the education of the boy, Émile, by a new plan, that of rejecting the formal teaching of the schools and permitting him to grow up and be educated according to nature. The volume was extensively read, and made a deep impression throughout all Europe, but was particularly influential among the thinkers of Switzerland. Gathering up the current idea of his age that the "state of nature" was the ideal one, and the one in which men had been intended to live; that the organization of society had created inequalities which prevented man from realizing his real self; and that human duty called for a return to the "state of nature," whatever that might be; Rousseau stated them in terms of the education of the boy, Émile. Despite its many exaggerations, much faulty reasoning, and many imperfections, the book had a tremendous influence on Europe in laying bare the defects and abuses of the formal and ecclesiastical education of the time. Though Rousseau's enthusiasm took the form of theory run mad, and the educational plan he proposed was largely impossible, he nevertheless popularized education. He also contributed much to changing the point of view in instruction from subject-matter to the child to be taught, and the nature of instruction from formal religious doctrine, preparatory for life hereafter, to the study of the life and universe amid which man lives here. The iconoclastic nature of Rousseau's volume may be inferred from its opening sentence, where he says: "Everything is good as it comes from the hand of the author of nature; everything degenerates in the hands of man."

Among those most deeply influenced by Rousseau's book was a young German Swiss by the name of Johann Heinrich Pestalozzi, who was born and brought up in Zurich. Inspired by Rousseau's writings, he spent the early part of his life trying to render service to the poor, and the latter part in working out for himself a theory and method of instruction based on the natural development of the child. Trying to educate his own child according to Rousseau's plan, he not only discovered its impracticability but also that the only way to improve on it was to study the children themselves. Accordingly he opened a school and home on his farm at Neuhof, in 1774. Here he took in fifty abandoned children, to whom he taught reading, writing, and arithmetic, gave them moral discourses, and trained them in gardening, farming, and cheese-making. It was an attempt to regenerate beggars by means of education, which Pestalozzi firmly believed could be done. At the end of two years he had spent all the money he and his wife possessed, and the school closed in failure — a blessing in disguise — though with Pestalozzi's faith in the power of education unshaken. Of this experiment he wrote: "For years I have lived in the midst of fifty little beggars, sharing in my poverty my bread with them, living like a beggar myself in order to teach beggars to live like men."

Turning next to writing, while continuing to farm, Pestalozzi now tried to express his faith in education in printed form. His *Leonard and Gertrude* (1781) was a wonderfully beautiful story of Swiss peasant life, and of the genius and sympathy and love of a woman amid degrading surroundings. From a wretched place the village of Bonnal, under Pestalozzi's pen, was transformed by the power of education. The book was a great success from the first, and for it Pestalozzi was made a "citizen" of the French Republic, along with Washington, Madison, Kosciusko, Wilberforce, and Tom Paine. He continued to farm and to think, though nearly starving, until 1798, when the opportunity for which he was really fitted came.

Pestalozzi's educational experiments. In 1798 "The Helvetic Republic" was proclaimed, an event which divided Pestalozzi's life into two parts. Up to this time he had been interested wholly in the philanthropic aspect of education, believing that the poor could be regenerated through education and labor. From this time on he interested himself in the teaching aspect of the problem, in the working out and formulation of a teaching method based on the natural development of the child, and in training others to teach. Much to the disgust of the authorities of the new Swiss Government, citizen Pestalozzi applied for service as a schoolteacher. The opportunity to render such service soon came.

That autumn the French troops invaded Switzerland, and, in putting down the stubborn resistance of the three German cantons, they shot down a large number of the people. Orphans to the number of 169 were left in the little town of Stanz, and citizen Pestalozzi was given charge of them. For six months he was father, mother, teacher, and nurse. Then, worn out himself, the orphanage was changed into a hospital. A little later he became a schoolmaster in Burgdorf; was dismissed; became a teacher in another school; and finally, in 1800, opened a school himself in an old castle there. He provided separate teachers for drawing and singing, geography and history, language and arithmetic, and gymnastics. The year following the school was enlarged into a teachers' training school, the government extending him aid in return for giving Swiss teachers one month of training as teachers in his school. Here he wrote and published *How Gertrude teaches her Children*, which explained his methods and forms his most important pedagogical work; a *Guide for teaching Spelling and Reading;* and a *Book for Mothers*, devoted to a description of "object teaching." In 1805, the castle being needed by the government, Pestalozzi moved to Yverdon, where he opened an Institute, and where the next twenty years of his life were spent and his greatest success achieved.

The contribution of Pestalozzi. The great contribution of Pestalozzi lay in that, following the lead of Rousseau, he rejected the teaching of mere words and facts, which had characterized all elementary education up to near the close of the eighteenth century, and tried instead to reduce the educational process to a well-organized routine, based on the natural and orderly development of the instincts, capacities, and powers of the growing child. Taking Rousseau's idea of a return to nature, he tried to apply it to the education of children. This led to his rejection of what he called the "empty chattering of mere words" and "outward show" in the instruction in reading and the catechism, and the introduction in their place of real studies, based on observation, experimentation, and reasoning. "Sense impression" became his watchword. As he expressed it, he "tried to organize and psychologize the educational process" by harmonizing it with the natural development of the child. To this end he carefully studied children, and developed his methods experimentally as a result of his observation. To such an extreme was this idea carried at Burgdorf and Yverdon that all results of preceding educators and writers were rejected, for fear that error might creep in. Read nothing, discover everything, and prove all things, came to be the working guides of himself and his teachers.

The development of man he believed to be organic, and to proceed according to law. It was the work of the teacher to discover these laws of development and to assist nature in securing "a natural, symmetrical, and harmonious development" of all the "faculties" of the child. Real education must develop the child as a whole — mentally, physically, morally — and called for the training of the head and the hand and the heart. The only proper means for developing the powers of the child was use, and hence education must guide and stimulate self-activity, be based on intuition and exercise, and the sense impressions must be organized and directed. Education, too, if it is to follow the organic development of the child, must observe the proper progress

PESTALOZZI MONUMENT AT YVERDON

A picture of this monument occupies a prominent place in every
schoolroom in Switzerland

PESTALOZZI AT STANZ

of child development and be graded, so that each step of the process shall grow out of the preceding and grow into the following stage. To accomplish these ends the training must be all-round and harmonious; much liberty must be allowed the child in learning; education must proceed largely by doing instead of by words; the method of learning must be largely analytical; real objects and ideas must precede symbols and words; and finally the organization and correlation of what is learned must be looked after by the teacher.

Still more, Pestalozzi possessed a deep and abiding faith, new at the time, in the power of education as a means of regenerating society. He had begun his work by trying to "teach beggars to live like men," and his belief in the potency of education in working this transformation, so touchingly expressed in his *Leonard and Gertrude*, never left him. He believed that each human being could be raised through the influence of education to the level of an intellectually free and morally independent life, and that every human being was entitled to the right to attain such freedom and independence. The way to this lay through the full use of his developing powers, under the guidance of a teacher, and not through a process of repeating words and learning by heart. Not only the intellectual qualities of perception, judgment, and reasoning need exercise, but the moral powers as well. To provide such exercise and direction was the work of the school.

Pestalozzi also resented the brutal discipline which for ages had characterized all school instruction, believed it by its very nature immoral, and tried to substitute for this a strict but loving discipline — a "thinking love," he calls it — and to make the school as nearly as possible like a gentle and refined home. To a Swiss father, who on visiting his school exclaimed, "Why, this is not a school, but a family," Pestalozzi answered that such a statement was the greatest praise he could have given him.

The consequences of these ideas. The educational consequences of these new ideas were very large. They in time gave aim and purpose to the elementary school of the nineteenth century, transforming it from an instrument of the Church for church ends, to an instrument of society to be used for its own regeneration and the advancement of the welfare of all. The introduction of the study of natural objects in place of words, and much talking about what was seen and studied instead of parrot-like reproductions of the words of a book, revolutionized both the methods and the subject-matter of instruction in the developing elementary school. Observation and investigation tended to supersede mere memorizing; class discussion and thinking to supersede the reciting of the words of the book; thinking about what was being done to supersede routine learning; and class instruction to supersede the wasteful individual teaching which had for so long characterized all school work. It meant the reorganization of the work of elementary education on a modern basis, with class organization and group instruction.

The work of Pestalozzi also meant the introduction of new subject-matter for instruction, the organization of new teaching subjects for the elementary school, and the redirection of the elementary education of children. Observation led to the development of elementary-science study, and the study of home geography; talking about what was observed led to the study of language usage, as distinct from the older study of grammar; and counting and measuring led to the study of number, and hence to a new type of primary arithmetic. The reading of the school also changed both in character and purpose. In other words, in place of an elementary education based on reading, a little writing and spelling, and the catechism, all of a memoritor type with religious ends in view, a new primary school, much more secular in character, was created by the work of Pestalozzi. This new school was based on the study of real objects, learning through sense impressions, the individual expression of ideas, child activity, and the development of the child's powers in an orderly way. In fact, "the development of the faculties" of the child became a by-word with Pestalozzi and his followers.

Pestalozzi's deep abiding faith in the power of education to regenerate society was highly influential in Switzerland, throughout Western Europe, and later in America in showing how to deal with orphans, vagrants, and those suffering from physical defects or in need of reformation, by providing for such a combination of intellectual and industrial training.

The spread and influence of Pestalozzi's work. So famous did the work of Pestalozzi become that his schools at Burgdorf and Yverdon came to be "show places," even in a land filled with natural wonders. Observers and students came from all over Europe to see and to teach in his school. In particular the educators of Prussia were attracted by his work, and, earlier than other nations, saw the far-reaching significance of his discoveries. Herbart visited his school as early as 1799, when but a young man of twenty-three, and wrote a very sympathetic description of his new methods. Froebel spent the years 1808 to 1810 as a teacher at Yverdon, when he was a young man of twenty-six to eight. "It soon became evident to me," wrote Froebel, "that 'Pestalozzi' was to be the watchword of my life."

Many Swiss teachers were trained by Pestalozzi, and these spread his work and ideas over Switzerland. Particularly in German Switzerland did his ideas take root and reorganize education. Of his Swiss followers one of the most influential was Emanuel Fellenberg, who, adopting Pestalozzi's idea of combined intellectual and industrial training, developed a combined intellectual and manual-labor school at Hofwyl, near Berne, which he conducted very successfully from 1806 to 1844. By 1829, when his work was first made known to American educators through the articles of William Woodbridge, his school included:

1. A farm of about six hundred acres.
2. Workshops for manufacturing clothing and tools.
3. A printing and lithographing establishment.

4. A literary institution for the education of the well-to-do.

5. A lower school which trained for handicrafts and middle-class occupations.

6. An agricultural school for the education of the poor as farm laborers, and as teachers for the rural schools.

Fellenberg's work was widely copied in Switzerland, Germany, England, and the United States, and contained the germ-idea of both agricultural and reformatory education.

Pestalozzi's ideas in Prussia. It was in Prussia that Pestalozzi's ideas made the deepest impression, and there that they were most successfully transplanted and carried out. As early as 1803 an envoy, sent by the Prussian king, reported favorably on the methods used by Pestalozzi, and in 1804 Pestalozzian methods were authorized for the primary schools of Prussia. In 1807–08, after the severe defeat inflicted on Prussia by Napoleon, the German philosopher Fichte, who had taught in Zurich and knew Pestalozzi, exploited Pestalozzi's work in Berlin, and emphasized the importance of reorganizing the work of the common schools of Prussia, as a phase of the work of national regeneration, along the lines laid down by him. To popular education, Fichte declared, must the nation turn to develop new strength to face the future. As a result the civil service was put on an efficiency basis; the two-class school system, shown in the accompanying drawing, was reorganized and freed from clerical con-

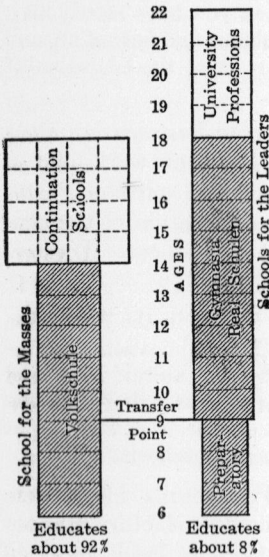

FIG. 51. THE GERMAN STATE SCHOOL SYSTEMS

Compare with Fig. 45, page 235, and note the difference between a European two-class school system and the American democratic educational ladder.

trol; and the basis of the strong military state which set Europe afire in 1914 was laid.

The Prussian Government now sent seventeen teachers to Switzerland to spend three years, at the expense of the Government, in studying Pestalozzi's ideas and methods, and they were particularly enjoined that they were not sent primarily to get the mechanical side of this method, but to

warm yourselves at the sacred fire which burns in the heart of this man, so full of strength and love, whose work has remained so far below what he originally desired, below the essential ideas of his life, of which the method is only a feeble product.

You will have reached perfection when you have clearly seen that education is an art, and the most sublime and holy of all, and in what connection it is with the great art of the education of nations.

On their return these, and others, spread Pestalozzian ideas throughout Prussia, and so effective was their work, and so readily did the Prussian people catch the spirit of Pestalozzi's endeavors, that at the Berlin celebration of the centennial of his birth, in 1846, the German educator Diesterweg said:

By these men and these means, men trained in the Institution at Yverdon under Pestalozzi, the study of his publications, and the applications of his methods in the model and normal schools of Prussia, after 1808, was the present Prussian, or rather Prussian-Pestalozzian school system established, for he is entitled to at least one-half the fame of the German popular schools.

Pestalozzianism in England. Pestalozzi's ideas were also carried to England, but in no such satisfactory manner as to the German States. Where German lands received both the method and the spirit, the English obtained only the form. The introduction into England was due chiefly to the Reverend Charles Mayo and his sister Elizabeth, but England was at that time so deeply immersed in monitorial instruction that the country was not in a frame of mind to profit greatly from the new ideas. Mayo spent the years 1819–22 at Yverdon, when Pestalozzi's institute was in its decline, rent by dissensions, and rapidly approaching its end. On his return to England he opened a private Pestalozzian school for children of the wealthy. His sister shortly afterward published a Pestalozzian manual for teachers, called *Lessons on Objects*, but missed the spirit of Pestalozzi's work. The lessons were formal, scientific, far too detailed and analytical, and much beyond the comprehension of children.

For example, if common salt were the "object" for the lesson, the children would be expected to learn its chemical composition, its uses, how and where found in nature, how mined and refined, that its crystalline form is cubical, that it varies in color from white to bluish and reddish, that it is transparent to translucent, that it is soluble in water and saline in taste, that it imparts a yellow color to a flame, etc., without more contact with a piece of real salt than seeing the "specimen" passed around by the teacher. "Object teaching" soon became the great educational fad in England, and was later brought to the United States. The effect of this instruction was to "formalize" the Pestalozzian movement in England, and in consequence much of the finer spirit and significance of Pestalozzi's work was lost.

The Mayos were prominent in the Infant-School movement, which made such great headway in England after about 1820, and in 1836 they helped organize "The Home and Colonial Infant Society" to spread the idea at home and abroad. This Society adopted the English interpretation of Pestalozzian methods, established a Model Infant School and a Training College for teachers, and had an important influence in introducing the English type of formalized Pestalozzianism into the schools of the United States.

III. Early American Travelers and Official Reports

Early American travelers. Our first contact with the educational thought and practices of continental Europe came through some half-dozen Americans who studied at the Prussian university of Göttingen, then almost unknown outside of German lands, before 1820. Our first contact with the work of Pestalozzi in Switzerland came through Joseph Naef, one of Pestalozzi's teachers, who came to America and taught a private school in Philadelphia for a time between 1806 and 1809, and who later wandered westward and for a short time taught in a little communistic colony at New Harmony, Indiana. So little had been done, though, in developing public education with us before 1810, south of New England and New York, that Naef's work remained almost unknown, while those who had studied at Göttingen influenced educational development, even in the colleges of the time, but very little.

Our first real contact with continental European ideas and accomplishments in education came in 1819, through the publication in this country of *A Year in Europe*, written by Professor John Griscom, of New York, who had spent the year 1818–19 in visiting the schools, colleges, and charitable institutions of Great Britain, Holland, France, Switzerland, and Italy. His description of his visit to Pestalozzi awakened some interest, and his volume was read by the leading thinkers of the day. Our city and state school systems, though, were as yet hardly under way, Lancastrianism was at its height, and Griscom's work influenced our common-school development scarcely at all. Griscom's description of the high school at Edinburgh, though, probably gave the name to the new school at Boston (p. 190) and to the American secondary school as well.

The chief influence of the book proved to be along the lines of reformatory and charitable education, in which we were just making a beginning. Griscom told what had been done along these lines in Europe. This information was welcomed by the few Americans interested in such development and came as a valuable contribution at the time.

Another early American traveler was William C. Woodbridge, of New England, who spent the year 1820 and the years 1825–29 in Europe. It was he who, through his enthusiastic "Letters," published in Russell's *American Journal of Education,* and elsewhere, first really brought the work of the Swiss reformers — Pestalozzi and Fellenberg — to the attention of American teachers. After his return he published two textbooks on geography (1824, 1833), based on Pestalozzian methods, and it was he who inspired Lowell Mason to offer his services, in 1836, to introduce music into the schools of Boston. This was probably the first teaching of music in the schools of the United States, so successful with us up to that time had been the Calvinistic idea of the repression as irreligious of all joyful and artistic instincts. Even this start was a failure, and it was a quarter of a century later before music and drawing became generally recognized as subjects of study, even in the better city schools.

Cousin's Report on German education. The first document describing European schools which made any deep impression on those then engaged in organizing our American state school systems was an English translation of the famous *Report on the Condition of Public Instruction in Germany, and particularly Prussia,* made to the French Government by Victor Cousin, in 1831 and publicly printed the next year. This *Report* was reprinted in England, in 1834, and the first half of it, explaining the administrative organization of Prussian education and the Prussian system of people's schools, was reprinted in New York City, in 1835.

After the overthrow of the old restored monarchy in France, in 1830, a new government was set up, supported by the leading thinkers of the time. One of the most important measures to which attention was at once turned was the creation of a state school system for France. Cousin was sent to Prussia to study what was then the best state school system in Europe, and so convincing was his *Report* that, despite bitter national antipathies, it carried conviction throughout France and was deeply influential in securing the creation of the first French national schools, in 1833. The church control of the school committees was broken, the examination of teachers was required, thirty new normal schools to train teachers were established, state aid for primary and infant schools was provided, freedom of religious instruction was guaranteed, recommendation was changed to obligation, and both state and local supervision were instituted. The modern state school system of France dates from the Law of 1833, and this from Cousin's *Report*.

Influence of Cousin's Report in the United States. The translation of Cousin's *Report* into English and the publication of half of it in the United States came just as our new state school systems were beginning to take form, and just as the battle for state control was in full swing. Its convincing description of the strong Prussian state school organization, under a state minister, and with state control over so many matters, was everywhere of value in this country. It gave support to the demands of the few leaders of the time who were struggling to reduce the rampant district system to some semblance of order, and who were trying to organize the thousands of little community school systems in each State into one state school system, under some form of centralized control. Though actually influencing legislation in but one or two of our States, the two main ideas gained from it were the importance of some form of centralized state control, and the training of teachers in state normal schools. These influences were evident chiefly in Michigan and Massachusetts.

The publication of the *Report* came just as Michigan was organizing to enter the Union as a State, and two leaders there — John D. Pierce, a minister who became the first head of the state school system, and General Isaac E. Crary, chairman of the committee on education in the constitutional convention — obtained a copy of it and were deeply impressed by Cousin's statements. They discussed together "the fundamental principles which were deemed important for the convention to adopt," and it was agreed by them that education "should be made a distinct branch of the government, and that the constitution ought to provide for an officer who should have the whole matter in charge and thus keep its importance perpetually before the public mind."

Largely as a result of their efforts Michigan was the first State to take the 16th section school lands, given by the National Government for schools, from the control of the townships and place them under the control of the State, and likewise the first State to create the appointive office (a pure Prussian imitation) of State Superintendent of Public Instruction. The first constitution also made very definite provision for a state system of schools and a state university.

A later superintendent of public instruction in Michigan, writing in 1852 on the history of the system, said that "the system of public instruction which was intended to be established by the framers of the constitution, the conception of the office, its province, its powers, and duties were derived from Prussia." That Cousin's *Report* influenced the class-organization or class-work of the Michigan schools, or the schools of any other State for that matter, is a contention recently advanced which the facts scarcely warrant.

In Massachusetts the *Report* came just in time to give useful support to Brooks, Carter, Mann, and the few others interested who were trying there to secure the establishment of the first American state normal school. The normal-school idea in America, though, as we shall point out a little later, was of native American growth, and had clearly taken form before Prussian normal schools were known of in this country. The descriptions of the Prussian training schools for teachers only awakened a new support and helped along more rapidly a movement which was then well under way as a purely native development.

Stowe's Report on Elementary Education in Europe. In 1829 there was formed at Cincinnati the "Western Academic Institute and Board of Education," and for a decade this was practically the only active organization for education in the State of Ohio. It was a private propaganda organization, and included in its membership such men as Lyman Beecher, Samuel Lewis, and Professor Calvin E. Stowe. Money was raised, an agent (Lewis) was sent to visit the schools of the State, reports as to conditions were prepared, and delegations were sent to the legislature to urge action. When Professor Stowe started for Europe, in 1836, to buy a library for the Lane Theological Seminary, with which he was connected, the "Institute" induced the legislature of Ohio to commission him to examine and report on the systems of elementary instruction found there. The result was his celebrated *Report on Elementary Education in Europe*, made to the legislature in 1837.

This was the first report on European educational conditions by an American which attracted general attention. In it he contrasted educational conditions in Ohio with those of Prussia and Würtemberg, with particular reference to the organization and thoroughness of the instruction, and the maintenance of institutions for imparting to prospective teachers some knowledge of the science and art of teaching. The meager legal requirements in Ohio of instruction in reading and writing and arithmetic, with school trustees frequently forbidding instruction in any higher branches; the untrained and poorly educated teachers, and the absence in the State of any means of training teachers; he contrasted with the enriched elementary-school curriculum, the Pestalozzian methods, and the well-informed and trained teachers of Prussia and Würtemberg. The *Report* commanded the admiration of legislators and educators, was widely read, and "not a little of the advancement in common schools," says Barnard, "during the next twenty years may be traced to this Report." The legislature of Ohio ordered ten thousand copies of it printed, and a copy sent to every school district in the State. It was later ordered reprinted and circulated by vote of the legislatures of Pennsylvania, Massachusetts, Michigan, North Carolina, and Virginia.

In his summary Professor Stowe said:

But perhaps some will be ready to say, "The scheme is indeed an excellent one, provided only it were practicable; but the idea of introducing so extensive and complete a course of study into our common schools is entirely visionary, and can never be realized."

I answer, that it is no theory that I have been exhibiting, but a matter of fact, a copy of actual practice. The above system is no visionary scheme, emanating from the closet of a recluse, but a sketch of the course of instruction now actually pursued by thousands of schoolmasters, in the best district schools that have ever been organized. It can be done; for it has been done — it is now done: and it ought to be done. If it can be done in Europe, I believe it can be done in the United States: if it can be done in Prussia, I know it can be done in Ohio.

To show how much influence this *Report* had with legislatures in Ohio it might be added that it was not until 1848 that grammar and geography were added to the narrow elementary-school curriculum, not until 1853 that the rate-bill was abandoned and the schools made free, and almost three quarters of a century before the first state normal school was established by the State.

Barnard, Bache, and Dr. Julius. In the years 1835-37 Henry Barnard visited the schools of the different countries of Europe, and from this visit dates his interest in introducing into our state school systems the best of European organization and practices, — an interest he retained all his active life. He made no special report at the time of his visit, but through the pages of the educational journals which he edited, for the next forty years, he continued to set before his readers interesting descriptions of educational organization and practices in other states and lands. He also gathered together the important parts of all these reports and issued them in book form, in 1854, under the title *National Education in Europe*.

In 1836 the trustees of the newly founded Girard College, at Philadelphia, an institution for the education of orphans, sent Professor A. D. Bache "to visit all establishments in Europe resembling Girard College." On his return, in 1839, his *Report on Education in Europe* was printed. In this he devoted about two hundred pages to an enthusiastic description of Pestalozzian methods as he had seen them in the schools of Holland, and also described the German *Gymnasium*.

In 1835 a Dr. H. Julius, of Hamburg, crossed the ocean with the Reverend Charles Brooks, of Hingham, Massachusetts, and during the forty-one days of the passage from Liverpool to New York, described to him the Prussian system of elementary schools. Through Brooks's efforts Dr. Julius was invited to give an account of the Prussian system of education before the committee on education of the Massachusetts legislature, but "his delineations, though clear and judicious, were so brief as led to no action." What he had to say was printed by the State, and later on reprinted by New York State. There is no evidence that what Dr. Julius said had much influence, except with the Reverend Mr. Brooks, but upon him the Prussian idea of institutions for training teachers made a deep impression, as we shall see a little further on.

Mann's Famous Seventh Report. In 1843 Horace Mann spent some months visiting schools in Great Britain, Belgium, Holland, the German States, and France, and on his return devoted his *Seventh Report* (1843) to a description and appraisal of what he had seen, but with particular reference to the studies taught, classification of pupils, methods of teaching, teachers, discipline, and the training of teachers. Of this Report Hinsdale writes:

Read half a century after it was written, the *Seventh Report* impresses the reader as being the work of an open-minded man, who is making a hurried examination of educational institutions that were before known to him only at second hand. The matter is copious; facts and ideas fairly crowd the pages. The writer is evidently anxious to discover and report the exact truth. He wants to show his countrymen the schools just as he sees them. He has no prejudices against things that are foreign. The writer not only has a first-hand interest in the subject, but is also conscious that he is writing things new and strange to his audience. . . . We are so familiar with these things now that we may wonder at Mr. Mann's enthusiasm over them; but we must remember that a half century has wrought great changes in American schools, changes that in some measure have grown out of the very document we are reading.

Mr. Mann ranked the schools of the different countries
he visited in the following order: Prussia, Saxony, the western and southern German states, Holland, Scotland, Ireland,
France, Belgium, and, lowest of all, England.   The lack of
a national system of education in England, in which the
whole people participated, he felt was full of admonition to
the people of Massachusetts, as it was a condition toward
which they were drifting before the work of Carter and the
organization of the State Board of Education.   The schools
of the German States, with their Pestalozzian methods and
subject-matter, trained and well-informed teachers, oral instruction, mild discipline, class organization, normal schools
for teachers, and intelligent supervision, particularly won
his enthusiastic approval. "There are many things abroad
which we at home should do well to imitate," he wrote,
"things, some of which are here as yet matters of specula-
tion and theory, but which, there, have long been in operation and are now producing a harvest of rich and abundant
blessings."

His controversy with the Boston schoolmasters.   This
Report might have exerted no greater influence than other
previous *Reports*, and possibly even less, had it not been the
last straw to the Boston school principals, many of whom
had appropriated to themselves the Secretary's previous
sharp criticism of school conditions in Massachusetts. There
had been no comparisons made in the *Report* between the
schools of Massachusetts and those of Prussia and Saxony,
or of Boston with Hamburg or Dresden, but the Boston masters, many of whom shared the opposition that the creation of the State Board of Education had awakened, and
stung by such expressions in the *Report* as "ignorance of
teachers," and "sleepy supervision," felt called upon to attack the *Report* in a very personal and offensive manner. A
committee of the Principals' Association accordingly issued
a book of 144 pages, attacking and replying to the *Report* of
Mr. Mann.   Two months later Mr. Mann replied, in a
volume of 176 pages, in which he not only vindicated him-

self and what he had written, and pointed out the difficulties with which he had to contend arising from unintelligent
criticism, but, feeling that the attack on him had been un-
provoked and uncalled for, he retaliated on his assailants
with terrible severity. Though he objected to severe punishment for children, he apparently had no objection to giving a sound drubbing to a body of schoolmasters. Part of
the masters later replied to Mr. Mann's reply, and he again
responded to them in kind. This ended the controversy,
public opinion being too thoroughly against the schoolmasters to warrant its further continuance.

The result of this unexpected public debate was to attract very much more attention to Mr. Mann's *Seventh
Report* than would otherwise have been given to it, to fix the
attention of the public generally on the need for educational
improvement, and to add to Mr. Mann's importance in the
history of American education. In particular it gave support to the recently established normal schools, and to the
efforts of a few to improve instruction by the adoption of a
better classification of pupils and Pestalozzian methods and
subject-matter. The result was that Mr. Mann's report on
European school practices proved to be the most influential
of all the *Reports* on education in Europe.

The Fellenberg manual-labor movement. The one European idea which we did adopt almost bodily, because we
had no previous development of the kind, and because we
found it so well suited to early democratic conditions among
a people of little wealth, was the Pestalozzian idea, worked
out by Fellenberg and his followers at Hofwyl, in Switzerland, of combining manual labor with schooling. Early in
our national history the interest in farming was strong, the
first farmers' journals were established, and there soon arose
a demand for special schools for farmers' sons. The advantages, both pecuniary and educational, of combining schooling and farming made a strong appeal in the days when
money was scarce and opportunities limited, and such
schools, drawing their inspiration from the very successful

school of Fellenberg, were founded first in Connecticut, in 1819; Maine in 1821; Massachusetts in 1824; New York in 1827; and New Jersey in 1830. The purpose in each was to unite training in agriculture with the studies of the school, and thus give to farmers' boys a double type of training. The idea was soon extended to the rapidly rising mechanical pursuits, and manual-labor institutions of a mechanical type also arose. The Oneida School of Science and Industry, the Genesee Manual-Labor School, the Aurora Manual-Labor Seminary, and the Rensselaer School, all in New York, were among the most important of these early institutions. The Andover Theological Seminary also adopted the plan, and by 1835 the manual-labor-school idea had been tried in a dozen States, extending from Maine to Illinois. Many of the institutions thus founded became colleges later on, as for example the Indiana Baptist Manual-Labor Institute, which later became Franklin College; the Wabash Manual-Labor Seminary, in Indiana, which later became Wabash College; and the Knox Manual-Labor College, in Illinois, which later became Knox College. In 1831 the short-lived "Manual Labor Society for Promoting Manual Labor in Literary Institutions" was formed in New York to promote the idea. This Society also added gymnastics to its program, and the early recognition of the value of physical training in the schools of the United States is in part due to the interest awakened in it by the work of this Society. In 1833 the governor of Indiana recommended to the legislature the establishment of manual-labor academies to train teachers for the schools of the State, and in 1836 a resolution was offered in the United States Senate proposing "a grant of public lands to one or more colleges in each of the new States for educating the poor upon the manual-labor system."

The manual-labor idea, however, was short-lived in this country. The rise of cities and wealth and social classes was against the idea, and the opening up of cheap and rich farms to the westward, with the change of the East from agriculture to manufacturing, turned the agricultural aspect of the movement aside for a generation. When it reappeared again in the Central West it came in the form of a new demand for colleges to teach agriculture and mechanic arts, but with the manual-labor idea omitted.

General result of these foreign influences. The general result of these various observations by travelers and official *Reports*, extending over nearly a quarter of a century in time; and the work of the newer educational journals, particularly the publication work of Henry Barnard; was to give to American educators some knowledge of different and better school organizations elsewhere. In particular they gave strong support to the movement, already well under way, to organize the many local school systems into state school systems, subjecting them to state oversight and control; further stimulated the movement, already well begun, to grade and classify the schools in a more satisfactory manner; helped to inaugurate a movement for the introduction of Pestalozzian methods to replace the wasteful individual and the mechanical Lancastrian plans which had for so long been in use; and gave material assistance to the few leaders in Massachusetts and New York who were urging the establishment by the State of professional training for teachers for the educational service. The distinctively state school organization provided for in the Michigan constitution of 1835, and the creation of the first state normal schools in the United States in Massachusetts, in 1838, are in part directly traceable to the influence of German practice, as described in these Reports. The one idea we for a time tried to copy and adapt to our needs was the Fellenberg manual-labor school for combining instruction in agriculture with the study of books. The later introduction of a form of Pestalozzian procedure into our normal schools and city school systems, and later into all our schools, to which we next turn, also is traceable in part to the interest awakened in better classroom practice by the descriptions of Pestalozzian instruction in other lands.

That we at this time adopted the German *Volkschule*, as has recently been asserted, an examination of the evidence will show was hardly the case. Not only did we not adopt its curriculum, or spirit, or method of instruction, but we did not adopt even its graded system. The *Volkschule* is a definite eight-year school, while we worked out and have ever since retained seven-year, eight-year, and nine-year elementary schools, in different parts of the United States. That the elementary school we developed was in general an eight-year school, as in the German *Volkschule*, was due to the school age of children and to a perfectly natural native development, rather than to any copying of foreign models. The great thing we got from the study of Prussian schools was not a borrowing or imitation of any part or feature — our own development had been proceeding naturally and steadily toward the lines we eventually followed, long before we knew of Prussian work — but rather a marked stimulus to a further and faster development along lines which were already well under way.

QUESTIONS FOR DISCUSSION

1. Explain why we remained isolated educationally for so long.
2. Is there any evidence that the common tendency of new democracies to reject world experience and knowledge influenced us also?
3. State the essential defects in the educational plan of Rousseau.
4. State the change in the nature of the instruction from that of the church schools to that of Pestalozzi.
5. Compare Pestalozzi's ideas as to child development with modern ideas.
6. Explain the educational significance of "self-activity," "sense impression," and "harmonious development."
7. How far was Pestalozzi right as to the power of education to give men intellectual and moral freedom?
8. What do you understand Pestalozzi to have meant by "the development of the faculties"?
9. State how the work of Pestalozzi was important in showing the world how to deal with orphans and defectives.
10. Show how the germs of agricultural and technical education lay in the work of Fellenberg.
11. Contrast the German and the American school systems, as shown in the figures on pages 235 and 268.

12. How do you explain the fact that the Germans got the spirit of Pestalozzi's work so much better than did the English?
13. Show why Naef influenced American development so little.
14. Point out the Prussian influences and characteristics in the early organization of education in Michigan.
15. How do you explain the failure of Stowe's report to exert a greater influence on practice in Ohio?
16. How do you explain our failure to take up Pestalozzian ideas in instruction more rapidly?
17. Explain the reasons for the popularity of the manual-labor idea, about 1825, and its failure to maintain this popularity.

TOPICS FOR INVESTIGATION AND REPORT

1. Character of early educational journalism.
2. Influence of the ideas of Rousseau.
3. The educational contributions of Pestalozzi.
4. Fellenberg's school at Hofwyl. (Barnard.)
5. *Leonard and Gertrude.* Read and characterize.
6. The English system of Object Teaching.
7. The Manual Labor idea in the United States. (Anderson; Barnard; Monroe.)
8. Mr. Mann's *Seventh Report.*
9. Stowe's *Report on Education in Europe.*
10. Pestalozzi Institute at Yverdon.

SELECTED REFERENCES

*Anderson, L. F. "The Manual Labor School Movement"; in *Educational Review*, vol. 46; pp. 369–88. (Nov., 1913.)

A very good historical article on the Fellenberg movement in the United States.

Barnard, Henry, Editor. *The American Journal of Education.* 31 vols. Consult *Analytical Index* to; 128 pp. Published by United States Bureau of Education, Washington, 1892.

*Barnard, Henry. *National Education in Europe, 1854.* C. W. Bardeen, Syracuse.

Reprints of extracts from many of the early Reports.

*Barnard, Henry. *Pestalozzi and his Educational System.* 745 pp. C. W. Bardeen, Syracuse, 1906.

His life, educational principles, and methods, with sketches of several of his assistants. A standard volume of source material regarding the work of Pestalozzi and the Pestalozzian movement, both in Europe and America.

Griscom, John. "Fellenberg and Hofwyl"; in *Barnard's Journal*, vol. 31, pp. 269–80.

An extract from Griscom's *Year in Europe*.

*Guimps, Roger de. *Pestalozzi; his Aim and Work.* 320 pp. C. W. Bardeen, Syracuse, 1894.

> A standard biography, written in a very interesting style, and from the personal point of view.

*Hinsdale, B. A. "Notes on the History of Foreign Influence upon Education in the United States"; in *Report of the United States Commissioner of Education*, 1897–98, vol. I, pp. 591–629.

> Very good on English, French, and German influence, and contains much valuable material.

*Holman, H. *Pestalozzi, his Life and Work.* Longmans, Green & Co., New York, 1908.

> A very useful volume for the general student.

*Krüsi, Hermann, Jr. *Life and Work of Pestalozzi.* 248 pp. American Book Co., Cincinnati, 1875.

> A valuable work, by the Oswego teacher.

*Monroe, Paul. *Cyclopedia of Education.* The Macmillan Co., New York, 1911–13.

> The following articles are specially important:
> 1. "Fellenberg, P. E."; vol. II, pp. 590–91.
> 2. "Pestalozzi, J. H."; vol. IV, pp. 655–59.

*Parker, S. C. *History of Modern Elementary Education.* 506 pp. Ginn & Co., Boston, 1912.

> Chapter XIII is very good on the Pestalozzian movement in Europe and America, and Chapter XIV on Pestalozzian industrial education for juvenile reform.

*Pestalozzi, J. H. *Leonard and Gertrude.* Translated and abridged by Eva Channing. 181 pp. D. C. Heath Co., Boston, 1888.

> A charming story; one which every teacher ought to read.

Pestalozzi, J. H. *How Gertrude teaches her Children.* 256 pp. C. W. Bardeen, Syracuse, 1894.

> This volume contains the essentials of Pestalozzi's ideas and methods, and shows how his methods were developed. Written in a somewhat uninteresting style.

Pine, John. "The Origin of the University of the State of New York"; in *Educational Review*, vol. 37, pp. 284–92. (March, 1909.)

Pinloche, A. *Pestalozzi and the Foundation of the Modern Elementary School.* 306 pp. Chas. Scribner's Sons, New York, 1901.

> A rather technical evaluation of his work and influence.

* Quick, R. H. *Essays on Educational Reformers.* 566 pp. 2d revised edition. D. Appleton & Co., New York, 1890.

> Contains a very well-written chapter on Pestalozzi and his ideas.

Snedden, D. S. *American Juvenile Reform Schools.* 206 pp. Teachers College Contributions to Education, No. 12, New York, 1907.

> Contains a brief historical statement, and an excellent account of recent tendencies.

CHAPTER X

THE REORGANIZATION OF ELEMENTARY EDUCATION

I. The Rise of the Normal School

Beginnings of the teacher-training idea. The first training class for teachers organized in the world was a small local school organized by Father Démia, at Lyons, France, in 1672. Stimulated into activity by the results of the Protestant Revolt, he had begun schools in his parish to teach reading and the catechism to the children of his parishioners. Not being satisfied with the volunteer teachers he could obtain, he organized them into a class that he might impart to them the ideas he had as to teaching. The first real normal school was that founded at Rheims, France, in 1685, by Abbé de la Salle, to educate and train teachers for the schools of the order he had founded — "The Brothers of the Christian Schools" — to give free religious primary education to the children of the working classes of France. He later founded a second school of the kind in Paris, and called each institution a "Seminary for Schoolmasters." In addition to imparting a general education of the type of the time and a thorough grounding in religion, his student teachers were trained to teach in practice-schools, under the direction of experienced teachers.

The beginning of teacher-training in German lands was Francke's *Seminarium Præceptorum*, established at Halle, Prussia, in 1697. In 1738 Julius Hecker, one of Francke's teachers, established the first regular seminary for teachers in Prussia, and in 1748 he established a private *Lehrerseminar* in Berlin. In these two institutions he first showed the German people the possibilities of special training for teachers. It was not, however, until 1819 that the Prussian Government established normal schools to train teachers for its elementary or peoples' schools.

In 1808, as a part of the reorganization of higher education in France by Napoleon, the *École Normale Supérieure*
(higher normal school) of France was created, and between
1831 and 1833 thirty new normal schools were established
by the new French government.   Pestalozzi had trained
teachers in his methods of instruction at Burgdorf and Yverdon, from 1800 to 1825, but the Swiss did little with the idea
until later.   Both the Lancastrian and the Bell monitorial
systems of education in England, which developed about the
beginning of the nineteenth century, had trained their monitors for teachers, but the first "Training College" for teachers in England dates from 1835.

Of all this development, excepting the work of Pestalozzi, we in America were ignorant until about 1835.   By
that time we were so well on the way toward the creation
of native American training schools that the knowledge
of what Prussia and France had done, which came in then
through the Reports of Cousin, Julius, and Stowe, merely
stimulated a few enthusiastic workers to help carry more
rapidly into effect the establishment of the first training
schools for American teachers.

The Independent American development.   As early as
the founding of Franklin's *Academy* at Philadelphia (p. 185)
in 1756, one of the purposes specified in its establishment
was "that others of the lesser sort might be trained as
teachers."   In an article in the *Massachusetts Magazine*, for
June, 1789, on "The Importance of Studying the English
Language Grammatically," the author recommends the
establishment of institutions to prepare "young gentle-
men for schoolkeeping."   In a commencement address at
Yale College, in 1816, on "The State of Education in Connecticut," by Denison Olmstead, a plan for "an academy
for schoolmasters" was outlined and urged, to prepare in-
tending teachers for "the organization and government of
a school."   In 1823 two papers appeared, one by William
Russell, urging the establishment of such schools, and in
1825 two more, and to these four papers Mr. Barnard traces

much of the early interest in teacher training in the United States. As early as 1820 Mr. James G. Carter (p. 164), often called the "Father of the Massachusetts School System and of Normal Schools," published a pamphlet in which he suggested an "institution for the training of teachers," and during 1824–25 he published numerous newspaper articles and public appeals for the establishment of such an institution. In 1827 he showed his faith in such schools by opening one himself, at Lancaster, Massachusetts, and petitioning the legislature of the State for aid. This was probably the second school of its kind in America.

From this time on many articles, widely scattered in place of publication, appeared urging that something be done by the States in the matter. The demand which now arose for teacher-training institutions was only another phase of the new democratic movement throughout the country, which was calling for both votes and schools. The general enlightenment of the people having been conceived as essential to the protection and preservation of republican institutions, it was important, as Governor Clinton expressed it, that the "mind and morals of the rising and perhaps the destinies of all future generations, be not entrusted to the guardianship of incompetence."

Our first teacher-training school. The first teacher-training school in America was established privately, in 1823, by the Reverend Samuel R. Hall, who opened a tuition school for training teachers at Concord, Vermont. This he continued there until 1830; at Andover, Massachusetts, until 1837; and at Plymouth, New Hampshire, until 1840. He offered a three-years' course, based on a common-school education, which reviewed the common-school branches; studied much mathematics, some book chemistry and natural philosophy, logic, astronomy, evidences of Christianity, moral and intellectual philosophy; and, in the third term of the third year, took up a new study which he called the "Art of Teaching." Practice teaching was obtained by teaching during the winter in the rural schools. It was the typical academy training of the time, with the Art of Teaching added. Without a professional book to guide him, and relying only on his experience in teaching, Hall tried to tell his pupils how to organize and manage a school. To make clear his ideas he wrote out a series of *Lectures on School-keeping*, which some friends induced him to publish. This appeared in 1829, and was the first professional book in English issued in America. It was a success from the first, illustrating the rising professional interest of the time. The acting superintendent of common schools of New York ordered ten thousand copies of it for distribution throughout the State, and a committee on education in Kentucky recommended that the same be done for that State.

The academies begin teacher-training. The Lancastrian higher schools in New York and elsewhere had, by 1810, evolved classes for educating monitors as teachers, and Governor Clinton, in 1826, recommended to the legislature of New York the establishment by the State of "a seminary for the education of teachers in the monitorial system of instruction." In 1827, he recommended the creation of "a central school in each county for the education of teachers." Again, in 1828, he recommended the establishment of county monitorial high schools, "a measure so well calculated to raise the character of our schoolmasters and to double the power of our artisans by giving them a scientific education."

Still earlier (1821) the Board of Regents of the State of New York had declared that it was to the academies of the State "that we must look for a supply of teachers for the common school," and the committee of the legislature, to whom Governor Clinton's recommendations had been referred, thought as had the Regents. The result was the New York law of 1827, appropriating state aid to the academies "to promote the education of teachers." In the *Annual Report* of the Regents for 1828 we find the statement that

the academies have become, in the opinion of the Regents, what it has always been desirable they should be, fit Seminaries for imparting instruction in the higher branches of English education, and especially for qualifying teachers of Common Schools.

In the *Report* for 1831 two academies report "Principles of Teaching" as a new subject of study, and by 1835 five were offering instruction in this new subject. In 1834 the New York Legislature enacted "the first law in this country making provision for the professional education of teachers for common schools." After providing for state aid to one academy in each of the eight judicial districts of the State, the law reads:

> The trustees of academies to which any distribution of money shall be made by virtue of this act shall cause the same to be expended in educating teachers of common schools in such manner and under such regulations as said Regents shall prescribe.

Excepting the Lancastrian monitorial schools, and the private schools of Hall and Carter, this was the first form of the normal school idea in the United States. In this form the training of teachers was continued in New York State until the establishment of the first State Normal School, at Albany, in 1844, with David Page as principal. In 1849 teacher-training in the academies was reëstablished, and still exists in the high schools of the State.

The training of teachers in the academies now became common everywhere. Among the older and more important ones, Phillips Andover, for example, introduced an English course primarily to train teachers, and many other New England academies did the same. To the south and westward many academies also added instruction intended for teachers, and several offered instruction for teachers on the manual-labor part-time plan. In Indiana, Governor Noble, in 1833, recommended to the legislature, "that seminaries be fitted to instruct and prepare teachers," and suggested that state aid be granted to one or more such institutions "for the preparation of young men as teachers for the township schools on the manual labor system."

The training offered was almost entirely academic, as it

was also in the first state normal schools as well, there being as yet no professional body of knowledge to teach. There was as yet no organized psychology; child study had not been thought of; and there was no organized history of education, applied psychology, philosophy of education, or methodology of instruction. Principles of teaching and school management, taught by lectures and almost entirely out of the personal experience of the principal of the school, was about all of professional instruction there was to give. This constituted one study, and the remainder of the time was given to reviews of the common-school subjects and to advanced academic studies.

Our first state normal schools. The publication of the Reports by Cousin (1835) and Stowe (1837), with their descriptions of the teacher-training seminaries of Prussia, together with the contact of Dr. Julius and the Reverend Charles Brooks (1845), united to give valuable support to the efforts of Carter, Mann, and a few others in Massachusetts who were laboring to inaugurate such schools there. Carter, in particular, had been at work on the idea for a decade and a half, and on his election to the legislature, in 1835, he began a campaign that resulted in the creation of the State Board of Education in 1837, and the first American state normal schools in 1838. Though the law gave no name to these new institutions, they soon settled down to that of Normal Schools — a distinctively French term.

While Carter worked with the legislature, Brooks worked with the people, traveling over two thousand miles in his chaise and at his own expense throughout Massachusetts, during the years 1835–38, explaining the Prussian system of teacher-training and the Massachusetts need for such, and everywhere awakening interest in the idea by his enthusiastic portrayal. Finally a citizen of Boston, Mr. Edmund Dwight, authorized Mr. Mann to say to the legislature that he would personally give $10,000 for the project, if the State of Massachusetts would give a similar amount. A bill to this effect was put through by Carter, then chairman

REV. SAMUEL R. HALL
(1795–1877)
Principal of the First Private
Normal School
Concord, Vt.

CYRUS PIERCE
(1790–1860)
Principal of the First American
State Normal School
Lexington, Mass.

THE FIRST NORMAL SCHOOL PRINCIPALS IN THE UNITED STATES

REV. CHARLES BROOKS
(1795–1872)
Prominent in the establishment
of the First Normal Schools

of the committee on education in the State Senate, and the new State Board of Education was authorized to expend the money "in qualifying teachers for the common schools of Massachusetts." No schools were created and no plans were laid down, everything being left to Mr. Mann and the Board to decide. After mature deliberation it was determined not to follow the New York plan of aiding academies, but instead to create special state schools for the purpose, as had been done in France and in German lands.

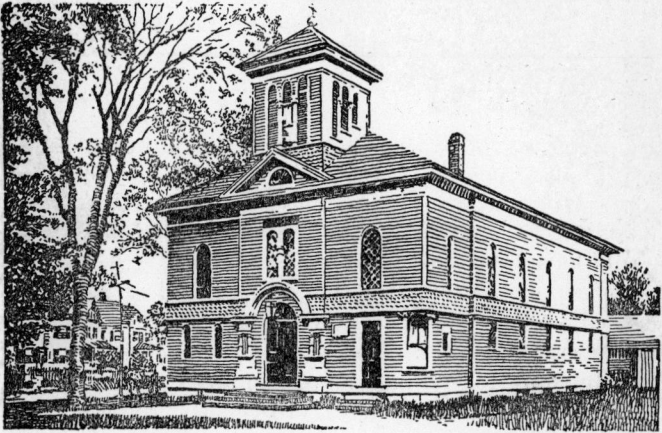

FIG. 52. WHERE THE FIRST STATE NORMAL SCHOOL IN AMERICA OPENED

On July 3, 1839, the first state normal school in the United States was opened in the town hall at Lexington, Massachusetts, with one instructor and three students. At the close of the first quarter there were but twelve students, and at the end of three years but thirty-one. The course of instruction was one year in length, but could be extended to two years. It was much the same as Hall's earlier one, but the distinctive feature of the school was the addition of a Model School, in which the students observed and taught.

The opening of this first school was not particularly aus-

picious. Few knew what such a school was to be. Many
teachers regarded its creation as derogatory to them. Many
academies did not especially welcome its competition. Not
a note of congratulation welcomed the new principal to his
post. Only a few zealots in the cause of reform looked upon
its opening with favor. Much depended on the new principal, and of him Horace Mann later wrote: "Had it not
been for Mr. Cyrus Pierce, I consider that the cause of normal schools would have failed, or have been postponed for
an indefinite period." As it was the new schools had to
weather legislative storms for a decade before they became
firmly established as parts of the school system of the State.
It is indeed fortunate that this new institution was created
and its period of trial carried through in Massachusetts,
under the care of so able an advocate and protector as Mr.
Mann. Massachusetts was without doubt the only State
in the Union where state normal schools could have been
established at so early a date, or where, if established, they
would have been allowed to remain.

On September 5th, 1839, the State Board of Education
opened another normal school at Barre, and the third at
Bridgewater, in 1840. Speaking at the dedication of the
first building for normal school purposes erected in the
United States, at Bridgewater, in 1846, Mr. Mann revealed

FIG. 53. THE FIRST STATE NORMAL SCHOOL BUILDING IN AMERICA
At Bridgewater, Massachusetts. Dedicated by Horace Mann, in 1846.

the deep interest he felt in the establishment of normal schools, in the following words:

> I believe the Normal schools to be a new instrumentality in the advancement of the race. I believe that without them free schools themselves would be shorn of their strength and their healing power, and would at length become mere charity schools, and thus die out in fact and in form. Neither the art of printing, nor the trial by jury, nor a free press, nor free suffrage, can long exist to any beneficial and salutary purpose without schools for the training of teachers; for if the character and qualifications of teachers be allowed to degenerate, the free schools will become pauper schools, and the pauper schools will produce pauper souls, and the free press will become a false and licentious press, and ignorant voters will become venal voters, and through the medium and guise of republican forms an oligarchy of profligate and flagitious men will govern the land; nay, the universal diffusion and ultimate triumph of all-glorious Christianity itself must await the time when knowledge shall be diffused among men through the instrumentality of good schools. Coiled up in this institution, as in a spring, there is a vigor whose uncoiling may wheel the spheres.

Further development and change in character. The States which established normal schools, before 1860, and their order of establishment were:

1839. Massachusetts (1st).	1854. Massachusetts (4th).
1839. Massachusetts (2d).	1854. Rhode Island.
1840. Massachusetts (3d).	1855. New Jersey.
1844. New York.	1857. Illinois.
1849. Connecticut.	1859. Pennsylvania.
1849. Michigan.	1860. Minnesota.

The year 1860 thus found the United States with twelve state normal schools, in nine States (see map, p. 242), and six private schools organized for the same purpose. By 1865 the number had increased to twenty state schools, and thereafter, for reasons which we will next describe, the development of both public and private normal schools was rapid. Their development, compared with the growth of the United States, is shown in the figure on the following page. Teacher-

training also changed markedly in character, after about
1860, with the rise of a new methodology of instruction,
which we shall next describe.

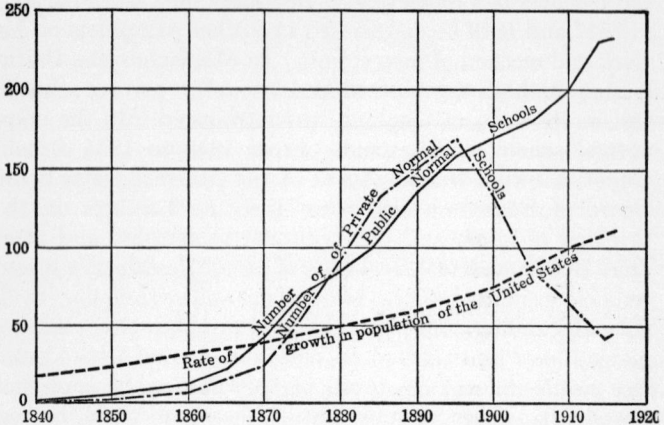

FIG. 54. GROWTH OF PUBLIC AND PRIVATE NORMAL SCHOOLS IN THE
UNITED STATES

High-school training classes not included.

II. THE INTRODUCTION OF PESTALOZZIAN METHODS

Early beginnings. Up to about 1860 there had been no
general adoption in the United States of Pestalozzian ideas
as to instruction, aside from primary arithmetic, though
much had been written on his work in Switzerland, and the
various *Reports* by American travelers abroad had extolled
the Pestalozzian-Prussian elementary-school instruction.
The introduction of Infant Schools, after 1818, had done
something to bring about a more rational conception as to
the educational process (p. 100), particularly as to teaching
reading and numbers, and the publication of Warren Colburn's *First Lessons in Arithmetic on the Plan of Pestalozzi*, in 1821, had gradually substituted mental arithmetic
for ciphering sums in the lower grades of our schools. The
new educational journals (p. 260) and many magazine

articles had also done much to familiarize schoolmen with the ideas and practices of the Swiss reformer.

As early as 1839 Henry Barnard had distributed among the teachers of Connecticut a pamphlet on Pestalozzi, and in 1847 and 1849 he distributed two other pamphlets on his work and method of instruction. In Massachusetts, Pestalozzian methods were introduced into a few private schools, and in 1848 object teaching was introduced into the state normal school at Westfield. From 1848 to 1854 Arnold Guyot, a Swiss, was an Agent of the Massachusetts State Board of Education and State Institute Lecturer on the teaching of home and observational geography, and after 1852 Hermann Krüsi, Jr., a son of one of Pestalozzi's teachers, held a similar position for drawing and arithmetic. Still, notwithstanding these promising beginnings, the work remained local and exerted no real influence on school practice elsewhere, and up to about 1860 it may be said that Pestalozzian ideas, though adopted here and there, had as yet made no deep impression in the United States.

The Oswego Movement marks the real introduction. The real introduction of Pestalozzian ideas and methods is due to the energy and initiative of Edward A. Sheldon, of Oswego, New York, and so thoroughly did he do the work that in a few years every one was talking in terms of Pestalozzian procedure, and the ideas and methods he introduced had spread all over the country.

Mr. Sheldon began, much as had Pestalozzi himself, by establishing, in 1848, a school in Oswego for poor and neglected children. Following English terminology it was called a "ragged school," and was composed of "120 rude and untrained Irish boys and girls between the ages of 5 and 21." In 1851 Mr. Sheldon was elected superintendent of the schools of Syracuse, but in 1853 was recalled to Oswego to become its first superintendent. Himself a careful student, familiar with the pedagogical literature of the day, he soon eliminated much of the textbook memorizing and began to give his teachers training in teaching by better methods.

Somewhere about 1860 Mr. Sheldon saw, in the museum at Toronto, Canada, a full set of the models, objects, method-materials, and publications of the English Home and Colonial Infant Society, which, it will be remembered (p. 270), had adopted the formal type of Pestalozzian work introduced into England by the Mayos. His interest now fully awakened, he set about reshaping the training of his teachers after the plans of the English Society. The necessary books and apparatus were imported from England, in 1860, and the next year the Board of Education of Oswego dignified the work he was doing by creating a city normal school to train teachers in the new methods for the schools of the city. The Board also (1861) obtained permission for Miss Margaret E. M. Jones, a teacher in the English Training College of the Society, to come to Oswego and establish the work. On her return to England in 1862, Hermann Krüsi, Jr., who had taught in the Home and Colonial Infant Society Training College in England for five years, and who had been in the United States for ten years, teaching in a private school and acting as institute lecturer on drawing and arithmetic for the Massachusetts Board of Education, was secured to continue the training Miss Jones had started.

The English formalized Pestalozzian methods were soon firmly established in the Oswego schools, and so well was the work there advertised, and so important did the movement become, that it for a time completely overshadowed the Swiss and German type of Pestalozzian instruction which had been introduced into Massachusetts, and here and there into schools in other States. In 1862 a committee of prominent educators accepted an invitation to visit and examine the Oswego schools, and they made a favorable report on the work. In 1863 Mr. Sheldon explained his work before the National Teachers' Association. After this, "object teaching" held a place of first importance on the program of this and other teachers' associations for at least a decade. In 1864 the National Teachers' Association appointed a committee to investigate the system, and this committee reported favorably the following year.   In 1863 the State of New York granted $3000 a year aid to the Oswego school, and in 1866 took it over as a State Normal School.

Visitors now came in numbers to see the new work, "oral instruction" and "object teaching" became the great new ideas in education, and Oswego teachers were sought by city school systems and new normal schools all over the northern part of the United States.   For a decade and a half Oswego was distinctively the training school for normal school instructors and city school supervisors, and the "striking personalities" which Mr. Sheldon gathered and held together for years, and the enthusiasm for the new work which his teachers imparted to others, gave his school a deserved national reputation.   As a recent writer has well said, "he shaped a coherent course of study and turned out a large group of teachers who thought teaching, on Oswego lines, the greatest thing in the world."   What the so-called "Oswego Movement" in our educational history really meant may be shown most easily by indicating the changes in the nature of instruction which came as a result of it.

Oral and objective teaching.   In the first place it meant a very great change in the character of the teaching process itself.   As we have seen, colonial and early national education was characterized by individual reciting.   The pupil did his work at his seat, and the teacher heard him read or looked over his work or the sums on his slate or paper.   The next advance step was to class organization, which we traced in Chapter VIII, but the teacher or the assistant teacher still heard recitations from subject matter which the children had learned, that is memorized, from a book.   Many of the early geographies and histories had even been constructed on the plan of the older Catechism, that is on a question and answer basis.   The *System of Geography* by Nathaniel Dwight, an early and a very popular book, illustrates the plan.   It was a volume of 215 pages, beginning with Europe and ending with America, and all of the Catechism type. The following, relating to France, is illustrative:

Q. What is the situation and extent of France?
A. It is situated between 42 and 51 degrees of north latitude, and between 5 degrees west and 8 degrees of east longitude. It is 600 miles long and 500 broad.
Q. How is France bounded?
A. It is bounded by the English Channel and the Netherlands on the north; by Germany, Switzerland, and Italy on the east; by the Mediterranean and the Pyrenean Mountains, south; and by the Bay of Biscay, west.
Q. How is France divided?
A. Into 21 provinces formerly, and lately into 83 departments.
Q. From what is the name France derived?
A. It is derived from a German word signifying *free men.*

There was nothing for the child to do but memorize such subject-matter, or for the teacher but to see that the pupils knew the answers to the questions. Up to the middle of the nineteenth century, at least, and much later in most schools, the dominant characteristic of instruction was the recitation, in which the pupils merely recited what had been learned from their textbooks. It was school-keeping, not teaching, that teachers were engaged in.

The Pestalozzian form of instruction, based on sense-perception, reasoning, and individual judgment, called for a complete change in classroom procedure. What Pestalozzi tried most of all to do was to get children to use their senses and their minds, to look carefully, to count, to observe forms, to get, by means of their five important senses, clear impressions and ideas as to objects and life in the world about them, and then to think over what they had seen and be able to answer his questions, because they had observed carefully and reasoned clearly. Pestalozzi thus clearly subordinated the printed book to the use of the child's senses, and the repetition of mere words to clear ideas about things. Pestalozzi thus became one of the first real teachers.

This was an entirely new process, and for the first time in history a real "technique of instruction" was now called for. Dependence on the words of the text could no longer be relied upon. The oral instruction of a class group, using real objects, called for teaching skill. The class must be kept naturally interested and under control, the essential elements to be taught must be kept clearly in the mind of the teacher, the teacher must raise the right kind of questions, in the right order, to carry the class thinking along to the right conclusions, and, since so much of this type of instruction was not down in books, it called for a much more extended knowledge of the subject on the part of the teacher than the old type of school-keeping had done. The teacher must now both know and be able to organize and direct. Class lessons must be thought out in advance, and teacher-preparation in itself meant a great change in teaching procedure. Emancipated from dependence on the words of a text, and able to stand before a class full of a subject and able to question freely, teachers became conscious of a new strength and a professional skill unknown in the days of textbook reciting. It is not to be wondered that the teachers leaving Oswego went out feeling that teaching, by the Oswego methods, was the greatest thing in the world.

Language instruction. From such teaching oral language lessons, once so rare and now so common, naturally followed as a matter of course. Pupils trained to observe and think naturally come to be able to express. Boys and girls who are full of a subject have little difficulty in telling what they have seen or know. Free exercise in oral expression — oral language work — thus entered the school. Pestalozzi made it one of the great features of his teaching. Stowe and Mann had called attention to it as an important element of the instruction in the Prussian people's school. Some start had been made in introducing such instruction into the schools of Massachusetts, but it was left to Oswego to demonstrate clearly the importance of oral language in the instruction of children. Oral language work thus came in as a new subject for instruction in the primary grades, and, to a degree, oral and written language work tended to replace the former great emphasis on English grammar in the upper grades of the elementary school.

From oral language work, once made a feature of instruction, the teaching of correct speech-usage came naturally to the front, and usage, rather than learning the rules of grammar, came to be depended upon as the chief means for teaching English. Virtually a new subject of instruction was thus added to the elementary-school course as a result of the oral and objective teaching introduced into our schools between 1860 and 1875.

Object teaching leads to elementary science. Another new and most valuable subject of instruction also came in now as an outgrowth of oral and objective teaching, and this was the study of nature. The first step in the process was the object-lesson idea, popularized in England after 1830 by Miss Mayo's book, and in this country after 1860 by the work at Oswego. Thousands of lessons were written out on all forms of natural objects, many far too technical and too scientific to be of much interest or value to children, and these were taught by the teachers.

Under the influence of William T. Harris, who became superintendent of schools in St. Louis in 1868, an important change was made from the scattered object lessons on all sorts of scientific subjects to a much more logically organized study of the different sciences. He published, in 1871, an extremely well-organized course of study for the orderly study of the different sciences, and one thoroughly characteristic of his logical, metaphysical mind. Due in part to his high standing as a school superintendent, and in part to his course of study being a marked improvement over the English-Oswego object-lesson work, this type of course of study was widely copied, became very popular in our schools for the next generation, and did much to introduce science instruction into our schools. Oral lessons in physiology were also introduced into all the grades, and this subject,

DR. EDWARD A. SHELDON
(1823-1897)

Superintendent of Schools, Oswego, N.Y.
Principal of the Oswego State Normal School

PROFESSOR HERMANN KRÜSI
(1817-1902)

Born at Yverdon, Son of Pestalozzi's
assistant. For a quarter of a
century a teacher at Oswego

TWO LEADERS IN THE INTRODUCTION OF PESTALOZZIAN IDEAS

DR. WILLIAM T. HARRIS
(1835–1908)

Teacher and Principal of Schools, St. Louis, 1857–1867
Superintendent of Schools, St. Louis, 1867–1880
U.S. Commissioner of Education, 1889–1906

COL. FRANCIS W. PARKER
(1837–1902)

Supt. of Schools, Quincy, Mass., 1875–1880
Asst. Supt. of Schools, Boston, 1880–1883
Prin. Cook County Normal School, Chicago, 1883–1899

due to its importance, soon tended to separate itself off as a new study.

The next step, and a relatively recent one, was the development of the modern nature-study idea. By this is meant, for the lower grades at least, "a simple observational study of common natural objects and processes for the sake of personal acquaintance with the things which appeal to human interest directly, and independently of relations to organized science," and to include object lessons, observation, picnics, stories told and read, awakening a love of nature, and finally a more serious study of selected simple phases of agriculture, geology, and the physical and biological sciences. Thus, by a process of evolution, we have obtained another new and very important study — two, if we count physiology and the more recent development of health instruction as a separate subject — as an outgrowth of the objective and oral instruction which goes back in its origin to Pestalozzi and the *Émile* of Rousseau.

Instruction in geography revolutionized. Oral and objective teaching also led to great changes in the character of instruction in geography. The old geography was fact-geography — astronomical, physical, natural, and political — and some of the earlier, briefer compends, as we have pointed out, were of the question and answer type. The early work by Morse fixed the type of text and the nature of the instruction. Definitions, all kinds of political and statistical data, boundaries, capitals, products, exports and imports, and similar more or less useless information, filled the texts. This was learned and recited by the pupils, and the teacher's task was to see that it was memorized. Such geography has been called ship-captain or mail-clerk geography.

Objective and oral teaching, applied to geography, wrought a vast change in the character of the instruction. Following Rousseau's idea of "back-to-nature" and Pestalozzi's plans for instruction, the new study of home geography was developed, and from the immediate surroundings geographical instruction was extended to the region thereabout. This called for observation out-of-doors, the study of type forms, and the substitution of the physical and human aspects of geography for the political and statistical. The German, Carl Ritter, developed this new type of geography, between 1817 and 1859, and especially home geography after the ideas of Pestalozzi.

In 1848 the Massachusetts State Board of Education brought to this country a Swiss by the name of Arnold Guyot, who had been a pupil under Ritter, and who for the next six years was an institute lecturer and state inspector for Massachusetts, and later did similar work in New Jersey. He addressed thousands of teachers on the needed reforms and proper methods, and later, through his beautifully illustrated textbooks and a detailed method-guide for teachers, all published about 1866, tended to fix the new type of instruction among the more progressive teachers of the time. An Oswego teacher helped him prepare his books, the aims of which he stated to be "to fill the young with vivid pictures of nature in such regions of the globe as may be considered great geographical types." The work of Colonel Francis W. Parker in training teachers, his *How to Teach Geography* (1889), and the textbooks by Frye (1895), continued the work of Guyot, improving on it and bringing geographical teaching down to its modern form. We thus have a direct line of descent from Rousseau through Pestalozzi, Ritter, Guyot, Parker, and Frye to modern practices.

Mental arithmetic. Before Pestalozzi, arithmetic had meant ciphering, and either commercial counting or the solution of complicated problems. Pestalozzi replaced ciphering with simple and rapid mental calculations. Counting beans, boys, sticks, lines, mountain peaks, and holes in the lace curtains or spots on the wall-paper of the castle, formed the basis for his arithmetic. The number chart shown here was for long a prominent feature in all Pestalozzian schools, the purpose being to keep before the pupil's perception the number combinations from one to ten. Concrete number ideas, and not words about numbers, were what Pestalozzi was trying to teach.   He held that the mental processes of the pupil were the most important part of arithmetical study, and that the quickness, accuracy, judging, and reasoning developed by such work was of prime

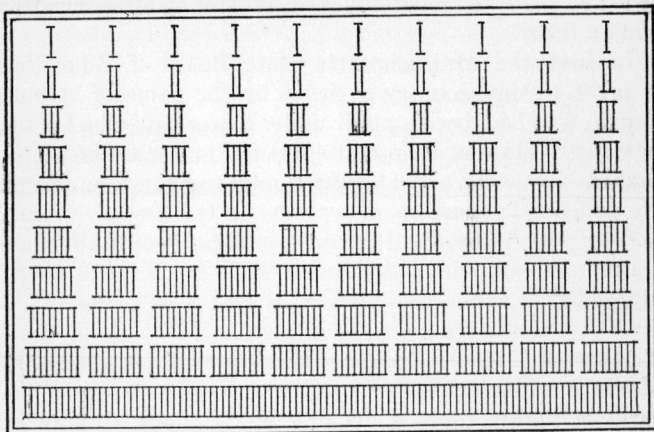

FIG. 55. A PESTALOZZIAN NUMBER CHART

importance in the education of children.   He accordingly discarded sand-tables, paper, and slates for ciphering, and trained the pupils to solve mentally rather complicated problems with whole numbers and fractions.   Visitors to his school were astonished at the skill displayed by the children in the use of the four fundamental operations in arithmetic.   Mental arithmetic, being a very practical subject, Pestalozzian ideas and plans were soon adopted generally in the schools of Switzerland, Holland, the German States, and England.   After the close of Pestalozzi's school in Switzerland, in 1825, Reiner, who had taught arithmetic there, went to England and became a teacher in the Training College of the Home and Colonial Infant Society.

Pestalozzian mental arithmetic was the first of the new subjects to reach us, coming through Warren Colburn's *First*

Lessons in Arithmetic on the Plan of Pestalozzi, published in Boston, in 1821. The publication of this book marked our first adoption of Pestalozzian ideas in teaching, and was the only phase of Pestalozzianism to be widely adopted before 1860. The book contained a multitude of simple problems, to be solved mentally, and many of these were stated in particularly attractive form. The following extracts are illustrative:

> How many hands have a boy and a clock?
> Four rivers ran through the Garden of Eden, and one through Babylon; how many more ran through Eden than Babylon?
> Judas, one of the twelve Apostles, hung himself; how many were left?
> Miss Fanny Woodbury was born in 1791, and died in 1814; Miss Hannah Adams lived to be 53 years older; how old was Hannah Adams?
> At $2.50 a yard, what will $2\frac{1}{2}$ yards of cloth cost?

This book must be ranked with Webster's *Speller* as one of the greatest American textbooks. Mental arithmetic, by 1850, had become one of the most important subjects of the school, and everywhere Colburn's book was in use. The sale of the book was enormous, and its influence great. Like all successful textbooks, it set a new standard and had many imitators. One of these, Barnard's *A Treatise on Arithmetic*, published at Hartford, in 1830, was the first American arithmetic to contain any pictures to aid beginners in mastering the subject. The following is an illustration from this book.

> 5. One stage has four horses. How many horses have two stages?

> 6. Then 2 times 4, or *twice* 4 are how many?

The Grube idea. In 1842 a German, by the name of Grube, tried to improve on the teaching of arithmetic thus developed by applying to it another Pestalozzian principle, namely, that of reducing each subject to its elements, and then making a thorough study of each element before proceeding to the next. His idea had all the characteristics of logical German thoroughness, carried to a typical German extreme. Fortunately the method was not exploited in this country until 1870, when it was explained in a paper by Louis Soldan, then a teacher in St. Louis, a school system then under the leadership of Dr. Harris and at the front in all movements intended to improve instruction. The paper was republished in many States, from New England to California, and soon marked out a new line for the teaching of primary arithmetic. By 1885 even the rural schools of the United States had adopted the Grube idea, and it is only since about 1900 that we have turned back once more to the better ideas of Pestalozzian teaching as represented in Colburn's book and its modern successors.

The essential idea of Grube's method was intense thoroughness in teaching every element. The number one was taught for days before going to number two, and two in all possible and imaginary combinations before taking up three, and so on. The entire first year was devoted to teaching the numbers one to ten, and the second year the numbers to one hundred. The method was extremely absurd, and so clearly away from the better teaching of Colburn that one wonders how American teachers came to take up so completely the Grube idea.

Writing, drawing, and music. Grube's work in organizing a subject so as to proceed by carefully graded stages from the simplest element to the more and more complex illustrated another Pestalozzian idea, viz., that the teaching process could eventually be so "mechanized" that there would be a regular A, B, C, for each type of instruction, which, once learned, would give perfection to a teacher. This idea Pestalozzi strove, unsuccessfully, to work out. In reading it led to the alphabet-syllable-word — A, B, C, ba, ca, ra; bat, cat, rat — method of teaching, long retained

by us, but early discarded by the Germans for the word
method, and now replaced in this country by a combined
word and sound method for teaching beginners to read. In
arithmetic the idea led eventually to the absurd Grube
method.   In object lessons it led to a detailed study and

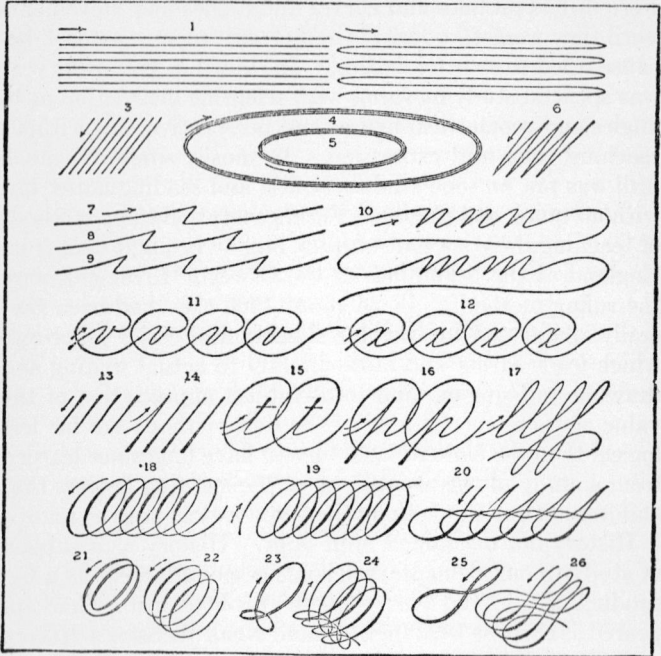

Fig. 56. Early Spencerian Writing Exercises

(From *Spencerian Penmanship No. 4, Revised*. Copyright. American Book Company,
publishers.)

analysis of properties and characteristics, and to an absurd
— for children — scientific classification of objects.

When applied to the new subjects of writing, drawing, and
music, which really came in as elementary school subjects
after about 1845 in Massachusetts, and more generally only
with the Oswego work after 1860, we get this Pestalozzian

principle in its extreme form.   For a generation the teaching of these newer subjects was formal, mechanical, lifeless, and largely ineffective because of the attempt to present the subjects logically to children, and to analyze each subject into its elements.   Before children began really to write they were drilled on lines and curves and angles and movements until they were thoroughly tired of writing as a subject because it led to so little writing.   In drawing, year after year was spent in studying form, with scientific instruction as to angles and geometrical figures and perspective, but without reaching color and expression.   In music, similarly, much drill was put on tone studies, scales, and reading notes, but without much real singing.   For a generation these methods of teaching these special subjects, largely brought over from England at the beginnings of the Oswego Movement, were the ruling methods.   Since about 1900 they had been generally abandoned for the far simpler and easier procedure which leads earlier and more directly to actual writing and drawing and singing, and to a childish appreciation of the value of these special arts.   The new methods are far less logical than the earlier plans, but we have long since learned from a study of the psychology of the learning process that children do not think along the same logical lines as adults.

History not developed until later.   History as a subject of study in our elementary schools came in largely as a by-product of the Civil War.   Goodrich's little history had appeared as early as 1822 (p. 219), and Noah Webster's *History of the United States* in 1832.   Before that time such history as had been taught had been brought in incidentally under geography and in reading.   Vermont, in 1827, was probably the first State to add history to the required list of elementary school subjects.   Massachusetts, the same year, added the subject for the schools of the larger towns and the cities, but did not include it for all until 1857.   In most of the older Northern States history was added to the list of required subjects shortly after the close of the Civil War, though many cities had added it to their course of study at an earlier date. The purpose from the first was to emphasize American accomplishments, with the chief stress on the memorization of facts relating to our national heroes, wars, and political struggles. The dominant purpose was the development of patriotism and an enthusiasm for the Union.

Rousseau had declared history to be a subject of no importance for children, and Pestalozzi had done practically nothing with it. Neither had the followers of Pestalozzi anywhere, so with the introduction of Pestalozzianism at Oswego and elsewhere, instruction in history was not included. It was added generally about this time, but, being unaffected by the new Pestalozzian ideas as to instruction, it began to be taught by the old memory methods of its earlier ancestor, geography. The reorganization of history instruction did not come until near the end of the nineteenth century, under the inspiration of a new German influence, to be described in the next division of this chapter. The reorganization of reading, and the creation of a methodology for instruction in both history and literature, also date from the coming of this new influence.

The normal school finds its place. The great change which took place in the character of elementary-school education between 1850 and 1880 will now be evident. The Civil War had checked material development. As a people we had neither the money nor the public interest necessary to expand the school system along material lines, or to add new types of schools. In organization our schools stood very much in 1880 as they had in 1850, the chief change being that the lines marked out as to organization and grading and supervision by the better and more progressive city school systems by 1850 had, by 1880, been extended to even the smaller towns. Instead, the great educational development of these three decades was within. New subjects of study were introduced, the teaching of the older ones was revolutionized, and a technique, a methodology, for instruction in each subject, except history and literature, was worked out. Where before the ability to organize and discipline a school had constituted the chief art of instruction, now the ability to teach scientifically took its place as the prime professional requisite. A "science and art of teaching" now arose, and the new subject of Pedagogy began to take form and secure recognition.

The normal school now found its place, and Figure 54, showing its development, reveals how rapidly the movement to establish these schools gained headway after about 1865 for public normal schools, and after about 1870 for the private tuition schools. The National Normal University, at Lebanon, Ohio; the Valparaiso Normal School, in Indiana; and the Northern Illinois Normal School, at Dixon, are types of dozens of such private low-tuition schools, which had thousands of students and were good money-makers for their owners. These illustrate the great interest awakened by the work at Oswego and elsewhere in the effort to psychologize the educational process and to reduce the teaching process to rule and method.

Psychology becomes the master science. The new conception of the child as a slowly developing personality, demanding subject-matter and method suited to his stage of development, and the new conception of teaching as that of directing education instead of hearing recitations and "keeping school," now replaced the earlier knowledge-conception of school work. Psychology soon became the guiding science of the school, and, imparting to would-be teachers the methodology of instruction in the different subjects, the great work of the normal school. A little later, in the early nineties, the natural successor of this movement — child study — made its appearance, and for a time almost monopolized the educational field. It was now sought to ascertain much more fully how and in what ways childish personality developed. Children were observed and questioned and tabulated for all sorts of traits, opinions, and information; the "questionnaire" was used by the child-study enthusiasts to gather all kinds of data, and much useful as well as much worthless information was gathered as to child nature and ideas. Though carried on in all parts of the United States, the work of G. Stanley Hall and his students, at Clark University, formed the leading center of the movement, and the *Pedagogical Seminary* was founded to disseminate the results.

The new normal-trained woman teacher now began to be markedly in evidence and, after 1880, the displacement of men teachers was rapid in all parts of the country. This new teacher brought with her to the school a new concep-

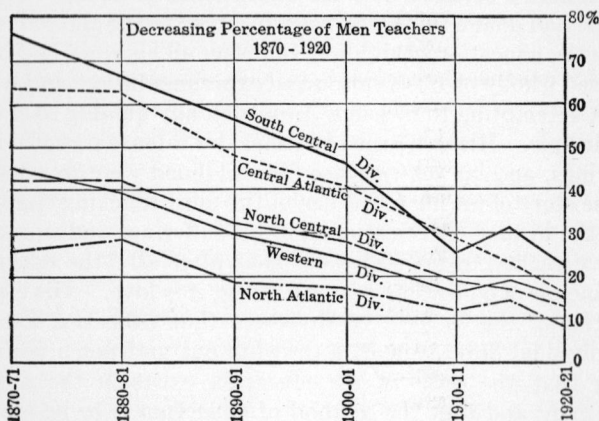

FIG. 57. THE DECREASING PERCENTAGE OF MEN TEACHERS

tion of childhood, a new and a minute methodology, and a new enthusiasm, all of which were valuable additions, though for a time often carried to a ridiculous extreme. Problems had to be analyzed just so, pupils must answer just so, and thinking must proceed in approved order and be stated in proper form. Each problem to be solved must first be analyzed in correct English into a correct statement, short-cut though correct replies were not allowed, while such errors as the multiplication of children by dimes or the division of dollars by horses were almost unpardonable. The spirit of instruction was often lost in a too strict observance of the form. These defects and excesses, almost always the accompaniment of any new movement which strongly influences the course of educational development, in time largely disappeared, and both methodology and child study fell into their proper places as parts, but not the whole, of the science of education.

III. New Ideas from Herbartian Sources

Where Pestalozzi left the educational problem. Pestalozzi had done a wonderful work in reorganizing and redirecting the education of children, but after all his work had been based wholly on observation and experimentation, and without attempting to measure it up with any guiding scientific principle. His unwearied patience, his intense personal sufferings, and his self-sacrifice for childhood were wonderful. The story of his life forms one of the most touching chapters in the history of education, and his sufferings and successes gave reality to his statement that after all "the essential principle of education is not teaching; it is love." His elaboration of the thought of Rousseau that education was an individual development, a drawing out and not a pouring in; that the basis of all education exists in the nature of man; and that the method of education is to be sought and not constructed, were his great contributions. These ideas led him to emphasize sense perception and expression; to formulate the rule that in teaching we must proceed from the simple to the complex, and from the concrete to the abstract; and to construct a "faculty psychology" which conceived of education as "a harmonious development" of the different "faculties" of the mind. It was at this point that Pestalozzi left the problem, and in this form that we received it by way of England in the sixties.

The work of Herbart. Taking up the problem as Pestalozzi left it, a German by the name of Johann Friedrich Herbart (1776–1841) carried it forward by organizing a truer psychology for the whole educational process, by erecting a new aim in instruction, by formulating new steps in method, and by showing the place and the importance of properly organized instruction in history and literature in the education of the child. Though the two men were entirely different in type, and worked along entirely different lines, the connection between Herbart and Pestalozzi was, nevertheless, close. Herbart had visited Pestalozzi at Burgdorf, in 1799, just after graduating from Jena and while acting as a tutor for three Swiss boys, and had written a very sympathetic description of his school and his theory of instruction. Herbart was one of the first of the Germans to understand and appreciate "the genial and noble Pestalozzi."

The two men, however, approached the educational problem from entirely different angles. Pestalozzi gave nearly all his long life to teaching and human service, while Herbart taught only as a traveling private tutor for three years, and later a class of twenty children in his university practice school. Pestalozzi was a social reformer, a visionary, and an impractical enthusiast, but was possessed of a remarkable intuitive insight into child nature. Herbart, on the other hand, was a well-trained scholarly thinker, who spent the most of his life in the peaceful occupation of a professor of philosophy in a German university. The son of a well-educated public official, Herbart was himself educated at the *Gymnasium* of Oldenburg and the University of Jena. After spending three years as a tutor, he became, at the age of twenty-six, an under teacher at the University of Göttingen. At the age of thirty-three he was called to become professor of philosophy at Königsburg, and from the age of fifty-seven to his death at sixty-five he was again a professor at Göttingen. It was while at Königsburg, between 1810 and 1832, and as an appendix to his work as professor of philosophy, that he organized a small practice school, conducted a Pedagogical Seminar, and worked out his educational theory and method. His work was a careful, scholarly attempt at the organization of education as a science, carried out amid the peace and quiet which a university atmosphere almost alone affords. He addressed himself chiefly to three things: (1) the aim, (2) the content, and (3) the method of instruction.

The aim and the content of education. Locke had set up as the aim of education the ideal of a physically sound gentleman. Rousseau had declared his aim to be to prepare his boy for life by developing naturally his inborn capacities. Pestalozzi had sought to regenerate society by means of education, and to prepare children for society by a "harmonious training" of their "faculties." Herbart rejected alike the conventional-social education of Locke, the natural and unsocial education of Rousseau, and the "faculty-psychology" conception of education of Pestalozzi. Instead he conceived of the mind as a unity, rather than divided into "faculties," and the aim of education as broadly social rather than personal. The purpose of education, he said, was to prepare men to live properly in organized society, and hence the chief aim in education was not conventional fitness, natural development, mere knowledge, nor personal mental power, but personal character and social morality. This being the case, the educator should analyze the interests and occupations and social responsibilities of men as they are grouped in organized society, and, from such analyses, deduce the means and the method of instruction. Man's interests, he said, come from two main sources — his contact with the things in his environment (real things, sense-impressions), and from his relations with human beings (social intercourse). His social responsibilities and duties are determined by the nature of the social organization of which he forms a part.

Pestalozzi had provided fairly well for the first group of contacts, through his instruction in objects, home geography, numbers, and geometric form. For the second group of contacts Pestalozzi had developed only oral language, and to this Herbart now added the two important studies of literature and history, and history with the emphasis on the social rather than the political side. Two new elementary

school subjects were thus developed, each important in revealing to man his place in the social whole. History in
particular Herbart conceived to be a study of the first importance for revealing proper human relationships, and
leading men to social and national "good-will."

The chief purpose of education Herbart held to be to develop personal character and to prepare for social usefulness.
These virtues, he held, proceeded from enough of the right
kind of knowledge, properly interpreted to the pupil so that
clear ideas as to relationships might be formed. To impart
this knowledge interest must be awakened, and to arouse
interest in the many kinds of knowledge needed, a "many-
sided" development must take place. From full knowledge, and with proper instruction by the teacher, clear
ideas or concepts might be formed, and clear ideas ought to
lead to right action, and right action to personal character
— the aim of all instruction. Herbart was the first writer
on education to place the great emphasis on proper instruction, and to exalt teaching and proper teaching-procedure
instead of mere knowledge or intellectual discipline. He
thus conceived of the educational process as a science in
itself, having a definite content and method, and worthy of
special study by those who desire to teach.

Herbartian method. With these ideas as to the aim and
content of instruction, Herbart worked out a theory of the
instructional process and a method of instruction. Interest
he held to be of first importance as a prerequisite to good
instruction. If given spontaneously, well and good; but,
if necessary, forced interest must be resorted to. Skill in
instruction is in part to be determined by the ability of the
teacher to secure interest without resorting to force on the
one hand or sugar-coating of the subject on the other.
Taking Pestalozzi's idea that the purpose of the teacher was
to give pupils new experiences through contacts with real
things, without assuming that the pupils already had such,
Herbart elaborated the process by which new knowledge is
assimilated in terms of what one already knows, and from

his elaboration of this principle the doctrine of apperception — that is, the apperceiving or comprehending of new knowledge in terms of the old — has been fixed as an important principle in educational psychology. Good instruction, then, involves first putting the child into a proper frame of mind to apperceive the new knowledge, and hence this becomes a corner stone of all good teaching method.

Herbart did not always rely on such methods, holding that the "committing to memory" of certain necessary facts often was necessary, but he held that the mere memorizing of isolated facts, which had characterized school instruction for ages, had little value for either educational or moral ends. The teaching of mere facts often was very necessary, but such instruction called for a methodical organization of the facts by the teacher, so as to make their learning contribute to some definite purpose. This called for a purpose in instruction; the organization of the facts necessary to be taught so as to select the most useful ones; the connection of these so as to establish the principle which was the purpose of the instruction; and training in systematic thinking by applying the principle to new problems of the type being studied. The carrying out of such ideas meant the careful organization of the teaching process and teaching method, to secure certain predetermined ends in child development, instead of mere miscellaneous memorizing and school-keeping.

The Herbartian movement in Germany. Herbart died in 1841, without having awakened any general interest in his ideas, and they remained virtually unnoticed until 1865. In that year a professor at Leipzig, Tuiskon Ziller (1817–1883), published a book setting forth Herbart's idea of instruction as a moral force. This attracted much attention, and led to the formation (1868) of a scientific society for the study of Herbart's ideas. Ziller and his followers now elaborated Herbart's ideas, advanced the theory of culture-epochs in child development, the theory of concentration in studies, and elaborated the four steps in the process of instruction, as described by Herbart, into the five formal steps of the modern Herbartian school.

In 1874 a pedagogical seminary and practice school was organized at the University of Jena, and in 1885 this came under the direction of Professor William Rein, a pupil of Ziller's, who developed the practice school according to the ideas of Ziller. A detailed course of study for this school, filling two large volumes, was worked out, and the practice lessons given were thoroughly planned beforehand and the methods employed were subjected to a searching analysis after the lesson had been given.

Herbartian ideas reach the United States. Between 1885 and 1890 a number of Americans, many of them graduates of the state normal school at Normal, Illinois, studied in Jena, and returning brought back to the United States this Ziller-Rein-Jena brand of Herbartian ideas and practices. Charles De Garmo's *Essentials of Methods*, published in 1889, marked the beginning of the introduction of these ideas into this country. In 1892 Charles A. McMurry published his *General Method*, and in 1897, with his brother, Frank, published the *Method in the Recitation*. These three books probably have done more to popularize Herbartian ideas and introduce them into the normal schools and colleges of the United States than all other influences combined. Another important influence was the "National Herbart Society," founded in 1892 by students returning from Jena, in imitation of the similar German society. For the first few years of its existence its publications were devoted to a discussion of interest, apperception, correlation, recitation methods, moral education, the culture-epoch theory, training for citizenship, the social function of history and geography, and similar subjects. This Society is still rendering good service under the name of the "National Society for the Study of Education," though its earlier Herbartian character now has disappeared.

Herbartian ideas took like wildfire over the United States, but particularly in the normal schools of the Upper Missis-

sippi Valley. Methods of instruction in history and literature, and a new psychology, were now added to the normal
school professional instruction. New courses of study for
the training schools were now worked out, in which the elementary school subjects were divided into drill subjects,
content subjects, and motor-activity subjects. Apperception, correlation, social purpose, moral education, and recitation methods became new words to conjure with. From
the normal schools these ideas spread rapidly to the better
city school systems of the time, and soon found their way
into courses of study everywhere. Practice schools and the
model lessons in dozens of normal schools were remodeled
after the pattern of those at Jena, and for a decade Herbartian ideas and child study vied with one another for the
place of first importance in educational thinking. The Herbartian wave of the nineties resembled the Pestalozzian
enthusiasm of the sixties. Each for a time furnished the
new ideas in education, each introduced elements of importance into our elementary-school instruction, each deeply
influenced the training of teachers in our normal schools by
giving a new turn to the instruction there, and each gradually settled down into its proper place in our educational
practice and history.

To the Herbartians we are indebted in particular for important new conceptions as to the teaching of history and
literature, which have modified all our subsequent procedure; for the introduction of history teaching in some form
into all the elementary-school grades; for the emphasis on a
new social point of view in the teaching of history and geography; the emphasis on the moral aim in instruction; a new
and a truer educational psychology; and a better organization of the technique of classroom instruction. With the
introduction of normal child activities, which came from
another source about this same time, our elementary school
curriculum as we now have it was practically complete, and
the elementary school of 1850 had been completely made
over to form the elementary school of 1900.

IV. The Kindergarten, Play, and Manual Activities

To another German, Friedrich Froebel, we are indebted, directly or indirectly, for three other additions to elementary education — the kindergarten, the play idea, and handwork activities.

Origin of the kindergarten. Of German parentage, the son of a rural clergyman, early estranged from his parents, retiring and introspective by nature, having led a most unhappy childhood, and apprenticed to a forester without his wishes being consulted, at twenty-three Froebel decided to become a school teacher and visited Pestalozzi in Switzerland. Two years later he became the tutor of three boys, and then spent the years 1808–10 as a student and teacher in Pestalozzi's institute at Yverdon. During his years there Froebel was deeply impressed with the great value of music and play in the education of children, and of all that he carried away from Pestalozzi's institution these ideas were most persistent. After serving in a variety of occupations — student, soldier against Napoleon, and curator in a museum of mineralogy — he finally opened a little private school, in 1816, which he conducted for a decade along Pestalozzian lines. In this the play idea, music, and the self-activity of the pupils were uppermost. The school was a failure, financially, but while conducting it Froebel thought out and published (1826) his most important pedagogical work — *The Education of Man.*

Gradually Froebel became convinced that the most needed reform in education concerned the early years of childhood. His own youth had been most unhappy, and to this phase of education he now addressed himself. After a period as a teacher in Switzerland he returned to Germany and opened a school for little children in which plays, games, songs, and occupations involving self-activity were the dominating characteristics, and in 1840 he hit upon the name *Kindergarten* for it. In 1843 his *Mutter- und Kose-Lieder,* a book of fifty songs and games, was published.

JOHANN FRIEDRICH HERBART
(1776–1841)
Organizer of the Psychology of Instruction

FRIEDRICH WILHELM FROEBEL
(1782–1852)
Founder of the Kindergarten

A KINDERGARTEN GROUP

(Courtesy Adelphi Academy)

Spread of the kindergarten idea.   After a series of unsuccessful efforts to bring his new idea to the attention of
educators, Froebel, himself a rather feminine type, became
discouraged and resolved to address himself henceforth to
women, as they seemed much more capable of understanding him, and to the training of teachers in the new ideas.
Froebel was fortunate in securing as one of his most ardent
disciples, just before his death, the Baroness Bertha von
Marenholtz Bülow-Wendhausen (1810–93), who did more
than any other person to make his work known.   Meeting,
in 1849, the man mentioned to her as "an old fool," she understood him, and spent the remainder of her life in bringing
to the attention of the world the work of this unworldly man
who did not know how to make it known for himself.   In
1851 the Prussian Government, fearing some revolutionary
designs in the new idea, forbade kindergartens in Prussia, so
the Baroness went to London and lectured there on Froebel's ideas, organizing kindergartens in the English "ragged
schools."   She later expounded Froebelian ideas in Paris,
Italy, Switzerland, Holland, Belgium, and (after 1860, when
the prohibition was removed) in Germany.   In 1870 she
founded a kindergarten training college in Dresden.   Many
of her writings have been translated into English, and published in the United States.

In this country the kindergarten idea has met with a cor-
dial reception.   The first kindergarten in the United States
was a German kindergarten, established at Watertown,
Wisconsin, in 1855, by Mrs. Carl Schurz, a pupil of Froebel.
During the next fifteen years some ten other kindergartens
were organized in German-speaking communities.   The
first English-speaking kindergarten was opened privately in
Boston, in 1860, by Miss Elizabeth Peabody.   In 1868 a
private training school for kindergartners was opened in
Boston, largely through Miss Peabody's influence, by Madame Matilde Kriege and her daughter, who had recently
arrived from Germany.   In 1872 Miss Marie Boelte opened
a similar teacher-training school in New York City, and in

1873 her pupil, Miss Susan Blow, accepted the invitation of Superintendent William T. Harris, of St. Louis, to go there and open the first public school kindergarten in the United States. St. Louis, then perhaps the most prominent city school system in the country, soon became a center from which public kindergarten ideas were diffused. The first kindergarten in Chicago was opened in 1874, and by 1880 some 300 kindergartens and 10 kindergarten training schools, mostly private undertakings, had been opened in the cities of thirty of the States of the Union. By 1890 philanthropic kindergarten associations to provide and support kindergartens had been organized in most of the larger cities, and after that date our city schools rapidly began to adopt the kindergarten as a part of the public school system, and thus add, at the bottom, one more rung to our educational ladder. To-day there are approximately 9000 public and 1500 private kindergartens in the cities of the United States, and training in kindergarten principles and practices is now given by many of our state normal schools.

The kindergarten idea. The dominant idea in the kindergarten is natural but directed self-activity, focused upon educational, social, and moral ends. Froebel believed in the continuity of a child's life from infancy onward, and that self-activity, determined by the child's interests and desires and intelligently directed, was essential to the unfolding of the child's inborn capacities. He saw, more clearly than any one before him had done, the unutilized wealth of the child's world, that the child's chief characteristic is self-activity, the desirability of the child finding himself through play, and that the work of the school during these early years was to supplement the family by drawing out the child and awakening the ideal side of his nature. To these ends doing, self-activity, and expression became fundamental to the kindergarten, and movement, gesture, directed play, song, color, the story, and the human activities a part of kindergarten technique. Nature study and school gardening were given a prominent place, and motor activity much called into play. Advancing far beyond Pestalozzi's principle of sense impressions, which, and as we have seen under object lessons, was largely passive learning, Froebel insisted on motor activity and learning by doing.

Froebel, as well as Herbart, also saw the social importance of education, and that man must realize himself not independently amid nature, as Rousseau had said, but as a social animal in coöperation with his fellowmen. Hence he made his schoolroom a miniature of society, a place where courtesy and helpfulness and social coöperation were prominent features. This social and at times reverent atmosphere of the kindergarten has always been a marked characteristic of its work. To bring out social ideas many dramatic games, such as shoemaker, carpenter, smith, and farmer, were devised and set to music. The "story" by the teacher was made prominent, and this was retold in language, acted, sung, and often worked out constructively in clay, blocks, or paper. Other games to develop skill were worked out, and use was made of sand, clay, paper, cardboard, and color. The "gifts" and "occupations" which Froebel devised were intended to develop constructive and æsthetic power, and to provide for connection and development they were arranged into an organized series of playthings. Individual development as its aim, motor expression as its method, and social coöperation as its means were the characteristic ideas of this new school for little children.

Since Froebel's day we have learned much about children that was then unknown, especially as to the muscular and nervous organization and development of children, and with this new knowledge the tendency has been to enlarge the "gifts" and change their nature, to introduce new "occupations," elaborate the kindergarten program of daily exercises, and to give the kindergarten more of an out-of-door character.

The Montessori method. Another recent development of the kindergarten idea, which a decade ago created quite a furore in many countries, is the scheme of child-training

devised by Madame Maria Montessori, at Rome.   Many
Montessori schools have been opened in the United States,
and the method has been heralded as a great improvement
over the kindergarten.   A more critical examination of her
ideas has led, however, to their somewhat general rejection
by most American educators, and it is probable that a decade
hence Montessori schools will have largely disappeared as a
school for normal-minded children.   Based on an outgrown
faculty psychology, a psychologically unsound plan for sense
training, and involving a too early start in the formal arts of
learning, the method has been generally decided to be distinctly inferior to the modern Americanized kindergarten.
Its best features have been drawn from the work of Seguin,
Madame Montessori herself having been a teacher of defectives at Rome, and the method has its greatest value for
subnormal children.

The contribution of the kindergarten.   Wholly aside from
the specific training given children during the year, year
and a half, or two years of training, the addition of the kindergarten to our American education has been a force of very
large significance and usefulness.   The idea that the child is
primarily an active and not a learning animal has been given
new emphasis, and that education comes chiefly by doing
has been given new force.   The idea that a child's chief
business is play, so different from our early Calvinistic
conception, has been of large educational value.   The elimination of book education and harsh discipline in the kindergarten has been an idea that has slowly but gradually
extended upward into the lower grades of the elementary
school.   The play and game idea brought in by the kindergarten has also been exceedingly useful in slowly changing
the character of the physical training exercises of the upper
grades and of the high school from the stiff *Turnen* and military type of bodily exercises, brought in by the Germans
after their great migration to America began, to the free
play and competitive games which we now have quite generally developed.

To-day, largely as a result of the spreading of the kinder-garten spirit, we are coming to recognize play and games at something like their real social, moral, and educational values, wholly aside from their benefits as concern physical welfare, and to schedule play as a regular subject in our school programs. Music, too, has attained new emphasis since the coming of the kindergarten, and methods of teach-ing music more in harmony with kindergarten ideas have been introduced into the upper grades of our schools.

Instruction in the manual activities. Froebel not only introduced constructive work — paper folding, weaving, needlework, and work with sand and clay and color — into the kindergarten, but he also proposed to extend and de-velop such work for the upper years of schooling in a school for hand training, which he outlined but did not establish. His proposed plan included the elements of the so-called manual-training idea, developed later, and he justified such instruction on the same educational grounds that we ad-vance to-day. It was not to teach a boy a trade, as Rous-seau had advocated, or to train children in sense-perception, as Pestalozzi had employed all his manual activities, but as a form of educational expression, and for the purpose of developing creative power within the child. The idea was advocated by a number of thinkers, about 1850 to 1860, but the movement finally took its rise in Finland, Sweden, and Russia.

The first country to organize such work as a part of its school instruction was Finland, where, as early as 1858, Uno Cygnaeus (1810–88) outlined a course for manual training involving bench and metal work, wood-carving, and basket-weaving. In 1866 Finland made some form of man-ual work compulsory for boys in all its rural schools, and in its training colleges for male teachers. In 1872 the govern-ment of Sweden decided to introduce sloyd work into its schools, partly to counteract the bad physical and moral effects of city congestion, and partly to revivify the declin-ing home industries of the people. A sloyd school was es-

tablished at Näs, in 1872, to train teachers, and in this a few
of our early manual training teachers studied. In 1877 the
work was added to the Folk School instruction of Sweden.
At first the old native sloyd occupations were followed, such
as carpentering, turning, wood-carving, brush-making, book-
binding, and work in copper and iron, but later the industrial element gave way to a well-organized course in educational tool work for boys from twelve to fifteen years of
age, after the Finnish plan.

Manual training reaches the United States. The first
introduction of the United States to this new form of instruction came through the exhibit made by the Russian Government, at the Centennial Exhibition in 1876, of the work in
wood and iron done by the pupils at the Imperial Technical
School at St. Petersburg. This was a type of work especially adapted to secondary school instruction. The St.
Louis Manual Training High School, founded in 1880 in
connection with Washington University, first gave expression to this new form of education, and formed a type for
the organization of such schools elsewhere. Privately supported schools of this type were organized in Chicago,
Toledo, Cincinnati, and Cleveland before 1886, and the first
public manual-training high schools were established in Baltimore in 1884, Philadelphia in 1885, and Omaha in 1886.
The shopwork, based for long on the "Russian system," included wood-turning, joinery, pattern-making, forging,
foundry and machine work. The first high school to provide sewing, cooking, dressmaking, and millinery for girls
was the one at Toledo, established in 1886, though private
classes had been organized earlier in a number of cities.
This type of high school has developed rapidly with us, and
to-day the tendency is strong to introduce such courses into
all our high schools.

The introduction of manual work into the elementary
schools came a little later and a little more slowly, but now is
very general. As early as 1880 the Workingmen's School,
founded by the Ethical Culture Society of New York, had

provided a kindergarten and had extended the kindergarten constructive-work idea upward, in the form of simple woodworking, into its elementary school. In the public schools, experimental classes in elementary school woodworking were tried in one school in Boston, as early as 1882, the expense being borne by Mrs. Quincy A. Shaw. In 1888 the city took over these classes. In 1886 Mr. Gustav Larson was brought to Boston from Sweden to introduce Swedish sloyd, and a teacher-training school which has been very influential was established there in 1889. In 1876 Massachusetts permitted cities to provide instruction in sewing, and Springfield introduced such instruction in 1884, and elementary school instruction in knifework in 1886. In 1882 Montclair, New Jersey, introduced manual training into its elementary schools, and in 1885 the State of New Jersey first offered state aid to induce the extension of the idea. In 1885 Philadelphia added cooking and sewing to its

FIG. 58. REDIRECTED MANUAL TRAINING

A boy at Portland, Oregon, mending his shoe, instead of making a mortise-joint.

elementary schools, having done so in the girls' high school five years earlier. In 1888 the City of New York added drawing, sewing, cooking, and woodworking to its elementary school course of study. By 1890 approximately forty cities, nearly all of them in the North Atlantic group of States, had introduced work in manual training into their elementary schools, and from these beginnings the movement has extended to practically all cities and to many towns and rural communities.

From about 1885 to 1888 the manual-training idea was under heavy fire, the papers at the meeting of the Department of Superintendence of the National Education Association, in 1887 and 1888, being a culmination of the discussion. The new work was then advocated on the grounds of formal discipline — that it trained the reasoning, exercised the powers of observation, and strengthened the will. The "exercises," true to such a conception, were formal and uniform for all. With the breakdown of the "faculty psychology," and the abandonment in large part of the doctrine of formal discipline in the training of the mind, the whole manual-training work has had to be reshaped. As the writings of Pestalozzi, Herbart, and Froebel were studied more closely, and with the new light on child development gained from child-study and the newer psychology, manual training came to be conceived of in its proper light as a means of individual expression, and to be extended to new forms, materials, colors, and new practical and artistic ends. To-day the instruction in manual work in all its forms has been further changed to make it an educational instrument for interpreting the fields of art and industry in terms of their social significance and usefulness.

The elementary school now reorganized and complete. Excepting instruction in agriculture, which came in recently as an outgrowth of nature study, and in response to an economic demand, the elementary course of study of 1900 contained all the elements of this course to-day. The changes and additions, and the variations in relative emphasis and in teachers' methods in each subject, are shown in the chart opposite. It was a vastly changed course of study, though, from that of 1850, both as to content and methods. The beginning of these changes goes back to the work of Pestalozzi, though his contributions and those of Herbart, Froebel, and their disciples and followers are so interwoven in the educational practice of to-day that it is in most cases impos-

1775	1825	1850	1875	1900
READING Spelling Writing Catechism BIBLE Arithmetic	READING* Declamation SPELLING* Writing Good Behavior Manners & Morals ARITHMETIC*	READING DECLAMATION SPELLING WRITING Manners Conduct MENTAL ARITH.* CIPHERING	READING Literary Selections SPELLING PENMANSHIP* Conduct PRIMARY ARITH. ADVANCED ARITH.	READING* LITERATURE* Spelling Writing* ...... ARITHMETIC
	Bookkeeping GRAMMAR Geography	Bookkeeping Elem. Language GRAMMAR Geography History U.S.	Oral Language* GRAMMAR Home Geography* TEXT GEOGRAPHY U.S. HISTORY Constitution	ORAL LANGUAGE Grammar Home Geography TEXT GEOGRAPHY* History Stories* TEXT HISTORY*
	Sewing and Knitting	Object Lessons	Object Lessons* Elementary Science* Drawing* Music* Physical Exercises	Nature Study* Elem. Science Drawing* Music* Play Physical Training* Sewing Cooking Manual Training

CAPITALS = Most important subjects. *Italics* = Subjects of medium importance. Roman = Least important subjects.

* = New methods of teaching now employed.

FIG. 59. THE EVOLUTION OF OUR ELEMENTARY-SCHOOL CURRICULUM, AND OF METHODS OF TEACHING.

sible to trace them or separate them out one from the other. Our elementary school instruction of to-day remains, as before, a sturdy native development, but deeply influenced, since 1860, by the best ideas of the great European theorists and reformers.

In the great reorganization and redirection of elementary education, which took place between 1860 and 1900, probably no American was more influential than Colonel Francis W. Parker (1837–1902). After some years in teaching, he spent the years 1872 to 1875 in study in Germany. On his return he was superintendent of schools at Quincy, Massachusetts, from 1875 to 1880, and from 1883 to 1899 was principal of the Cook County Normal School, at Chicago. It was he who introduced Germanized Pestalozzian-Ritter methods of teaching geography; he who strongly advocated the Herbartian plan for concentration of instruction about a central core, which he worked out for geography; he who insisted so strongly on the Froebelian principle of self-expression as the best way to develop the thinking process; and he who saw educational problems so clearly from the standpoint of the child that he, and the pupils he trained, did much to bring about the reorganization in elementary education which had been worked out by 1900. Since that time the most influential constructive critic has been Professor John Dewey, to whom we shall refer a little later on.

QUESTIONS FOR DISCUSSION

1. How do you explain the long-continued objection to teacher-training?
2. Contrast the early New York academy plan and the Massachusetts state school plan for training teachers.
3. Why is it probable that the state normal school could hardly have arisen, at the time it did, in any other State than Massachusetts?
4. How do you explain the large and immediate success of Mr. Sheldon?
5. Contrast "oral and objective teaching" with the former "individual instruction."
6. Show how complete a change in classroom procedure this involved.
7. Show how Pestalozzian ideas necessitated a "technique of instruction."

8. Why is it that Pestalozzian ideas as to language and arithmetic instruction have so slowly influenced the teaching of grammar, language, and arithmetic?

9. How do you explain the decline in importance of the once-popular mental arithmetic?

10. Show why the Grube idea as to number-teaching was absurd.

11. How do you explain the small interest in United States history until after the Civil War?

12. How do you explain the decrease in men teachers at about the same time that the normal schools developed most rapidly?

13. Show how Child Study was a natural development from the Pestalozzian psychology and methodology.

14. Explain what is meant by the statements that Herbart rejected:
    (a) The conventional social idea of Locke.
    (b) The unsocial ideal of Rousseau.
    (c) The "faculty-psychology" conception of Pestalozzi.

15. Explain what is meant by saying that Herbart conceived of education as broadly social rather than personal.

16. Show in what ways and to what extent Herbart:
    (a) Enlarged our conception of the educational process.
    (b) Improved the instruction content and process.

17. Explain why Herbartian ideas took so much more quickly in the United States than did Pestalozzianism.

18. State the essentials of the kindergarten idea, and the psychology behind it.

19. State the contribution of the kindergarten idea to American education.

20. Show the connection between the sense impression ideas to Pestalozzi, the self-activity of Froebel, and the manual activities of the modern elementary school.

21. Show how a faculty psychology and set and uniform manual training exercises stood and fell together.

22. State the new method in instruction indicated by the * for each subject in the table on page 327.

TOPICS FOR INVESTIGATION AND REPORT

1. Early work of Carter and Hall in establishing normal schools.
2. David Page and the Albany normal school. (Barnard.)
3. Teacher training in the academies.
4. Change in character of arithmetical instruction produced by Colburn's book.
5. Work and influence of the Oswego normal school. (Hollis.)
6. The Pestalozzian movement in the United States. (Monroe.)
7. Work and influence of the St. Louis city school system under William T. Harris.
8. The change in geography teaching during the last century.

9. The change in arithmetical teaching during the last century.
10. The change in teaching of reading during the last century.
11. The Child Study movement in American education.
12. Change in the character of the kindergarten since its introduction.
13. Change in the character of manual training instruction since its introduction.

SELECTED REFERENCES

Barnard, Henry, Editor. *The American Journal of Education*, 31 vols. Consult *Analytical Index* to; 128 pp. Published by United States Bureau of Education, Washington, 1892.

*Bowen, H. C. *Froebel and Education through Self-Activity*. 209 pp. Chas. Scribner's Sons, New York, 1893.

An excellent historical account.

De Garmo, Chas. *Herbart and the Herbartians*. 268 pp. Chas. Scribner's Sons, New York, 1895.

Traces the development of the movement in Germany and America.

Dewey, John and Evelyn. *Schools of To-morrow*. 316 pp. E. P. Dutton & Co., New York, 1915.

Chapter X gives a good criticism of the new Montessori work, and compares it with the more psychologically sound kindergarten.

*Gordy, J. P. *Rise and Growth of the Normal School Idea in the United States*. 145 pp. Circular of Information, United States Bureau of Education, No. 8, 1891.

An important contribution.

Harris, William T. "Twenty Years of Progress in Education"; in *Proceedings of the National Education Association*, 1892, pp. 56–61.

*Hollis, A. P. *The Oswego Movement*. 136 pp. D. C. Heath & Co., Boston, 1898.

The contribution of the Oswego Normal School to educational progress in the United States, through its work in introducing Pestalozzian methods.

Jones, L. H. "E. A. Sheldon"; in *Educational Review*, vol. 14, pp. 428–32. (Dec., 1897.)

An appreciative sketch.

*Monroe, Paul. *Cyclopedia of Education*. The Macmillan Co., New York, 1911–13.

The following articles are particularly important:
1. "Child Study"; vol. I, pp. 615–21.
2. "Froebel, F."; vol. II, pp. 713–23.
3. "Herbart, J. F."; vol. III, pp. 250–53.
4. "Kindergarten, The"; vol. III, 598–606.
5. "Manual Training"; vol. IV, pp. 124–28.
6. "Normal School"; vol. IV, pp. 481.
7. "Object Teaching"; vol. IV, pp. 523–25.
8. "Parker, F. W."; vol. IV, pp. 606–07.
Also see articles on Arithmetic, Geography, etc.

*Monroe, Walter S. *Development of Arithmetic as a School Subject.* 170 pp. United States Bureau of Education, Bulletin No. 10, Washington, 1917.

An excellent collection of very interesting illustrative material. The chapters deal with colonial arithmetic, the ciphering-book period, Colburn's Pestalozzian arithmetic, influence of Colburn, and recent tendencies. The volume also gives the table of contents of the most important early arithmetics.

Monroe, Will S. "Joseph Neef and Pestalozzianism in America"; in *Education,* vol. 14, p. 479. (April, 1894.)

*Monroe, Will S. *History of the Pestalozzian Movement in the United States.* 244 pp. C. W. Bardeen, Syracuse, 1907.

An important work. Good on early movements — Oswego, St. Louis — and with good bibliography.

*Parker, S. C. *History of Modern Elementary Education.* 506 pp. Ginn & Co., Boston, 1912.

Chapter XV is very good on Pestalozzian object teaching and oral instruction, and Chapter XVI on Pestalozzian formalism and degenerate object teaching, while Chapters XVII and XVIII are very detailed and readable accounts of the Herbartian and Froebelian movements in education.

Phillips, C. A. "Development of Methods in teaching Modern Elementary Geography"; in *Elementary School Teacher,* vol. 10, pp. 427–39, 501–15.

*Reeder, R. R. *Historical Development of School Readers.* 92 pp. Columbia University *Contributions to Philosophy, Psychology, and Education,* vol. VIII, No. 2. New York, 1900.

A good description of early readers, and of the evolution of modern methods of teaching reading.

Smith, D. E. "The Development of American Arithmetic"; in *Educational Review,* vol. 52, pp. 109–18. (Sept., 1916.)

Historical sketch of influences and results.

*Vandewalker, N. C. *The Kindergarten in American Education.* 274 pp. The Macmillan Co., New York, 1908.

A very important historical account of the kindergarten movement in the United States.

CHAPTER XI

NEW MODIFYING FORCES

WE have now traced the evolution of the American public school from the beginnings of education at public expense down through the educational reorganization which took place within the school between 1860 and 1900, and have shown how the native American elementary school was modified and expanded and changed in character as the result of new educational ideas which came to us from abroad. Since 1860, too, but particularly since about 1885 to 1890, our schools have also been profoundly modified in character and changed in direction by forces other then educational, and to these we next turn. In doing so we shall need to go back and pick up the beginnings of these new forces, trace briefly their development, and point out their far-reaching influence on our educational aims and procedure. The two great new forces to which we refer were foreign immigration and the industrial revolution. These two combined produced vast social changes which in turn have necessitated important changes in our educational aims and practices.

I. Changes in the Character of our People

Our original stock. In previous chapters it has been shown that in all our early educational traditions and procedure we were essentially English. The Dutch parochial school had been established in a few towns in New Amsterdam, but most of these had lapsed or been superseded by English schools after New Amsterdam passed to the control of the English. Some Lutheran Swedes had settled along the Delaware and established there their type of schools, but in time these were assimilated by the English around them and they, too, became English-speaking schools. Only in Pennsylvania was there any marked grouping of non-English-speaking peoples. We were in origin, and by the time of the American Revolution certainly had become, an English-type colony, speaking the English language, following English customs and observances, adopting English law and English habits in morality and Sunday observances, and such schools as existed were, always excepting the Germans of Pennsylvania, almost entirely English-speaking schools.

Some conception as to the character of our original population may be obtained from the records of the first Federal Census, taken in 1790. It was not customary then, as it is now, to note down the country in which each person was born and the nationality of the parents, but an

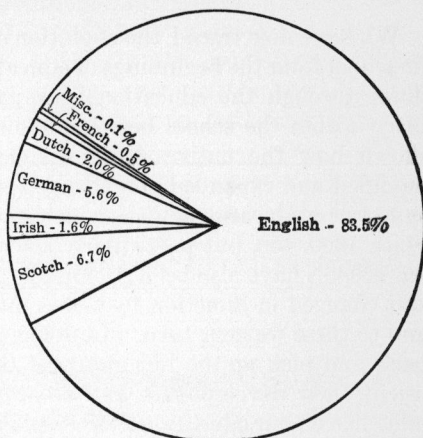

FIG. 60. NATIONALITY OF THE WHITE POPULATION, AS SHOWN BY THE FAMILY NAMES IN THE CENSUS OF 1790

analysis has been made of the names of all persons appearing on the lists of this first census to determine their original nationality. The result is shown, for the white population, in the accompanying drawing. This shows that 83.5 per cent of the population possessed names indicating pure English origin, and that 91.8 per cent had names which pointed to their having come from the British Isles. The next largest name-nationality was the German, with 5.6 per cent, and these were found chiefly in Pennsylvania, where they constituted 26.1 per cent of the total population. Next were those having Dutch names, who constituted 2 per cent of the whole population, and 16.1 per cent of the population of New York. No other nationality constituted over one half of one per cent of the total. The New England States then were almost as English as England itself, 93 to 96 per cent of the names being pure English, and 98.5 to 99.8 per cent being from the British Isles.

The stream of immigrants begins. Up to 1820 the annual immigration into the United States was quite small, mostly English in character, and no records as to it were taken by the Government. In 1820, the first year for which records were kept, the number coming was only 8385, and it was not until 1825 that the number of immigrants reached fifty thousand, and not until 1842 that it reached one hundred thousand. Excepting only two years during our Civil War, the immigration to the United States, since 1845, has never been less than one hundred thousand. Between 1847 and 1857 inclusive, the number coming was in no year less than two hundred thousand, and in 1854 the number was 427,833. Since 1903 the numbers have ranged from three quarters of a million to one and one quarter millions each year, and the total immigration from 1820 to 1914 has been 32,102,671. Compared with this vast movement of peoples to a new world the migrations of the Germanic tribes — Angles, Saxons, Jutes, Goths, Visigoths, Ostrogoths, Vandals, Sueves, Danes, Burgundians, Huns — into the old Roman Empire in the fourth and fifth centuries pale into insignificance. No such great movement of peoples was ever known before in history.

Up to 1825 at least, the immigrants coming to the United States continued to be largely English, Scotch, and Protestant Irish, with a few Protestant Germans to the Eastern cities and to Pennsylvania. These fitted in easily with the existing population, and awakened but little notice and no fear. Between 1820 and 1840 both the German and the Irish immigration increased rapidly, and Irish Catholics from central and southern Ireland began to replace the northern Protestant Irish of the earlier migration. It was during the period from 1830 to 1850 that the Catholic parochial-school question first began to appear in cities of the North Atlantic group of States, and the controversy over the secularization of American education was brought to the front.

The north and west of Europe migrations. The years 1846–48 were years when the potato crop of Ireland was almost a complete failure, and, driven out by famine and by the oppressive system of landlordism which prevailed, great numbers of Irish immigrants came to the United States to find a new home. They settled chiefly in the cities of the North Atlantic group of States. Between 1845 and 1855 a million and a quarter came, and again, in 1882, following another famine, Irish immigration reached another high point. In all, over four millions of Irish have come to us since 1820, and they still constitute ten per cent of all our foreign-born people. Unlike the other North and West of Europe peoples, Ireland had a high degree of illiteracy. The census of 1841 showed that fifty-three per cent of the people of Ireland over five years of age were unable to read and write. Less than one half of those who came in the early migration, and scarcely one quarter of those who came later, could read and write, and the coming of such large numbers of people, poor and uneducated, who would ultimately become citizens and voters, awakened a solicitude for our political future among the people of the northeastern part of the United States which materially aided in the establishment there of public education and the development of state oversight and control.

About this time the United States also began to receive large numbers of Germans. Up to 1830 the number of this nationality arriving had been negligible, as the government at home had been satisfactory. After 1835, however, with the growing narrowness of the German state governments, German immigration began a constant increase, and after the unsuccessful German revolutions of 1848 great numbers of liberty-loving Germans, chiefly from the South German States, left the Fatherland and came to this country. During the decade from 1846 to 1855 over a million and a quarter came, settling in the cities of the eastern part of the United States and the cities and farming regions of the upper Mississippi Valley. After the establishment of the Imperial German Government, in 1870, and the definite embarkation of this Government on an aggressive military policy, large numbers of Germans left the Empire and came to us, approximately two millions arriving between 1881 and 1895. In all, a total of about five and a quarter million Germans, the best and most liberty-loving of the German people, have come to this country since 1820.

Unlike the Irish who came earlier, the Germans were a picked and a well-educated class, the earlier ones having left Germany largely because of political and religious oppression, and the later ones largely to escape forced military service. The early Germans usually came in groups, formed settlements by themselves, held themselves aloof, and for a time constituted a segregated intellectual aristocracy among our people. They too awakened considerable alarm, as they, for a time, showed but little disposition to become a part of our national life.

During the middle years of the nineteenth century large numbers of English came, in all a total of about three and a half millions having arrived since 1820. After 1840 Scandinavians, attracted by the free farms of the Northwest, also began to appear, though they did not reach the great period of their migration until the decade of the eighties. In all nearly two million Scandinavians have come to our shores.

While these different peoples frequently settled in groups and for a time retained their foreign language, manners, and customs, they have not been particularly difficult to assimilate. Of all these early immigrants the Germans have shown the greatest resistance to the assimilative process. All except the Irish came from countries which embraced the Protestant Reformation (see map, Fig. 1, page 7), where general education prevailed, and where progressive methods in agriculture, trade, and manufacturing had begun to

supersede primitive methods. All were from race stock
not very different from our own, and all possessed courage,
initiative, intelligence, adaptability, and self-reliance to a
great degree. The willingness, good-nature, and executive
qualities of the Irish; the intellectual thoroughness of the
German; the respect for law and order of the English; and the
thrift, sobriety, and industry of the Scandinavians have
been good additions to our national life.

Change in character of our immigration. After about
1882 the character of our immigration changed in a very remarkable manner.
Immigration from
the North and West
of Europe began
to decline rather
abruptly, and in its
place immigration
from the South and
East of Europe set
in. This soon de-
veloped into a great
stream. Practically
no Italians came to
us before 1870, but
by 1890 they were
coming at the rate
of twenty thousand
a year, and during
the five-year period

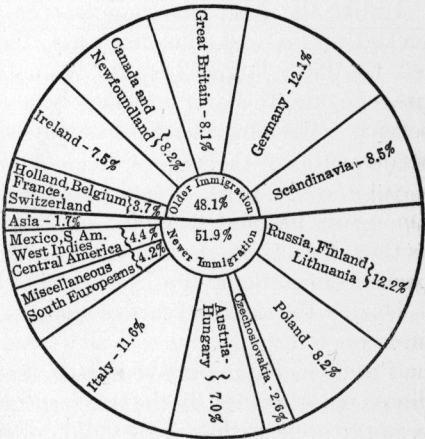

Fig. 61. Foreign-born in the United States
as shown by the Census of 1920

1906–10 as many as 1,186,100 arrived. After 1880, in
addition, people from all parts of that medley of races
which formerly constituted the Austro-Hungarian Empire
— Poles, Bohemians, Moravians, Slovaks, Slovenes, Ruthe-
nians, Dalmatians, Croatians, Bosnians, Magyars, and Aus-
trians; Serbs, Bulgars, Roumanians, Montenegrins, and
Albanians from the Balkans; Slavs, Poles, and Jews from
Russia; and Japanese and Koreans from the Far East, be-

gan to come in numbers.   After 1900, Finns and Lithuanians
from the North, driven out by Russian persecution; and
Greeks, Syrians, Armenians, and Turks from the South,
have come in shiploads to our shores.   French Canadians
also have crossed the border in large numbers and crowded
into the mill-towns of New England.   As a result we had, in
1910, thirteen and a half millions of foreign-born people in
our population, distributed as shown in Figure 62, of whom
practically forty per cent had come from the South and East
of Europe.   Of the immigration since 1900 almost eighty
per cent has come from there.   In addition to these thirteen
and a half millions of foreign-born, an additional nine and
a half million were native-born, but the children of foreign
parents, and of another six million one parent was foreign-
born.

These Southern and Eastern Europeans were of a very
different type from the North and West Europeans who preceded them.   Largely illiterate, docile, lacking in initiative, and almost wholly without the Anglo-Saxon conceptions of righteousness, liberty, law, order, public decency, and
government, their coming has served to dilute tremendously
our national stock and to weaken and corrupt our political
life.   Settling largely in the cities of the North, the agricultural regions of the Middle and the Far West, and the mining districts of the mountain regions, they have created
serious problems in housing and living, moral and sanitary
conditions, and honest and decent government, while popular education has everywhere been made more difficult by
their presence.   The result has been that in many sections
of our country foreign manners, customs, observances, and
language have tended to supplant native ways and the English speech, while the so-called "melting-pot" has had more
than it could handle.   The new peoples, and especially
those from the South and East of Europe, have come so fast
that we have been unable to absorb and assimilate them,
and our national life, for the past quarter of a century, has
been afflicted with a serious case of racial indigestion.

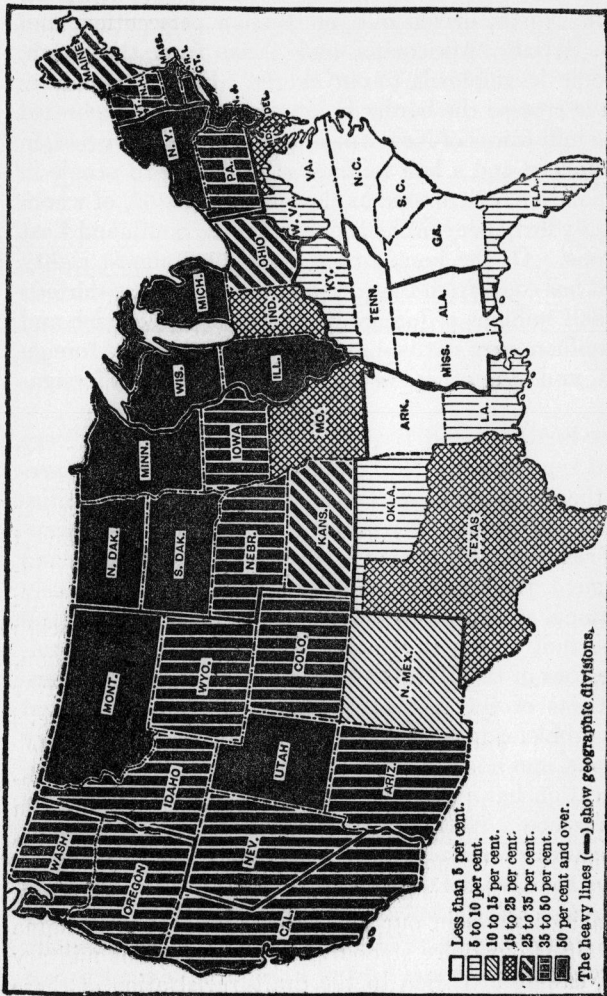

Fig. 62. Distribution of the Foreign-Born, by States

Showing the percentage of foreign-born whites, and native whites of foreign or mixed parentage combined, in the total population, 1910, by States.

Less than 5 per cent.
5 to 10 per cent.
10 to 15 per cent.
15 to 25 per cent.
25 to 35 per cent.
35 to 50 per cent.
50 per cent and over.

The heavy lines (——) show geographic divisions.

The United States to-day a great cosmopolitan mixture.
The result of this great world-wide movement of peoples is
that the United States to-day represents the most cosmopolitan mixture of peoples and races to be found anywhere on the
face of the earth.   Only in the Southern States is there an
absence of a large percentage of foreign-born, and there the
problem of the negro and his education takes the place of the
foreign-born educational problem.

How great the American mixture is we scarcely realize
until we take stock of our neighbors.   We buy our groceries
of Knudsen and Larsen, our meats of Klieber and Engel-
meier, our bread of Rudolf Krause, Petar Petarovich delivers our milk, Giuseppe Battali removes our garbage, Swen
Swensen delivers our ice, Takahira Matsui is our cook, and
Nicholas Androvsky has recently taken the place of Pancho
Garcia as our gardener.   We occasionally take dinner at a
café managed by Schiavetti and Montagnini, we buy our
haberdashery of Moses Ickelheimer, Isaac Rosenstein is our
tailor, Azniv Arakelian sells us our cigars, and Thirmutis
Poulis supplies our wants in ice cream and candies.   Timo-
thy Mehegan represents our ward in the city council, Patrick
O'Grady is the policeman on our beat, Nellie O'Brien teaches
our little girl at school, Nels Petersen is our postman,
Vladimir Constantinovitch is our street-sweeper, Lazar
Obichan reads our electric meter, Lorenzo Guercio sells
potted plants and flowers on the corner, Mahmoud Bey
peddles second-grade fruit past our door, and Alexis Grab-
lowsky mends and presses our suits and cleans our hats in
a little shop two blocks down the street.   The service ga-
rage, run by Pestarino and Pozzi, looks after our car, Emil
Frankfurter is the cashier at our bank, Kleanthis Vassar-
dakis shines shoes in our office building, and Wilhelmina
Weinstein is our office stenographer.   The recent military
poster, calling attention to the draft registration of those
18 to 45, was repeated in fifteen different languages on
the sheet.   The casualty list in the morning paper as we
write announces that, among others, such representative

American citizens as Rudolph Kochensparger, Robert Emmet O'Hanlon, Ralph McGregor, John Jones, Rastus Brown, Pietro Sturla, Rafael Gonzales, Dominico Sebatino, Ignace Olzanski, Diego Lemos, and Manthos Zakis have made the supreme sacrifice on the battle-fields of France in defense of the civilization of the world. If our earlier statesmen were concerned at the coming of the Irish and the Germans, well may we be alarmed at the deluge of diverse peoples which has poured into this Nation during the past forty years.

Assimilation and amalgamation. The problem which has faced and still faces the United States is that of assimilating these thousands of foreigners into our national life and citizenship. We must do this or lose our national character. The German tried to solve the problem with his subject peoples by coercion, and failed; the French and English hold their colonials by kind, considerate, and good government; we have either neglected the problem entirely or have trusted to our schools to handle the children and to our labor unions to initiate the adults. As a result, the census of 1910 showed that we had among us ten millions of foreign-born who professed no allegiance to the land of their adoption, and a large percentage of this number could neither read nor write English. Still worse, many of the number live in foreign settlements or foreign quarters in our cities, where they can get along without even speaking the English language, and their children not infrequently are sent to a non-English-speaking parochial school. Of the 11,726,506 immigrants who came to us during the four years preceding the outbreak of the World War, 26.5 per cent were unable to read and write any language, and not over 12 per cent could speak English.

In view of the large migrations of diverse peoples to us since 1845 we were fortunate, indeed, that before that time we had settled in the affirmative the question of general education at public expense; that we had provided for English schools, even for the Germans of Pennsylvania;

and that we had definitely eliminated the sectarian school
from our program for public education.   A common English
language, our common law and political institutions, our
common democratic life, our newspaper habit, our free social intercourse, our common free schools, our ease of communication, our tolerance of other peoples, and the general absence of a priesthood bent on holding nationalities together
for religious ends — all these have helped us in the assimilation of other races.   On the other hand, the process has been
retarded by the coming of such numbers, by city congregation and segregation, by the coming of so many male
adults without their wives and children, by the work of the
Germans in trying to preserve their language and racial habits and *Kultur*, and by the work of the Catholic and Lutheran
churches in endeavoring to hold nationalities together.

The greatest success in assimilating the new peoples who
have come to us has been made by the school and the labor
unions, but up to recent years the school has reached only
the children of those classes bringing their families with
them and who have not been attracted by the foreign-language parochial school.   With these children the results
have in general been remarkable, and the schools have proved
to be our greatest agency for unifying the diverse elements
of our population.   Even under the best circumstances,
though, it requires time to so assimilate the foreign-born
that they come to have our conceptions of law and order
and government, and come to act in harmony with the spirit
and purpose of our American national ideals.   After this end
has been attained, which usually requires two or three generations, the amalgamation of the descendants of these
peoples into our evolving American racial stock may take
place through intermarriage and the mixture of blood.   Assimilation is a blending of civilizations and customs to create
that homogeneity necessary for citizenship and national feeling, and may be promoted by education and social institutions and wise legislation; amalgamation is a blending of
races and bloods, and is a process of centuries.   Through

the assimilation of all our diverse elements we are preparing
the way for that future amalgamation of racial elements
which will in time produce the American race.

II. THE INDUSTRIAL REVOLUTION

Industrial changes since 1850.   In Chapter IV, under the
heading "Rise of Manufacturing," we traced somewhat
briefly the beginnings of manufacturing in the United States,
and pointed out how the application of steam, the perfecting
of inventions, and the development of transportation revolutionized the industrial methods of our people of the northeastern part of the United States, between 1820 and 1850.
We also pointed out how these industrial changes and the
rise of the factory system meant the beginnings of the breaking up of home and village industry, the inauguration of a
cityward movement of the population, the rise of entirely
new educational and social problems, the ultimate concentration of manufacturing in large establishments, and the
consequent rise of the city to a very important place in our
national life.

The changes which had been accomplished by 1850,
though, or even by 1860, were but the beginnings of a vast
change in the nature of our national life which has since
gone forward with ever-increasing rapidity, and has extended
to all parts of the Nation.   As a result the United States
stands to-day as the greatest manufacturing country of the
whole world.   There are few things connected with the
wonderful development of our country since 1850 which
stand out more prominently than the amazing rapidity with
which we have gone to the front as a manufacturing nation.
Awakening to the wonderful possibilities which the vast
native resources in iron, coal, timber, and mineral wealth
of the country gave us; utilizing the best European, and
especially the best English manufacturing experience; and
applying new technical knowledge, which in 1860 we had
scarcely begun to teach, — Yankee ingenuity and energy
and brains have since pushed American products to the front

by leaps and bounds. In textiles, in iron and steel products, and in high-grade tools and machinery in particular, our American products successfully compete throughout the world. In coal production, the lumber industry, and in agriculture the United States to-day stands first. The packing and exporting of meats and meat products has also become a great national industry, and American refrigerated beef and bacon and hams are sent to all quarters of the globe. In hundreds of specialized industries, such as the manufacture of furniture, desks, typewriters, office conveniences, automobiles, motor-cycles, bicycles, farm tractors, reapers and threshers, locomotives, printing-presses, sewing machines, surgical instruments, edge tools, electrical goods, plumbing supplies, phonographs, rifles, explosives, cotton goods, and shoes, American manufactured articles supply not only the home market, but are exported all over the world. Scarcely a year has passed, during the last forty at least, that American inventive genius and energy and labor combined have not wrested from other nations a world-lead in some new article of manufacture, and the result of the World War promises to be that the leadership in many new lines will pass to us. Particularly do we promise to gain at the expense of Germany in such large and important lines as the manufacture of dyes and chemicals, in which for so long the Germans had the lead.

Vast changes since Lincoln's day. We can perhaps get a better idea of the tremendous industrial development of the United States since 1860 if we try to picture to ourselves the things with which Lincoln was unacquainted. When he died, in 1865, the world was relatively simple and undeveloped, and business methods were old-fashioned compared with what we know to-day. If Lincoln were to return now and walk down Pennsylvania Avenue, in Washington, he would be astonished at the things he would see. Buildings more than three or four stories high would be new, as the steel-frame building was unknown in 1865. The large plate-glass show windows of the stores, the electroliers along the

curb, the moving-picture establishments, the electric eleva-
tors in the buildings, the beautiful shops, and especially the
big department stores would be things in his day unknown.
The smooth-paved streets and cement sidewalks would be
new to him. The fast-moving electric street-cars and motor-
vehicles would fill him with wonder. Even a boy on a bi-
cycle would be a curiosity. Entering the White House, the
sanitary plumbing, steam heating, electric lights, electric
fans, telephones, typewriters, modern office furniture and
filing devices, the Edison phonograph and dictaphone, and
the fountain pen would have to be explained to him. In his
day plumbing was in its beginnings, coal-oil lamps and gas-
jets were just coming into use, and the steel pen had but
recently superseded the quill. There were stenographers
then, but all letters and papers were still written out by hand.
As for communication, messenger boys with written notes
ran everywhere on foot, and the transaction of all kinds of
business was exceedingly slow. The telegraph had recently
been installed, but it still required two weeks to get news
from England, and two months from Manila or Valparaiso.

The steel rail, the steel bridge, fast vestibuled trains, high-
powered locomotives, transcontinental railways, dining-
cars, refrigerator cars, artificial ice, friction matches, repeating rifles, machine guns, smokeless powder, submarines,
dynamite, money orders, special-delivery stamps, weather
reports and flags, the parcels post, gasoline engines, electric
motors, type-setting machines, chemical fire engines, self-
winding watches, player-pianos, the cable, the wireless, the
traction engine, the cream separator, the twine binder, the
caterpillar tractor, — these and hundreds of other inventions in common use, which now simplify life and add to our
convenience and pleasure, were all alike unknown. The
cause and mode of transmission of the great diseases which
decimated armies and cities — plague, cholera, malaria, yellow fever, typhoid fever, typhus, and dysentery — were all
unknown. Anæsthetics, sanitary plumbing, paved streets,
sleeping-cars, and through railways were just coming in when

Lincoln died, while such terms as "bacteria," "eugenics," "evolution," and "sanitation" were seldom used or entirely unknown. Much of what every one ate or wore was still manufactured in the home, the apprenticeship system still ruled in almost all lines, and every youngster still had "chores" to do and enough physical and manual activity to answer all human needs. Life was still relatively simple, agriculture was still the great industry of the people, and 77.8 per cent of the people of the Nation still lived on the farms. But 16.1 per cent had settled in cities of 8000 or more inhabitants, and there were but 141 of these in the entire United States.

Changes in the nature of living. Since 1865 vast and far-reaching changes have taken place in the nature and character of our living, with the result that we live to-day, in many respects, in an entirely new world. During the past hundred years steam and steel, and during the past forty years electricity and medical science, have wrought an alteration in human living greater than was wrought in all the time from the Crusades up to a hundred years ago.

Along with the far-reaching industrial transformation has come a tremendous increase in the sum of our common human knowledge. The applications of science have become so numerous, books and magazines have so multiplied and cheapened, trade and industry have become so specialized, all kinds of life have been so increased in complexity, and the inter-relationships of mankind have been so extended and have grown so intricate, that what one needs to know to-day has been greatly increased over what was the case half to three quarters of a century ago. Once the ability to read and write and cipher distinguished the educated from the uneducated man; to-day the man who knows only these simple arts is an uneducated man, hardly fitted to meet the struggle for existence in which he is placed, and certainly not fitted to participate in the complex industrial and political life of which he now forms a part.

Since 1860 cities have greatly increased in number and in

the complexity of their life. From 141 of 8000 inhabitants or over in 1860, there are over 1200 of over 10,000 to-day, and some 15,000 incorporated towns and cities of all sizes. Approximately one half our people to-day live in incorporated towns or cities, as against one sixth sixty years ago. Great numbers of people of all kinds have congregated together in the cities, as the industrial life of the Nation has developed, and within recent decades entire new cities have been built and developed to supply the needs of the workers in some one or two lines or a group of related industries.

Rural life also greatly changed. The effects of the industrial revolution have not been confined to the cities alone, but have extended to all parts of our national life. Life in the rural districts has experienced an almost equally great change in character and direction. During the past thirty years in particular there have been marked alterations in the character of life on the farm. Nearly everywhere the harsh conditions and limitations of the earlier period have been modified, everywhere the applications of science and the products of the press have made their way and rendered life easier and created new interests, everywhere new medical and sanitary knowledge have made rural life more desirable, and everywhere the old isolation and the narrow provincialism of the rural classes are passing away. The great world-wide increase in city population and in the number engaged in the manufacturing industries, all of whom are food and clothing consumers but not producers, coupled with a world-wide increase in the standard of living and the per capita food and clothing consumption of the people, have created much greater demands for fruits, grains, meats, hides, cotton, and wool than heretofore. The general introduction of scientific processes and methods and machinery, the development of farming on a large scale, and the opening of world-wide markets due to the perfecting of means of transportation, have alike combined to change farming from a self-subsistence industry and make of it a profitable business undertaking. Near our large cities, intensive truck gardening has been extensively developed, and in this our foreign-born have been particularly successful. New agricultural regions have been opened, new grains and fruits introduced into old regions, new methods of marketing and preserving demonstrated, and new bookkeeping methods have been employed. Largely as a result of the work of the new agricultural colleges, agricultural education has been placed on a firm foundation, and practical and helpful assistance has been extended to farmers all over the United States.

Within recent years a marked change in the character of the farming population itself has taken place. In the richest agricultural sections of our country the earlier sturdy type of American farmer is everywhere giving way to the tenant farmer, because he is leasing his farm and moving to the town or city to live more comfortably and to give his children better educational and social advantages. From thirty to forty per cent of the farms in the North Central States, and from fifty to sixty-five per cent of the farms in the South, are to-day let out to tenant farmers. Still more, the foreign-born tenant is rapidly displacing the native-born, and Italians, Austro-Huns, Poles, Slavs, Bulgars, Serbs, Armenians, and Japanese, and in the South Italians and negroes, are to-day replacing the well-to-do native farmer of an earlier period, and it is probable that the movement of these new peoples to the farms is as yet only in its beginnings. Capable agriculturists, thrifty and economical, they pass successively from farm laborer to tenant, and from tenant to owner. The agricultural consequences of these changes in the character of our rural population may not be very significant, but the educational and social consequences are very important and very far-reaching.

III. Effect of these Changes on the Home

Changes in the character of industry. With the great industrial development of our country, and the concentration of industries about certain centers of population where cheap labor is plentiful, the character of home life has altered greatly. To these centers both the country resident and the immigrant have been attracted in large numbers. The opportunities for gaining a livelihood there at easier or more remunerative labor have drawn to these population-centers many who have found great difficulty in adjusting themselves to the new and peculiar life. The most energetic and capable of our people, as well as the most vicious and corrupt, have seen larger opportunity for success in the city and have left better home-life conditions to join the city throngs.

The modern city is essentially a center of trade and industry, and home life and home conditions must inevitably be determined and conditioned by this fact. The increasing specialization in all fields of labor has divided the people into dozens of more or less clearly defined classes, and the increasing centralization of trade and industry has concentrated business in the hands of a relatively small number of people. All standards of business efficiency indicate that this should be the case, but as a result of it the small merchant and employer are fast giving way to large mercantile and commercial concerns. No longer can a man save up a few thousand dollars and start in business for himself with much chance of success. The employee tends to remain an employee; the wage-earner tends to remain a wage-earner. New discoveries and improved machinery and methods have greatly increased the complexity of the industrial process in all lines of work, and the worker in every field of trade and industry tends more and more to become a cog in the machine, and to lose sight of his part in the industrial processes and his place in our industrial and civic and national life.

The effect of such conditions on the family has been very noticeable, and in some respects very unfortunate. Under the older village and rural-life conditions a large family was an asset, as every boy and girl could help about the house and farm from an early age. In doing this they received much valuable education and training. City life, though, has changed a large family from an asset to a serious liability, and the result is shown in the large number of small or childless families found there. Only among the foreign-born and in rural communities does one any longer find large families common. The native American, and the more thoughtful citizen generally, tends to limit the size of his family to the few children he can clothe and educate according to his standard of life.

Changes in the character of home life. As a result of the changes of living incident to the change from an agricultural to an industrial society, and the rapid development of city-life conditions, the home life has greatly altered in character. Once it was a center where the rudiments of almost all the trades and industries of life were practiced, and where both boy and girl obtained many valuable life experiences. In the villages, blacksmiths, wagon-makers, cabinet-makers, harness-makers, shoemakers, millers, and saw-mill workers carried on most of the fundamental trades. In their small establishments the complete industrial processes were carried through, and could be seen and learned. In the homes girls were taught to sew, make hats and clothing, cook, bake, wash, iron, mend, and clean the house. On the farm the boy learned to plant, cultivate, and reap the crops, care for and feed the horses and stock, watch and learn to read the signs of the weather, mend wagons and harness, make simple repairs, and go to town on errands. The boy in town as well had the daily "chores" to attend to.

These conditions, within the past half-century, have largely passed away. Since about 1890 the process of change has been particularly rapid. The farm is no longer the center of industry it used to be. Purchases at city stores supply much that formerly required hand labor. Both the farmer and his wife have been freed from much that used to constitute the drudgery of life, and have been given much new time to read and think and travel. In the villages the small artisans and their apprentices have almost completely disappeared. Wagons now come from South Bend, furniture is made largely in Grand Rapids, harness comes largely from New York State, and shoes from the cities of eastern Mas-

sachusetts, while flour is ground in large mills in a few industrial centers. The telephone, the delivery wagon, the
elevator, gas and electricity, running water, the bakery and
delicatessen shop, the steam laundry, and the large department store have taken from children their "chores" and
from their parents much hard labor. As a result homes in
our cities have come to be little more than places where
families eat and sleep and children grow up.

There are many compensating advantages, it must be
remembered, for the losses the home has sustained. Children grow up under much more sanitary conditions than
formerly, are better cared for, have far greater educational
advantages provided for them, learn much more from their
surroundings, are not so overworked, and have opportunities which children did not have in an earlier day. Still, a
boy or girl under modern living conditions has so little of the
old-fashioned home-life, so little useful manual activity, and
acquires so much information through the eye and the ear
and the senses and so little by actual doing, that the problem
of providing a proper environment and education for town
and city children, and of utilizing their excess leisure time in
profitable activities, has become one of the most serious as
well as one of the most difficult social and educational problems now before us.

The home, nevertheless, has gained. Despite the concentration of industry and business in the hands of a small
percentage of our people, the virtual abolition of apprenticeship, the concentration of manufacturing in large establishments where specialized labor is the rule, and the prevalence
of much poverty and wretchedness among certain classes of
our people, society as a whole is by no means the worse for
the change, and in particular the poor have not been growing poorer. The drudgery and wasteful toil of life have
been greatly mitigated. People have leisure for personal
enjoyment previously unknown. The trolley-car, the automobile, and the "movies" have brought rest, recreation, and
enjoyment to millions of people who in previous times knew

only work, and whose pleasures consisted chiefly of neighborhood gossip, church attendance, and drink. Wages have
increased faster than the cost of living, the advantages of
education have been multiplied and extended, health conditions in home and shop and town are better than ever
known before, much more is done for people by the corpora-
tions and the State than formerly, and the standard of com-
fort for those even in the humblest circumstances has advanced beyond all previous conception. The poorest work-
man to-day can enjoy in his home lighting undreamed of in
the days of tallow candles, warmth beyond the power of the
the old smoky soft-coal grate, kitchen conveniences and an
ease in kitchen work that our New England forefathers probably would have thought sinful, and sanitary conditions and
conveniences beyond the reach of the wealthiest even half
a century ago. If the owner of the poorest tenement house
in our cities to-day were to install the kind of plumbing
which was good enough for George Washington, we should
lock him up. The family as a unit has gained tremendously
by the changes of the past forty to fifty years; the losses
have come to the children and to society and government.

Weakening of the old educative influences. As an accompaniment of the far-reaching nature of these recent
changes in the character of our living and of our population,
there has followed a general weakening of the old social
customs and traditions which once exercised so strong a
restraining and educative influence on the young. Children
formerly, much more than now, were taught reverence,
courtesy, respect, proper demeanor, obedience, honesty,
fidelity, and virtue, and both boys and girls were trained in
useful employments. The Church, too, was a much more
potent factor in the lives of both old and young than it is
to-day. The young were trained to go to Sunday School
and Church, and Sunday was observed as a day of rest and
religious devotion. The minister was generally respected
and looked up to by both parents and children. A religious
sanction for conduct was often set forth. Communities

were small and homogeneous in character, and every one's actions were every one's business. The community code of conduct and community sentiment exercised strong restraints. The positive convictions of the older members served to check the tendencies toward waywardness in both boys and girls, while the number of opportunities to go wrong were much fewer than they are to-day. Along certain lines these early restraining influences were highly educative, served to keep many a boy and girl in the path of rectitude, and helped to train them for an honest and a respectable life.

Changes that have taken place. In some of our smaller and older communities these conditions still in part persist, though much modified by the character of present-day life, but in the cities, towns, and the newer parts of the country these older educative influences and traditions have largely broken down, or have entirely ceased to exist. The little homogeneous communities, with their limited outlook and local spirit, have been changed in character by the coming of a much more cosmopolitan population, semi-urban conditions, and a much freer and easier life. The Church has lost much of its hold and influence over the young, and frequently the parents give it only nominal allegiance. Thousands of children are growing up to-day without any kind of religious training, and the former general knowledge of Biblical history and characters has largely passed away. New sects and religions, as well as new nationalities and races of people, have come among us, and within a generation the character of Sunday observance has greatly changed. The attitude of the people generally toward the old problems has been materially altered. Parents everywhere are less strict than they used to be. The discipline of the young in obedience and proper demeanor is no longer fashionable, and the attitude of thousands of communities to-day, as expressed in their life, their newspapers, their city government, and their general failure to enforce obedience to law, is really opposed to righteousness and good citizenship. The home, altogether too often, is unintelligent and neglectful in the handling of children, and not infrequently it has abdicated entirely and turned the whole matter of the education and discipline of the young over to the public school to handle.

The effect of all these changes in our mode of living is written large on our national life. The social and industrial revolutions which we have experienced have been far-reaching in their consequences. The home and life conditions of an earlier period are gone, never to return. This country has passed through that stage of its national development. Instead, we now form a part of a new and vastly more complex world civilization, in competition with the best brains of all mankind, with a great and an ever-increasing specialization of human effort taking place on all sides, and with new and ever more difficult social, commercial, industrial, educational, and human-life problems awaiting solution. We have given up our earlier isolation and independence, — social, political, and industrial, — and have become dependent even for the necessities of life upon the commerce of remote regions and distant peoples. For us the world has become both larger and smaller than it used to be, and its parts are linked up with our future welfare to an extent never known before. The Spanish War did much to destroy our earlier isolation and independence; the great World War has cast us upon the middle of the world stage.

IV. EFFECT OF THESE CHANGES ON THE SCHOOL

New national needs make new demands. It is impossible to understand the present complexity of American public education, and the many new lines of educational effort being put into practice in our schools, except in the light of the great social and industrial and home-life changes of the past half-century which we have just traced. It is these vast and far-reaching social and industrial and home-life changes which have been behind the changes in direction which our public schools have taken during the past quarter of a century, and which underlie the most pressing problems in educational readjustment of the present. It is as true to-day as when public schools began that the nature of the national need must determine the character of the education provided. As civilization increases in complexity, education must broaden its activities and increase in efficiency.

Our schools are essentially time- and labor-saving devices, created by us to serve democracy's needs. To convey to the next generation the knowledge and accumulated experience of the past, important as this may be, we now see is neither the only nor the chief function of public education. Instead, our schools, within the past quarter-century, have been asked to prepare their children more definitely for personal usefulness in life, and the future citizen more directly for the to-morrow of our complex national and international existence. Instead of mere teaching institutions, engaged in imparting book-information and imposing discipline, our schools have been asked to grasp the significance of their social relationships, to transform themselves more fully into institutions for the improvement of democracy, and to prepare the young who attend them for greater social efficiency by teaching more that is directly useful and by training them better for citizenship in a democracy such as ours.

A new lengthening of the period of dependence. As modern city-life conditions have come more and more to surround both boys and girls, depriving them of the training and education which earlier farm and village life once gave, the school has been called to take upon itself the task of giving training in those industrial experiences and social activities which once formed so important a part of the education of American youths. With the breakdown of the old home and village industries, the passing of the old "chores," and the coming of the factory system and city-life conditions, it has come to be desirable that children should not engage in productive labor. On the contrary, all recent thinking and legislation have been opposed to their doing so. Both the interests of organized labor and the interests of the

Nation have set against child-labor. Even from an economic point of view, all studies which have been made as to the money-value of an education have shown the importance of children remaining in school as long as they are able to use with advantage the educational opportunities provided.

Wages of Two Groups of Brooklyn Citizens

	Those who left school at 14; Yearly Salary	Those who left school at 18; Yearly Salary
When 14 years of age	$200	$ 0
" 16 " " "	250	0
" 18 " " "	350	500
" 20 " " "	475	750
" 22 " " "	575	1,000
" 24 " " "	600	1,150
" 25 " " "	688	1,550
Total Salary 11 years	$5,112.50	
Total Salary 7 years		$7,337.50

Fig. 63. What Four Years in School paid

Notice that at twenty-five years of age the better-educated boys are receiving $900 per year more salary and have already, in seven years, received $2250 more than the boys who left school at fourteen years have received for eleven years' work. (From a United States Bureau of Education chart at the Panama Pacific Exposition, based on a study by the Brooklyn Teachers' Association.)

It has at last come to be a generally accepted principle that it is better for children and for society that they should remain in school until they are at least sixteen years of age. As a result, child life everywhere has recently experienced a new lengthening of the period of dependence and training, and all national interests now indicate that the period devoted to preparing for life's work should be further lengthened rather than shortened.

Everywhere the right of the State to compel communities to maintain not only the old common school, but special types of schools and advanced training, has been asserted and sustained by the courts. Conversely, the corollary to this assertion of authority, the right of the State to compel children to partake of the educational advantages provided, has also been asserted and sustained by the courts.

New social and national problems. As our social life has become broader and more complex, a longer period of guidance has become necessary to prepare for proper participation in it. As our industrial life has become more diversified, its parts narrower, and its processes more concealed, new and more extended training has been called for to prepare the worker for his task, to reveal to him something of the intricacy and interdependence of our modern social and industrial life, and to point out to him the necessity of each man's part in the social and industrial whole. With the ever-increasing subdivision and specialization of labor, the danger from class subdivision has been constantly increasing, and more and more has been thrown upon the school the task of instilling into all a social and political consciousness that will lead to unity amid our great diversity, and to united action for the preservation and improvement of our democratic institutions. As large numbers of the foreign-born have come to our shores, and particularly from countries where general education is not common and where the Anglo-Saxon conception of law, order, government, and public and private decency do not prevail, a new and still greater burden has been placed on all the educative forces of society to try to impart to these new peoples, and their children, something of the method and the meaning of our democratic life. As the children of these new classes have crowded into our public schools, our school systems have been compelled to pay more attention to the needs of these new elements in our population, and to direct their attention less exclusively to satisfying the needs of the well-to-do classes of society. Education has in consequence recently turned away still more from its earlier aristocratic nature, and has become more and more democratic in character. It is only as schools serve as instruments for the perpetuation and improvement of our democratic life that the general education of all at public expense can be justified.

Beginnings of the change. The period following 1860 was a period of internal reorganization of our elementary education. As has been shown, the school then became more clearly conscious of itself, and reorganized its teaching work along lines dictated by the new psychology of instruction which had come to us from abroad. The thorough adoption

of this new psychological point of view covered the period
from 1860 up to about 1900. Beginning back about 1880
to 1885, however, our schools began to experience a new but
steady change in purpose and direction along the lines of
the new social and democratic forces, though it is only since
about 1900 that any marked and rapid changes have set in.

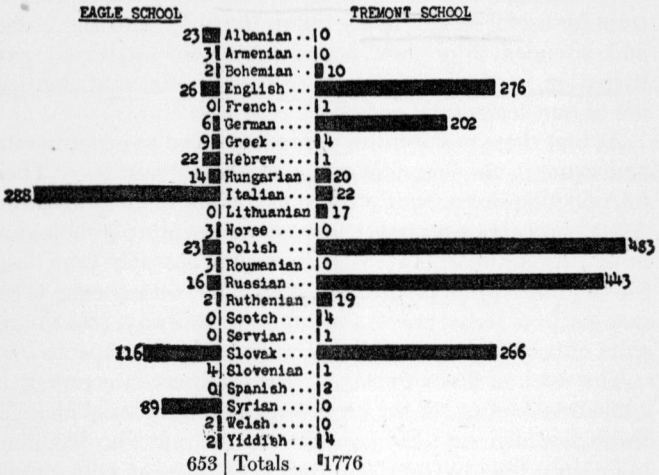

EAGLE SCHOOL		TREMONT SCHOOL
23	Albanian	0
3	Armenian	0
2	Bohemian	10
26	English	276
0	French	1
6	German	202
9	Greek	4
22	Hebrew	1
14	Hungarian	20
288	Italian	22
0	Lithuanian	17
3	Norse	0
23	Polish	483
3	Roumanian	0
16	Russian	443
2	Ruthenian	19
0	Scotch	4
0	Servian	1
116	Slovak	266
4	Slovenian	1
0	Spanish	2
89	Syrian	0
2	Welsh	0
2	Yiddish	4
653	Totals	1776

Fig. 64. Distribution by Nationalities of Pupils in two
Elementary Schools in Cleveland

From Miller's *The School and the Immigrant Child*, p. 34. Cleveland Foundation Survey
Volume. Reproduced by permission.

The old limited book-subject curriculum, both elementary
and secondary, could no longer meet the changing character
of our national life, and new studies began to be introduced.
Drawing, clay modeling, color work, nature-study, sewing,
cooking, and manual training were introduced here and there
into city elementary schools, and the sciences and the manual and home arts into the high schools. This was done
despite the objections of many conservative teachers and
citizens, and much ridicule from the public press. Many
spoke sneeringly of the new subjects as representing the

"fads and frills" of education, but they slowly made a place for themselves and have ever since remained. The cities, as in practically all other educational advances, were the leaders in introducing these new subjects and in attempting to transform their schools from mere disciplinary institutions, where drill was given in the mastery of the rudiments of knowledge, into institutions of democracy calculated to train for useful service in the office, the shop, and the home, and intended to prepare young people for intelligent participation in the increasingly complex social and political life of our democratic society.

At first these new studies were introduced as experiments, and came in as new drill and disciplinary studies. Their introduction was generally defended on disciplinary grounds. An attempt also was made to organize a definite psychological procedure for instruction in each, as had recently been done for the older fundamental subjects. In consequence these new subjects for a time made but slow headway, and the results obtained were not always what had been expected.

The work of John Dewey. The foremost interpreter, in educational terms, of the great social and industrial changes through which we have passed, and the one who has done more since 1895 to think out and state for us an educational philosophy suited to the changed and changing conditions in our national life, is John Dewey (1859–   ), for many years head of the School of Education at the University of Chicago, but more recently Professor of Philosophy at Columbia University. His work, both experimental and theoretical, has tended both to psychologize and socialize American education; to give to it a practical content, along scientific and industrial lines; and to interpret to the child the new social conditions of modern society by connecting the activities of the school closely with those of real life. Believing that the public school is the chief remedy for the ills of society, he has tried to change the work of the school so as to make it a miniature of society itself. Social efficiency, and not mere knowledge, he conceives to be the end, and this social efficiency is to be produced through participation in the activities of an institution of society, the school. The different parts of the school system thus become a unified institution, in which children are taught how to live amid the complexities of modern social life.

Education, therefore, in Dewey's conception, involves not merely learning, but play, construction, use of tools, contact with nature, expression, and activity, and the school should be a place where children are working rather than listening, learning life by living life, and becoming acquainted with social institutions and industrial processes by studying them. The work of the school is in large part to reduce the complexity of modern life to such terms as children can understand, and to introduce the child to modern life through simplified experiences. Its primary business may be said to be to train children in coöperative and mutually helpful living. The virtues of a school, as Dewey points out, are learning by doing; the use of muscles, sight and feeling, as well as hearing; and the employment of energy, originality, and initiative. The virtues of the school in the past were the colorless, negative virtues of obedience, docility, and submission. Mere obedience and the careful performance of imposed tasks he holds to be not only a poor preparation for social and industrial efficiency, but a poor preparation for democratic society and government as well. Responsibility for good government, with us, rests with all, and the school should prepare for the political life of to-morrow by training its pupils to meet responsibilities, developing initiative, awakening social insight, and causing each to shoulder a fair share of the work of government in the school.

Remarkable progress since 1898. The Spanish-American War of 1898 served to awaken us as a Nation and to shake us out of our earlier national isolation and contentment. Among other things it revealed to us something of the position we should probably be called upon to occupy in world affairs. Both it and the Russo-Japanese War which followed served particularly to concentrate attention on the advantages of general education, as it was "the man behind the gun" who won in each war. For the two decades following the Spanish-American War our country experienced an unprecedented period of industrial development and national prosperity, while the immigration of peoples further removed from our racial stock reached a maximum. The specialization of labor and the introduction of labor-saving machinery took place to an extent before unknown; city conditions became even more complex and potentially more dangerous; villages grew more urban, and a more cosmopolitan attitude began to pervade our whole life; the national feeling was intensified; and the national and state governments were called upon to do many things for the benefit of the people never attempted before.

In consequence, since 1898, public education has awakened a public interest before unknown. Since 1900 the Southern States have experienced the greatest educational awakening in their history — an awakening to be compared with that of Mann in Massachusetts and Barnard in Connecticut and Rhode Island. Everywhere state educational commissions and city school surveys have evidenced a new critical attitude on the part of the public. Much new educational legislation has been enacted; permission has been changed to obligation; minimum requirements have been laid down by the States in many new directions; and new subjects of instruction have been added by law. Courses of study have been entirely made over, and new types of textbooks have appeared. The democratic American high school has been transformed into a truly national institution. New normal schools have been founded, and higher requirements have been ordered for those desiring to teach. College departments of education have increased from nine in 1890 (first permanent chair in 1873) to something like four hundred to-day. Private gifts to colleges and universities have exceeded anything known before in any land. School taxes have been increased, old school funds have been more carefully guarded, and new constitutional provisions

as to education have been added.   Compulsory education
has begun to be a reality, and child-labor laws to be enforced.
A new interest in child-welfare and child-hygiene has arisen,
evidencing a commendable desire to look after the bodies
as well as the minds of our children.   The education of the defective and the delinquent, and the education of the foreign-
born everywhere, have received new attention.   In recent
years a new and an extensive national interest in agricultural,
industrial, vocational, and household education has become
clearly evident.   However much we may have lost interest
in the old problems of faith and religion, the American people
has come to believe thoroughly in education as the best
means for the preservation and advancement of the national welfare.   In the chapters which follow the changes
and additions and expansions which have accompanied the
educational evolution of the past quarter-century will be set
forth in some detail.

QUESTIONS FOR DISCUSSION

1. Show how the fact that all the earlier immigrants, except the Irish,
   came from lands which had accepted the Protestant Reformation
   ideas as to education made their assimilation easier.
2. Explain why the recent South and East of Europe immigration has
   served to dilute our national stock, and weaken and corrupt our
   political life.
3. Show how we have left the problem of adult assimilation largely to
   the labor unions and the political boss.
4. Canada allowed Quebec to retain its French language on entering the
   Union of Canada, with bad results.   Show what might have been the
   result had we allowed Pennsylvania to remain a German-language State.
5. Why is it much more dangerous when any foreign element collects
   in colonies than if it scatters?
6. Show why the extensive changes in home life since 1860 have necessitated a different type of education, and changed the large family
   from an asset to a liability.
7. What are the effects of the foreign-born tenant farmer on rural social
   life and the rural school?
8. It is often stated that the coming of so many foreign-born to America
   has tended to decrease the size of native American families.   Why
   should it?
9. Show how the vast industrial and commercial development has tended

to limit individual opportunities, and made broader education for all necessary.

10. Show how the elimination of waste and drudgery and disease has also made larger educational opportunities desirable.
11. How do you account for the change in the character of home training and discipline?
12. Would schools have advanced in importance as they have done had the industrial revolution not taken place? Why?
13. Why is more extended education called for as "industrial life becomes more diversified, its parts narrower, and its processes more concealed?"
14. Point out the social significance of the educational work of John Dewey.
15. Explain why the social and national changes since the Spanish American War should have led especially to the expansion of the high school.
16. Point out the value, in the new order of society, of each group of school subjects listed on page 370.

SELECTED REFERENCES

Betts, Geo. H. *Social Principles of Education.* 318 pp. Chas. Scribner's Sons, New York, 1912.

Chapter V, on institutional modes of experience, forms quite simple collateral reading for this chapter.

Bogart, E. L. *The Economic History of the United States.* 522 pp. Longmans, Green & Co., New York, 1908.

Part IV gives a very good sketch of agricultural and industrial development since 1860.

*Commons, John. *Races and Immigrants in America.* 242 pp. The Macmillan Co., New York, 1907.

A very readable volume. Chapters I to IV and IX are especially valuable as supplemental to this chapter.

*Dewey, John. *The School and Social Progress.* 130 pp. University of Chicago Press. 1899.

Lecture I, on the School and Social Progress, is an excellent statement of the problem.

Draper, A. S. "The Adaptation of Schools to Industry and Efficiency," in *Proceedings of the National Education Association*, 1908, pp. 65–78.

A good article on elementary-school waste, and the lack of balance and adaptation to national needs of elementary-school programs of study.

*Ellis, A. C. *The Money Value of Education.* 52 pp. Illustrated by charts. United States Bureau of Education, Bulletin No. 22, Washington, 1917.

A very valuable document showing the relation of education to individual success.

Ellwood, C. A. *Sociology and Modern Social Problems.* 394 pp. 2d ed.; American Book Co., New York, 1913.

> Chapter VIII, on the problem of the modern family; Chapter X, on the immigration problem; and Chapter XII, on the problem of the modern city, form good supplemental reading along the lines of part of this chapter.

*Fletcher, H. J. "Our Divided Country"; in *Atlantic Monthly,* vol. 117, pp. 223–33. (Feb., 1916.)

> An excellent article on the problem of the assimilation of our foreign-born.

Gibbins, H. de B. *Economic and Industrial Progress of the Century.* 594 pp. Chambers, London, 1901.

> A well-written volume on the progress made by the world during the nineteenth century.

Hyde, Wm. deW. "Social Mission of the Public School"; in *Educational Review,* vol. 12, pp. 221–35. (Oct., 1896.)

> An old, but a very good article.

Roberts, Peter. *Immigrant Races in North America.* 109 pp. Y.M.C.A. Press, New York, 1910.

> A brief and important volume, classifying and describing our immigrant people.

*Ross, E. A. *The Old World in the New.* 327 pp. Century Co., New York, 1914.

> An excellent work, classifying and describing the larger immigrant groups. Chapters 9–11, on the economic, social, and political effects of immigration, particularly good and useful.

*Ross, E. A. "The Value Rank of the American People"; in *Independent,* for Nov. 10, 1904. Also in his *Foundations of Sociology,* chap. XI.

> Characteristics; education; decimation; dilution.

Smith, W. R. *Introduction to Educational Sociology.* 412 pp. Houghton Mifflin Co., Boston, 1917.

> Chapter IV, on the family, good on the losses and new demands.

*Suzzallo, Henry. "Education as a Social Study"; in *School Review,* vol. 16, pp. 330–40. (May, 1908.)

> An excellent article on education and democracy.

U.S. Census Bureau. *A Century of Population Growth.* 303 pp. Washington, Government Printing Office, 1909.

> A very valuable volume, covering the changes from 1790 to 1900.

Warne, F. J. *The Immigrant Invasion.* 335 pp. Dodd, Mead & Co., New York, 1913.

> An illustrated and very interesting description of the older and newer immigrants.

CHAPTER XII

NEW EDUCATIONAL CONCEPTIONS AND EXTENSIONS

I. NEW CONCEPTION OF THE EDUCATIONAL PROCESS

The old knowledge conception. Our earlier school work was carried on on the unexpressed assumption that children were alike in needs and capacities, and that the training necessary for citizenship and life consisted in their acquiring certain book-knowledge which the school sought to impart. While some children were able to remain longer in school than were others, and consequently could climb higher on the educational ladder, the type of training while ascending the ladder was practically the same for all. Only in the high school were some options allowed. The knowledge aim, as we have seen, everywhere dominated instruction. Knowledge and civic virtue came to be regarded as somewhat synonymous, and disciplinary drill was the main purpose of the teaching process.

The psychological conception of the educational process, evolved between 1860 and 1890, also was based on an assumption that the mind could be trained by a uniform procedure. By means of selected subject-matter, now to be psychologically organized and presented, teachers would be able to drill the attention, will, memory, imagination, feelings, judgment, reasoning, ability in observation and sense discrimination, and other "powers of the mind," and thus awaken the egoistic and social feelings, stimulate the higher sentiments, and develop the moral character of the children so taught. By such means the citizenship-aim of education would be realized. The mind of the child was conceived of as consisting of a number of more or less water-tight compartments, or "faculties," the drilling of which was the business of education.

Courses of instruction were now much more minutely out-lined than before; the work for each grade was quite definitely laid down; the kind, amount, and order of subject-matter to be learned, by all pupils in all parts of the city, and regardless of age, past experience, future prospects, or physical or mental condition, was uniformly prescribed for all; and the examination test at the end of the term became the almost uniform proof that what had been outlined had or had not been mastered. Such courses of study and such conceptions of the educational process came to be the prevailing type between about 1870 and 1890, and are still found here and there in cities and villages which have not been touched by the newer conceptions of education.

Newer conceptions of educational work.   From the discussion in the preceding chapter, regarding changed social, industrial, and national conditions, the reader will have seen why such a knowledge conception of education ultimately must give way to newer and sounder ideas as to the nature and purpose of public education.   To meet the newer conditions of our national life not only must the direction of educational effort be changed, but also the education of different classes of children must take somewhat different directions.

Beginning here and there, back in the decade of the eighties, and becoming a clearly defined movement after about 1900, new courses of study and teaching directions appeared which indicated that those responsible for the conduct of the school systems were actuated by new conceptions as to the nature and purpose of the educational process.   Recognizing that the needs of society and the community were ever changing and growing, and that the needs of pupils, both by classes and individually varied much, the courses which were then outlined came to include alternatives and options, and to permit variations in the work done in different rooms and schools.   The excess of drill which had characterized earlier school work came to be replaced by lessons in subjects involving expression and appreciation, such as art, music,

NEW EDUCATIONAL CONCEPTIONS 367

manual work, domestic training, play, and humane education; the kindergarten and the kindergarten spirit began to effect changes in the character of the work of the receiving class and of the first grade or two of the elementary school; the discipline of the school everywhere became milder, and pupil-coöperation schemes for training in self-control arose; subjects which prepared better for efficient participation in the work of democratic society, such as hygiene, community civics, industrial studies, and thrift, were added; the social relationships of the classroom and school were directed, through studies in conduct and manners, toward the preparation of more socially efficient men and women; and the commercial and industrial life of the community began to be utilized to give point to the instruction in manual training, local history, civics, geography, and other related studies.

The main duty of the teacher, under these newer courses, came to be that of guiding and directing the normal processes of thought and action on the part of the pupils, of extending their appreciation in new directions, of connecting the work of the school with life in a better way, of widening the horizons of the thinking and the ambitious among the children, and of stimulating them to develop for themselves larger and better ideals for life and service. Instead of being fixed and largely finished products, this new type of courses of study remained plastic, to be changed in any direction and at any time that the best interests of the children might seem to require.

The new center of gravity. The most marked change between this newer type of course of study and the older type was the shifting of the center of gravity from that of the subject-matter of instruction to that of the child to be taught. The children of a particular community who presented themselves for education, and not the more or less traditional subject-matter of instruction, now came to be the real educational problem. The school, in consequence, began to change from that of a place where children prepare for life by learning certain traditional things, to a place where children live life and are daily brought into contact with such real industrial, social, community, and life experiences as will best prepare them for the harder problems of living which lie just ahead.

Viewed from the angle of child needs and child welfare the school became a new institution. Knowledge now came to be conceived of as life experience and inner conviction, and not as the memorization of the accumulated learning of the past; as a tool to do something with, and not as a finished product in itself. It came to be seen that facts possess but little real importance until they have been put to use. Child welfare and social welfare were perceived to be closely inter-twined. To train children for and to introduce them into membership in the little community of which they form a part, and from this to extend their sense of membership outward to the life of the State, the Nation, and to world civilization; to awaken guiding moral impulses; to fill them with the spirit of service; and to train them for effective self-direction; — these became the great tasks of the modern school.

The teacher in the new type of school. The teacher under the earlier type of school was essentially a drill master and a disciplinarian. It was his business to see that his pupils learned what was set before them, and to keep order. In the period between 1860 and 1900 it came to be conceived of as the teacher's chief function so to impart the selected subject-matter of instruction as to introduce it to the mind of the child by the most approved psychological procedure. The function of the teacher, though rendered much more important, still remained that of an instructor rather than that of a guide to instruction.

While retaining both of these earlier aims as important — drill where drill is needed, and proper psychological procedure in the teaching process — the newer conceptions as to school work went beyond either of these earlier aims. Both principals and teachers came to be expected to think over their work of instruction in the light of their local prob-

lems, with a view to adapting and adjusting the school work
to the particular needs and capacities of the pupils to be instructed.   Teaching now becomes a finer art and a still more
difficult psychological process than before.   Individual results, as well as group results, now were aimed at.   The
teacher proposed problems to the pupils, and then guided
them in examining and studying them.   Problems involving
life-situations became of greatest value.   In each case the
solving became the main thing; not the memorizing of some
one else's solution.

Both principals and teachers now came to stand as stim-
uli to individual activity, as whetstones upon which those
stimulated could bring their thinking to a keener edge, and
as critics by whose help young people might develop their
ability to reason accurately and well.   The aim of instruction became that of fitting young people, by any means
suited to their needs and capacities, to meet the responsibilities of life; to train them to stand on their own feet; to
develop in them the ability to do their own thinking; and
to prepare them for civic and social efficiency in the national life of to-morrow.

The spirit of the modern school.   Such, in brief, are the
actuating motives which have come to underlie the work of
the efficiently directed modern school.   The school often falls
far short of such ideals in the results it is able to achieve,
but such at least, consciously or unconsciously, are the actuating motives of its work.   Its aim is not mere knowledge,
except as knowledge will be useful; not mental discipline,
of the drill sort, but a discipline of the whole life; not a head
full of facts, but a head full of ideas; not rules of conduct
learned, but the ability to conduct one's self properly; not a
pupil knowing civics, but one who can think over civic questions; and not so much a learned as a well-trained output.

Through community civics, studies in science and industry, studies of community life, the study of community
health problems, studies of home needs, domestic science,
manual training, drawing, music, thrift training, manners

and conduct, play and games, as well as through a reorganization and redirection of the work in the older subjects — arithmetic, geography, language study, literature, history — the modern school aims to train pupils for greater social usefulness and to give them a more intelligent grasp of the social and industrial, as well as the moral and civic, structure of our modern democratic life.

The studies which have come to characterize the modern elementary school may now be classified under the following headings:

Drill Subjects	Content Subjects	Expression Subjects
Reading	Literature	Kindergarten Work
Writing	Geography	Music
Spelling	History	Manual Arts
Language	Civic Studies	Domestic Arts
Arithmetic	Manners and Conduct	Plays and Games
	Nature Study	School Gardening
	Agriculture	Vocational Subjects

The order of arrangement is not only almost the order of the historical introduction of the different subjects into the elementary school, but the three groups also represent the three great periods of our elementary school development. The drill subjects characterized the earlier school; the content subjects, excepting the last, the period of development between 1860 and 1890; and the expression subjects the modern elementary school development.

II. Necessary Adjustments and Differentiations

The average child. Up to relatively recently all our school work has been adjusted to meet the needs of the so-called "average child." As children of average capacity usually do reasonably well under courses of study constructed with average needs in view, the results for a long time were not noticeably bad. Teachers tried hard to bring all their pupils "up to grade." Those who could not master the subject-matter were in time promoted anyway, while the bright pupils marked time. The teacher naturally labored

most with those who had the most difficulty with their
studies. The figure below shows the results of such instruction in a city where the courses of study and the promotional
plans were arranged and carried out to meet the needs of the
great mass of the city's children. The great bulk of the

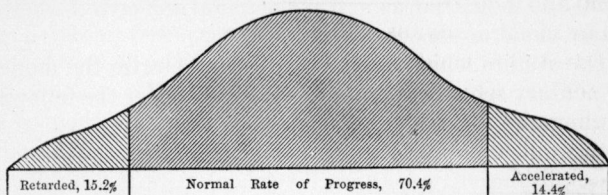

FIG. 65. PROMOTIONAL RESULTS IN A CITY FOLLOWING A COURSE OF
STUDY ADJUSTED TO THE AVERAGE CAPACITY OF THE PUPILS

From Cubberley's *Public School Administration*, p. 295.

pupils, it will be seen, made normal progress, while approximately equal percentages were ahead and behind their
grade. In an average school of 42 pupils in that city, 6
would be ahead of grade, 29 on grade, and 7 below grade.
This represents what may still be said to be an average and
a tolerably satisfactory condition. In many school systems
the percentage of retarded pupils is much higher, and the
number who are ahead much lower than in the school system here shown.

Children whom average courses do not fit. For some of
the children, though, it has been found that some or all of
the school work either is too difficult, or is entirely unsuited
to their needs. As a result they fail to make proper progress,
and gradually drop farther and farther behind. In the city
shown in the diagram, 15.2 per cent of the children were in
this class. One often finds such children two, three, or four
years over age for their grades, and accomplishing little in
school that is of value to them. On the other hand, for
some children the work is entirely too easy. Such children
can do their school work in short time and without half trying, and in consequence fall into habits of idleness by not

being worked to capacity. Often, too, these more capable children are held back by teachers, in part because their capacity is not recognized, and in part to keep their grade progress nearer to their age progress. The result is that they are actually retarded, even though they are "up to grade."

The effect of uniform and average courses of study on both classes of children has been found to be distinctly bad. On the one hand, the pupils who are held for years in the lower grades instead of advancing, too large for their seats, often unfit associates for the smaller children, and usually accomplishing little because the school work is too difficult for them or is not suited to their needs, are being prepared by the school to join the ranks of the inefficient and unsuccessful and dissatisfied in our working world. When one considers with what a meager life-equipment these young people eventually leave school, and what a poor preparation they have for social efficiency or intelligent citizenship, the bad results of unsuitable school work become evident. If the school can do better by these children it is its duty, as a social institution, to do so. To learn to succeed is one of the purposes of going to school. On the other hand, bright children are held back when they ought to be put into more advanced work, better suited to their needs and more likely to awaken their interest and enthusiasm. To learn to dawdle and loaf is not the purpose of education.

We thus see that we really have at least three well-recognized groups or types of children in our schools with which to deal — the below-average, the average, and the above-average. While these three classes have in a way for a long time been recognized, it is only relatively recently that we have begun to pay any particular attention to the needs of the two non-average groups. For some time we continued to educate the average child, hoping to bring the slower pupil up by a little extra attention, and letting the bright child rather shift for himself.

Flexible grading and promotion plans. The earliest and

most common attempt to remedy conditions arising from
the discovery that uniform courses of study were not fully
adjusted to the needs of all, was along the lines of coaching
the backward children by an assistant teacher. This plan
goes back to the days of the usher, or assistant teacher
(p. 229), and in its modern form was employed by Colonel
Parker at Quincy, Massachusetts, in the late seventies, and
still later was more fully applied at Batavia, New York.

Sept.	Oct.	Nov.	Dec.	Jan.	Feb.	Mar.	Apr.	May	June

FIG. 66. THE BATAVIA PLAN

Showing a half-year's progress for all pupils under this plan. The coaching of the slow
pupils by the assistant teacher makes this equality of progress possible. In North Denver this
plan was reversed, the assistant teacher working with the brighter pupils. (From Cubberley's *Public School Administration*, p. 302.)

The Batavia form became known, and about ten years ago
was tried in many parts of the United States. The plan
is well shown in the above drawing. The idea was to use
the assistant teacher to coach the laggards and bring them
up to grade, so that all might be promoted together.

The next plan tried was that of breaking up the yearly
grade system, which we had evolved, so as to make promotion easier and more frequent. The essential feature of this
plan consisted in providing semi-annual, or even quarterly
promotions, so that children might be advanced one half or
one quarter of a year's work, or be set back that amount
as conditions might seem to indicate as desirable. This
provided two grades, an A and B, for each school year, and
pupils failing of promotion need repeat only a half-year instead of a whole year of school work. Both of these ideas
were put into use after about 1875 to 1880, and the semi-
annual promotion has since become an established institu-

tion in our American schools.   The Batavia plan has met
with only limited favor.

Since about 1900 the problem has been approached from a
different angle, by the organization of what are variously
known as *supplementary classes, over-age classes, or ungraded
classes*, one or more such classes being provided for in each
large school building.   To such classes are sent the over-
aged, the "left-overs," those behind due to illness or absence, those who need special coaching to enable them to
understand some school subject or to make up some deficiencies, or those ahead and about ready to jump a grade.
Such pupils may remain in such classes all day, or only during the time they are receiving extra teaching, and for only a
few weeks or for quite a long time.   For pupils for whom
such classes are adapted they render the double service of
instructing them better and of relieving the regular class
teacher of their care.   Their purpose is not only to make the
graded system more flexible, and thus break up somewhat
the so-called "lock-step" of the public school, but also to
meet the needs of both the dull and the bright children, by
providing special instruction better adapted to their stage
of progress than is the regular instruction of the average
school grade.   As a matter of experience the brighter children usually receive but little direct help from such classes, as
they are used almost entirely for the dull or retarded pupils.
The average pupils who remain with the grade teacher receive better instruction because the more time-consuming
cases have been removed from the room.

Parallel courses of study.   None of these plans, however,
make any specific provision for the regular advancement of
the pupils capable of going ahead much faster than the
average.   Since about 1895 the wants of this class have been
somewhat recognized, and a number of different plans have
been evolved and put into operation, in different parts of the
United States, the purpose of which has been to provide
better for the needs of the brighter pupils in the school.
The address of President Eliot, of Harvard, before the Na-

tional Education Association, in 1892, on "Undesirable and Desirable Uniformity in Schools," did much to stimulate thinking as to the desirability of providing better for the needs of the more capable children.   The uniformity in grading and promotion he condemned as "suppressing individual differences instead of developing them and leaving

A Basal Course 8 Years	1		2		3		4		5		6		7		8	
	1	2	3	4	5	6	7	8	9	10	11	12	13	14	15	16	17	18	19	20	21	22	23

B Parallel Course 6 Years	1	2	3	4	5	6	7	8	9	10	11	12	13	14	15	16	17
	1		2		3		4		5		6	

FIG. 67. THE NEW CAMBRIDGE PLAN

Two parallel elementary-school courses, with one third more work assigned for each year in Course B than in Course A. (From Cubberley's *Public School Administration*, p. 304.)

individual capacities undiscovered and untrained, thus robbing the individual of happiness and serviceableness, and society of the fruits it might have enjoyed from the special endowments of thousands of its members."

The Cambridge, Massachusetts, plan, shown in the above drawing, is a 1910 revision of a still earlier plan inaugurated there to meet such needs as President Eliot had described. The essential features of it are two parallel courses of study, one of eight years for the average pupil, and a parallel course of six years in length for the gifted pupil, with natural transfer points which make it possible for a pupil to take any amount of time from six to eight, or even more, years to complete the course.   The Cambridge plan is typical of a number of somewhat similar parallel-course plans which have been evolved, the purpose of all of which has been to enable the more capable pupils to advance more rapidly.

Differentiated courses of study. About 1898 an experiment was begun at Baltimore, by Superintendent Van

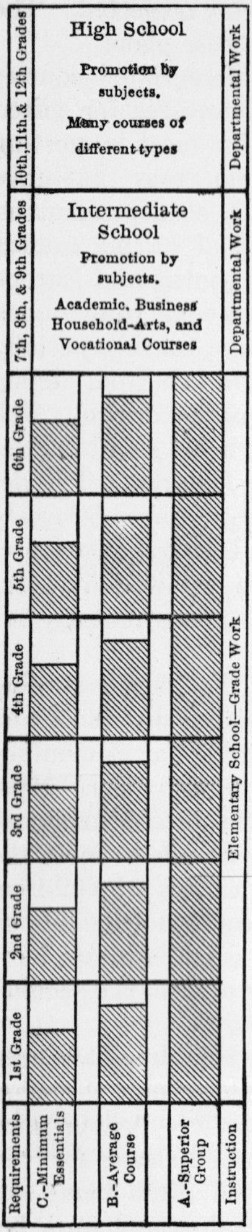

FIG. 68. THE DIFFERENTIATED-COURSE PLAN

The accompanying figure shows the plan as followed in Santa Barbara, California. The Baltimore plan was essentially the same. (From Cubberley's *Public School Administration*, p. 306.)

Requirements	1st Grade	2nd Grade	3rd Grade	4th Grade	5th Grade	6th Grade	7th, 8th, & 9th Grades	10th, 11th, & 12th Grades
C.-Minimum Essentials							Intermediate School — Promotion by subjects. Academic, Business, Household-Arts, and Vocational Courses	High School — Promotion by subjects. Many courses of different types
B.-Average Course								
A.-Superior Group								
Instruction	Elementary School—Grade Work						Departmental Work	Departmental Work

Sickle, and about the same time a somewhat similar one was tried for a short time at Santa Barbara, California, both of which were very important viewed from the standpoint of the best interests of our democratic life. Similar experiments have since been tried and are still in use in a number of places. The essential idea underlying each is that children are different not only in mental capacity but in future possibilities as well; that they fall roughly into three groups — the slow, the average, and the gifted; that a course of study for each group should be worked out which is up to but not beyond the capacities of the pupils of each group to accomplish; that transfer from one group to the other, in either direction, should be easy; that during the first six years of school life the courses should vary in the amount of work done, but not in the time consumed; and that, after this preliminary sorting period, the largest possible opportunities should be given to the gifted group to move rapidly, take extra studies, and enjoy extra educational advantages, the other groups at the same time not being neglected. The adjoining diagram shows the nature of these plans.

The prime idea underlying these differentiated courses has been that of providing better advantages for gifted children, and as such they are among the most interesting experiments for the improvement of democracy that have been made. No form of government is so dependent on intelligence as is a democracy. Instead of having leaders trained for us in separate schools, as in continental Europe (see Fig. 51, page 268), they must with us come from among the mass of our citizenship. A democracy, too, is especially in need of leaders to guide the mass, and it is from among its gifted children that the leaders must be drawn. The future welfare of this Nation depends, in no small degree, upon the right education of our gifted children. The degree to which our civilization moves forward depends largely upon the work of creative thinkers and leaders in science, trades, industry, government, education, art, morality, and religion. Moderate ability can follow, or can imitate, but superior ability must point the way.

Differentiated classes and schools. The flexible-grading idea may be said to have become common by 1890, and parallel and differentiated courses of study for elementary pupils have been introduced almost entirely since 1900. Largely since 1900, too, we have seen the establishment of a number of special types of classes or schools to meet the educational needs of these different classes of children. Realizing that the three large groups could not include all classes in need of special training, our school systems have begun the organization of special classes to meet the peculiar needs of small percentages of their children.

In a few places special classes for gifted children have been organized, though most of this special educational effort has been placed at the other end of the scale. Among such extra educational efforts may be mentioned classes for children markedly over age, these children often being advanced into selected upper-class and high-school work be-

cause of their age, and regardless of their failure to be promoted; special classes for non-English-speaking children,
to teach them the use of the language; ship schools, in the
ports, to train boys for the sea, and at the same time impart
to them a general elementary school training; industrial
classes, where certain types of industrial work are substituted for academic branches less useful and particularly
difficult for such types of children; special art and music
schools, where pupils showing special aptitude for drawing
or music may receive special attention; and home schools,
where girls of upper grammar-school age may receive special
preparation for home-keeping.

The effect of the introduction of these specialized classes
has been to reduce waste, speed up the rate of production,
and increase the value of the output of our schools.   The
condition of our schools before about 1890, and to a certain
degree this condition still persists, was that of a manufacturing establishment running on a low grade of efficiency.   The
waste of material was great and the output small and costly
— in part because the workmen in the establishment were
not supplied with enough of the right kind of tools; in part
because the supervision emphasized wrong points in manufacture; but largely because the establishment was not
equipped with enough pieces of special type machinery,
located in special shops or units of the manufacturing plant,
to enable it to meet modern manufacturing conditions.
Since 1890, through the introduction of flexible promotions,
parallel courses of study, differentiated courses, and special-
type classes and schools, we have been engaged in improving
the business by speeding it up, supplying it with new and
specialized machinery, saving wastes, and increasing the
rate and the value to society of the output.   The public
schools of the United States are, in a sense, a manufactory,
doing a half-billion dollar business each year in trying to
prepare future citizens for usefulness and efficiency in life.
As such we have recently been engaged in applying to it
some of the same principles of specialized production and

manufacturing efficiency which control in other lines of the manufacturing business.

All these changes are significant of the great shift in direction which has come over American education since the decade of the eighties. Then every one was talking about subject-matter, psychological procedure, and the "faculties" of the mind, and uniformity in educational output was the prevailing educational conception. The forty years which have elapsed, with the consequent social and industrial and political changes through which our Nation has passed, have witnessed a complete alteration in attitude, and the child to be educated has been brought to the front in our educational thinking. To-day child welfare, rather than subject-matter, occupies the center of the stage, while our educational practice is directed by a truer psychology than the decade of the eighties knew.

III. The Education of Delinquents

Compulsory school-attendance legislation. In the earlier days of our educational development we dealt with school delinquents much as the Church of the time dealt with religious delinquents. They were simply left outside the pale. As the Church could not be wrong and the difficulty must of course lie with the sinner, so the school felt itself to be right and the difficulty to be with the children who found the school unattractive and did not attend. Both Church and school have since seen fit to revise this judgment, as well as their methods of dealing with the young.

Though Massachusetts and Connecticut had had colonial laws requiring school attendance, these in time fell into disuse, and the first modern compulsory-attendance law was enacted by Massachusetts, in 1852. This required all children between the ages of eight and fourteen to attend school for twelve weeks each year, six weeks of which must be consecutive. A number of other States and Territories in time followed Massachusetts' lead, those before 1885 being as follows:

1864. District of Columbia.
1867. Vermont.
1871. New Hampshire.
    Washington Territory.
1872. Connecticut.
    New Mexico Territory.
1873. Nevada.
1874. New York.
    Kansas.
    California.

1875. Maine.
    New Jersey.
1876. Wyoming Territory.
1877. Ohio.
1879. Wisconsin.
1883. Rhode Island.
    Illinois.
    Dakota Territory.
    Montana Territory.

Six other Western States and Territories were added by 1890, and by 1900 nearly all the Northern and Western States had enacted some form of a school-attendance law. As late as 1890, though, but one State, Connecticut, had required attendance at school during the entire period the schools were in session. All the other States had followed the Massachusetts plan, requiring attendance for from twelve to twenty weeks, only a portion of which need be consecutive.

Since 1900, and due more to the activity of persons concerned with social legislation and those interested in improving the physical and moral welfare of children than to educators themselves, there has been a general revision of the compulsory education laws of our States and the enactment of much new child-welfare and anti-child-labor legislation. As a result of this the labor of young children has been greatly restricted; work in many industries has been prohibited entirely, because of the danger to life and health; compulsory education has been extended in a majority of the States to cover the full school year; poverty, or dependent parents, in many States no longer serves as an excuse for non-attendance; often those having physical or mental defects also are included in the compulsion to attend, if their wants can be provided for; the school census has been changed so as to aid in the location of children of compulsory-school age; and special officers have been authorized or ordered appointed to assist school authorities in enforcing the compulsory-attendance and child-labor laws. Having taxed their citizens to provide schools, the States have now required the children to attend and partake of the advantages provided. The schools, too, have made a close study of retarded pupils, because of the close connection found to exist between retardation in school and truancy and juvenile delinquency.

One result of this legislation. One of the results of all this legislation has been to throw, during the past quarter of a century, an entirely new burden on the schools. These laws have brought into the schools not only the truant and the incorrigible, who under former conditions either left early or were expelled, but also many children of the foreign-born who have no aptitude for book learning, and many children of inferior mental qualities who do not profit by ordinary class-room procedure. Still more, they have brought into the school the crippled, tubercular, deaf, epileptic, and blind, as well as the sick, needy, and physically unfit. By steadily raising the age at which children may leave school from ten or twelve up to fourteen and sixteen, our schools have come to contain many children who, having no natural aptitude for study, would at once, unless specially handled, become a nuisance in the school and tend to demoralize schoolroom procedure. These laws have thrown upon the school a new burden in the form of public expectancy for results, whereas a compulsory-education law cannot create capacity to profit from education. Under the earlier educational conditions the school, unable to handle or educate such children, expelled them or let them drop from school and no longer concerned itself about them; now the public expects the school to get results with them. Consequently, within the past twenty-five years the whole attitude of the school toward such children has undergone a change, and an attempt has been made to salvage them and turn back to society as many of them as possible, trained for some form of social and personal usefulness.

Enlarging the educational opportunities of the schools. With the recent tendency of our States to insist on the education of all children until they are sixteen years of age, and for all the time the schools are in session, the need for modifications in schoolroom procedure to meet the needs of the children thus brought in has recently become very pressing. The result has been not only the establishment of differentiated and parallel courses of study, and special-type schools, but also, in our better organized school systems, the provision of such a large number of different types of school opportunities that somewhere in the school system every boy and girl may find the type of education suited to his or her peculiar needs. Where this cannot be done locally, due to the small size of the school system, it should be done by the county or by the State. Otherwise compulsory-education laws will only force children into schools from which they will get little of value and in which they will often prove troublesome, with a resulting increase of over-age children, refractory cases, and corporal punishment, and at the same time defeat the social and citizenship aims of the schools. It may cost more to train such children properly than it does the so-called normal children, but it is cheaper for society in the long run that the schools should do it.

Double nature of the problem. Accordingly our schools have undertaken to organize new types of special classes to meet these new educational needs, and also to redirect some of their older instruction. The problem is a double one — first, that of providing for the needs of the classes forced in or forced to remain; and second, that of preventing the development of delinquency among other children of the school.

For the first class the remedy has been found largely in the differentiated courses of study we have just described; the organization of elementary industrial school work; the organization of non-English-speaking and over-age classes; the liberal use of play and school gardening; training in government and self-control; and particularly the use of the newer expression studies which involve the elements underlying the trades of modern industrial society. For the sec-

ond class of children, those who early exhibit a tendency to
be wayward, the problem is one of weighting down the
wrong path by making it hard to follow, and of lighting up
the right path by giving to it the rewards and social approval
of the school as an institution.

New types of schools needed. In addition to the differentiations in courses and classes, and the new types of
schools and instruction, indicated above, the handling of
cases showing tendencies toward truancy and waywardness
and incorrigibility involve the creation of one special type of
class and two types of central schools. The first may be
organized in any graded school building; the second has been
organized in many cities, and could be organized for a
county as a whole. The third has been organized by a few
cities, and the need could also be met by providing a few
state schools of the type. These may be described, briefly,
as follows:

1. *The disciplinary class.* A special class, usually organized in
the regular school building, to which refractory children of either
sex may be assigned for an indefinite period, in part to relieve the
regular classroom of these troublesome cases, and in part to adjust
the school work and discipline to the needs of such children. These
classes are kept small, are individual in their instruction, are taught
by particularly capable teachers, and often have benches, tools,
and other equipment in the room for teaching some of the expression subjects. Their purpose is to handle, in an efficient and orderly
manner, and to turn back if possible into the main current of the
school, those who have begun to manifest difficulty in fitting into
the work of the ordinary class. When this cannot be done, the
pupils may later be transferred to an industrial, or other type of
special class or school.

2. *The parental school.* To this school those who cannot be controlled in the disciplinary classes may be sent. Incorrigible pupils
from all the schools of a county are sometimes sent to one central
county parental school, or a city and county may unite in maintaining such a school. Some of these children, too, can be turned
back into the regular current of the school, but a larger percentage
than in the disciplinary classes will be unable to profit there.
Many can best be directed into the next type of school.

3. Central schools for peculiar boys and girls. The sexes now are
arranged for separately, pupils are gathered into these schools
largely on the basis of age, and without regard to school-grade
advancement, and the effort is to discover in what lines such peculiar children may be made useful to society. Such schools emphasize instruction in music, industrial art, manual and domestic
activities, play, dramatics, and group-organization and construc-
tional and pre-vocational activities. Some of the pupils later can
be sent to a regular trade school, public or private, while many
will pass out into life at the end of the compulsory-school period.
For such children instruction which leads toward such trades or
occupations as carpentry, bricklaying, plastering, cement work,
plumbing, electrical work, automobile repairing, and acting as
chauffeur, gardener, waiter, baker, cook, and seamstress, has been
found quite satisfactory.

State industrial schools. With a few pupils all these
types of specialized instruction will fail, and such will need
to be committed to a state school of a reformatory type, now
usually known as a State Industrial School. Of all children
enrolled in public and private schools of all kinds in the
United States, in 1918, approximately 1 in 350 was in a
State Industrial School. In these schools the sexes, and in
the Southern States the two races also, are usually kept in
separate institutions.

Reformatory education is only a century old. The first
juvenile reform school was founded at Birmingham, England, in 1817, and the second was the New York House of
Refuge, founded in 1824. But few additional schools were
founded before 1850, but by 1900 there were 90 such schools
in the United States, and by 1916 we had 121 state institutions, with 49,009 boys and 12,819 girls who had been
committed to them. Many of these were illiterate, and
many were feeble-minded or of low mentality. With the
latter class the public school was doomed to fail from the
first.

Two types of state institutions exist. The earlier institutions were almost entirely for the older and more depraved
children, the commitment of some crime usually being a

prerequisite to being sent to the school. Recently other state institutions have been founded to handle the more youthful and less serious offenders, and these cover much the same ground as the central city schools for peculiar and over-age children, described above. The idea in this latter type of school is cure through reëducation, rather than confinement and punishment.

The next step in the state system of education for delinquents is the penitentiary for youthful first offenders. Such institutions have recently been established in a few States, and while not usually thought of as being part of the state educational system, in reality they should be so considered and conducted.

IV. THE EDUCATION OF DEFECTIVES

Change in public attitude. On page 271 we mentioned very briefly the beginnings of special instruction of the deaf, blind, and feeble-minded in the United States. At first the feasibility of such instruction was doubted, the work in most cases began privately, and it was some time before our people came to see the need for such instruction or to be willing to pay for it. The first institutions were small, and the pupils taught were commonly exhibited in public to show what could be done, and to awaken interest in the work.

Up to about 1850 only a few States had taken up the consideration of the education of their defective children, but to-day the education of defectives forms so important a part of the state's educational system that no book on public education in the United States would be considered complete without at least a brief statement regarding the origin and development of such special schools. The change in attitude toward educating such classes has come about as a part of the changed attitude of society on many questions involving human and social welfare. We now see that it is better for the State, as well as for the unfortunates themselves, that they be cared for properly and educated, as far as can be done, for self-respect, self-support, and some form of social usefulness. An uneducated defective is a dependent on some one or on society, and finds but little real enjoyment in life; an educated defective usually becomes able to support and care for himself, and sometimes to care for others in addition. So convinced have we at last become of the value of education for defectives that our American States are now somewhat generally requiring the attendance of defectives, after certain specified ages, at a state institution or a public-school class specialized for their training.

FIG. 69. REV. THOMAS H. GALLAUDET TEACHING THE
DEAF AND DUMB

From a *bas-relief* on the monument of Gallaudet, erected by the deaf and dumb of the United States, in the grounds of the American Asylum, at Hartford, Connecticut.

Education of the deaf. The beginnings of this work were made at Hartford, Connecticut, in 1817, by the Reverend Thomas H. Gallaudet. The school opened with seven pupils, and enrolled thirty-three during the year. In 1819 Massachusetts provided for the education of twenty pupils at Hartford, at state expense, and New Hampshire and Vermont soon adopted the same policy. In 1823 Kentucky established the first state school for the education of the deaf, and Ohio followed in 1827. Each obtained teachers

from the Hartford school. From these beginnings, the movement has grown until to-day all but five of our American States support one or more special state schools for the education of the deaf. In 1916 there were 69 state schools for the education of the deaf in the United States, with approximately twelve thousand pupils enrolled, and with a cost for maintenance of approximately $320 per pupil per year. In addition there is maintained at Washington the only institution for the higher education of the deaf in the world — Gallaudet College.

Gallaudet, in establishing his Hartford school, followed the method he saw in France, which was the sign method. Among the things which Horace Mann saw in German lands, and commented upon favorably in his famous *Seventh Report*, was a new method of teaching the deaf. This was a pure oral method, using speech and lip reading, and excluding all signs and finger spelling. Mann considered this method much superior to that used in the schools of the United States. It will be remembered that this Report was received with anything but an open-minded attitude (p. 278) and as the teachers of the deaf did not agree with Mr. Mann, no change took place until 1867, when the Massachusetts legislature established the first oral-method school in the United States. This created much opposition and discussion, but the method slowly made headway, and is to-day the one in general use with all normal-minded deaf.

State institutions cannot conveniently receive such children before they are twelve years of age, whereas deaf children who are to learn to speak and read the lips should begin to receive instruction at the age of three or four. In 1869 the first city day-school for the oral instruction of little deaf children in the United States was organized in Boston, and very appropriately named the Horace Mann School. For the next twenty years there was much controversy as to the desirability of cities establishing such schools. In 1890 the "American Association to Promote the Teaching of Speech to the Deaf" was organized in New York, under the presidency of Dr. Alexander Graham Bell, and the influence of this Society and of Dr. Bell on the establishment of day schools for the oral instruction of deaf children has been deep and lasting. By 1916, there were seventy-one cities in fifteen states which maintained, as a part of the city public school system, day schools where little deaf children were trained to speak and to read the lips, and fitted for further public school education and for social usefulness and happiness. The education of the deaf is one of the most difficult undertakings in our entire educational plan, but when successful the results to society are large. It has been found that normal-minded deaf children can be trained for any line of work which does not involve hearing.

Education of the blind. The education of the blind began in France in 1784, England in 1791, Austria in 1804, Prussia in 1806, Holland in 1808, Sweden in 1810, Denmark in 1811, and Scotland in 1812. The first American institutions were opened in Boston and New York in 1832, and Philadelphia in 1833. All were private institutions, and general interest in the education of the blind was awakened later by exhibiting the pupils trained in these institutions before legislatures and bodies of citizens. The first book for the blind was printed at Paris, in 1786. In 1873 Congress began to aid the American Printing House for the Blind, at Louisville, Kentucky. Partly because of this, and partly because the Post-Office Department carries books for the blind free, America has printed more books and built up better libraries for the blind than has any other country. Practically all state libraries, and many city libraries, contain special libraries for the blind.

As with the deaf, the object in the education of the blind is to change them from dependents to self-sustaining men and women, and to promote their happiness as well. They are taught to read from books the print of which consists of a series of raised points, the alphabet of which is shown opposite. Besides learning to read, and being instructed orally from books, industrial work naturally plays an important

part in their training. The chief industries in which the
blind eventually find employment are basketry, weaving,
hammock-making, carpet-weaving, cordage work, mattress-
making, upholstering, broom- and brush-making, toy-mak-

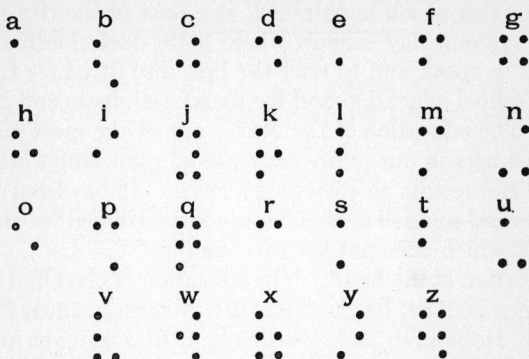

FIG. 70. THE AMERICAN BRAILLE ALPHABET FOR THE BLIND

Devised in 1825, and now used all over the world. The alphabet is made
by using parts of a six-point type :: A letter is capitalized by prefixing
to it the two lower points, with a little space before the letter, thus for
capital B.. :.

ing, and chair-caning, though the wonderful results recently
achieved in the reëducation of blinded soldiers promises to
open up many new opportunities and lines of instruction.
The blind showing musical talent are educated as musicians,
organists, etc., or as piano-tuners, while still others of special
ability become teachers and ministers. We have recently
had a United States Senator who was blind. A century ago
the blind were dependents, and the adult blind lived largely
in almshouses; to-day most of the normal-minded blind care
for themselves, and some have families of their own. The
United States Census Reports now show relatively few
adult blind in almshouses.

There are at present fifty-eight state or state-aided schools
for the blind in the United States, and three private schools.
Ten cities also maintain one or more schools for the blind as

parts of the city school system. The first kindergarten for the blind was established in Germany, in 1861; and the first school for the colored blind by North Carolina, in 1869. The first public city school for the blind was established by New York in 1909. By 1913 this city had opened eleven additional classes for blind children, and two classes for children with contagious eye diseases. The cost per pupil per year is about $375 in institutions, and $175 in city-school classes.

Education of the feeble-minded. Before the nineteenth century the feeble-minded and idiotic were the jokes of society, and no one thought of being able to do anything for them. In 1811 Napoleon ordered a census of such individuals, and in 1816 the first school for their training was founded at Salzburg, in Austria. The school was unsuccessful, and closed in 1835. The real beginning of the training of the feeble-minded was made in France by Edouard Seguin, "The Apostle of the Idiot," in 1837, when he began a lifelong study of such people. By 1845 three or four institutions for their study and training had been opened in Switzerland and Great Britain, and for a time it was thought that idiocy might be cured. Gallaudet had tried to educate such children at Hartford, about 1820, and a class for idiots was established at the Blind Asylum in Boston, in 1848. The interest aroused resulted in the creation of the Massachusetts School for Idiotic and Feeble-Minded Youth, in 1851, the first institution of its kind in the United States. By 1875 seven state and two private institutions had been established in this country, but until about 1890 the movement for the education of the feeble-minded had made but little real headway. Within the past ten years, as the social consequences of feeble-mindedness and idiocy have been brought to the attention of our people, a new interest in the institutional care of the worst cases, and the education within the range of their possibilities of the higher grade of feeble-minded children, has been awakened. As a result we have to-day thirty-eight state institutions in twenty-nine States, and twenty-eight private institutions in fifteen

States, for the institutional care and education of the distinctively feeble-minded.

In 1867 the first city school class to train children of low-grade intelligence was organized in Germany, and all the larger cities of Germany have since organized such special classes. Norway followed with a similar city organization in 1874, and England, Switzerland, and Austria about 1892. In 1893, the first American city, Providence, organized special instruction for children of low intelligence. Boston and Springfield did the same in 1898, and New York City in 1900. Since then 118 American cities, up to 1916, had organized school classes for the segregation and training of

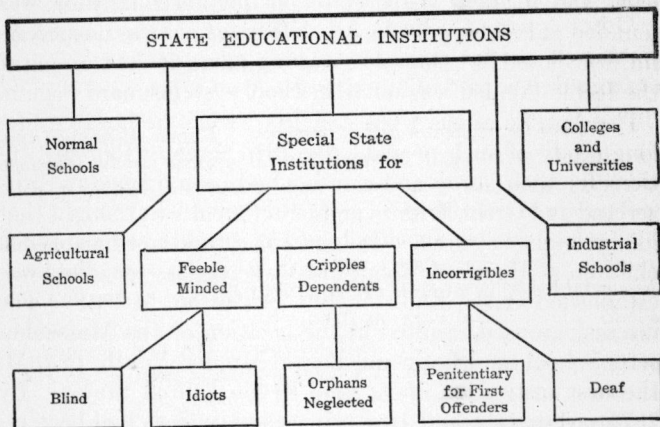

Fig. 71. Educational Institutions Maintained by the State

As state educational institutions, other than public schools.

the higher grades of children of low mental capacity. In the state institutions approximately thirty-three thousand feeble-minded persons are being cared for, and about nine hundred in private institutions. The 118 cities were educating, in special classes, 16,524 children of this type in 1916. As studies show that approximately two per cent of all school children are of such low-grade intelligence that they need special classes, and that at least two persons in each thousand are definitely feeble-minded or idiotic, it will be seen that but a small percentage of those who should be educated separately or confined in institutions are as yet under proper educational or institutional care.

The education of these children was at first largely of the old drill-subject type, but more recently has been shifted largely to the expression-type of studies, with special emphasis on preparation, for the higher grades of such children, which will fit them into the occupations mentioned under the heading of *Central Schools for Peculiar Boys and Girls* (p. 384). The different types of state institutions now provided are as shown in the figure on the preceding page.

Other types of schools for defectives. Other types of special classes for children suffering from defects, recently organized as a part of our city school systems, are:

1. Classes for stutterers and stammerers. Pupils suffering from speech defects are sent to small special classes, under teachers specially trained for such service, and by slow and careful speech-training are educated to speak properly. From one to two per cent of all school-children would be helped by such special-class speech training. Such classes are common in European cities, and have been established in a number of American cities, since the first one was founded in New York, in 1909.

2. Special schools for crippled children. The first attempt to educate crippled children in schools especially adapted to their needs was made in Munich, in 1832. The model school in Europe for the education of cripples was established in Copenhagen, in 1872. The work was begun privately in New York City, in 1861. In 1898 the London School Board undertook to provide classes for crippled children. In January, 1899, the city of Chicago established the first public school for crippled children in the United States. In 1898 there was organized in New York City "The Guild for Crippled Children of the Poor," and in 1900 the "Crippled Children's East Side Free School" began work. During the next six years a number of other private-aid organizations also opened schools for crippled children, and in 1906 the New York City Board of Education began the organization of such special classes in the public schools. By 1912 the city was educating, in

23 special classes, about 450 of the estimated 18,000 crippled children in the city. In 1907 Massachusetts opened the first state institution for the care and education of crippled and deformed children in the United States.

3. *Open-air classes.* This type of class has come in with the recent new interest in health education, it being designed to enable physically run-down children to continue their education and at the same time regain health and physical vitality. Such classes are held in the open air, the children are well fed and warmly clad, the hygienic conditions are closely supervised, and the instruction is carefully adjusted to the needs and capacities of the children. The first open-air school was organized in Berlin, in 1904, London opened its first open-air school in 1907, and the first in the United States was opened at Providence, in 1908. Boston and New York City opened similar schools the same year, and Chicago in 1909. The movement spread rapidly, and by 1912 forty-four American cities had organized similar special classes. The number of these is probably in excess of one hundred to-day.

In this country the classes have so far been confined largely to helping tubercular children, but in the European cities much more has been done than with us in caring for and improving children suffering from various forms of physical debility and subnormal vitality. So far we have met the needs of but very few with such schools, as statistics show from three to five per cent of our school-children are in need of such treatment as these open-air schools provide.

V. CHILD HEALTH AND WELFARE

The new interest in health. The education and care of tubercular children and children of low physical vitality, while valuable, is but a small part of the health problem which a modern school system has within recent years been called upon to face. The discovery and isolation of bacteria; the vast amount of new knowledge which has come to us as to the transmission and possibilities for the elimination of many diseases; the spread of information as to sanitary science and preventive medicine; the change in emphasis in medical practice from curative to preventative and remedial; the closer crowding together of all classes of people in cities; the change of habits for many from life in the open to

life in the factory, shop, and apartment; and the growing
realization of the economic value to the nation of its manhood and womanhood; have all
alike combined with modern
humanitarianism and applied
Christianity to make us take a
new interest in child health and
proper child development. European nations have so far done
much more in school health
work than has the United
States, though a very commendable beginning has been
made here.

Net average worth of a person	
Age	*Worth*
0	$90
5	950
10	2000
20	4000
30	4100
40	3650
50	2900
60	1650
70	15
80	−700

(Calculations by Dr. William Farr,
formerly Registrar of Vital Statistics
for Great Britain)

Medical inspection and health supervision. Medical inspection of schools began in France, in 1837, though genuine
medical inspection, in a modern sense, was not begun in
France until 1879. The pioneer country was Sweden,
where health officers were assigned to each large school as
early as 1868. Norway made such appointments optional
in 1885, and obligatory in 1891. Belgium began the work
in 1874. Tests of eyesight were begun in Dresden in 1867,
Frankfort-on-Main appointed the first German school physi-
cian in 1888. England first employed school nurses in
1887; and, in 1907, following the revelations as to low physical vitality growing out of the Boer War, adopted a mandatory medical inspection and health development act applying to England and Wales, and the year following Scotland
did the same. Argentine and Chili both instituted such
service in 1888, and Japan made medical inspection compulsory and universal in 1898.

In the United States the work was begun voluntarily in
Boston, in 1894, following a series of epidemics. Chicago organized medical inspection in 1895, New York City in 1897,
and Philadelphia in 1898. From these larger cities the idea
spread to the smaller ones, at first slowly, and then very
rapidly. By 1911 as many as 411 cities had provided medi-

AN OPEN-AIR CLASS IN CHICAGO IN WINTER
(Courtesy Elizabeth McCormick Memorial Fund of Chicago)

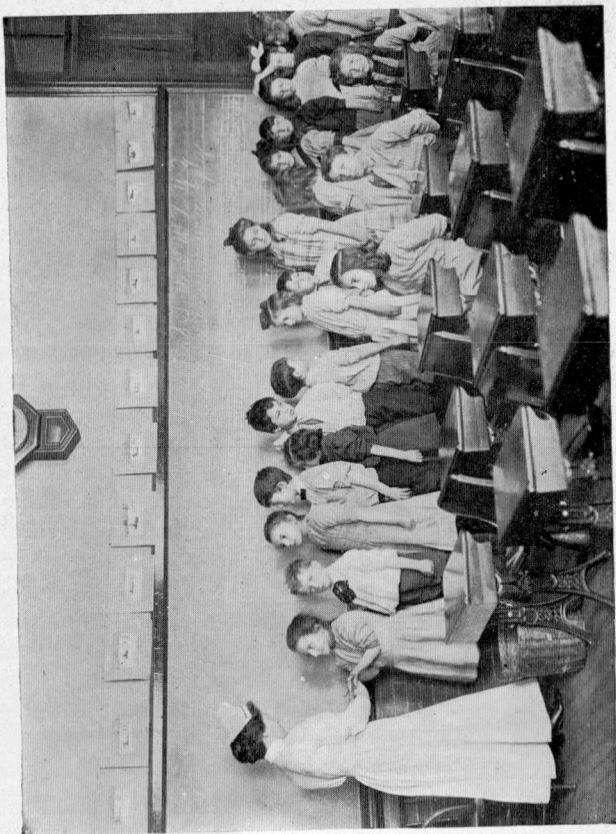

MEDICAL INSPECTION IN THE SCHOOL.

cal inspection, and the number to-day is probably near a thousand. The first school nurse in the United States was employed in New York City, in 1902, and the idea at once proved to be of great value. By 1911 as many as 415 school nurses had been employed in American cities, and the number has increased very rapidly since that date. In 1906 Massachusetts adopted the first state medical inspection law, and by 1911 twenty States had enacted such legislation. In 1912 Minnesota organized the first "State Division of Health Supervision of Schools" in the United States, and this plan has since been followed by other States.

The recent army-draft medical examinations have given us a rude shock as to the physical condition of our young men. In the first draft, approximately one in four of the young men between the ages of 21 and 30, the time when a young man should be in the prime of physical condition, were rejected for the army because of physical defects which would incapacitate them for the life of a soldier. Others who were accepted have had to be placed in development battalions to bring them up to physical standard. Had our young women between the same ages been called up for important national duty there is reason to think that an even larger percentage among them would have been rejected. Such tests of the nation's physical stamina are startling, and there is every reason to expect that these revelations as to the physical incapacity of our young men, together with the many recent studies of rural and city health conditions, will give a new emphasis to constructive health work in our schools.

From mere medical inspection to detect contagious diseases, in which the movement everywhere began, it was next extended to tests for eyesight and hearing, to be made by teachers or physicians, and has since been enlarged to include physical examinations to detect hidden diseases and a constructive health program for the schools.

The work has come to include eye, ear, nose, throat, and teeth, as well as general physical examinations; the supervi-

sion of the teaching of hygiene in the schools, and to a certain
extent the physical training and playground activities; and
a constructive program for the development of the health
and physical welfare of all children.   The value of the work
in reducing physical defects among school-children may be
seen from the following:

PERCENTAGE OF PUPILS HAVING PHYSICAL DEFECTS

Years		Percentage
1912–13	████████████████████████████████	69.0
1913–14	██████████████████████	50.8
1914–15	█████████████████	40.0
1915–16	██████████████	35.0
1916–17	████████████	30.0

RESULTS OF FIVE YEARS' WORK OF THE HEALTH SERVICE AT READING,
PENNSYLVANIA, UNDER THE LAW OF 1911

This work can now be carried on as satisfactorily in small
cities and in county-unit school systems as in the larger
places, and some knowledge of health needs and some ability
to detect disease is every year becoming increasingly important for teachers.   Child hygiene is a new study which
teachers need to take up.

Play and playground activities.   Closely related to the
health supervision of our schools is the play and playground
work of the children, itself also a recent educational development.   Probably the first playground organized in the United
States especially for children was provided by the Children's
Mission in Boston, in 1886.   Two summer playgrounds
were established privately in Philadelphia, in 1893, a sand
garden in Providence in 1894, and a summer playground in
Chicago in 1897.   The first public playground was organized
in Chicago in 1898.   By 1911, 257 cities reported 1543 playgrounds as in operation, and 75 other cities known to have
playgrounds did not report.   The number has increased
rapidly since 1911, and to-day organized play and playground directors are generally recognized necessities in the
proper education of children.

At first the tendency was to provide separate grounds and

management, under a city playground commission, but within the past eight to ten years the tendency has been to place the direction of playgrounds under the school department of the city, and to organize and schedule play as a regular school subject. The inclination has also been marked, within recent years, to get away from the German type of *Turnen* exercises, and all highly organized types of group games; to permit of much free play and to use play not only for physical development but also to develop mental and moral qualities, and above all the ability to play the game fairly and to lose cheerfully. It is this type of play which has done so much for the English boy, and which the German boy has never known. Still more, we now open the playgrounds, under paid teachers and playground directors, after school hours, on Saturdays and Sundays, and especially during the long summer vacation. The value of games and sports in sustaining the morale and physical stamina of the Allied armies on the Western Front was a new demonstration of the value of directed play.

Vacation schools. Another recent educational development, also along the line of child welfare, has been the organization of vacation schools. The first vacation school of which there is any record was held in the old First Church of Boston, as a private affair, in 1866. Its purpose was solely to get the children off the streets and under good influences. From 1868 to 1876 certain citizens voluntarily supported a vacation school at Providence, which the School Committee permitted to be held in one of the school buildings. In 1894 Providence again began such schools, and in 1900 the city school authorities adopted them as a regular part of the city school system. The first city to establish vacation schools as a part of its city school organization was Newark, in 1885. In 1894 "The New York Society for Improving the Condition of the Poor" was permitted to open four vacation schools in the city, and in 1897 the vacation school idea was adopted by the Board of Education and the schools taken over. In Cleveland, "The Ladies' Aid Society of the Old

Stone Church" established the first vacation school, in 1895, and in 1903 these volunteer schools were taken over by the city. In Chicago the Associated Charities in 1896, the University Settlement in 1897, and the Chicago Women's Clubs in 1898 opened vacation schools, and these have since been taken over by the city.

Almost everywhere, prior to 1900, vacation schools had their beginning in the voluntary effort of philanthropic organizations, being taken over later by the city school department. The early beginnings of these schools reminds one of the early public school societies for the establishment of the first free schools. Within the past ten years the vacation school idea has been accepted generally by our cities, and such schools are now maintained in hundreds of places. Begun first to take children off the streets, the idea has now changed to that of offering real instruction as well, though usually with more emphasis on the expression studies than is given in the regular winter schools. Manual training, domestic science, music, story-telling, nature-study, gardening, personal and community hygiene, local history and geography, excursions on Saturdays, play, swimming, and marching and drills occupy a large part of the instruction. The term is usually six weeks, though there was a noticeable tendency, after 1915, to extend the term to cover the entire summer vacation period, thus organizing the schools on an all-year four-quarter basis. Cleveland, Gary, and a few other places definitely provided such all-year schools. In many places the high school work has been extended as well, and either a six-weeks review school or a summer quarter has been provided.

School gardening. This is another recent activity undertaken by the school. The work began as an economic measure in Germany, in the first half of the nineteenth century, and was in time adopted quite generally by the state school systems of the different European nations, largely as a food-production measure. France and Denmark have in the past forty years made wonderful successes with such instruction.

In this country the movement is little more than two decades old. The first school garden with us was the Wild Flower Garden, established at Roxbury, Massachusetts, in 1891. The gardens established, in 1897, by the National Cash Register Company, of Dayton, Ohio, for the children of its employees, were among the first real school gardens in this country. At first, school officials saw little in the idea, and practically all gardens organized before about ten years ago were by private agencies. Only since about 1910 have the public schools become interested in the idea as an educational undertaking. After the outbreak of the World War, and the increasing world-wide scarcity of food which followed, the National Food Administration began an energetic campaign to stimulate the organization of school gardens as a food-production measure. In 1918 the United States Bureau of Education appointed a national organizer of school gardens, and an Educational Land Army of boys and girls was formed, under command of the President of the United States. The impetus thus given to the establishment of these gardens, together with the many valuable educational aspects of the work, promise to make school gardening with us, a new elementary school subject of large importance.

School gardening comes in naturally as a phase of the vacation school work, described above, as the gardens planted in the spring can be cared for during the summer as a part of the work of the vacation school. Wholly aside from the money-value and food-production aspects of the work, now most emphasized, the work makes a strong appeal from a purely educational point of view. To many city children it is almost the only contact they ever get with nature; to some it is a type of education in which they become deeply interested; and to many it means good and healthful exercise, under proper conditions, in the fresh air and sunshine. The nature-study value of the observation of how plants germinate, grow, and mature; the lessons in social coöperation which gardening can be made to teach; the industrial experience coming from the money value of the products raised; the efforts to excel developed by competition in production; the withdrawal of children from the games and vices of the streets; and the possibilities offered by the work for carrying over a vacation-school interest, — all are features of the school gardening movement which are of much moral and social as well as educational value.

VI. Significance of this Work

It will have been noted that all the extensions of educational effort which we have described in this chapter are recent in origin, both with us and in other parts of the world. The oldest of these special efforts, that of the education of the deaf, goes back less than a century, while the great development of state institutions for the education of delinquents and defectives has come since 1875. The earlier interest in defectives may, in a general way, be said to have been a phase of the great humanitarian movement which followed the Napoleonic wars, and found expression in education, poor relief, workingmen's societies, the protection of children, and anti-slavery propaganda.

Beginning about 1875 to 1880, and not becoming prominent until after about 1890 to 1900, a new interest in education and child welfare has become evident in all lands having what may be called an advanced type of civilization. The new interest is less humanitarian than the earlier, and is more an outgrowth of the changed conditions in the national life. There is a new consciousness of social needs, in part a truer Christian conception of one's duty to his fellow men, and a new feeling of need for the transformation of all possible dependents into independent members of society. The result has been a great expansion of public educational effort, as shown in the chart given opposite. In addition, with us, the new interest in providing so many new types of educational effort has arisen in large part because our American communities have come to see that, having committed themselves to the idea of educating all children, it is only fair and

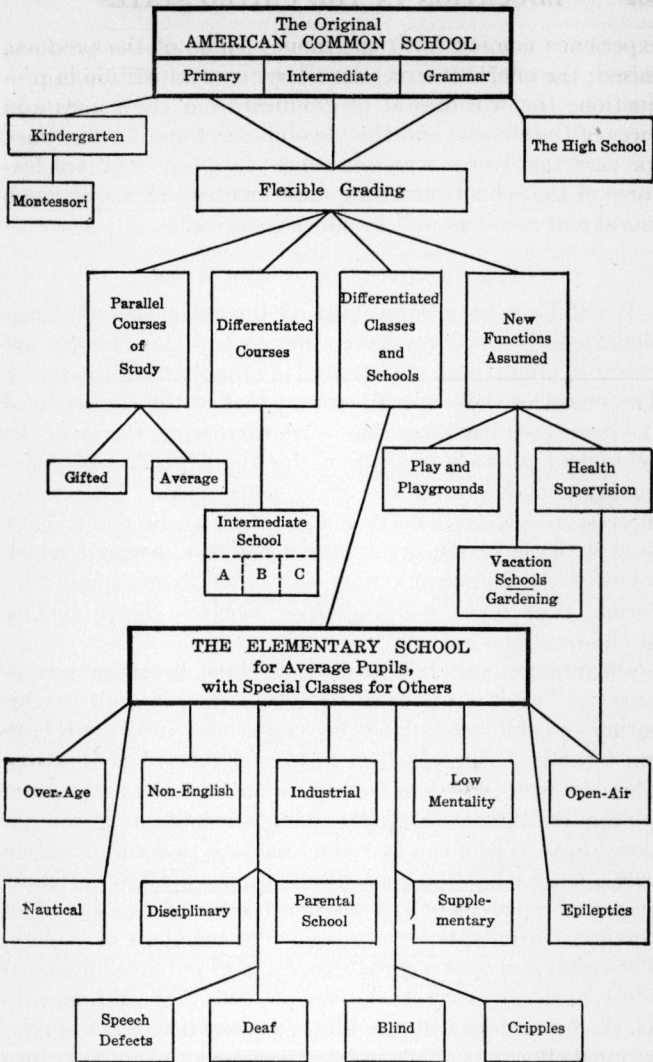

FIG. 72. EVOLUTION OF THE EXTENSIONS OF AMERICAN PUBLIC EDUCATION

wise that there should be provided such a variety of schools, classes, and courses that every boy and girl may obtain in our schools, local or state, an education of such a type as each can use to the greatest personal and social advantage. The fact that we have recently come to see that many different types of schools and classes are required to provide adequately for the needs of all has been felt to be no reasonable ground for discrimination between children.

QUESTIONS FOR DISCUSSION

1. Explain what you understand is meant by a "faculty psychology," and show the educational consequences of such a conception.
2. What is meant by pupil-coöperation schemes for training in self-control?
3. Contrast the earlier book-knowledge conception of education and the newer child-to-be-educated conception.
4. Contrast the knowledge-as-experience conception with the knowledge-as-memorized-learning conception of education.
5. Contrast the training and work of a teacher in these two types of schools.
6. State the dominating ideas of the modern school.
7. State the advantages and disadvantages of "average courses" of study.
8. In what way are over-age and retarded children being prepared to join the ranks of the unsuccessful and dissatisfied of our working world?
9. Does a uniform literary-type course of study tend to awaken ambitions which can never be fulfilled? Why?
10. Do differentiated courses and schools tend to prevent such disappointments, and if so, how?
11. Show that President Eliot's contention in his 1912 address was or was not correct.
12. Show how the breakdown of the old apprentice system has (a) made the educational problem more difficult, and (b) caused us to raise the compulsory school age.
13. Show how the increase of immigration has made compulsory attendance more necessary, and also compelled an enlargement of educational opportunity.
14. How do you account for the recent great interest in the education of delinquents and defectives?
15. Contrast the educational results of play and the lack of it, with American and English boys on the one hand, and German boys on the other.

16. How do you account for the long neglect of child welfare, contrasted with the recent interest in it as seen in health work, playgrounds, etc.?
17. Show how education beyond the elements has up to recently been for the few.
18. Indicate the educational consequences of accepting the idea that all children are to be given as good an education as their needs require.

TOPICS FOR INVESTIGATION AND REPORT

1. History of the compulsory-education movement in the United States.
2. Nature of the compulsory school-attendance law in your State, and what provisions exist for enforcing it?
3. The organization and work of some parental school.
4. The location, organization, work, and cost, in your State, of:
   (a) The State Industrial School or Schools.
   (b) The State School for training of the Deaf.
   (c) The State School for training of the Blind.
   (d) The State School for training of the Feeble-Minded.
   (e) The State School for training of Orphan Children.
5. The work of some city day school for the oral instruction of the deaf.
6. Organization and work of some day school for crippled children.
7. Organization and work of some open-air classes.
8. Organization and work of some city school health department.
9. Work of a school dental clinic.
10. The work of the school nurse.
11. School feeding.
12. Health work in the schools of England and the United States compared.
13. Education of the Ne'er do Wells.
14. Work of some city industrial school.
15. Work of some city home training school.
16. School and public playgrounds.
17. The organization and work of some vacation school.
18. School gardening.

SELECTED REFERENCES

Adams, G. S. "Recent Progress in Training Delinquent Children"; in *Report of the United States Commissioner of Education*, 1913, vol. I, pp. 481-97.

On the work of juvenile courts, probation officers, detention homes, and the relation of feeble-mindedness to delinquency.

*Allen, E. A. "Education of Defectives"; in Butler, N.M., *Education in the United States*, pp. 771-820. J. B. Lyon Co., Albany, 1900.

A well-written statement covering schools for the education of the deaf, blind, feeble-minded, and juvenile offenders.

*Ayres, May, Williams, J. F., and Wood, T. D. *Healthful Schools.* 292 pp.
Houghton Mifflin Co., Boston, 1918.

> Good chapters on medical inspection, play, exceptional children, and school feeding.

Betts, Geo. H. *Social Principles of Education.* 319 pp. Chas. Scribner's
Sons, New York, 1912.

> Chapter VII deals with education for play and use of leisure, and forms simple col-
> lateral reading for this chapter.

Cook, W. A. "A Brief Survey of the Development of Compulsory Education in the United States"; in *Elementary School Teacher,* vol. 12, pp.
331–35. (March, 1912.)

> A historical survey.

Cooley, E. G. "The Adjustment of the School System to the Changed
Conditions of the Twentieth Century"; in *Proceedings of the National
Education Association,* 1909, pp. 404–10.

> Need of better adjustment of education to class needs, worker, etc.

*Cubberley, E. P. *Public School Administration.* 479 pp. Houghton
Mifflin Co., Boston, 1916.

> Chapters XVII and XVIII, on "Types of and Adjustments and Differentiations in
> Courses of Study," present more expanded treatment on the first two sections of this
> chapter. Selected bibliography.

†Dewey, John and Evelyn. *Schools of To-morrow.* 316 pp. E. P. Dutton
Co., New York, 1915.

> Chapter IV describes a number of attempts at the reorganization of the curriculum
> and Chapter V play as a school study.

*Dooley, W. H. *The Education of the Ne'er-do-Well.* 164 pp. Houghton
Mifflin Co., Boston, 1916.

> Special needs of this class of children; adaptations of school work; and a constructive
> program for their instruction.

*Draper, A. S. *American Education.* 382 pp. Houghton Mifflin Co.,
Boston, 1909.

> The address on "Illiteracy and Compulsory Education," pp. 61–73, forms good sup-
> plemental reading for this chapter.

Dresslar, F. B. "Methods and Means of Health Teaching in the United
States" ; in *Report of the United States Commissioner of Education,* 1913,
vol. I, pp. 415–34.

> A good descriptive article on health service, hygiene, and the work of doctors and
> nurses.

*Eliot, Chas. W. "Undesirable and Desirable Uniformity in Schools"; in
Educational Reform, pp. 273–300. Century Co., New York, 1898.
Also in *Proceedings of the National Education Association,* 1892.

> The address cited in this chapter.

Hailman, W. N. *The Elementary Industrial School at Cleveland.* 19 pp.
United States Bureau of Education, Bulletin No. 39. Washington, 1913.

> A brief description and outline of work.

Hiatt, J. S.   *The Truant Problem and the Parental School.*   35 pp.   United States Bureau of Education, Bulletin No. 29.   Washington, 1915.

Study of conditions in different cities.

*Hoag, E. B., and Terman, L. M.   *Health Work in the Schools.*   321 pp. Houghton Mifflin Co., Boston, 1914.

An excellent book on health supervision, health teaching, open-air schools, and school housekeeping.

Jarvis, C. D.   *Gardening in Elementary School.*   74 pp.   United States Bureau of Education, Bulletin No. 40.   Washington, 1916.

Why and how gardening should be introduced as a study, and the promotion of the work.

Kingsley, S. C., and Dresslar, F. B.   *Open-Air Schools.*   280 pp.   United States Bureau of Education, Bulletin No. 23.   Washington, 1916.

A well-illustrated volume on open-air schools and health work for children.

*Mendelsohn, S.   "Summer Idleness and Juvenile Delinquency"; in *Educational Review,* vol. 50, pp. 24–35.   (June, 1915.)

A very able article.   Points out the need of greater use of the school plant.

*Mitchell, D.   *Schools and Classes for Exceptional Children.*   122 pp. Cleveland Education Survey, 1916.

Describes the special classes and schools in and needed by such a city.

*Monroe, J. P.   "The Grievance of the Average Boy against the Average School"; in *New Demands in Education,* pp. 3–25.   Doubleday, Page & Co., New York, 1912.

A good statement from the point of view of the boy.

*Monroe, Paul.   *Cyclopedia of Education.*   5 vols.   The Macmillan Co., New York, 1911-13.

The following articles are especially important:
1. "Attendance, Compulsory"; vol. I, pp. 285–95.
2. "Blind, Education of"; vol. I, pp. 395–401.
3. "Crippled Children, Education of"; vol. II, pp. 230–34.
4. "Deaf, Education of"; vol. II, pp. 257–65.
5. "Deaf Blind, Education of"; vol. II, pp. 265–70.
6. "Defectives, Education of"; vol. II, pp. 275–79.
7. "Gardens, School"; vol. III, pp. 10–12.
8. "Medical Inspection"; vol. IV, pp. 182–88.
9. "Open-Air Schools"; vol. IV, pp. 548–51.
10. "Playgrounds"; vol. IV, pp. 728–30.
11. "Reform Schools"; vol. V, pp. 130–33.
12. "Special Classes"; vol. V, pp. 384–86.
13. "Speech Defects"; vol. V, pp. 389–91.
14. "Teeth, Hygiene of"; vol. V, pp. 554–55.
15. "Vacation Schools"; vol. V, pp. 701–02.

*Moore, E. C.   *What is Education?*   354 pp.   Ginn & Co., Boston, 1915.

The first two essays, on "What is Education," and "What is Knowledge," form good supplemental reading for the first two sections of this chapter.

*National Society. *The City School as a Community Center.* **72 pp.** *Tenth Year-Book* of the National Society for the Scientific Study of Education, Part I, 1911.

> Contains three good papers on vacation playgrounds, organized athletics, and evening recreation centers.

*Snedden, D. "The Public School and Juvenile Delinquency"; in *Educational Review,* vol. 33, pp. 374–85. (April, 1907.)

> An excellent article on the handling of juvenile delinquents, and the place and work of the public school in the process.

Solenberger, E. R. *Public School Classes for Crippled Children.* 51 pp. United States Bureau of Education, Bulletin No. 10. Washington, 1918.

> Describes existing classes, and illustrates work.

Smith, C. O. *Garden Clubs in the Schools of Englewood, New Jersey.* 44 pp. United States Bureau of Education, Bulletin No. 26. Washington, 1917.

> Describes their origin and illustrates the work done.

*Terman, L. M. *Hygiene of the School Child.* 417 pp. Houghton Mifflin Co., Boston, 1914.

> An excellent book for teachers along the lines of child welfare.

Trowbridge, Ada W. *The Home School.* 95 pp. Houghton Mifflin Co., Boston, 1913.

> A very interesting description of the work and the ideas underlying the school for training in home arts, established at Providence, Rhode Island.

Van Sickle, J. H., Witmer, L., and Ayres, L. P. *Provisions for Exceptional Children in Public Schools.* 92 pp. United States Bureau of Education, Bulletin No. 4. Washington, 1911.

> Classifies exceptional children, and describes work done for them in thirty-nine American cities.

CHAPTER XIII

NEW DIRECTIONS OF EDUCATIONAL EFFORT

I. The Expansion of the High School

Great recent development. The diagram, on page 192, showing the development of the Latin grammar school, academy, and high school; and the map on page 198, showing the high schools established by 1860, alike indicate the slow development of the free public high school in the United States. Though begun in 1821, the public high school, up to 1860, had made but little headway except in regions where New England people had gone. The Civil War checked further development for two decades, but after about 1880 to 1885 a rapid growth of the American high school began. While no accurate figures are available, there were probably about 500 high schools in the United States by 1870, about 800 by 1880 (in cities 244), while by 1890, the first year for which complete statistics were collected by the United States Bureau of Education, the number was 2526. Since then the development has been as follows:

Year	Free public high schools	Teachers	Students	Per cent of pupils in:	
				Public high schools	Private high schools
1889–90	2,526	9,120	202,968	68.13	31.87
1894–95	4,712	14,122	350,099	74.74	25.26
1899–00	6,005	20,372	519,251	82.41	17.59
1904–05	7,576	28,461	679,702	86.38	13.62
1909–10	10,213	41,667	915,061	88.63	11.37
1914–15	11,674	62,519	1,328,984	89.55	10.45
1919–20	14,326	97,654	1,857,155	91.00	9.00

Unlike the development before 1860, the recent marked increase in the number of high schools has been true of all parts of our country, West as well as East, and South as well as North.   Before 1900 the development was more marked in the North; since 1900 in the South and West. The period up to 1860, and to a certain extent up to about 1880, was an experimental period.   The new school had to find its work and become established, and the people had to grow accustomed to the idea of the support of higher schools as a proper function of a democratic State.   By 1880 not only had we at last become convinced as to the need of extending education upward, for democratic ends, but by that time the industrial and social changes coming in our national life were making it evident that the further development and progress of our democracy would be seriously hampered unless the amount of education extended to our youths was both materially increased and changed in character.   Since about 1885 to 1890 our people generally seem to have accepted the idea that a secondary school education, at public expense, should be placed within the reach of as many of our youth as is possible.   After about this time legal and legislative objection to the establishment of high schools largely ceased, and many new laws providing for union schools and taxation for support appear on the statute books of our States.

Change in character of the school.   Along with this rapid development of the high school — in number of schools, teachers, and students, and the superseding of the old academy and the private high school by tax-supported institutions under public control — has also come a marked change in the character of the high school itself.   The course of study, before 1860, was essentially a book-study course, usually three years in length, and the same for all students. Reading, writing, geography, arithmetic, bookkeeping, history and Constitution of the United States, and English grammar, all of which have since been dropped back into the upper grades of the elementary school, were commonly taught in the high schools before 1860.   In addition, ancient and modern history, rhetoric, logic, intellectual and moral philosophy, natural philosophy, astronomy, algebra, geometry, trigonometry, Latin, and Greek were usually included. This list of high school subjects, as well as the floor plans of the high school buildings of the time (see floor plans for the Providence school, page 195, which are typical), show that the high school was essentially a place to study and recite.

While not originally begun with the idea of preparing young people for college (see statement of purposes in establishing the high schools in Boston and New York, page 191), this soon became one of the important purposes of our high schools, thus making of them a part of our educational ladder and the transition institution between the common school and the college.   Up to the time of the Civil War, however, but eight high school subjects (page 234) had found a place in the entrance requirements of the colleges of the time, and but six more were added up to 1875.   Since then the number has been greatly increased by adding new high-school subjects to the list.   Of the fourteen accepted by 1875, but two — physical geography (1870) and physical science (1872) — were other than book and recitation subjects, and for some time both of these were taught from text-books and without laboratory equipment.   Since 1890 laboratory science, and since 1900 manual, domestic, and agricultural subjects, have found a large place in the college-entrance list.

Development of new courses and schools.   After about 1880 the introduction of new subjects was so rapid that the old course of study became overcrowded, resulting in:

(a) the extension of the high school course to four years;
(b) the introduction of options and electives in the course; and
(c) the creation of a number of parallel four-year courses, such as

      (1) the ancient classical course;
      (2) the modern classical course;
      (3) the English-history course;

    (4) the scientific course;
    (5) the business course;
    (6) the manual arts course;
    (7) the household arts course;
    (8) the agricultural course;
    (9) the teacher-training course;
  (10) special vocational courses.

In addition to this multiplication of courses, in many cases separate high schools for teaching some one or more of the courses given above have also been developed, with the result that we have to-day:

(1) The general culture high school, being the successor, though now greatly modified both in subject-matter and spirit, of the original general high school.

(2) The cosmopolitan high school, offering in one building, or group of buildings, many or all of the different courses of study mentioned above.

(3) The manual-training high school, first begun as a part of our public school system in 1884 (page 324), but now more commonly developed in connection with (2).

(4) The household-arts high school, usually provided for as a course under (2) or (3), but sometimes organized separately.

(5) The commercial high school, for training for business life. Begun as a separate course in many high schools in the seventies. Since 1898 a number of commercial high schools have been organized in the more important of our commercial cities.

(6) The agricultural high school, first established in connection with the University of Minnesota, in 1888. By 1898 there were ten such schools in the United States. Since 1900 the development of the agricultural high schools has been more rapid than has been the case with any other previous type of high school. By 1909 there were 60 separate agricultural high schools, and agricultural courses were offered in 346 other high schools. The number of high schools to-day offering agricultural instruction is probably in excess of one thousand.

(7) Trade and industrial schools, of high-school grade, for vocational training. This represents our most recent development. With national aid for such schools and courses, this type of school promises to increase very rapidly.

Experience has shown that in some places and cases it is better that one or more of the above types of special high schools exist separately, while in other cases it is better that such courses be combined in what is now commonly spoken of as the cosmopolitan American high school. In their beginnings new types of education often prosper better if organized in separate schools; after the work has been established, and accepted as a legitimate form of educational effort it has been found wise to combine a number of different types of education in one school, thus enabling the high school to offer to each pupil a wider range of choice in studies. The American high school, unlike the secondary school of Europe, is preëminently a place for trying out young people, developing tastes, testing capacities, opening up life opportunities, and discovering along what lines pupils show enough special aptitude to warrant further education and training. The same principles that apply to the differentiation of elementary school courses to meet individual needs, as stated in the preceding chapter, apply with even greater force to pupils between the ages of fourteen and eighteen. This involves freedom from hard and fixed courses of study, a rich and varied offering of courses from which to select, and intelligent guidance of pupils toward preparation for a life of useful service.

New conceptions as to educational needs. As our civilization grows in complexity, as the ramifications of our social and industrial life become more extended, as production becomes more specialized and the ability to change vocations more limited, as our political life becomes wider and the duties and obligations of citizenship more important, as our place in world affairs becomes larger, and as the privileges conferred and the responsibility for proper living resting on each individual in society increase, the nature and extent of the education offered as preparation for life must correspondingly increase. An education which was entirely satisfactory to meet the needs of the simpler form of our social and industrial national life of the sixties or the eighties is utterly inadequate for the complex life of the twentieth century. All this has come to be generally recognized to-day, and in consequence our American States are providing for the further establishment of more high schools and new types of high schools, extending the compulsory school age upward, and offering the advantages of secondary education to as many of our children as can advantageously use what the schools have to give.

II. THE DEVELOPMENT OF VOCATIONAL EDUCATION

Vocational education in Europe and the United States. For more than half a century the leading countries of Western Europe, in an effort to readjust their age-old apprenticeship system of training to modern conditions of manufacture, have given careful attention to the education of such of their children as were destined for the vocations of the industrial world. Germany, Austria, Switzerland, and France have been leaders, with Germany most prominent of all. No small part of the great progress made by that country in securing world-wide trade, before the World War, was due to the extensive and thorough system of vocational education worked out for German youths. The marked economic progress of Switzerland during the past quarter-century has likewise been due in large part to that type of education which would enable her, by skillful artisanship, to make the most of her very limited resources. France has profited greatly, during the past half-century also, from vocational education along the lines of agriculture and industrial art. In Denmark, agricultural education has remade the nation since the days of its humiliation and spoliation at the hands of Prussia.

In the United States but little attention has been given to educating for the vocations of life until within the past ten years, though modern manufacturing conditions had before this destroyed the old apprenticeship type of training. Endowed with enormous natural resources, not being pressed for the means of subsistence by a rapidly expanding population on a limited land area, able to draw on Europe for both cheap manual labor and technically-educated workers, largely isolated and self-sufficient as a nation, lacking a merchant marine, not be-ing thrown into severe competition for interna-tional trade, and able to sell our products to na-tions anxious to buy them and willing to come for them in their own ships, we have not up to recently felt any particular need for anything other than a good common-school edu-cation or a general high-school education for our workers. The commercial course in the high school, the manual training schools and courses, and some instruction in draw-

Fig. 73. The Destruction of the Trades in Modern Industry

Under the old conditions of apprenticeship a boy learned all the processes and became a tailor. To-day, in a thoroughly organized clothing factory, thirty-nine different persons perform different spe-cialized operations in the manufacture of a coat.

ing and creative art have been felt to be about all we needed to provide.

Beginnings of vocational education with us.   Largely within the past ten years, due in part to our expanding com-merce and increasing competition in world trade, in part to the new educational impulses arising out of our new world position following the Spanish-American War, in part to the increasing world-wide demand for foodstuffs and manu-factured articles, and in part to a growing realization of the many advantages that would accrue to us as a nation and to our workers as individuals if we were to provide better and more specific types of education for those who are to labor, we have at last turned our attention in a really serious manner to the many problems surrounding the establish-ment of schools of secondary grade for the vocational edu-cation of our workers.

Due to our early national importance in agriculture, and the endowment in each State of a college of agriculture by the Federal Government, in 1862 (page 210), it was natural that in this country agricultural education for pupils of high school age should have been the first of the vocational subjects to be developed.   The first publicly-supported agricultural high school, as was stated above, was founded in 1888, and since 1900 instruction in agriculture has become an established feature of American school life.   In several of our American States, as for example Alabama, Georgia, Virginia, Oklahoma, and Massachusetts, a number of state agricultural high schools have been established by the legislature.   In other States, among them Wisconsin, Michigan, and Maryland, county high schools of agriculture have been established, and these receive state aid for support.   Many of the agricultural colleges also maintain an agricultural high school as a part of their work, and a number of cities have recently added courses in agriculture to their high schools.   Still more, instruction in elementary agriculture has, largely in the past fifteen years, been added by law to the courses of instruction in the rural and village schools in many of our States.

The first trade school in the United States was established privately in New York City, in 1881, and by 1900 some half-dozen schools of the trade or industrial type had been established privately in different parts of the country.   Due in part to the whole idea being new, and in part to the suspicion of organized labor that such schools were not being founded for any purpose favorable to them, the development of trade education came slowly.

The National Commission on Vocational Education.   The fifteen years from 1902 to 1917 was a period of investigation, discussion, and growing interest.   Commercial bodies and manufacturers' organizations sent school and business experts to Europe to investigate and report on the work of vocational schools in the different European nations; state commissions made investigations and reports; and much propaganda work was done by volunteer societies interested in establishing vocational education. In 1906 Massachusetts led the way by creating a State Commission on Industrial Education, with power to superintend the creation and maintenance of industrial schools for boys and girls, and appropriated state aid therefor. In 1907 Wisconsin enacted the first trade-school law, authorizing the creation of industrial schools by the cities of the State. The Milwaukee School of Trades, established earlier, now was taken over and made a part of the city school system, and a number of trade schools were established in other cities. In 1909 New York similarly permitted the organization of trade schools in cities. Back in 1902 the Manhattan Trade School for Girls had been organized privately in New York City, and the work of this school did much to awaken public interest in trade education. In 1910 it was made a part of the free public school system of the city.

Had we depended upon isolated state and local action, though, it would have been at least a generation, and probably longer, before anything approaching a national system of vocational education would have been evolved. Realizing the slow rate of local action, those interested in the movement urged the creation at once of a national system of vocational schools, with national aid to the States for their maintenance. The Davis bill of 1907, and the Page bill of 1912, were unsuccessful attempts to secure national encouragement for the movement. Finally Congress, in 1913, provided for a Presidential Commission to investigate the matter and to report on the desirability and feasibility of national aid for the promotion of vocational training. After a careful investigation this commission reported, in June, 1914, and submitted a plan for gradually increasing national aid to the States to assist them in developing and maintaining what will virtually become a national system of agricultural, trade, and vocational education.

The commission's findings. The commission found that there were, in 1910, in round numbers, 12,500,000 persons

engaged in agriculture in the United States, of whom not
over one per cent had had any adequate preparation for
farming; and that there were 14,250,000 persons engaged in
manufacturing and mechanical pursuits, not one per cent of
whom had had any opportunity for adequate training.   In
the whole United States there were fewer trade schools, of
all kinds, than existed in the little German kingdom of
Bavaria, a State about the size of South Carolina; while the
one Bavarian city of Munich, a city about the size of Pitts-
burgh, had more trade schools than were to be found in all
the larger cities of the United States, put together.   The
commission further found that there were 25,000,000 persons
in this country, eighteen years of age or over, engaged in
farming, mining, manufacturing, mechanical pursuits, and in
trade and transportation, and concerning these the Report
said:

If we assume that a system of vocational education, pursued
through the years of the past, would have increased the wage-
earning capacity of each of these persons to the extent of only ten
cents a day, this would have made an increase of wages for the
group of $2,500,000 a day, or $750,000,000 a year, with all that
this would mean to the wealth and life of the nation.

This is a very moderate estimate, and the facts would probably
show a difference between the earning power of the vocationally
trained and the vocationally untrained of at least twenty-five
cents a day.   This would indicate a waste of wages, through lack
of training, amounting to $6,250,000 every day, or $1,875,000,000
for the year.

The commission estimated that a million new young people were required annually by our industries, and that it
would need three years of vocational education, beyond the
elementary school age, to prepare them for efficient service.   This would require that three million young people of
secondary school age be continually enrolled in schools offering some form of vocational training.   This is approximately three times the number of young people to-day enrolled in all public and private high schools in the United

States. In addition, the untrained adult workers now in farming and industry also need some form of adult or extension education to enable them to do more effective work. The commission further pointed out that there were in this country, in 1910, 7,220,298 young people between the ages of fourteen and eighteen years, only 1,032,461 of whom were enrolled in a high school of any type, public or private, day or evening, and few of those enrolled were pursuing studies of a technical type. True to our ancient traditions, our high schools were still largely book-study schools, preparing for political activity and the learned professions, and not for the vocations in which the majority of men and working women must earn their living. Continuing, the commission said:

At present this vast body of over seven million youths represents on the whole an untrained army, needing vocational training to make it efficient. It has been estimated that the total cost of bringing a child from birth to the age of 18 is $4000, or $220 per year, of which about $60 per year comes from the State. If we assume that it would require on the average an additional outlay of $150 per person to prepare each properly for usefulness, so that society might realize more fully upon its vocational and civic possibilities, certainly no business man would hesitate for a moment to thus secure the protection of the sum of $4000.

Since commercial prosperity depends largely upon the skill and well-being of our workers, the outlook for American commerce in competition with our more enterprising neighbors, under present conditions, is not very promising.

It is even more short-sighted of the State and Nation to neglect these investments, since national success is dependent not alone on returns in dollars and cents, but in civic and social well-being.

The Smith-Hughes Bill. Bills to carry out the recommendations of the commission were at once introduced in both branches of Congress, in the Senate by Senator Hoke Smith, in the House by Representative Hughes. President Wilson early expressed himself as favoring the proposed legislation. After some delay, due in part to the outbreak of the World War, the bill was finally passed, and approved by the President on February 23, 1917.

The law provided for the creation of a Federal Board for Vocational Education; acceptance of the law by the States; national aid to the States for the salaries of teachers in the schools created, which aid the States must duplicate, dollar for dollar; federal supervision of work and expenditure; and national studies and investigations regarding needs in agriculture, home economics, industry, trade, commerce, and courses of instruction. The courses must be given in public schools; must be for those over fourteen years of age, and be of less than college grade; and must be primarily intended for those who are preparing to enter or have entered a trade or useful industrial pursuit. Both full-time and part-time classes are provided for.

The national aid is divided into four funds, as follows:

1. For the purpose of coöperating with the States in paying the salaries of teachers, supervisors, and directors of agricultural subjects, to be allotted to the States in the proportion which their rural population bears to the total rural population of the United States.

2. For the purpose of coöperating with the States in paying the salaries of teachers of trades, home economics, and industrial subjects, to be allotted to the States in the proportion which their urban population bears to the total urban population of the United States.

3. For the purpose of coöperating with the States in preparing teachers, supervisors, and directors of agricultural subjects and teachers of trade and industrial and home economics subjects, to be allotted to the States in the proportion which their population bears to the total population of the United States.

4. For making or coöperating in studies, investigations, and reports as to needs and courses in agriculture, home economics, trades, industries, and commerce.

The sums appropriated by Congress increase each year for nine years, when the maximum will be reached, and are as shown in the accompanying table. The bill has met with general acceptance everywhere, and promises in a decade to give us a really national system of vocational training. In all probability, before 1926 is reached, the work will have so

Year	For agricultural education	For trade, home economics, and industrial education	For training teachers of both	For investigations	Total national aid
1917–18	$500,000	$500,000	$500,000	$200,000	$1,700,000
1918–19	750,000	750,000	700,000	200,000	2,400,000
1919–20	1,000,000	1,000,000	900,000	200,000	3,100,000
1920–21	1,250,000	1,250,000	1,000,000	200,000	3,700,000
1921–22	1,500,000	1,500,000	1,000,000	200,000	4,200,000
1922–23	1,750,000	1,750,000	1,000,000	200,000	4,700,000
1923–24	2,000,000	2,000,000	1,000,000	200,000	5,200,000
1924–25	2,500,000	2,500,000	1,000,000	200,000	6,200,000
1925–26*	3,000,000	3,000,000	1,000,000	200,000	7,200,000

* Reaches the maximum this year, and continues at this sum.

justified the expenditure that the appropriations of national aid will be further increased.

The American high school, as a result of nearly a century of progress and evolution, now has evolved into an American system of secondary education, in turn leading to entrance to higher schools or to life occupations and professions, somewhat as shown on the following chart.

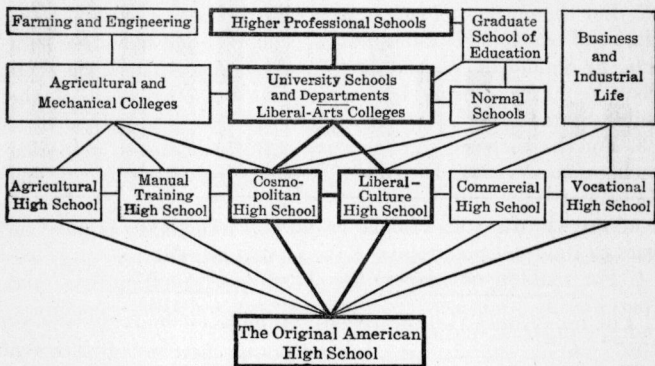

FIG. 74. THE RECENT EXPANSION OF THE HIGH SCHOOL AND THE COLLEGE

Vocational guidance. Under earlier conditions such a thing as the vocational guidance of youth was unnecessary, but with the growing complexity of industrial society and the minute subdivision of the old trades, vocational guidance has recently assumed an entirely new importance. The idea underlying it is not primarily to find jobs for young people, but rather to provide parents and pupils with information as to the demands and opportunities in the different life careers, and the best means of preparing for and entering them. The real purpose is to sort out capacities and adaptabilities, to prolong preparation in school, and to steer young people away from vocations for which they have no natural aptitude and from essentially "blind-alley" occupations."

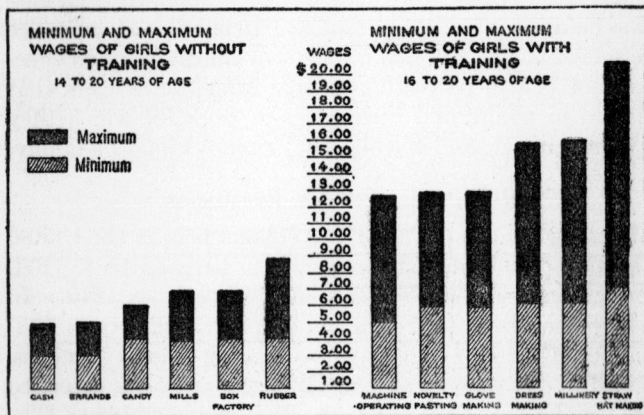

FIG. 75. WHAT VOCATIONAL TRAINING AND GUIDANCE CAN DO

In training girls for better occupations and guiding them away from "blind-alley" jobs.
(From a chart in Ellis's *Money Value of Education*, p. 26.)

The movement is quite recent, going back scarcely beyond 1907, when a bureau for advising young men in the choice of a vocation was opened in Boston. In 1909 this grew into a Vocational Bureau, which soon became connected in its work with the public schools, business houses, and manufacturing establishments. Lectures as to careers were given to the upper classes in the elementary schools; printed matter as to vocations was distributed; vocational counselors were appointed in all the schools, and pupil record-cards were made out. Boston soon became the center of the movement, and from there it has spread rapidly all over the United States. By 1910 thirty-five cities were at work on the idea. To-day it is an educational conception accepted generally, and schools everywhere are thinking and acting on the idea.

The study of life-careers for boys and girls has been introduced into many schools, and intelligent planning for one's life-work has been emphasized. Instead of leaving school and accepting the first job that offers, regardless of adaptability or the future it may hold or its influence on life and health, the attempt is made to save boys and girls from mistakes before it is too late to change. In giving such guidance the school is not only making its own education more effective, but is also protecting society from the dangers that arise when adults find themselves in work for which they have no aptitude and in which they cannot support a family.

III. Public School Extension

Evening schools. The first evening school in the United States was established in Louisville, as early as 1834. Baltimore organized six evening schools as early as 1840. In 1847 the new Board of Education for New York City (p. 178) was permitted by law to organize evening schools for males, as well as day schools, and similar permission was extended for females, in 1848, and to Brooklyn, in 1850. The first general state law for evening schools was enacted by Ohio, in 1839, and evening schools were opened in Cincinnati the following year. Massachusetts followed with a similar optional law in 1847. In 1855 Cincinnati also opened evening schools for girls. The first public evening high school was opened in Cincinnati, in 1856, and similar schools were opened in New York City in 1866, Chicago and St. Louis in 1868, Philadelphia in 1869, and Boston in 1870. By 1870 there were 60 public evening high schools in the United States, and a number of evening elementary schools. By 1881 32 cities were providing evening schools; by 1900,

165; by 1909, 233; and by 1916 the number had increased to 458, with 647,861 pupils enrolled. That even this number makes as yet no adequate provision for the education of our approximately 10,000,000 young people between the ages of fourteen and twenty may be seen from the following chart.

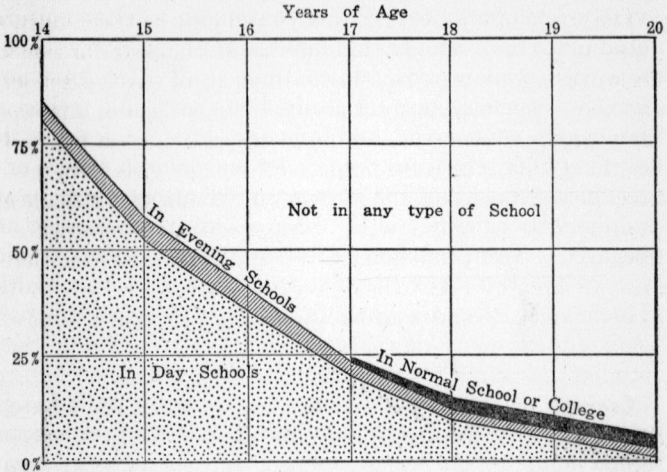

FIG. 76. SCHOOL ATTENDANCE OF AMERICAN CHILDREN, FOURTEEN TO TWENTY YEARS OF AGE

Based on an estimate made by the United States Bureau of Education in 1907 (Bulletin No. 1, 1907, p. 29), and based on conditions then existing. Since the World War the percentage not in any school doubtless has increased. In evening schools all classes are counted, — public, private, Y.M.C.A., Y.W.C.A., etc. Public and private day schools, both elementary and secondary, also are counted.

Originally evening schools were begun to provide education for those unable to attend during the day, and such continued to be their important function up to about 1900. Since that time, however, the evening school, both elementary and high, has been greatly expanded and materially changed in character. With the more general enforcement of compulsory education, the urgent need for providing duplicate elementary schools for children at work during the day has in large part disappeared, as such children are now required to attend day elementary schools until they are fourteen to sixteen years of age. In consequence, evening elementary schools are now chiefly useful, in States enforcing a good compulsory-education law, in providing the foreign-born with the elements of an English education. As this change has come, the evening high schools have grown vastly in importance. While continuing to offer cultural studies for those who have completed the elementary schools and wish, while working, to continue study, they have now largely become schools for study along scientific, technical, home arts, commercial, and industrial lines. A few use the evening high schools to prepare for entrance to college or a technical school, but the large majority attend them to attain greater efficiency in the occupations in which they are engaged. Technical, home arts, trade, and business studies are in greatest demand. The enactment of the Smith-Hughes bill is certain to result in a further marked expansion of the evening high school along vocational lines. Such studies as applied mathematics, navigation, mechanical drawing, machine design, engineering subjects, physics, chemistry, the various trades, automobile work, salesmanship, home economics, accounting, business management, and similar studies, now hold a prominent place in evening high school work.

By way of illustration, one city of 65,000 inhabitants, located in the upper Mississippi Valley, offered the following work in its evening vocational school in 1917–18:

For Boys

I. Woodwork.
 1. Wood-turning and pattern-making.
 2. Cabinet-making, finishing.
 3. Carpentry, joinery, stair-building.
II. Printing.
 1. Composition.
 2. Presswork.
 3. Proof-Reading.

For Boys

III. Electrical work.
 1. Electrical wiring.
 2. Electric signs.
 3. Installation, maintenance, operation, and repairing motors and generators.
IV. Metal-work.
 1. Forging.
 2. Plumbing.
 3. Sheet-metal work.

For Boys

IV. Metal-work *(continued)*.
    4. Auto repairing.
    5. Machine-shop practice.
V. Commercial illustrating and design.
VI. Draughting.
    1. Mechanical drawing.
    2. Architectural drafting.
    3. Making and reading blue-prints.
    4. Sheet-metal draughting.
    5. Machine designing.

Both Sexes

Two-year commercial course open to 8th grade graduates.

For Girls

1. Millinery.
2. Home-making.
3. Dressmaking.
4. Cooking, catering.
5. Applied art and design.
6. Salesmanship.
7. Machine operating.
8. Dry cleaning, dyeing.

Academic Work, both sexes

1. English.
2. Applied mathematics.
3. Applied science.
4. Industrial geography
5. History.
6. Citizenship.

Adult education. Compared with England and France, the United States has as yet done but little with adult education. What has been done has been chiefly along the lines of evening school classes for adults, evening lectures in the schoolhouses on topics of general interest, some efforts here and there at the elimination of adult illiteracy, farmers' institutes conducted by the agricultural colleges, and some university extension work by the state universities. What has been done so far, though, marks but a beginning of what the coming decade is certain to demand as new phases of the educational service. As new national needs arise, the conception of public education must broaden to meet them. Some of the more important phases of recent educational extension may be mentioned.

Adult illiterates. The World War brought seriously to our attention what our Census statistics had for some time been showing, viz. that we have among us a large body of illiterate adult males who possess little or no ability to use the English language. Many, though naturalized, we now find know and care little for us or our democratic institutions and government. The chart showing the nativity of the foreign-born in 1910 (p. 337) reveals something of the char-

acter of the immigrants we have among us.   The two circular charts below show the character of the male voting population in the United States, and the ability of the foreign-born
to use our common language, as shown by the Census
of 1920.   The situation disclosed by these charts is not a

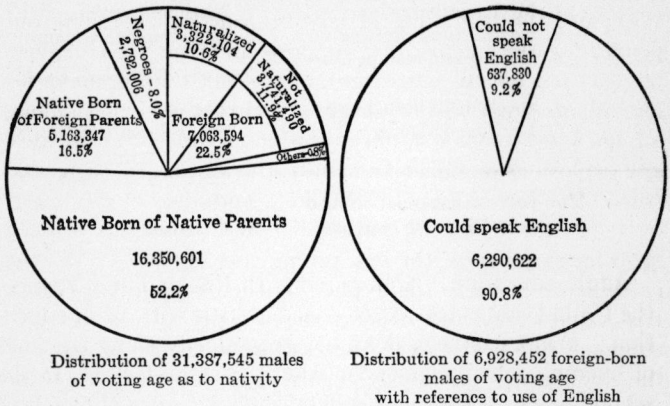

Distribution of 31,387,545 males   Distribution of 6,928,452 foreign-born
of voting age as to nativity   males of voting age
                                                with reference to use of English

FIG. 77. DISTRIBUTION OF THE MALE VOTING POPULATION OF THE UNITED
STATES, AS TO BIRTH AND ABILITY TO SPEAK ENGLISH. (FROM THE CEN-
SUS OF 1920).

particularly agreeable one.   Still more, the problem is worst
in our large cities, where assimilation is most difficult.   The
Census of 1920 showed that, for the ten largest cities of the
country, the percentage of the population in each which
could not speak English was as follows:

	Per Cent		Per Cent
St. Louis	5.5	Los Angeles	9.8
Boston	6.0	New York	10.6
Baltimore	8.1	Chicago	11.2
Philadelphia	8.1	Detroit	11.7
Pittsburgh	8.7	Cleveland	15.0

In our recent army draft eight per cent of all the young men
called up could understand no English, and an almost equal
additional number could understand so little as scarcely to

be able to follow commands.   Such conditions are a serious menace to our national welfare.

While providing schooling for such of the children of the foreign-born as choose to attend public rather than parochial schools, we have, through all our history, left to chance the Americanization of the adults.   The outbreak of the World War, and the beginning of hostile propaganda among our people by the agents of Germany and Austria-Hungary, brought forcibly to our attention the fact that we have for long reposed in a false security.   A long list of strikes among foreign-born colonies in our munition factories; "accidents" and explosions on docks and ships; the burning of barns and crops; the formation of "leagues" and "societies" interested in other than our national welfare; meetings of alien races for racial ends; the new prominence of the I.W.W.; the prominence given to the hyphen by the German-Americans, Irish-Americans, and others; the activity of the foreign-language press, and even the traitorous nature of some of the newspapers previously regarded as American; — these and many other happenings led us quickly to see that we had in the past been very negligent, and that we are now facing a vast social problem involving our national security and unity and the preservation of our national ideals.   National safety and national welfare alike demand that our schools now engage in a systematic and organized endeavor to educate the foreign-born in the principles and ideals of our democracy, and to make English our one common tongue.   In a recent bulletin on the subject the danger was well stated in the following words:

The government of the United States is a government by representation, and its integrity and effectiveness depend upon the intelligence of all the people.   This intelligence rests mainly upon the easy transfer of thought and information from one person to another by means of the spoken word and the printed page.   In an illiterate community the sense of civic responsibility is at its lowest, and disease, social isolation, and industrial inefficiency are found in highest degree.

It is difficult for those who can read easily to form even a bare conception of the mental limitations of the illiterate, the near-illiterate, and the non-reader. It is still harder to appreciate the material handicaps to earning a livelihood entailed by illiteracy. While illiteracy does not necessarily imply ignorance, it does predicate lack of information, comprehension, and understanding. It increases prejudice, suspicion, and passion, and diminishes natural appreciation and power to coöperate; yet coöperation is the essence of modern civilization, and inability to coöperate is the basis of race hatred. So that illiteracy is clearly a topic for national solicitude, and its eradication a proper subject for governmental action.

Citizenship classes. In 1915–16, under the lead of the United States Bureau of Education, our cities made the beginnings, through their adult citizenship classes, of what now seems destined to grow into a great campaign for the better assimilation of the adult foreign-born, and the stamping-out not only of illiteracy, but of the lack of ability to use and understand the English language as well. We have in the past cared little as to whether those coming among us became naturalized or not, and we have even admitted those still owing allegiance to other nations to important positions in local, state, and even national governmental work. We have had legal requirements for naturalization, to be sure, but no facilities have been provided to enable the foreign-born to meet these requirements. We have required the ability to "understand English," and that the applicant be "attached to the principles of the Constitution," but we have provided no pre-

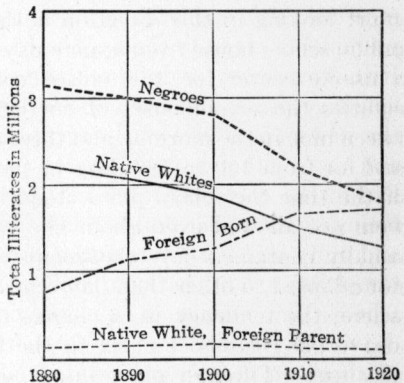

FIG. 78. WHO CONSTITUTE OUR
ILLITERATES

citizenship education, and the naturalization proceedings before judges, especially about election time, have too frequently been mere farces.

We see now that our schools must at once take on another new function, that of providing special classes and night schools, on an adequate scale, that will induct the foreign-born into the use of English as his common speech, and prepare him for naturalization by training him in the history and principles of our government, thus fitting him for proper membership in our national life by educating him along political, social, industrial, and sanitary lines. He, and she, must be educated for good citizenship if they are to remain among us.

The school as a community center. One important recent effort looking in this direction is the one to transform the public school house from a mere day school for children into a usable center for the entire community life. In the eighties the schoolhouses of our cities were used only between nine in the morning and three or four in the afternoon, and for from 150 to 180 days in the year. The remainder of the time the school plant stood idle, and boys and girls were not allowed even about the grounds. The buildings usually contained only classrooms and an office, and were not adapted to other than day-school uses. To-day, everywhere, the tendency is to change these earlier conditions, and to put the school plant to the largest possible community use. Through playgrounds, school gardens, vacation schools, and evening schools, our school grounds and school buildings in the cities and towns give much more service than formerly. As new school buildings have been erected and old ones rebuilt, they have been better fitted for use by the addition of an assembly hall, play rooms, a science room, a library room, and rooms for manual-training and household arts. Some also have workshops, baths, swimming-pools, and a gymnasium.

As this more extensive and more expensive equipment has been added to the schools; as the need for new efforts to assimilate the new classes in society has become evident; and as an increased participation in the functions of government through the initiative, referendum, recall, primary, and women's suffrage has come about, along with an increasing cosmopolitanism in our people; the demand has come that the public school, as the one great, active, unifying, non-racial, non-political, non-sectarian force in our national life, should take upon itself a new service and make of itself a center for the formation and education of community sentiment. As the school plant already belongs to the people, it has also been demanded that it be put to a more constant after-school use for the benefit of the community about it.

This has been done in many cities, and in a few rural communities as well. Starting almost entirely since 1900, statistics collected by the United States Bureau of Education show that 518 cities carried on community-center activities in their school buildings in 1915-16. These activities included lectures, on all kinds of human welfare topics, entertainments, adult society meetings, clubs for civic discussion, public meetings, dramatics, parties, social dancing, banquets, quiet reading and study, and the like. In 463 cities, for which the figures are complete, the school buildings were open on approximately 60,000 evenings, and the attendance was approximately 4,400,000 persons.

The aim has been to make the public school building a center for the life of the community; to extend the work of the school into the homes, and thus influence the civic and social welfare of the people; and to broaden the popular conception of education by making it a life-long process. A recent writer puts the matter well when he says:

When it is remembered that only ten per cent of the adult citizens have had a high school education, and only fifty per cent have ever completed the grammar grades, it becomes apparent that one of our great national needs is a popular university for the education of grown men and women. The public school as a community center is the answer to this national need. The community-center movement recognizes the fact that the mind matures more slowly than the body, and that education is a life-long process. While the public school is dedicated primarily to the welfare of the child, it is becoming daily more evident that the Nation's welfare requires it to be used for adults and youths as well. Notwithstanding the fact that it is our finest American invention and the most successful social enterprise undertaken, its golden age lies before it. It is now being discovered anew in its possibilities for larger service. The fact that all men desire knowledge is the fact which has justified the investment of $1,347,000,000 in the public school equipment; it is the fact which now justifies the use of this equipment for adults. In every part of the country there is a manifest tendency for the public school to develop into a house of the people to be used by them "for mutual aid in self-development." This is the significant fact at the heart of the community-center movement, and the touchstone of its value to the national welfare.

Agricultural extension. By an Act of Congress, approved May 8, 1914, and commonly known as the Smith-Lever Coöperative Agricultural Extension Act, Congress made the beginnings of what must ultimately prove to be a very important national movement for adult education along the lines of the improvement of agriculture and rural home-life. It provides for national aid to the States for "the diffusion among the people of useful and practical information on subjects relating to agriculture and home economics, and to encourage the application of the same," the work to be under the direction of the United States Department of Agriculture and to be done by the Agricultural Colleges in each State. The work must "consist of the giving of instruction and practical demonstrations in agriculture and home economics" to persons not attending the colleges. An important part of the educational work is to be through publications. For aiding the work the accompanying schedule of national aid to the States is provided.

The amount for printing and disseminating information is to be distributed evenly among the States, but the amount for extension work is to be distributed to the States in the proportion that the rural population in each State bears to the total rural population of the United States. Each

Year	For printing and distributing information	For rural extension work	Total national aid
1914–15	$480,000	–	$480,000
1915–16	480,000	$600,000	1,080,000
1916–17	480,000	1,100,000	1,580,000
1917–18	480,000	1,600,000	2,080,000
1918–19	480,000	2,100,000	2,580,000
1919–20	480,000	2,600,000	3,080,000
1920–21	480,000	3,100,000	3,580,000
1921–22	480,000	3,600,000	4,080,000
1922–23 *	480,000	4,100,000	4,580,000

* Reaches the maximum this year, and continues at this sum thereafter.

State must double, from state sources, all national aid received. The far-reaching future importance of this new educational effort toward improving crops, stocks, and rural home-life among our people can hardly be overestimated. The rural teacher should know and keep in touch with this new work.

IV. UNIVERSITY EXPANSION AND EXTENSION

Expansion of the original college. In Chapter VII we traced briefly the rise of the state university as the crown of the school system of the State, and the endowment by Congress, in 1862, of an entirely new type of higher instruction in the colleges of agriculture and mechanic arts. One of the earliest of these new institutions to become established, as well as one of the most heavily endowed, was Cornell University, in New York, opened in 1868. This institution, and the State University of Michigan, together rendered a very valuable pioneer service, during the quarter-century following the opening of Cornell, in marking out new lines of collegiate activity and new relationships between the colleges and the high schools beneath. At Cornell University instruction in science, agriculture, and engineering was placed on an entirely new footing, and the instruction in the

older subjects of the college curriculum was both broadened
and deepened.   Michigan was one of the first state universities to free itself from the hampering influences of state politics on the one hand and sectarian influences on the other;
to open its doors to women on the same terms as men (1870);
to begin the development of instruction in history (1857),
education (1879), and government (1881), with a view to
serving the State; and to examine and accredit the high
schools (1871) and receive pupils from accredited schools
into its freshman class without examination.

Before 1850 the colleges usually offered but one course,
based on Greek, Latin, and Mathematics, known as the
classical course, and leading to the A.B. degree.   Brown
offered a parallel course, without Greek and emphasizing
more modern studies, in 1851, leading to the Ph.B. degree.
Harvard organized the Lawrence Scientific School, in 1851,
with instruction in science, and leading to the B.S. degree,
and Yale made a similar organization in the Sheffield Scientific School, in 1852.   Dartmouth and Rochester also established courses for the B.S. degree in 1852, Michigan in 1853,
and Columbia a course for the Ph.B. degree in 1864.   By
1880 our colleges were offering three or four parallel courses,
much as the high schools did twenty years later.   These led
to different degrees — B.A., B.L., B.S., and Ph.B.   Graduate instruction was also organized, and courses leading to
the A.M., M.S., and Ph.D. degrees was in time provided.
The first Ph.D. degree granted in the United States was by
Yale, in 1851.   Few others were granted by our universities
before the opening of the first distinctively graduate university — Johns Hopkins, at Baltimore, in 1876.

Creation of new chairs and schools.   With the creation of
new chairs to represent new subjects of study, or subdivisions of old subjects, which became common after about
1875, the next tendency was to reorganize the colleges by
departments, such as Greek, Latin, English, history, mathematics, physics, biology, etc.   This became the common
form of organization for the larger universities after about

1890, and still continues. With the very rapid increase in the quantity of knowledge, and the subdivision of old subjects into many new chairs, the more recent tendency has been to re-group the university into a series of colleges and schools. To-day a large state university would include most or all of the following colleges, schools, or divisions, each subdivided into a number of departments or branches of knowledge, and often leading to separate degrees.

1. The college of liberal arts.
2. The college of engineering.
3. The college of agriculture.
4. The school of history and economics.
5. The school of pure science.
6. The school of education.
7. The school of household arts.
8. The school of fine arts.
9. The school of business administration.
10. The school of journalism.
11. The school of law.
12. The school of medicine.
13. The school of veterinary medicine.
14. The school of pharmacy.
15. The school of dentistry.
16. The school of forestry.
17. The school of mining.
18. The school of architecture.
19. The university-extension division.
20. The summer-session division.

Social significance of this great expansion. All this rapid development and subdivision of the university into schools and colleges indicates the assumption of new service for the welfare of the State. That the State has appreciated the service has been shown by a university development previously unknown. Since about 1885, when the state universities began to turn their attention to serving and advancing the welfare of the State, university attendance and revenues have advanced by leaps and bounds. During the same period the stimulating competition of such privately-endowed universities as Harvard, Yale, Columbia, Johns Hopkins, Tulane, Chicago, and Stanford has also made itself felt. The growth in student enrollment may be seen from the figures, at different dates, for a dozen of our larger state universities, as given on the following page.

Coincident with this rapid increase in students, faculty-schools, and courses has been the greatest number and amount of gifts of money to our universities ever given to

State University of	1885	1895	1905	1915
*California...........	197	1781	3294	6434
*Georgia............	184	299	483	651
*Illinois.............	247	814	3597	5439
Iowa...............	234	1133	1560	2680
Michigan	524	2818	3832	5833
*Minnesota.........	54	2171	3633	4484
*Missouri	573	614	1892	3140
*Nebraska..........	142	1397	2728	3832
*Ohio...............	64	805	1835	4599
Texas..............	151	630	1235	2574
Washington........	6	425	811	3249
*Wisconsin..........	313	1520	3010	5128

* The state agricultural college in these States is combined with the state university.

aid higher education in any land. Such gifts are evidence of the public appreciation of the valuable services to the State and Nation rendered by our colleges and universities, both publicly and privately endowed. The States, too, have put millions into the equipment and maintenance of these higher institutions, believing in them as creators of advanced public opinion and as training schools for the future leaders of the State. In a recent article in the *Atlantic Monthly*, President Pritchett wrote:

The rise of these great universities is the most epoch-making feature of our American civilization, and they are to become more and more the leaders, and the makers of our civilization. They are of the people. When a state university has gained solid ground, it means that the people of a whole state have turned their faces toward the light; it means that the whole system of state schools has been welded into an effective agent for civilization. Those who direct the purposes of these great enterprises of democracy cannot be too often reminded that the highest function of a university is to furnish standards for a democracy.

University extension. By way of rendering a still greater service to the people of the State, our state universities and agricultural colleges have recently made the beginnings of what seems destined to become a very important new fea-

ture of their state service.   By the development of study
centers, lecture courses, and scientific and technical instruction at many points within the State, by traveling exhibits,
traveling libraries, correspondence study, and by short

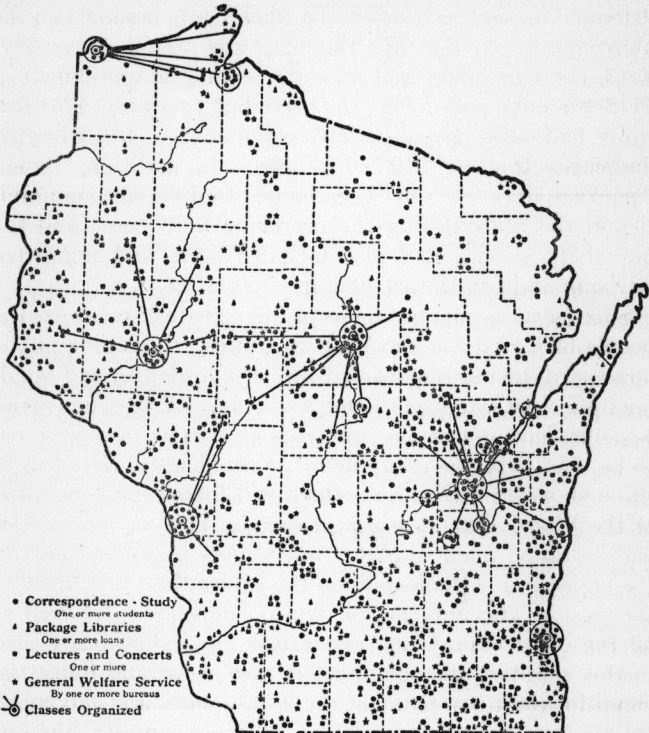

• Correspondence - Study
    One or more students
▲ Package Libraries
    One or more loans
■ Lectures and Concerts
    One or more
• General Welfare Service
    By one or more bureaus
⦵ Classes Organized

FIG. 79. UNIVERSITY EXTENSION WORK IN WISCONSIN

courses provided at public-school centers, our universities
and agricultural colleges have begun to extend the advantages of higher education to the people of the State who have
not been able to go to college.   To the work already begun we now have the agricultural extension work provided

for by the national government, through the Smith-Lever Bill (p. 430).

The University of Wisconsin has rendered notable service in this work, and may be considered as a type of the best and an example for development elsewhere. How it has extended its service to cover the whole State is shown on the above map. At the time this map was prepared, January, 1915, the University had an active extension enrollment of 7113 students, and during the preceding two years 1251 lectures had been given, in 525 communities, to estimated audiences totaling 370,750 people. In addition, 10,945 "package libraries" had been loaned to different communities in the State during the preceding four years, and the university service had also included state and municipal advising and health instruction.

Such service can be made of the greatest value to the people of a State in elevating standards, developing public opinion, diffusing general and special knowledge, and building up a more intelligent democratic life. With democracies so so dependent on learning and leadership as we now see them to be, and with the many intricate problems ahead of us in the new world civilization which will follow the conclusion of the World War, it is almost certain that our universities will be called upon to play a much more important part in the education of democracy in the future than they have in the past. The university-extension movement, as well as all the other educational expansions and extensions traced in this chapter, are significant of new social and industrial conditions and new national needs. As our social and political life becomes more intricate and more complex, and our world connections more extensive, education must broaden its work and enlarge its functions to prepare our people for the demands which lie ahead.

QUESTIONS FOR DISCUSSION

1. Show the connection between the recent rapid development of the high school and the social and industrial changes since 1860, described in Chapter XI.
2. What is the educational significance of the change of the high school from a book-study high school to a laboratory and shop high school?
3. What is the social meaning of the numerous parallel high school courses (p. 409) and schools (p. 410)?
4. Contrast the American and European high school in purpose.
5. Show the advantage, in a democracy, of a higher school to develop tastes and test capacities (p. 411).
6. Why should ours be free, when theirs is a tuition school?
7. Explain the breakdown of the old apprenticeship education.
8. Explain our long neglect of vocational training.
9. Explain our continued neglect of higher commercial training.
10. Explain our recent rapid acceptance of the agricultural high school, whereas the agricultural colleges for a long time faced much opposition.
11. Explain the continued emphasis by the high school of studies leading to the professions rather than the vocations, though so small a percentage of our people are needed in professional lines. How may vocational guidance help here?
12. Show the human and monetary value of vocational guidance.
13. Show the usefulness to the community and the nation of such evening-school instruction as is outlined on pp. 423-24.
14. How do you explain so large a percentage of young people, 14 to 20 years of age, not in any form of school (Fig. 76)?
15. How should we deal with the problem of adult illiteracy? What standards should we impose for naturalization?
16. Show how and why a people with one common language is safer and happier than one having many.
17. Explain how the public school is the natural center for community activities for advancing the public welfare.
18. Explain why agricultural and home-life extension is important enough to warrant national aid and state supervision.
19. Explain why university extension is so desirable in a democracy.
20. Explain the reasons for the very rapid and extensive expansion of our colleges since about 1885.
21. Show that the statement by President Pritchett (p. 434) is true.

TOPICS FOR INVESTIGATION AND REPORT

1. The organization and work of a large technical high school for girls.
2. The organization and work of a large technical high school for boys.

3. The organization and work of a county or district high school of agriculture.
4. The organization and work of an evening vocational school.
5. The need for vocational education in the United States.
6. The Smith-Hughes Bill plans and work so far organized in your state.
7. The organization and work of vocational guidance in some city school system.
8. The evening-school system of some large city.
9. The citizenship and adult-illiteracy classes organized in some city.
10. The community-center work in some city rendering good service.
11. The work done in agricultural extension in your state.
12. The university extension work done by your state university.
13. The library extension work organized by your state library.
14. The Report of the National Commission on Vocational Education.
15. Trade and industrial education in Germany before 1914.

SELECTED REFERENCES

Betts, Geo. H.   *Social Principles of Education.*   318 pp.   Chas. Scribner's Sons, New York, 1912.

Chapter VI, on "Education and Vocational Modes of Experience," deals with vocations and avocations in education, and forms simple collateral reading for this chapter.

*Bloomfield, Meyer.   *The Vocational Guidance of Youth.*   124 pp.   Houghton Mifflin Co., Boston, 1911.

A brief statement of the aims and purposes of the movement. A more detailed statement may be found in the same author's *Youth, School, and Vocation.* (Houghton Mifflin Company. 1916.)

Cubberley, E. P., and Elliott, E. C.   *State and County School Administration;* vol. II, *Source Book,* 729 pp.   The Macmillan Co., New York, 1915.

Chapter XV, on supplemental education, contains the following readings relating to this chapter:
    1. "The School House as a Social Center" ; W. Wilson.
    2. "The Wisconsin Free Library Commission."
    3. "Farmers' Institutes"; Hamilton.
    4. "University Extension" ; Van Hise.

*Dewey, John and Evelyn.   *Schools of To-morrow.*   316 pp.   E. P. Dutton & Co., New York, 1915.

A very interesting book, with good illustrations. Chapter VIII describes a social settlement school, and Chapter IX deals with the question of the place of vocational education in the school system.

*Farrington, F. E.   *Public Facilities for Educating Aliens.*   49 pp.   United States Bureau of Education, Bulletin No. 18, Washington, 1916.

The problem; conditions; statistics.

*Fletcher, H. J.   "Our Divided Country"; in *Atlantic Monthly,* vol. 117, pp. 223–32.   (Feb., 1916.)

An excellent article on the problem presented by our un-Americanized foreign-born.

Forbush, Wm. B. *The Coming Generation.* 402 pp. D. Appleton & Co., New York, 1912.

A readable account of the forces working for the betterment of American young people.

*Kellor, Frances A. "The Education of the Immigrant"; in *Educational Review*, vol. 48, pp. 21–36. (June, 1914.)

A very able and interesting article, pointing out the need of action.

*Kingsley, C. D. "The High-School Period as a Testing-Time"; in *Proceedings of the National Education Association*, 1913, pp. 49–55.

A good article on the high school as a testing-time, and the need for cosmopolitan high schools.

Lenz, Frank B. "The Education of the Immigrant"; in *Educational Review*, vol. 51, pp. 469–77. (May, 1916.)

The education of immigrant adults, by a Y.M.C.A. worker.

Lewis, Wm. D. *Democracy's High School.* 125 pp. Houghton Mifflin Co., Boston, 1914.

An interesting statement of the new national problems the high school must face, as these affect both the boy and the girl.

*Lutz, R. R. *Wage-Earning and Education.* 208 pp. Cleveland Education Survey, 1916.

A study of the industrial conditions and trade needs in one large American city.

*Monroe, Paul. *Cyclopedia of Education.* 5 vols. The Macmillan Co., New York, 1911–13.

The following articles are especially important:
1. "Agricultural Education"; vol. i, pp. 58–68.
2. "College, The American"; vol. ii, pp. 57–79.
3. "Evening Schools"; vol. ii, pp. 521–27.
4. "Household Arts in Education"; vol. iii, pp. 318–31.
5. "Illiteracy"; vol. iii, pp. 382–85.
6. "Immigration and Education"; vol. iii, pp. 390–95.
7. "Industrial Education"; vol. iii, pp. 425–43.
8. "University Extension"; vol. v, pp. 684–89.
9. "Vocational Education"; vol. v, pp. 740–42.

*National Society. *The City School as a Community Center.* 72 pp. Tenth Year-Book of the National Society for the Scientific Study of Education, Part i, 1911.

A series of eight papers on different aspects of the topic, and describing the work being done.

*Perry, C. A. *Wider Use of the School Plant.* 417 pp. Charities Publication Committee, New York, 1911.

The best single book on the schoolhouse as a community center. Many excellent illustrations.

*Perry, C. A. *Educational Extension.* 115 pp. Cleveland Education Survey, 1916.

Describes the needs and opportunities in a large city.

Perry, C. A. *The Extension of Public Education.* 67 pp. United States Bureau of Education, Bulletin No. 28, Washington, D.C.

A study in the wider use of school buildings. Many good illustrations. Bulletin No. 30, 1917, carries statistics down to 1915–16.

*Ross, E. A.   *Changing America.*   236 pp.   Century Co., New York, 1912.

Chapter X is a good general sketch on the state universities of the Middle West, and their influence.

*Talbot, W.   *Adult Illiteracy.*   90 pp.   United States Bureau of Education, Bulletin No. 55, Washington, 1916.

The distribution of; illiteracy of immigrants; and means for improving the situation.

Ward, E. J.   *The Social Center.*   359 pp.   D. Appleton & Co., New York, 1913.

A detailed description of the community-center movement in the United States.

*Weeks, Ruth M.   *The People's School.*   202 pp.   Houghton Mifflin Co., Boston, 1912.

A very interesting study in vocational training.   The problem, the vocation, trade-school training.

*Woolman, Mary.   "The Manhattan Trade School for Girls"; in *Educational Review*, vol. 30, pp. 178–88.   (Sept., 1905.)

A very interesting account of the beginnings of the school at New York, and of the types of work attempted.

Education of the Immigrant.   52 pp.   United States Bureau of Education, Bulletin No. 51, Washington, D.C., 1913.

A series of papers read at a public conference on the subject in New York City, May, 1913.

Illiteracy in the United States.   38 pp.   United States Bureau of Education, Bulletin No. 20, Washington, 1913.

The experiment for its elimination in the "moonlight schools" of eastern Kentucky, described and illustrated.

Report of the Committee on National Aid to Vocational Education.   House Document No. 1004, Sixty-third Congress.   Washington, 1915.

CHAPTER XIV

DESIRABLE EDUCATIONAL REORGANIZATIONS

Our progress toward scientific organization. Up to the days of Carter and Mann and Pierce in Massachusetts, and Barnard in Connecticut and Rhode Island, our school development had been almost entirely along the lines of securing legislation, first to permit, and later to require, the establishment of schools; of organizing an administrative machinery to look after the schools thus established; and of creating a public belief in education for democratic ends and a sentiment that would support further progress. The development was highly empirical, each community and State following the lines of least resistance, without much regard to underlying principles of action. Carter and Mann tried to give a better organization to the schools of Massachusetts, as did Barnard in the two States to the south, while Mann tried by his *Reports* and addresses, and Barnard by his *Journals* to introduce the better teaching methods which American travelers abroad had described, and which both had seen in European schools. The schoolmasters of the time largely resented change, however, and few who taught felt the need for any training, so it was not until the movement looking toward a more scientific basis for our school practice had had infused into it the psychology of Pestalozzi, the new ideas of Guyot and Krüsi, and particularly the enthusiasm of Sheldon, at Oswego, that we really set to work in earnest to psychologize instruction, train would-be teachers for teaching, and put schoolroom practice on something approaching a scientific basis. The period from 1860 to about 1885 to 1890 was with us the great period of "faculty"-psychology and subject methodology. This period was also marked by the firm establishment of the public

442 EDUCATION IN THE UNITED STATES

normal school, and the beginnings of the professional study
of education in our universities.

New directions during the past two decades. Since then
we have obtained some new ideas from abroad and have
worked out many new conceptions of the educational process at home, and as a result we to-day possess a truer psychology than Sheldon and his followers knew, while the
child-study movement has opened up entirely new conceptions as to the nature of child development. A new profession of teaching has been created, and the administration of
public education has been organized into a new professional
subject by our colleges and universities. Above all, our educational thinking has been colored through and through by
the new social and industrial forces which have become so
prominent during the past quarter-century, and as a result
we to-day think in terms of a new educational philosophy,
and direct the work of our schools along new lines and
toward new ends.

Within the past quarter of a century a number of new
educational conceptions have come to the front which have
already deeply modified our educational thinking and practices, and which promise to do more than any previous impulses to reorganize our educational work after a rational
plan, and to give scientific direction to our educational
procedure. These may be classified under the following
larger headings:

1. The scientific study of education.
2. The reorganization of school work.
3. The reorganization and redirection of rural and village education.
4. State educational reorganization.

We will consider each of these, briefly, in the above order.

I. The Scientific Study of Education

The overcrowded curriculum. From the diagram on
page 327, showing the evolution of our elementary-school
curriculum, it must be evident that, if the school subjects of

1825 or 1850 occupied all the time of the school, the many new subjects added since must seriously overburden the course of study, even after making all due allowance for better trained teachers, longer school terms, and better text-books and teaching appliances. The newer expression subjects (p. 370) also require better teaching preparation and more careful supervision than did the old book subjects. To the 1900 list should now be added school gardening, agriculture, play as a regular school subject, and a much greater emphasis on the social and industrial aspects of all our school work.

The result has been that our elementary school courses of study have become badly crowded and that teachers, especially in the upper grades, can no longer be expected to be qualified to teach satisfactorily all the subjects of the elementary school course. Nor would there be time in which to teach all the subjects in the old way, even admitting that the teacher was properly prepared to do so.

Early attempts at solving the problem. With the increase of new studies, the "over-burdening of the curriculum" had become a real live issue by 1890, and various attempts have since been made to solve the problem. In many places the introduction of the expression subjects was fought by calling them "fads and frills," and for a time they were kept out. This line of attack has now been given up except by a few of the older generation. It has been seen that abuse and ridicule are not arguments, while it has become increasingly evident that these same expression studies are not only valuable educational instruments in themselves, but also supply a real need under our changed conditions of living.

One of the earliest proposals for solving the over-burdened-curriculum difficulty was that we *concentrate* instruction about a few main subjects, and then *correlate* the other school work about these central subjects. Colonel Francis W. Parker (p. 328) was the leading advocate of this idea, and his book on the teaching of geography was to show how this could be done about geography as the central core.

The National Education Association's Committee of Fifteen, in its *Report* in 1895, devoted half the space to the correlation of elementary school subjects. During the nineties the terms *concentration* and *correlation* were terms to conjure with.

Eliminating useless subject-matter. Another plan pro-posed, and one that has proved very useful, has been to cut out parts of many of the subjects taught and to confine instruction to what is left. This has been done extensively. For example, we do not now teach a third as much arithmetic or grammar as we used to do; the facts in geography and the dates and battles of history are made much less prominent than they used to be; and bone and muscle and nerve physiology and the memorization of the Constitution have been displaced by hygiene and community civics. The tendency

In the midst of a meadow,
  Well stored with grass,
I've taken just two acres,
  To tether my ass:
Then how long must the cord be,
  That feeding all round;
He may n't graze less or more, than
  Two acres of ground. *Ans.* 55½ *yards.*

ONE OF THE PUZZLES WE NO LONGER TEACH

has been to eliminate the puzzles and little-used information, and to cut out all that is not useful for modern life needs. We thus not only simplify the teaching of the subject but make room for other subjects as well.

The Herbartians (p. 317) have been of much help here, as they have urged the teaching of "type studies," instead of hundreds of isolated facts. For example, in geography, a study of such types as coal-mining, a seaport, a railroad-center, the cotton industry, sheep and wool, shipping, transportation, and the interdependence of people, should take the place of learning great numbers of isolated facts. In history, instruction in such type studies as the internal development of our Nation, the development of the West, the growth of political parties, the rise of slavery, the evolution of transportation, the Monroe Doctrine, and the dominance of cotton in our early history and the effect of the invention of the cotton gin, should replace the chronological study of American annals. The same idea has been applied to science instruction, literature, civics, hygiene, and other studies. The work of Charles, Frank, and Lida McMurry has been very helpful along these lines.

Still more recently a committee of the National Education Association on "Economy of Time in Education" has made careful studies of possible eliminations, and the National Society for the Study of Education has made also valuable reports on "Minimum Essentials in Elementary School Subjects." All of these have been along the line of eliminating what is no longer important to teach, and should be studied by those interested in the problem.

The " project " idea. Another very important attempt at the solution of the problem has been along the line of abandoning largely the old subject-classification, and teaching "projects" instead. The work of John Dewey, in the experimental elementary school he conducted for some years (1896–1900) at Chicago, was pioneer work along this line. Making motor expression, social participation, and the industries of life the ideas around which instruction centered, and making the school reproduce the typical conditions of social life, he constructed a course of study based largely on occupations, projects, and social demands, and continually calling for expression rather than receptivity. In his school the work of the teacher was largely that of planning, guiding, and interposing "pedagogical interference" to direct the activities of the children along lines that would be helpful and educationally profitable. The old formal school subjects, with set times for classes, were replaced by studies, projects, and activities, into which were introduced number, speech, reading, writing, drawing, manual work, history, and geography, as needed to understand or work out the project of the day or week. The school resembled a combination of a kindergarten and a series of workshops more than an ordinary school.

Recently a number of attempts at reorganizing instruction on some form of the project, or pupil-activity basis, have been tried. The school of Mrs. Johnson, at Fairhope, Alabama, described by Dewey (see bibliography) forms a good modern example. There the elementary school course of study, instead of being made up of arithmetic, language, geography, history, etc., is organized under the headings of physical exercise, nature study, music, hand work, field geography, descriptive geography, reading, story-telling, sense culture, number, dramatization, and games. The experimental elementary school at the University of Missouri, also described by Dewey, divided the day's work equally among four activities — play, stories, observation, and hand work — and built its instruction around these four.

The new scientific study of the problem. Within the past decade an entirely new means of attacking the problem has been developed through what are known as scientific tests. The movement is as yet only in its infancy, but so important is it in terms of the future that it bids fair to change the whole character of the supervision of the instruction in our schools. The scientific purpose of the new movement has been to try to evolve, by the careful measurement of schools and children, a series of standards of measurement (measuring sticks for school work) and units of accomplishment (time and effort evaluations of instruction) which can be applied to schools anywhere to determine, scientifically, the economy or wastefulness and the efficiency or inefficiency of the work being done. On the basis of such information the effectiveness of all kinds of instruction can be measured, and schools in different places can be accurately compared. The leader in this movement has been Professor Edward L. Thorndike, of Teachers College, Columbia University.

These tests and measures we now know as Standard Scales. So forcibly has this new idea of measurement appealed to the younger school men that to-day probably hundreds of men and women are busy testing and perfecting scales for all kinds of measurements, new or improved scales are being proposed continually in the educational magazines, and a few very helpful books for the use of teachers have already been written on the subject. So far we have evolved fairly satisfactory scales for the measurement of:

Arithmetical ability.	English composition.
Reasoning skill.	Use of English.
Handwriting.	Silent reading.
Spelling.	Oral reading.
Drawing.	Geography.

For each of these subjects certain "standard scores," that is the amount of work with the tests which should be done by average pupils, of any age or grade, have been worked out.

A new ability to diagnose. With these standard tests and scores we can now measure an unknown class and say, rather definitely, that, for example, the class not only spells poorly but is 12 per cent below standard; that the class is 8 per cent ahead of its place in speed of writing, but 15 per cent below on quality; that the children are from 6 to 16 per cent above grade in the four simple arithmetical processes, but 21 per cent below in ability to reason on simple arithmetical problems; that they can read orally 16 per cent better than the average class, but are sadly deficient in thought-getting ability from silent reading; and that, in composition, they are 10 per cent below standard and can write much better than they can think. Still more, we can determine just where the difficulty lies, not only with schools or classes, but for individual pupils in classes as well, as may be seen from the pupil score card in Arithmetic, given on page 448.

Within the past five years these tests have been used in School Surveys in a number of American cities, and those responsible for the conduct of the schools were told, as a result of the tests, where their schools stood in the matter of instruction. Butte (1914), Salt Lake City (1915), Cleveland (1916), and Grand Rapids (1917) form good examples of the use of these tests to diagnose conditions. In Butte, for example, the schools were found ahead of where they should have been in all formal drill subjects, and below where they should have been in all subjects involving reasoning or expression. In Salt Lake City, the schools were found to rank high and above standard in all subjects in which

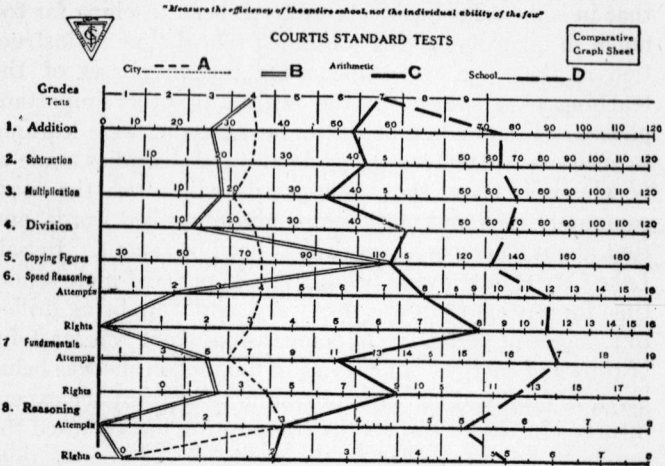

FIG. 80. A COURTIS SCORE CARD IN ARITHMETIC

From Cubberley's *Public School Administration*, p. 334.

In the figure above, curves A and B are of two individuals in the same class. From an Indiana school. Note that A is practically normal except in the last test (shown by the fact that the curve is almost a straight line and lies almost wholly within the boundaries of the fourth grade), while B is below grade in every test but one and is particularly weak on reasoning.

Curves C and D are two measurements of the same child, one in September and the other in June. From a Michigan school. Note the correction of many defects and the balance of the final score.

tests were given — spelling, composition, writing, reading, and arithmetic — but that the range of pupil abilities in classes and schools was too large, and that too much time was being given to these subjects at the expense of other studies. The Cleveland measurements showed much wrong emphasis in instruction, far too wide variations between schools and classes, and need of an entirely new type of school supervision to secure better results for the money expended. The schools of Grand Rapids, as a whole, were found near to where they should be, the attention needed being to individual schools, rather than to the school system as a whole.

Standard tests as a basis for course of study eliminations. The studies made with the use of the tests, too, have shown that in some school subjects we have been teaching far too much in quantity, giving too much school time to instruction in them, or over-emphasizing certain phases of the teaching of a subject to the neglect of other important phases. The children of Butte, for example, were learning to spell over 10,000 words, while all careful studies made of vocabularies show that 1000 words will cover the most commonly used and most commonly misspelled words, and that about 3500 words are all that need be taught. In Salt Lake City children were being given 25 per cent more school time for writing than was necessary, and were being drilled to a degree of perfection in penmanship which was wasteful of time and energy. In Cleveland too much time was being given to oral reading, without results to warrant the expenditure. In Grand Rapids the composition tests showed the pupils to be over-drilled in the mechanics of composition, but poor in ability to think. On the basis of such studies, combined with studies as to the social usefulness of the various parts of the different school subjects, and studies as to the pedagogy of instruction, we have already been able to do something in the revision of our elementary school curriculum that has lightened the load and materially improved the instruction of what remains.

By creating such measuring sticks for school work, both supervisors and teachers are given a far more definite aim than ever before for the work they are to do. Waste of energy through over- or under-emphasis of certain phases of the teaching process may be prevented. Principals and teachers can tell, from a glance at the results of standard tests, charted on a standard score card, whether or not any room or group of pupils is up to standard; what are the weak points; whether a room or a school is making progress;

and in what rooms the load and the teacher are not properly adjusted. Teachers, in particular, can know definitely what results are expected of them, and at all times whether or not they are accomplishing them. Even pupils can, in some subjects, score their own records on standard score cards, calculate their growth in accuracy and speed, and compare their writing with the standardized writing of a writing scale hung in the room.

The important underlying purpose in the creation of all such standards for measuring school work and for comparing the accomplishments of pupils, classes, schools, or school systems, is to give to supervisors and teachers means by which they may, quite definitely, measure the effectiveness of the work they do, and learn from the charted results where to shift the emphasis and how to improve the manufacturing process. Teaching without a measuring stick of standardized length, and without definite standards (standard scores, or norms) for the work of the different grades, is much like the old time luck-and-chance farming, and there is no reason to think that the introduction of well-tested standards for accomplishment in school work will not do for education what has been done for agriculture as a result of the application of scientific knowledge and methods. This recent development of tests and measures for instruction is a movement looking toward scientific accuracy in teaching, and is comparable in importance to the introduction of the idea, in the sixties, of an orderly psychological development in children, to which a methodology of instruction should be applied.

The measurement of intelligence. Within the past ten years we have also worked out and perfected another new and very important means whereby it is now possible to measure and classify children on the basis of their intellectual capacities. From the use so far made of this new measuring stick in retesting children once measured, at a later age, it is now confidently asserted that the degree of intelligence which a child has at six or eight or ten years of age is the degree of intelligence he will retain through life. That is, a child of 80 per cent of average intelligence at six years of age will remain close to 80 per cent the remainder of his life, and a child of 120 per cent will remain close to 120 per cent. Instead of being born free and equal, we are born free and unequal, and unequal we shall ever remain. The school, we now see, cannot make intelligence; it can only train and develop and make useful the intelligence which the child brings with him to school. This is a matter of his racial and family inheritance, and nothing within the gift of the schools or our democratic form of government. From the use of this new measuring stick, too, we have found that there can be no arbitrary classification of children into such groups as dull, average, and bright. Instead, children shade off from one classification into another, all the way from idiocy at one end of the scale to superior genius at the other. As might be expected, most children fall into the relatively normal class, the curve shading off somewhat evenly in either direction.

By means of a series of carefully selected and standardized mental tests, first worked out by Binet and Simon in France (1911), and revised and extended and adapted to use with American children by Terman (1916), we are now able to measure and give each child an intelligence rating (intelli-

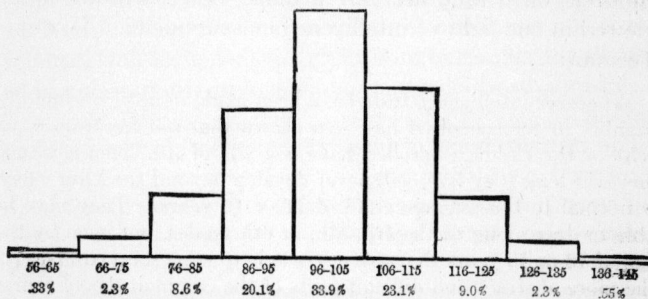

| 56-65 | 66-75 | 76-85 | 86-95 | 96-105 | 106-115 | 116-125 | 126-135 | 136-145 |
| .33% | 2.3% | 8.6% | 20.1% | 33.9% | 23.1% | 9.0% | 2.3% | .55% |

FIG. 81. THE DISTRIBUTION OF INTELLIGENCE AMONG CHILDREN

Based on the measurement of 905 unselected school children, 5 to 14 years of age. (From Terman's *The Measurement of Intelligence*, p. 66.)

gence quotient; I. Q.). From this rating (I. Q.) we know somewhat accurately the possibilities of the child in school work. Terman's studies showed that the distribution of the intelligence of children, between 5 and 14 years of age, is approximately as shown in the last diagram, the extremes in intelligence in the children he measured ranging from 56 to 145. On the basis of his work he suggested the following classification of children as to I. Q. and mental capacity.

I. Q.	*Classification*
Above 140............	Near genius or genius.
120–140..............	Very superior intelligence.
110–120..............	Superior intelligence.
90–110	**Normal, or average intelligence.**
80–90................	Dullness.
70–80................	Border-line deficiency, sometimes classifiable as dullness, often as feeble-mindedness.
Below 70.............	Definite feeble-mindedness.

Educational significance of intelligence measurements. The educational significance of this new means of measuring intelligence is very large. Questions relating to proper classification in school, grading, promotion, choice of studies, schoolroom procedure, vocational guidance, and the proper handling of subnormal children on the one hand and gifted children on the other, all acquire new meaning when viewed in the light of intelligence measurement. To quote Terman:

Wherever intelligence tests have been made in any considerable number in the schools it has been shown that not far from 2 per cent of the children enrolled have a grade of intelligence which, however long they live, will never develop beyond the level which is normal to the average child of 11 or 12 years. They may be able to drag along to the 4th, 5th, or 6th grades, but even by the age of 16 or 18 years they are never able to cope successfully with the more abstract and difficult parts of the common-school course of study. They may master a certain amount of rote learning, such as that involved in reading and in the manipulation of number combinations, but they cannot be taught to meet new conditions effectively, or to think, reason, and judge as normal persons do.

On the other hand, the number of children with very superior ability is approximately as great as the number of feeble-minded. The future well-being of this country hinges, in no small degree, upon the right education of these superior children. Psychological tests show that children of superior ability usually fail to reap any advantage whatever, in terms of promotion, from their superior intelligence. The large majority of superior children tested are found located below the school grade warranted by their intelligence level.

When these new tests of intelligence have been applied to the children who experience difficulty in getting along in the regular school a flood of light has been thrown on the problem. Low mentality, retardation in school, truancy, immorality, and criminal tendencies are all tied up closely together. It may now be confidently asserted, on the basis of tests so far made, that approximately 2 per cent of the children in our schools are of such low mentality that they probably never will attain to a grade of intelligence above that normal for a twelve-year-old child; that among the children in our reform (industrial) schools 20 to 30 per cent are feeble-minded, and another 20 to 25 per cent of low-grade mentality; that approximately 25 to 30 per cent of our criminals and 30 to 40 per cent of our prostitutes are feeble-minded. Of the low-grade-in-intelligence members of these classes, very few have ever progressed beyond the fifth grade in school. Lacking in the ability to foresee and weigh consequences, and unable to exercise self-restraint, every low-grade or feeble-minded girl is a potential prostitute, and every boy of the type a potential criminal.

Viewed in the light of this new knowledge, the importance of mental measurements to grade and classify intelligence, of the standard tests to determine lines of progress, and of all the special types of schools for delinquents and defectives mentioned in Chapter XII — differentiated course of study, over-age classes, non-English-speaking classes, supplemental coaching classes, industrial classes, home schools, disciplinary classes, parental schools, state industrial schools — acquire a new educational significance in the light of our recent discoveries as to the measurement and grading of intelligence. The recent development of standard scales and a scale for the grading of intelligence mark distinct forward steps in the improvement of our educational procedure. Just now they are both new, but as they are learned by teachers and principals, and their use made common, schoolroom methods will become more intelligent, children will be classified and taught better, and the needs of the slow on the one hand and the gifted on the other will be better cared for by our schools. Both represent important new steps forward in the process of making education a more scientific procedure.

II. The Reorganization of School Work

The 8-4 school as evolved by 1890. Our common-school system was an outgrowth of a great democratic movement, beginning in the early part of the nineteenth century, which created common tax-supported schools for democracy's ends. The college, on the other hand, has its roots back in the Middle Ages, and originally was founded to pass on to a small privileged class the inherited learning of the ages. In between the two there arose with us the academy, and this later was superseded by the public tax-supported high school. This, when created, unlike the common practice with higher schools in Europe (see Fig. 51, p. 268) was superimposed by democracy on the common school which had previously grown up. As was shown in the tabulation for twenty-five cities given on page 228, the parts of our school system at first possessed no fixed limits or length of course. Sometimes we found a three-year high school superimposed on anywhere from a six- to a nine-year elementary-school course of study, and sometimes a four-year school superimposed on schools of varying length below. In time the nine-year elementary school became common in the New

JOHN DEWEY

CHARLES WILLIAM ELIOT
President Emeritus of
Harvard University

England States, the seven-year elementary school in the Southern States, and the eight-year elementary schools elsewhere, with a three-year and later a four-year high-school course superimposed on top of each.

By 1890 the 8–4 plan of organization, shown in the chart on page 99, had become common everywhere, except in the South, the nine-year elementary school in New England being due to the admission of children to the lowest grade at five, instead of six. The high school was thus dovetailed in between the common school on the one side and the college on the other, as is shown in the left-hand plan given in Figure 82, page 460. A perfect educational ladder was thus provided by democracy, leading from the kindergarten at the bottom to the graduate or professional schools at the top. This all came about so naturally as the result of a slow native evolution, and seemed to fit so well the educational needs of the time, that no one for a time questioned the arrangement.

First questioning of the arrangement. In 1888 President Charles W. Eliot, of Harvard University, read a paper before the Department of Superintendence of the National Education Association on "Can School Programs be Shortened and Enriched?" and in 1892 followed this by another before the National Education Association on "Shortening and Enriching the Grammar School Course." These two papers started a discussion of a new educational problem, — that of the respective purposes and places in our educational system of the common elementary school, the high school, and the college. The discussion centered about the questions of shortening the instruction in the old drill subjects, the addition of new and more advanced studies in the upper grades of the elementary school, the specialization of the work of teachers there by the introduction of a departmental type of teaching for the sixth, seventh, and eighth school grades, and the shortening of the whole course of instruction so that boys might begin their professional study and life-work at an earlier age. These topics were much discussed for a decade and a half, and much careful thinking was given to them.

As a result, many schools, between about 1890 and 1905, reorganized the instruction in the upper grades by changing from the grade-teacher plan to a departmental type of instruction. A few new subjects, such as elementary algebra and geometry, elementary science, and Latin or a modern language were introduced, here and there, as new studies for selected classes in the upper grades, but usually there was no differentiation in courses, and no changes in the relation of the elementary school to the high school. The public school system still remained an 8–4 school system, with at best the five lower grades taught by the grade plan and the three upper by the departmental plan. The chief result of the discussion, though by no means a small one in itself, was to specialize more the work of the teachers in the upper elementary school grades, with a resulting improvement in the quality of the instruction.

One other result of importance was that the discussion aroused led to the appointment of three committees by the National Education Association, the reports of which were widely read and materially influenced subsequent thinking. These were:

Appointed	Committee	Reported
1891	Committee of Ten on Secondary School Studies	1893
1893	Committee of Fifteen on Elementary Education	1895
1895	Committee on College Entrance Requirements	1899

A new direction given the discussion. In 1901 Professor John Dewey, and in 1902 President Harper, at the meetings of conferences of academies and high schools at the University of Chicago, gave the discussion a new direction by questioning the organization of public education as then developed. President Harper proposed to condense and shorten the elementary school to six years, and then extend the high school to an equal length of time. For such a change he advanced many educational arguments. This proposal, too, brought forth much educational discussion.

A number of committees to consider it were appointed by
different educational associations, a number of reports were
prepared and printed, and many articles on the question
appeared in the educational magazines. The fact that, in
1900, two of the most progressive nations in the world,
France and Japan, had revised their national systems of
education and virtually limited elementary education to
six years, was quoted; and the educational exhibits at the
St. Louis Exposition, in 1904, made it conspicuously evident
that the United States was almost the only important nation
to prolong elementary education to eight or nine years. In
the Philippines, too, we had just organized a school system
built on a four-year elementary school.

General result of the discussion. The result of a decade
of discussion which followed this new proposal was a rather
general acceptance, at least by those who had participated
actively in it, of the idea of shortening the drill and funda-
mental-knowledge instruction of the elementary school to
six years, and the organization of all the instruction of
the following eight years — the seventh and eighth grades,
the four years of the high school period, and the first two
years of the college course — into some organized form of
secondary education, as is done in most European countries.
It gradually came to be felt that such an arrangement would
not only provide for better instruction, but that it would
be based on better psychological grounds than the 8–4 plan.
Under the plans proposed the first two years of the college
course would become more closely connected with the secondary school — perhaps an integral part of it — and the
university of the future would in consequence become a group
of professional schools, beginning at the present junior year.
The general result would be the enrichment of instruction,
the provision of larger educational opportunities at home
for the more ambitious pupils, and the capable student
would be able to finish college by the time he was twenty,
get his professional preparation made by twenty-three or
twenty-four, and thus enter upon his professional life at

least two years earlier than was then the case. The following statement, made by Professor Alexis F. Lange, in 1909, is expressive of the general result arrived at as the outcome of the discussion carried on between 1902 and 1909. He said:

The question is no longer, Shall the high school live unto itself; but, How shall it live with its neighbors on either side? . . . Education must become more continuous, not mechanically, but organically. The sixteen or more grades of our school system must come to stand approximately for as many adaptations to unbroken growth. The educational edifice erected by the nineteenth century still resembles too closely an irregular pyramid of three boxes, the tops and bottoms of which are perforated in order that the more acrobatic pupils may vault from the known to the unknown, and their teachers above and below may exchange maledictions. The twentieth century cannot accept this arrangement as final. The structure, as seen from the outside, may well remain intact; but the provisional tops and bottoms inside must be refitted, if not removed. Now, one essential in preparing for this task is to realize that adolescence begins at least two years earlier and ends about two years later than the inherited accidental high-school period. Divested of artificial meanings, secondary education is seen to cover not less than eight grades, instead of four.

Up to 1911 or 1912 the question of educational reorganization remained largely an academic question, though being increasingly subjected to critical analysis by practical school men to see if the reorganizations proposed could be carried out in practice. Along with this study of the problem of educational reorganization a number of other practical school problems, such as the acceleration of capable children, retardation and its causes, flexible grading, promotional schemes, courses of study eliminations, and parallel and differentiated courses of study to meet varying social and individual needs, now began to receive a hitherto unknown attention. Within the past half-dozen years not only these problems, but the earlier question of educational reorganization as well, have been put in a new light through the use of the new standard tests and the new ability to measure and grade intelligence. The desirability of some form of educational reorganization now stands forth clearer than ever before.

The 6-3-3 and 6-3-5 plans evolved. The result of this twenty-five years of discussion, the careful thought given to the practical administrative problems just mentioned above, the new light on our educational work obtained through the use of new measuring tests, and a growing consciousness that the problem of educational reorganization was a real one, with educational, social, and psychological bearings of far-reaching importance, have all combined recently to change the problem from an academic into a very practical issue. From the educational point of view the problem has become — Can any reorganization better fit the school to attract and retain a larger percentage of the older boys and girls who now drop out, and can a more flexible organization be devised to meet the needs alike of the slow, the gifted, and the peculiar? From a social point of view the problem has become — Can the instruction, by any reorganization, be adapted better to the needs of the different social classes, and thus meet better the social and industrial demands of our modern world? From the psychological point of view the problem has become — Can we adjust our school work better to the natural growth and mental-development periods of child life? From the democratic point of view the problem remains almost as stated by President Eliot, — Can we by any rearrangement meet better the needs of the gifted children, and thus permit them to progress more rapidly through school?

After the problem of reorganization had shaped itself in these ways, as a result of the long discussion, a number of important experiments in educational reorganization began. While these have varied somewhat, in different parts of the United States, the most common plan so far worked out, and one which contains the essential features of practically all the variations, is what has become known as the 6–3–3 plan, and is as shown by the right-hand diagram given in

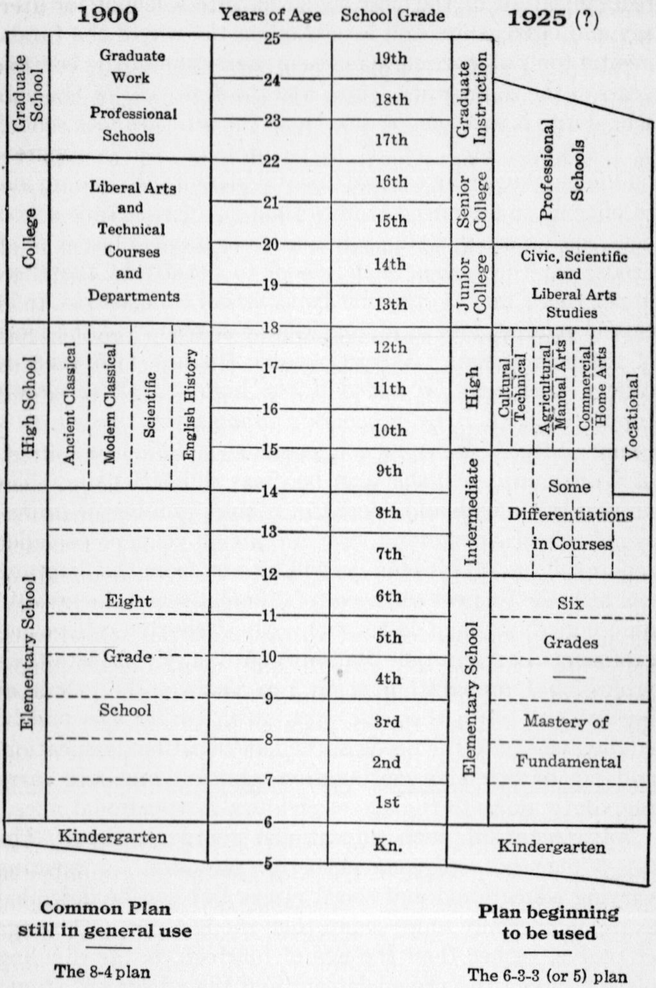

	1900	Years of Age	School Grade	1925 (?)
Graduate School	Graduate Work — Professional Schools	25 24 23 22	19th 18th 17th	Graduate Instruction — Professional Schools
College	Liberal Arts and Technical Courses and Departments	22 21 20 19 18	16th 15th 14th 13th	Senior College — Junior College — Civic, Scientific and Liberal Arts Studies
High School	Ancient Classical · Modern Classical · Scientific · English History	18 17 16 15	12th 11th 10th 9th	High — Cultural Technical · Agricultural Manual Arts · Commercial Home Arts · Vocational
		14 13 12	8th 7th	Intermediate — Some Differentiations in Courses
Elementary School	Eight Grade School	12 11 10 9 8 7 6	6th 5th 4th 3rd 2nd 1st	Elementary School — Six Grades — Mastery of Fundamental
	Kindergarten	6 5	Kn.	Kindergarten

Common Plan
still in general use

The 8-4 plan

Plan beginning
to be used

The 6-3-3 (or 5) plan

FIG. 82. THE REORGANIZATION OF AMERICAN EDUCATION

Figure 82. The essential features of the plan are (1) the reorganization of the first six years into a school for literacy and citizenship, and for attaining the use of the fundamental tools of learning; (2) the organization of the last two years of the elementary school and the first year of the high school into a new school, known as the intermediate school, or the junior high school, to be provided for in separate buildings, taught by a departmental plan of instruction, and to offer more advanced studies than the usual grade-school does, with some variations in courses to meet different pupil needs; (3) the formal high school to constitute the three upper years; and (4) the first two years of college work to be closely related, and in a sense complementary, to the work of the high school. Where possible the first two years of college work may be added to the high school, or closely connected with it by a separate organization known as a junior college. When so connected, as is done in a number of California cities, the plan becomes a 6–3–5 plan. The university then should consist of a large number of professional schools, beginning with the junior year, or so-called senior college. This plan, as will be seen from the diagram, can be made to meet the needs of different social classes with different educational destinations, can so shorten college and professional preparation that our youth may complete their professional preparation some two years earlier than at present and begin their life-work at an earlier age, can be adapted easily to the needs of the new vocational education, and can be fitted to continuation schools which will carry the youth along to the age of eighteen in vocational lines.

Advantages of such educational reorganization. The 6–3–3 plan not only makes better provision for meeting varying educational and social needs, but can be defended as psychologically more sound than the 8–4 plan. The age of twelve, rather than the age of fourteen, is the dividing place between the pre-adolescent and the adolescent stages of development, and the place where methods and types of instruction should change. By a rearrangement by means

of which each division of the school system is made to serve
a distinct educational, social, and psychological purpose, and
has a distinct outline of work shaped to meet such ends, the
school is made into a much more useful social institution.
Eight years, beginning at six, carries the child beyond the
period necessary for acquiring the tools of knowledge, and
beyond the natural division of his life which comes at the
dawn of adolescence.

Instead of being kept under grade teachers, grinding on
the tools of knowledge long past the period of interest in
such work, the child at twelve passes to a school organized
by subjects, taught by teachers with better preparation in
specialized lines, and better adapted to utilize that curiosity,
eagerness, plasticity, impressionability, and ambition toward adult goals which characterize the years from twelve
to fifteen or sixteen.   In such a school general courses, offering a survey of the fields of human knowledge, and some
opportunity to determine individual aptitudes, should be
the characteristics of the instruction.   There should also be
some options and differentiations in courses to meet the
needs of different types of children.

With such an introductory training pupils would be far
better fitted to enter and carry the work of the regular high
school which follows, or to turn to the trade and vocational
courses and become intelligent workers in our modern industrial society.   With such an educational reorganization
it should be the ambition of every community to see that
every normal pupil, before the compulsory school-years
have passed, shall have completed the six-year elementary
course and some line of study in the three-year intermediate
or junior high school.   In cities willing to organize their
schools on the 6–3–5 plan, as many California cities have
done, the completion of the fourteenth grade, at twenty,
should provide a good college education, well adapted either
to professional study or to the duties of municipal or political
life.

The Flexner " Modern School " proposal.   In 1916 President Eliot published a paper on the " Changes needed in American Secondary Education," in which he urged that "the best part of all human knowledge has come by exact and studied observation made through the senses," and that "the most important part of education has always been the training of the senses through which the best part of knowledge comes." He accordingly urged that our high schools give much more time to scientific and technical instruction in place of their excessive devotion to book-subject studies. This was followed, in 1917, by a paper on "A Modern School," by Abraham Flexner, of The General Education Board, which was in a way a constructive sequel to President Eliot's paper. In this he asserted that tradition largely determined what was taught in our high schools; showed that the great amount of time spent on Latin, literature, and mathematics did not produce results; and asserted that a modern school should make it much more important to young people to know, to care about, and to understand the physical and social world in which they live. To this end a modern secondary-school course of study should emphasize activities in four fields:

1. *Science* — This to be the central feature of the school.

2. *Industry* — The occupations and trades of the industrial world.

3. *Civics* — History, civic institutions, and the organization of society and government.

4. *Æsthetics* — Literature, languages, music, and art.

He also contended that the subjects of the high-school course were in need of revision to eliminate useless material and to add much-needed new material. Still further, he contended that all general education should be completed by the age of twenty, so that young people could enter on professional study or life-work by that age.

The latter paper brought forth much discussion, and some bitter criticism from the partisans of the old classical training. Finally a school, to carry out the experiment and evolve the kind of modern instruction described, was endowed by The General Education Board, in New York City, and placed under the direction of the Teachers College at Columbia University. The work to be done in this school will be well worth watching, as it is likely to work out important new lines in secondary-school instruction.

The Gary idea. Another educational reorganization, or rather the construction of a school system from the foundations along new lines, is represented by the school system recently built up at Gary, Indiana. This represents one of the most original pieces of constructive work ever attempted in American education, and contains many ideas of importance for our schools. Whether or not the Gary idea will, in time, become a common type of school one cannot now say, but it represents a type of social service of which few schools as at present organized are capable. In some form this idea has been adopted in a number of our cities.

At Gary the schools run on a four-quarter plan, each quarter of twelve weeks' duration; the school plant is a play-ground, garden, workshop, social center, library, and a traditional-type school all combined in one; the elementary-school and the high-school work are both given under the same roof; some of the high-school subjects begin as early as the fifth grade; specialization in the instruction and, in consequence, departmental instruction run through the schools; classes in special out-door activities and shop work are carried on at the same time as indoor classes, thus doubling the capacity of the school plant; the school day is eight hours long, with the school plant open also all day Saturday; continuation schools and social and recreational centers are conducted in the same plant in the evenings; and play and vocational work are important features of the instruction in all schools. Each school is, in effect, a world in itself, busily engaged in the work and play and government of the world, and so well do such activities and a highly flexible curriculum meet the needs of all classes that the need for most of the promotional machinery and special-type classes and schools found elsewhere is here eliminated.

Significance of the reorganization movement. It has been the effort to readjust the work of our inherited educational system to meet the changed conditions in our national life — social, industrial, political, religious, economic, scientific — brought about by the industrial revolution of the latter part of the nineteenth century, which has been behind all the discussion and the efforts at educational reorganization since President Eliot started the discussion thirty years ago. The question is as yet by no means settled, and further, the need for educational reorganizations is certain to be given new emphasis by the new position the United States will occupy in world affairs as a result of the World War. New committees will be appointed to consider the question, new experiments will be tried, new courses of study will be worked out, much old subject-matter will be eliminated, new textbooks will be written, and perhaps more than one new type of school will be perfected. The day of the simple uniform school system has gone forever, but underneath all the discussion and the present diversity in practice lies a serious attempt to create, by evolution from what we now have, a new and a better system of public education, better adapted to the needs of child life and the needs of the scientific, democratic, and industrial world in which we live.

III. The Reorganization and Redirection of Rural and Village Education

All progress sketched city progress. The reader probably has been impressed, before this, by the fact that practically all of the educational progress so far sketched as happening within the past half-century has been city progress. This, unfortunately for rural and village education, is only too true. The firm establishment of the Massachusetts district system in the States, described in Chapter VIII, and the fastening on the schools, as a result of the early democratic movement, of a political instead of an educational basis for the selection of county and state school superintendents, as described in Chapter VI, have together combined to deprive the rural and village schools of our country of any real educational leadership, and to keep rural and village education from making the progress needed to meet the changed conditions of rural and village life. The cities, by the early elimination of their school districts (p. 237) and elective superintendents, have been able to draw to the management of their school systems the keenest thinkers and the most capable administrators engaged in educational work. In any line of work involving good organization and adaptation to rapidly changing conditions, nothing counts for so much as good leadership at the top. Of this our city school systems have for long had a monopoly.

The rural and village schools of most of our States, cut off by law from securing such directive oversight from outside the county, and split up into thousands of little unrelated school districts, inspired by no unity of purpose and animated by no modern conception of educational work, have gone along without much change since the days of the sixties. Too often the little rural

FIG. 83. ONE OF THE LANDMARKS

school stands to-day as a forlorn and shrunken landmark of what used to be an important rural social and educational institution. The textbooks have been revised and made uniform, to be sure, but the new books adopted have been books written primarily with city and not rural needs in view. A uniform course of study has been introduced, usually of the formal and drill type, but until recently with but little adaptation to rural needs. Normal-trained teachers, trained for city grade work, have been employed, but they have taught in terms of city needs, and have de-

serted the rural school for a city position at the earliest
opportunity. Some formal agriculture has recently been
introduced into the course of study, but without provision
for its supervision or adequate facilities for the work, and
the city-trained teacher has usually not known what to do
with it. The natural result is that our rural and village
schools have remained bookish, their work unrelated to
farm life, and their influence away from the farm. In consequence, country people have largely lost interest in them,
and many have rented their farms and moved to town, in
large part to obtain better educational advantages for their
children.

The new rural-life problem. In the mean time, since the
days when the district system flourished in all its glory, and
when eighty per cent of our people lived on the farm or in
the little village and under rather simple living conditions, a
vast and far-reaching revolution has taken place in the
character of rural and village life. Inventions, labor-saving
machinery, steam, electricity, the automobile, improved
roads and means for transportation, rural mail delivery, the
increase of conveniences and comforts, the rise of the cheap
illustrated magazine, the circulation of the city daily paper,
new world interests, new agricultural knowledge, new and
more distant markets, commercial large-scale farming, the
rapid rise of farm tenantry, the influx of the foreign-born
into rural districts, the decay of the rural church, the dying
out of the old rural social life, the decline of the old farm
and village industries, the coming of a new type of tenant
farmer, the cityward migration of the best and the poorest of the rural population, the decline in interest in local
government as larger national and world interests have
come in, the intellectual revolution which has followed the
industrial revolution, — all these have combined to change
the whole face of the rural-life educational problem.

To one who has given little or no thought to the subject
it is hard to appreciate the great change in rural and village
life which has taken place within the past half-century. It

has been of far-reaching importance, and has touched every phase of rural life.   Almost nothing is now as it used to be; almost nothing is done as it was a half-century ago.   Nowhere has the social and industrial revolution wrought greater alterations than in the village or on the farm, and nowhere in our national life have the institutions of society made so little change to meet the new conditions.   The result has been the rapid development of a rural-life problem of large magnitude and of great social, economic, and educational consequences, the solution of which lies largely in the provision of a new type of rural and village school, and the reorganization and redirection of rural education.

Effect of these changes on the rural school.   Under the stress of these new life conditions the old supervision by the district school trustees has completely broken down, while the expanding scope of all education to-day has left the little independent district too small a unit to make any adequate provision for modern rural or village educational needs. Only in remote districts or in isolated country places does the district system longer render any important service.   The boy or girl on the farm or in the little village does not to-day receive a fair deal, and can never hope to receive as good an education as the city boy or girl so long as the outgrown district system continues to attempt the impossible, and so long as local political availability rather than educational training and competence rules in the selection of our county superintendents of schools.   If there is any clear and unmistakable lesson to be drawn from the administrative experience of our city school systems, it is that the prime essentials for good school organization and administration are the abolition of school-district control, the unification of all schools under one board and one superintendent for administration and supervision, larger units for school finance, and the entire elimination of party politics and local residence requirements in the selection of superintendents of schools.   If rural people could only understand how much better schools they could have, often for the same money, if

for the district system they substituted a much larger unit
for administration, the district system would soon be placed
where many other outgrown institutions of society have
been.

That the district system is wasteful of effort and funds,
results in great educational waste, is unprogressive to a high
degree, leads to an unwise multiplication of little schools,
does not provide adequately for the needs of country and
village boys and girls, and that any marked general educational progress is impossible under it, no longer admits of
successful contradiction. Here and there one occasionally
hears of a redirected rural or village school which is rendering a real service, but these are few in number, and the
progress made is too slow and too local to be of much value.

The school-consolidation movement. Having started the
mischief in the early days of its history, Massachusetts was
the first State to try to remedy the matter. As early as

FIG. 84. A CONSOLIDATED COMMUNITY-CENTER SCHOOL

Compare this with the schoolhouse shown on page 245 as a place for country boys
and girls to go to school.

1869 this State enacted legislation permitting the consolidation of school districts, and in 1882 finally abolished the
district system by law and restored the old town system
from which the district system had evolved (see drawing on
p. 42). After this abolition of the district system, the consolidation of schools in Massachusetts became more rapid,
and by about 1890 the idea spread to other States. Ohio,

in 1892, was the first State west of the Alleghenies to permit the union of two or more districts to form a consolidated school. Indiana began consolidation in 1901, and, largely due to its earlier abolition of the district system, the idea has made remarkable progress there. Many other States have experimented with the idea, though due to the difficulty of securing popular consent to the abandonment of a number of little districts, not much progress has been made in any strong district-system State.

The essential features of the consolidation plan are an agreement, usually by vote at an election called for the purpose, to abandon three, four, five, or more little district schools; to erect instead a good modern school building at some central place; to haul the children by wagon or automobile from their homes each day to this central school in the morning, and back home in the late afternoon; and at this central school to provide graded instruction, a partial or complete high school, agriculture, manual and domestic work, and many of the advantages now enjoyed by city children. Such a school can also be made a rural community-center school by adding an assembly hall, branch library room, and play-grounds. The picture on the preceding page shows such a school, containing six classrooms, an assembly hall, and library on the main floor, manual-training room, domestic-science room, an agricultural laboratory, toilet rooms, and indoor play-rooms in the basement.

County-unit consolidation. The trouble with all such voluntary consolidation of school districts lies in that consolidation proceedings are very hard to get started, district jealousies and district inertia usually prevent the union district being made large enough at the start, and but few voluntary unions can be secured. The left-hand figure in the drawing on the opposite page shows the usual result under a voluntary, district-vote plan. The one consolidated district may have cost ten years of popular education, and then probably is too small.

After nearly twenty years of trial and effort we now see

not only that voluntary consolidation is inadequate and too slow, but that the new rural educational demands require not only more rapid but also more extensive reorganization than voluntary effort can secure.   Only by the use of a unit as large as the county can the right kind of consolidation and the right type of school be provided, and this must be superimposed on the districts by general state law.   Such a county-unit consolidation is shown in the right-hand figure of the drawing below.

In this second case the county has been dealt with as a whole, and a county-unit school system has been substituted

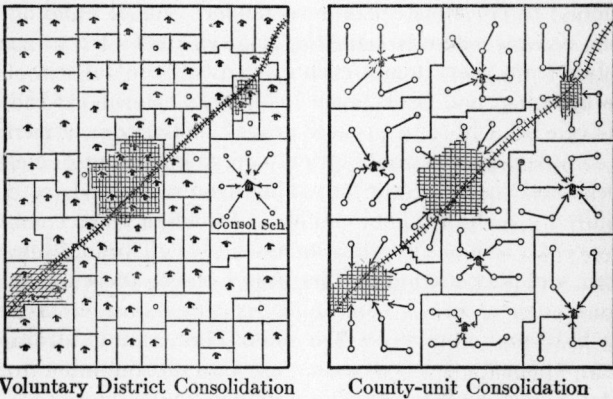

Voluntary District Consolidation   County-unit Consolidation

FIG. 85. RURAL EDUCATIONAL REORGANIZATION
Eighty-eight school districts consolidated into ten.

for the district systems of the other figure.   The central city school system may have been left under the control of its separate city board of education, though compelled to annex, for school purposes, a number of adjacent school districts. Otherwise the county has been consolidated by state law into one county school district; all the old small districts and their boards of district trustees have been abolished; and for the management of the new county school district

the people of the county have elected a county board of
education of five citizens, much as they elect a county
board of five supervisors to oversee county expenses, build
roads and bridges, and supervise the poor relief and county
hospital and poor farm. This county board of education is
exactly analogous to a city board of education, and has
substantially the same powers. It selects and appoints a
county superintendent of schools, being free to go anywhere
and pay what they feel they can afford to get the man or
woman they want for the office. With the aid of the
county superintendent the county board consolidates the
small scattered schools; erects larger and more modern
buildings at central points; provides "teacherages" for
each; changes district attendance lines as need for so doing
arises; establishes kindergartens and high schools in connection with these central schools; can reorganize the school
work by providing intermediate schools and departmental
organization; may provide for a county high school of agriculture and manual and household arts; establishes county
health supervision and employs a traveling county school
nurse; unites with the city in maintaining a parental school;
and provides assistant county superintendents who act as
supervisors of primary work, agriculture, household arts,
music and drawing, etc. The board also employs all teachers and principals, builds and repairs all schoolhouses, levies
one county school-tax for maintaining all schools, and otherwise conducts the schools of the county just as a city board
of education conducts the schools of a city. About the only
difference is that the schools are somewhat smaller than in
the city, are farther apart, and that the education is directed toward the farm and rural-life and home needs instead
of cityward and for city ends.

What such a reorganization would mean. Such county-
unit consolidation is by no means theoretical, but is found
well-developed in Maryland and Utah, and in a more or less
well-developed form in a number of Southern States. The
school system which the United States organized for Porto

Rico was organized on this plan. It has so many advantages, is so well adapted to meet the new rural-life problems, and under it rural education can so easily be redirected and enriched along the lines needed by rural and village boys and girls, that it or some modification of it now promises to be the coming form of educational organization for all territory lying outside the separately organized cities.

With about ten to fifteen such consolidated schools to an average Middle-West county, instead of eighty to a hundred and twenty little insignificant schools, or something like eight to twelve hundred such consolidated schools to an average State instead of eight to twelve thousand little district schools, the whole nature of rural life and education could be reshaped and redirected in a decade, and life on the farm and in the village would be given a new meaning. Such a change would also dispense with the need for the services of from 2500 to 3000 of the cheapest and most poorly educated rural teachers of the State, as well as some 24,000 to 36,000 district-school trustees — both of which would be educational gains of no small importance. In place of this army of school trustees, five citizens for each county, or about five hundred for a State, would manage much better than now all educational affairs of the rural and village schools. The Baltimore County, Maryland, county-unit school system, which has often been described, forms an interesting example of what can be accomplished by such an educational reorganization and redirection.

After a few years under such a county-unit reorganization each county would have a small number of modern-type consolidated schools, rendering effective rural service, and, if properly located, serving as centers for the community life. High-school education, directed toward rural- and village-life needs, would become common for all, instead of as at present only for city and town children; adequate professional supervision would direct the work; and the curriculum could be tied up closely with the rich life experiences of rural boys and girls. What now seems so wonderful and so exceptional, when carried through here and there by some especially intelligent and persuasive county superintendent, would then become the rule. The chief right of which the people of the rural districts would be deprived by such a reorganization would be the right to continue to mismanage and misdirect the education of their children by means of a system of school organization and administration the usefulness of which has long passed by.

IV. State Educational Reorganization

The chief state school officer. Closely related to the county educational reorganization which we have just sketched is the problem of state educational reorganization, which is fast coming to the front as another of our important educational reorganization questions. As was stated in Chapter VI, when we finally decided to establish the office of state school superintendent, we almost everywhere turned to popular election as the means for filling the office. As was explained on page 161, this at the time seemed the natural and proper method, as the office was then conceived of as being much like that of a State Auditor or State Land Agent. The early duties were almost wholly financial, statistical, clerical, and exhortatory; the office required no special professional knowledge; and any citizen possessing energy, a strong personality, and a belief in general education at public expense could fill it. Many of the most successful early state school officers were ministers or lawyers.

Since these earlier days the whole character of our popular education has changed, and education at public expense has been transformed into a great state, one might almost say, a great national interest. From a mere teaching institution the school has been raised to the foremost place as a constructive agent in our democratic life. Public education to-day represents our greatest national undertaking, and, aside from the army, our most highly organized public effort. Since the first establishment of state school systems permission has everywhere been changed to obligation;

functions formerly entrusted to the districts have been
taken over by the county or the State; new and far larger
demands have been made on communities; new aims and
purposes in instruction have been set up; and entirely new
problems in organization, administration, instruction, sanitation, and child welfare have been pushed to the front.
The different State School Codes have become bulky, and
school legislation has come to demand a professional knowledge and an expertness of judgment which formerly was not
required. The exhorter and the institute worker have come
to be needed less and less, and the student of education and
the trained administrator more and more. As a result, a
well-thought-out state educational policy is now a necessity
if intelligent progress is to be made.

Election and appointment of experts. Only in the cities,
though, has our administrative organization kept pace
with our educational development along other lines. The
school in its development, has outrun the thinking of those
who direct it in district, county, and State. Though the
expert and professional character of the office of State Superintendent of Public Instruction is now somewhat generally
recognized, the office itself, in most of our States, is still in a
backward state of development, and realizes but a small
fraction of its possible efficiency. In two thirds of our
American States we still trust to political nomination, and
the popular election of residents of the State willing to enter
political candidacy for the office, to secure the head of our
state school systems, though not employing the method to
select the state geologist, state horticultural commissioner,
state highway engineer, state entomologist, state forester,
secretary of the state board of health, or president of the
state university.

There is no reason, though, except the historical one, why
we should elect the head of the state school system and not
elect the other experts mentioned, or why we should appoint
them and not appoint the head of the state school system.
The argument so often advanced that by so doing we would

be taking the schools away from the people represents either
sheer ignorance or political claptrap, as a comparison with
the other experts mentioned at once reveals.   What the
people want is good government and efficient service from
their public servants, and it is axiomatic in government that
experts should be selected by an individual or by a small
responsible body, and not elected by the people themselves.
It is then the business of such an employing board to oversee the experts it selects, hold them strictly accountable for
results, protect them in the discharge of their duties from
injust attacks, and dismiss them whenever they cease to be
competent.

State school officer and president of university compared.
The situation can perhaps best be seen if we compare the
two offices of head of the state school system and president
of the state university.   Probably no position in the whole
state public service has greater possibilities for constructive
statesmanship than the position of state superintendent of
public instruction in one of our American States.   As a position it is, potentially at least, a more important one than
that of the president of the state university.   No president
of an American state university ever exercised a greater influence in a State or shaped to better advantage the destinies of the people by his labors than did Horace Mann in
Massachusetts.

The chief reason why one is appointed and the other
elected is that the college and the university have their roots
buried back in the Middle Ages, and appointment of the
rector, chancellor, or president has always been the rule,
whereas the office of state superintendent of schools is a
wholly modern creation.   When our American States
founded their state universities they organized them after
the pattern of the ages; when they created the new office of
head of their newly evolved democratic school system they
followed the new democratic idea of the people electing
every public official.   The governing body for the university
(board of trustees, or regents) has often been elected by

the people, but the president and professors have always been recognized as expert state servants, and appointed without reference to residence, politics, race, sex, or religion. Under such a plan our universities have made wonderful progress. Imagine the result, though, if you can, had the people nominated and elected, along political lines and always from among the citizens of the State, the president of the state university as they do the head of the state school system, and the heads of departments in the university as they do the heads of the county school systems in the State. It is hard to conceive what Republican Chemistry, Democratic Latin, Prohibitionist English, or Union-Labor History, would be like.

That the office of head of the state school system has not measured up with that of the presidency of the state university is a matter of common knowledge, and it has not done so largely because the office has for so long been afflicted with the blight of partisan politics; been one of the lowest-salaried positions within the gift of the State; and because political expediency, rather than any educational standard, has been the measuring stick used in selecting candidates for the position. The people seldom have an opportunity to vote for a really good man for the office, as the best men usually cannot be induced to become candidates. Of a few States where the office is elective this at times has not been true, but not of many, and usually not for long in any State. In some of our States the traditions of the office have settled down to merely that of a retiring job for some old and reasonably successful practitioner from the ranks, and in consequence has commanded but little respect or authority.

Lack of a consecutive state educational policy. As a result, few of our States to-day reveal, in their educational and legislative history, any evidence of having followed for any length of time a well-thought-out educational policy. Often the state oversight has been of a distinctively *laissez-faire* type, the officer acting largely as a clerk, statistical agent, tax distributor, and institute lecturer. School legislation has represented expediency, has been of the patch-work variety, and a conception of the State as an active and energetic agent for the improvement of educational conditions and the advancement of the public welfare has been entirely lacking.

When we turn to the State of Massachusetts we get an example of the opposite of these tendencies and results. Thanks perhaps to her strong aristocratic leanings, when the State Board of Education was created, in 1837, the State provided for the appointment by it of a Secretary to act as head of the school system, and not for the popular election of a chief state school officer. The result was the appointment of Horace Mann as the first Secretary, he holding the position, despite abuse and bitter attacks, until his election to succeed John Quincy Adams as a Member of Congress from Massachusetts, twelve years later. Had he been compelled to submit himself to the people every two or four years for reëlection, there were times when he could not have been reëlected, and had the office been an elective instead of an appointive one it is more than probable that Mann would have remained a lawyer and never been known as a school administrator.

Largely as a result of the Massachusetts conception of the importance of the chief state educational office, the leadership of that State in educational progress has been one of the marked features of our educational history. Since the establishment of the office of Secretary, in 1837, but nine persons have held the office up to the present time, and all have been educational leaders and statesmen of a high order. The present incumbent (1919; now called Commissioner of Education) was called to the position in 1916 from the head of the school system of Maine; his predecessor from a professorship of school administration at Teachers College, Columbia; and his predecessor from the position of assistant superintendent of the schools of Boston. One who has read the preceding chapters of this book cannot help but be impressed with the number of important educational advances which had their origin in Massachusetts, and the State has also been a leader in much other educational legislation which has not been mentioned. Though small in size and possessing no great natural resources, and for the past seventy-five years being slowly buried under a constantly increasing avalanche of foreign-born peoples who have corrupted her politics, diluted her citizenship, and often destroyed the charm of her villages, the State has persisted in a constructive educational policy which has been in large part her salvation. Had the selection of leaders for her schools been left to politics, it is hardly probable that the results would have been the same.

Democracy's need for leadership. No type of government has such need for trained leadership at the top as has a democracy, and no branch of the public service in a democracy is fraught with greater opportunities for constructive statesmanship than is public education. By it the next generation is moulded and the hopes and aspirations and ideals of the next generation are formed. To rise above office routine to the higher levels of constructive statesmanship is not easy, and calls for a high type of educational leader. Yet this higher level of leadership is what a state department of education should primarily represent. The improvement of society and the advancement of the public welfare through education is perhaps the greatest business of the State. A state board of education to determine policies and select leaders, and a chief state school officer (state superintendent, commissioner of education, or whatever title he may be given) to carry policies into execution and think in constructive terms for the schools, should be the center up to which and down from which ideas for the improvement of public education should come.

In both county and state the demand to-day is for intelligent professional leadership, that our people may receive greater return for the money they put into their schools, and that the children in them may receive a better-directed education than they are now receiving. The important steps in the process of securing these results consist in following the lines for reorganization which have been set forth in this chapter — namely, changing from guess-work to scientific procedure; the reorganization of school work to secure larger opportunities and greater effectiveness; the reorganization and redirection of rural and village as well as city educational procedure; the abolition of the outgrown district system for a larger administrative unit; the elimination of politics and popular election in the selection of experts; and the concentration of larger authority in the hands of those whose business it is to guard the rights and advance the educational welfare of our children.

National aid and oversight. Up to the close of the Civil War all our development had been by state action, except as the National Government had given land to the States for common schools and for a seminary of learning, and in 1862 had endowed with national land a college of agriculture and mechanic arts in each State. In 1866, at the first meeting of the new National Association of School Superintendents, afterwards the Department of Superintendence of the National Education Association, Mr. E. E. White, then State Commissioner of Education for Ohio, read a paper on a "National Bureau of Education." In response to a resolution then adopted Hon. James A. Garfield, then a Member of Congress from Ohio, introduced and sponsored a bill in Congress to create such a Bureau "to collect statistics and facts concerning the condition and progress of education in the several States and Territories, and to diffuse information respecting the organization and management of schools and school systems and methods of teaching." Instead, Congress, in 1867, created a National Department of Education, but two years later reduced the Department to the rank of a Bureau in the Interior Department, where it has since remained. Henry Barnard was appointed the first Commissioner, and William T. Harris held the office for seventeen years. Along the lines originally indicated the Bureau has rendered important service to the States, but now that our educational problems have assumed so many national aspects a Bureau of such limited scope is utterly inadequate to render the type of service we need to-day.

While the school systems which we have gradually developed are state school systems, some of the educational problems with which we have recently come face to face are too large, too extensive in their scope, and too far-reaching in their consequences to permit us to leave them longer to the States, unaided, to solve. State action, even at its best, is too slow and too uncertain, while some of our most pressing problems to-day are national in character and demand general and immediate action. The World War has brought forcibly to our attention some of our most serious weaknesses, and the need for early and general action stands revealed. This we are not likely to get, however, unless it is action by the Nation, such as has already been taken for the improvement of rural home-life, agriculture, and vocational education — action which will stir the States to immediate movement along similar lines, and under national guidance and control.

A pressing need to-day is that our national government shall undertake a national campaign to eliminate some of our national weaknesses and dangers. We must resolutely set to work, during the respite from the immigrant flood which the World War promises for a time to give us, to Americanize the foreign-born in our midst. We must abolish illiteracy, and make English our one language. A thorough health and physical education program should be instituted everywhere. Continuation schools should be provided generally, that will extend at least part-time vocational training up to the age of eighteen. The utter inadequacy of our present scheme for rural and village education stands revealed as never before, and the rebuilding and revitalizing of rural education is too large an undertaking to be made less than a national movement. The salaries paid teachers are inadequate, as is also the training for teaching. To meet these demands in any truly adequate manner calls for national aid, national supervision, and a national program of work. To secure this we need to transform, as is proposed in a bill now (1919) before Congress, our National Bureau of Education at Washington into a National Department of Education, and place all our different national educational efforts and aid under the direction of this Department. We must in future study our larger educational problems from a national point of view, rather than from a local one; we must extend sufficient national aid and direction to the States to stimulate them to activity; and we must enable them to cope adequately with the problems at hand.

QUESTIONS FOR DISCUSSION

1. Show how our educational thinking has been colored through and through by the new social and industrial forces of the past half-century.
2. Show the advantages of "type studies" in teaching.
3. Show how the "project" could be made useful in teaching.
4. What do you understand by (a) concentration, (b) correlation, and (c) pedagogical interference?
5. Show how it would be possible to organize a course of study around activities, as at Fairhope, Alabama (p. 446).
6. Show how the new standard measures: (a) mean ability to diagnose, (b) give a basis for course of study eliminations, and (c) mean more definite work in instruction.
7. What advantages would standardized records have over per cents in transferring records from school to school?
8. How could a series of student-records be made useful in the work of vocational guidance?
9. Show how the introduction of standard measures means as great an advance in instruction as did the introduction of the conception of an orderly psychological development in the sixties.
10. What new light do intelligence measurements throw on the question of differentiated courses of study and schools, as set forth in Chapter XII? What on the truancy problem? What on the problem of the education of "peculiar children"?
11. If not far from two per cent of our children are of very low-grade intelligence, have we as yet done much in providing special class instruction?
12. Show how the 6 3–3 plan provides better for the different social and intellectual classes of children in our schools than does the 8-4 plan.

13. Show how, with the 6–3–3 plan, it could be made possible to put all children of fair ability through the ninth grade before the end of the compulsory education period.
14. Does the statement of President Eliot (p. 463) appeal to you as true?
15. Show that the Flexner modern-school idea means as fundamental a reorganization of secondary education as would be an elementary-school course based on projects and activities.
16. Explain how the Gary plan differs from ordinary school work.
17. Why should we be giving so much consideration to educational reorganization now, whereas before 1888 we were fairly well satisfied with the schools we had evolved?
18. What do you understand by the rural-life problem?
19. Show why the rural school has been left behind in the educational progress of the past sixty years.
20. What do you understand by the redirection of rural education?
21. What are the fundamental needs of rural education to-day?
22. What do you understand to be meant by the term community-center rural school?
23. Show the advantages of county-unit organization for rural education.
24. State why the popular election of experts is always less likely to produce good public servants than is selection and appointment.

TOPICS FOR INVESTIGATION AND REPORT

1. The use, and character, and results of Standard Tests in any elementary-school subject.
2. Special classes for the training of those of low intelligence.
3. The organization and character of work in some 6–3–3 school system.
4. The Gary school system.
5. Typical conditions in rural education.
6. The organization and work of some good rural consolidated school.
7. The county-unit school systems of Maryland or Utah.
8. Fundamental needs in rural education.
9. The preëminent leadership, in our educational history, of the State of Massachusetts.
10. A comparison of national support to and services rendered by the National Department of Agriculture and the National Bureau of Education.

SELECTED REFERENCES

Ayers, L. P. "Economy of Time through testing the Course of Study"; in *Proceedings of the National Education Association*, 1913, pp. 241–46.

A brief but suggestive article dealing with the possibility of applying standards and measurements, so as to secure a more economical use of the time of pupils.

Bourne, R. S.   *The Gary Schools.*   200 pp., illustrated.   Houghton Mifflin Co., Boston, 1916.

A well-rounded description of the organization and work of these schools.

*Bunker, F. F.   *Reorganization of the Public School System.*   186 pp. United States Bureau of Education, Bulletin No. 8, Washington, 1916.

A very full and a very important discussion of the question.   Reviews the arguments and describes practices.   Chapters VII and VIII give a good idea of the changes required, and the new purposes in instruction.

Burris, W. P.   *The Public School System of Gary, Indiana.*   United States Bureau of Education, Bulletin No. 18, Washington, 1914.

A good and easily available description, giving plans, programs, and illustrations of the work done.

Cubberley, E. P.   *Public School Administration.*   479 pp.   Houghton Mifflin Co., Boston, 1916.

Chapter XIX, on Efficiency Experts and Testing Results, states briefly the educational significance of the new measuring movement.   Part III sets forth the lessons to be drawn from city educational experience, and the need for educational reorganization in relation to the office of state and county superintendents of schools.

*Cubberley, E. P.   "Desirable Reorganizations in American Education"; in *School and Society*, vol. II, pp. 397–402.   (Sept., 1915.)

Presents briefly the desirable administrative reorganizations needed.   A condensation of Part III of the above reference.

Cubberley, E. P.   *Rural Life and Education.*   367 pp.   Houghton Mifflin Co., Boston, 1914.

A study of the rural-school problem, as a phase of the rural-life problem, tracing the question in its historical development and describing the lines of its solution.

*Cubberley, E. P.   *The Improvement of Rural Schools.*   76 pp.   Houghton Mifflin Co., Boston, 1912.

A brief digest of the main ideas contained in the larger volume above.   Good for supplementary reading for this chapter.

*Cubberley, E. P., and Elliott, E. C.   "Rural School Administration"; in *Proceedings of the National Education Association*, 1914, pp. 244–50. Also in *School and Society*, vol. I, pp. 154–61.   (Jan. 30, 1915.)

A concise statement of the problem of rural educational reorganization, and the necessity for certain fundamental changes.

*Dewey, John and Evelyn.   *Schools of Tomorrow.*   316 pp.   E. P. Dutton & Co., New York, 1915.

A very interesting and a very well-written book, describing a number of reorganization experiments being carried out.   Chapter II describes the experiment of Mrs. Johnson, at Fairhope, Alabama; Chapter III the reorganized elementary school at the University of Missouri; and Chapters VII and X the work at Gary, Indiana.

Eliot, Chas. W.   "Can School Programs be Shortened and Enriched?" in *Proceedings of the National Education Association*, 1888; also in his *Educational Reform.*   Century Co., New York, 1898.

The paper which started the discussion as to educational reorganization.

Eliot, Chas. W. "Shortening and Enriching the Grammar-School Course"; in *Proceedings of the National Education Association*, 1892; also in his *Educational Reform*. Century Co., New York, 1898.

The second paper in the reorganization discussion.

Eliot, Chas. W. *Changes needed in American Secondary Education.* 29 pp. General Education Board, Occasional Papers, No. 2, New York, 1916.

Sets forth the needed changes in high-school work.

*Flexner, Abraham. *A Modern School.* 23 pp. General Education Board, Occasional Papers, No. 3, New York, 1917.

Outlines the modern school mentioned in the text. A constructive sequel to the preceding.

*Hardy, Edw. L. "The Reorganization of our Educational System"; in *School and Society*, vol. v, pp. 728–32. (June 23, 1917.)

Proposes a new 4–4–4–4 plan for a still more psychological reorganization of American education. A very able and thought-provoking paper.

Jessup, W. A. "Economy of Time in Arithmetic"; in *Proceedings of the National Education Association*, 1914, pp. 209–22.

A good type of a number of studies on economy of time in teaching.

Johnson, Chas. H. "The Social Significance of Various Movements for Industrial Education"; in *Educational Review*, vol. 37, pp. 160–80. (Feb., 1909.)

A very able article, showing the comparative position of the United States in such development.

*Judd, Chas. H. *Measuring the Work of the Public Schools.* 290 pp. Cleveland Education Survey, 1916.

An excellent volume, showing standard measures applied as a means of educational diagnosis to both elementary and high schools in a large city-school system.

*Monroe, W. S., DeVoss, J. C., and Kelly, F. J. *Educational Tests and Measurements.* 309 pp. Houghton Mifflin Co., Boston, 1917.

The standard guide to the use of the standard tests, and an explanation of the meaning of the results obtained.

*Monroe, Walter S. *Measuring the Results of Teaching.* 297 pp. Houghton Mifflin Co., Boston, 1918.

An excellent guide on the use and significance of the standard tests as applied to the measurement of teaching. A simplification and expansion of the above book. Written for the use of the grade teacher.

National Society. *Minimum Essentials in Elementary School Subjects.* Year-Books of the National Society for the Study of Education. 1st Report, 152 pp. Fourteenth Year-Book, Part i, 1915. 2d Report, 192 pp. Sixteenth Year-Book, Part i, 1917.

Two rather long reports, dealing with the reduction of the subject-matter of instruction in the common-school subjects.

National Society. *Report of the Committee on Economy of Time in Education*. Year-Books of the National Society for the Study of Education. 3d Report. Seventeenth Year-Book, Part I, 1918. 4th Report, 123 pp. Eighteenth Year-Book, Part II, 1919.

Two additional reports of the Committee, dealing with minimum essentials, purposes in instruction, and methods of work.

National Society. *Standards and Tests for the Measurement of the Efficiency of Schools and School Systems*. 160 pp. Fifteenth Year-Book of the National Society for the Study of Education, Part I, 1916.

Contains fifteen addresses on standard scales, and their applications to school work.

*Russell, Will. *Economy in Secondary Education*. 74 pp. Houghton Mifflin Co., Boston, 1916.

A splendid brief presentation of possible lines along which economy of time may be had.

Snedden, D. S. "The High School of Tomorrow"; in *School Review*, vol. 25, pp. 1-15. (Jan., 1917.)

An interesting and suggestive article on the high school of 1925.

*Terman, L. M. *The Measurement of Intelligence*. 362 pp. Houghton Mifflin Co., Boston, 1916.

Part I gives a simple explanation of the measurements, and points out their educational significance. Part II describes the measurements and explains how to give them.

*Terman, L. M. *The Intelligence of School Children*. Houghton Mifflin Co., Boston., 1919.

A very readable and valuable account of the results and significance of mental measurements. Written for the grade teacher.

*Wells, Dora. "The Lucy Flower Technical High School"; in *School Review*, vol. 22, pp. 611-19.

A very interesting description of a large technical school for girls.

CHAPTER XV

FUNDAMENTAL PRINCIPLES AND PROBLEMS

I. FUNDAMENTAL PRINCIPLES ESTABLISHED

The national system evolved. In the chapters preceding this one we have traced, in some detail, the evolution of our American public schools from the days of their infancy to the present, and have shown the connection between our more pressing present-day problems and our evolution during the past. Starting with a few little church school systems, founded as an outgrowth of Reformation fervor and convictions, we have, in the course of nearly three centuries of educational evolution, gradually transformed the school from an instrument of the church to a civil institution, and have built up what are in effect forty-eight different state school systems. While these vary somewhat in their form of organization and the scope of the system provided, they nevertheless have so much in common, are actuated by so many of the same national purposes, and follow so closely the same guiding principles, that we may easily say that we have evolved what is in spirit, if not in legal form, a national system of public education. This we feel, due to the thoroughly native character of the evolution which has taken place, is reasonably well suited to the needs of a great democratic society such as our own.

In the course of this long evolution, despite much conflict and irregular development in different parts of our country, we have at last come to a somewhat general acceptance of certain fundamental principles of action. These may now be said to have become fixed, not only in our traditions but in our laws and court decisions as well, and to represent the foundations upon which our public educational systems rest. In this final chapter it may be well to review briefly some of the more important of these guiding principles before taking up the problems which lie just ahead.

The essential nature of education. To the enthusiasts of the Protestant Reformation we owe the idea that the education of all is essential to the well-being of the State; that it is the duty of each parent to educate his child; and that the State may enforce this duty by appropriate legislation. First conceived of wholly for the welfare of the religious State, and so enforced in the Massachusetts Laws of 1642 and 1647, in the church-period legislation of the central colonies, and somewhat in the apprenticeship legislation of the southern colonies, the idea of the right of the State to enforce education to advance the welfare of the State in time became a fixed idea in the New England colonies, Rhode Island excepted, and from there was gradually spread, by the migration of New England people, all over the northeastern quarter of the United States. Becoming firmly established there by the middle of the nineteenth century, the idea spread, in the course of time, over the entire Union, and is now an accepted principle of action in all our American States.

In establishing schools of its own to enforce the obligation of education, the State has done so, not so much because it can educate better than can parents, though in most cases this is true, but because by itself taking charge of the conduct of schools the State can enforce better the obligation it imposes that each child shall be educated. Neither does the State establish schools because by state coöperative effort they can be established and conducted more economically than by private agencies, but rather that by so doing it may better exercise the State's inherent right to enforce a type of education looking specifically to the preservation and improvement of the State. With the passage of time, the growth of our Nation, and the extension of the suffrage to more and more diverse elements in our population, we have come to see clearly that an uneducated citizenship is a public peril, and to insist more strongly than before on the exercise of this fundamental right of the State. A natural corollary of this right to require education for the protection and improvement of the State is the right of the State to provide inspection to see that the obligation the State imposes is being fulfilled, and supervision to lead to the improvement of what is being done.

The right to tax to maintain. The provision of schools to enforce the obligation imposed by the State, though, requires money, and the better the schools provided the more they are likely to cost. Even state supervision of education, were the provision of schools left entirely to private or religious initiative, also would cost something. This cost must be defrayed from public funds, and these must come from individual, group, or general taxation.

Just how schools should be supported must be determined by a consideration as to their nature. If they are only or largely of personal or local benefit, such as telephone service, street-lighting, pavements, or streets, then they should be supported by individual or local taxation. Being conceived, though, as essential to the welfare of the State as a whole, then their support should be by the general taxation of all, and not from taxes or fees paid by the parents of the children educated. The establishment of this principle, that the wealth of the State must educate the children of the State, required time and effort, for it virtually meant the confiscation of a portion of the fruits of the labor of all men, and in proportion as they by hard labor and thrift had been able to accumulate a surplus, and the use of the part so confiscated to educate the children of the State, regardless of whether or not the particular parents of the children educated had any surplus wealth to be so confiscated.

This is an essential state service to which all owners of property must be subject, and no man can expect to escape his share for support by sending his children to a private or parochial school. This of course he is free to do, as we have so far in our history not seen any reason for limiting this right of choice, but the exercise of such freedom and choice cannot be expected to relieve him of his proper share for the support of so essential a state service as public education. Equally might he claim exemption from taxation for the maintenance of police because he is a law-abiding citizen, from the support of the fire department because he has built his house of concrete, and from taxation to purchase and maintain parks because he has attractive grounds around his home and does not visit the parks maintained by the public.

How far the State may go. How far the State may go in levying taxation to provide general educational advantages is another matter which we have decided shall be left to the State to determine. Our government is a government by majority rule, and we have gradually established it as a principle of public policy that what the majority, acting through its accredited representatives, once decide to be for the public welfare, can be ordered and provided. When this involves new lines of action not only new laws, but at times amendments to the constitution of the State are necessary, but, once a clear majority has decided that something in the interest of the public welfare should or should not be done, it is not difficult to alter whatever laws or constitutional provisions stand in the way. When this has been done the courts have uniformly decided that the will of the majority, so registered, shall prevail. The early school taxation laws, the laws for the extension of the high school, the provision of state normal schools, the first compulsory attendance laws, free textbook laws, laws for medical inspection and health supervision, — these and others have been tested in and upheld by the courts.

So it may be safely asserted to have become an established principle of our American educational policy that the State may provide, or order provided, if it deems that the welfare of the State will be better preserved or advanced, whatever form of educational effort, type of school, aspect of inspection or instruction, or extension of education may to it seem wise to add. The needs of our democracy are alone the test, and these needs are to be determined by majority action and in the majority interest, and not imposed by the rule or to meet the needs of a class.

There is every reason to feel that this fundamental principle of action has not as yet in any way reached the limits of its application, but rather that the future is almost certain to see a great extension of educational advantages into new directions to meet the needs of classes of our people not now adequately provided for. In the fields of night schools, vacation schools, play-grounds and directed play, community-center activities, adult education, public music, civic-welfare education, health supervision, child welfare, school and university extension, and vocational guidance, to mention a few of the more certain directions of future state educational activity, we are almost sure to see marked extensions of the right of the State, in the interests of the welfare of the State, exercised to provide or to order provided.

Schools to afford equal opportunity. Another principle which we have firmly established in our educational policy is that the schools provided shall afford not only equal opportunity for all in any one class or division of the school, but also that full opportunity for promising youths to rise shall be offered by the State, and that this opportunity, as well, shall be equally free and open to all. In other words, we decided early, and as a part of the great democratic movement in the early part of the nineteenth century, that we would institute a thoroughly democratic school system, and not in any way copy the aristocratic and monarchical two-class school systems of European States. Accordingly we early provided in our state constitutions and in our laws for free public schools, equally open to all. As soon as possible we abolished the rate-bill and the fuel tax, extended the free-school term, and provided free school supplies. We replaced the tuition academy with the free public high school, and superimposed it onto the common school we had developed to form an educational ladder which ambitious youths might climb. On top of the high school we superimposed the state college and university, similarly

tuition free.   We freed the schools from the pauper taint,
and opened the same or equivalent opportunities to girls as
well as boys.   To make the school as common in its advantages as possible we also early eliminated all trace of sectarian control.

As a result we have to-day, in each of our American
States, a school system free, non-sectarian, and equally open
to all children of the State, and which any child may attend,
at the expense of the State, as long as he can profitably partake of the educational advantages provided.   To reach an
increasing number of the State's children, and to retain
them longer in school, the State is continually broadening
its educational system by adding new schools and new types
of education, so that more may find in the schools educational advantages suited to their life needs.   In this way
we widen the educational pyramid by increasing the opportunities for more and more to rise, and thus secure a more
intelligent and a more enlightened democracy.   Under an
autocratic form of government this would not be desirable,
but in a democracy it is a prime necessity.

State may compel attendance.   The State, having adjudged the provision of education to be a public necessity,
to preserve and advance the welfare of the State, the natural corollary of such a position is the right of the State to
compel children to attend and to partake of the educational
advantages which have been provided.   The State may also
compel their parents, by severe penalties if need be, to see
that their children come to school for the period adjudged
by the State as the minimum term and minimum number of
years to be accepted.   We came to this position slowly and
hesitantly, but to-day we may be said to have arrived at the
point where we hold it the right of the State to compel each
child to attend school every day the schools are in session
and he is able to attend, and for a period extending up to at
least fourteen years of age, with every probability that in the
near future it will be extended up to sixteen.   Having conceived a common school education, at least, to be the birth-

right of every American boy and girl, the State has finally
stepped in to see that the children of the State are not prevented from obtaining their birthright. Nor can the State
admit the needs of the parents for the labor of their children
as an excuse for non-attendance, though the rejection of such
a plea involves obligations on the part of the State to provide, in the form of poor-relief, the earnings of which the
State by the exercise of compulsion deprives the parent.

The State may set standards. Any conception of the
State as an educational agent, interested in seeing that
schools are provided to preserve itself and to advance its
welfare, naturally involves the right of the State to fix the
minimum standards below which it will not allow any community or private or parochial school to fall. While either
too much liberty or too much state oversight may result in
weakness in the local school systems maintained, some state
oversight and control must be exercised if strength is to be
developed. In all such matters as types of schools and
classes which must be maintained; the language in which the
instruction is given; length of term to be provided; the care
of children which must be exercised; the hygienic conditions;
and the minimum rate of tax for schools which must be
raised locally, it is essentially the business of the State to fix
the minimum types, lengths, and amounts which will be
permitted, and through the exercise of state inspection and
state penalties to enforce these minimum demands. This
we have clearly settled both as a right and a duty in our
laws and our court decisions. It is also the right, as well as
the duty of the State, to raise these minima from time to
time, as changing conditions and new educational needs may
seem to require or as the increasing wealth of the State will
permit, and without waiting until all communities are able
to make such advances. To do this will often involve
reciprocal obligations on the part of the State, but these the
State must expect and be prepared to meet.

Carrying the idea still further, we have also come to accept as an established principle that it should be the business

of the State to formulate and carry out a constructive edu·
cational policy for the advancement of the welfare of the
State by means of public education.   Instead of being a
passive tax-gatherer, distributor of funds, and lawgiver, the
State, if it is to meet the educational problems of a modern
world, must become an active, energetic agent, working for
the moral, social, hygienic, industrial, and intellectual advancement of its people. The formulation of minimum standards from time to time, the protection of these standards from
being lowered by any private or sectarian agency, and the
stimulation of communities within the State to additional
educational activity, these have now come to be accepted
both as fundamental rights and duties of the State.

Public education not exclusive.   Unlike France, we have
never been driven to the necessity of making public education exclusive.   Instead, we have felt that the competition
of private and parochial schools, if better than the public
schools, is good for the public schools.   Especially in the
line of higher education have we profited by allowing the
freest competition between the privately endowed colleges
and the state universities.   As a result such privately endowed institutions as Harvard, Yale, Columbia, Princeton,
Johns Hopkins, Tulane, Chicago, and Stanford have fallen
in whole-heartedly with our state and national purposes
and have become really national universities.

On the other hand, our States have not as yet exercised
their accepted rights of supervision, and often have allowed
a competition from private and religious schools which was
not warranted by any ideas of state welfare.   In a few of our
American States this situation has recently been taken in
hand, and standards have been established which are clearly
within the right of the State to establish.   These involve
the requirement of instruction in the English language, the
provision of schools at least as good as the public schools
of the same community, and full coöperation with the public
school authorities in such matters as compulsory school
attendance and statistical reports.   These are legitimate

demands of the State; they have been upheld by our courts, and they should everywhere be enforced by our American Commonwealths.

The present conviction of our people. Slowly but certainly public education has been established as a great state, one might almost say, a great national, interest of the American people. They have conceived the education of all as essential to the well-being of the State, and have established state systems of public education to enforce the idea. The principle that the wealth of the State must educate the children of the State has been firmly established. The schools have been made free and equally open to all; education has been changed from a charity to a birthright; and a thoroughly democratic educational ladder has everywhere been provided. The corollary to free education, in the form of compulsion to attend, is now beginning to be systematically enforced. The school term has been lengthened, the instruction greatly enriched, new types of classes and schools provided, and new extensions of educational opportunity begun.

As a result of our long evolution we have finally developed a thoroughly native series of American state school systems, bound together by one common purpose, guided by the same set of established principles, and working for the same national ends. In consequence it may now be regarded as a settled conviction of our American people that the provision of a liberal system of free non-sectarian public schools, in which equal opportunity is provided for all, even though many different types of schools may be needed, is not only an inescapable obligation of our States to their future citizens, but also that nothing which the State does for its people contributes so much to the moral uplift, to a higher civic virtue, and to increased economic returns to the State as does a generous system of free public schools.

II. Education as a Constructive Tool

Our characteristic native development. We have evolved these fundamental principles of action, as has been said, only after long public discussion and conflict. Time was required to set forth the arguments and convince a majority of our people as to the desirability of accepting them, and still more time to permit the necessary extension from an acceptance in principle to an acceptance in reality. Still more, after their acceptance in a few States or a section of the Union, more time was required to permit the spread and general acceptance of the ideas by our people as a whole. As a result we have made progress but slowly and irregularly, and often a generation has been required to familiarize ourselves with and accept some new idea which has been a demonstrated success in other States or other lands.

Our educational development, as a result, has been slow and thoroughly native, and ideas reaching us from abroad have been carefully examined, questioned, tried, worked over, and adapted to our conditions before they have met with any general acceptance among our people. Consequently our American school systems are thoroughly "of the people, for the people, and by the people." This is both their strength and their weakness. They are thoroughly democratic in spirit and thoroughly representative of the best in our American development, but they also represent largely average opinion as to what ought to be accomplished and how things ought to be done. There are many improvements which ought to be carried out without delay, and which if made would add greatly to the effectiveness of our schools and consequently to our national strength, but which we shall probably have to wait for until a new generation arises, and achieve then only after a long process of popular agitation and discussion in which those in favor of the changes have out-argued those opposed.

National initiative without responsibility. The same "show me" spirit which has characterized our slow educational development has also characterized our instruction. We have thrown both teachers and pupils largely on their own resources, with the result that either the instruction has been very poor or both teachers and pupils have made marked development in initiative and in ability to care for themselves. The most prominent characteristic of many of our schools has been the former, but the latter has characterized so many schools, and so thoroughly characterizes our private and public life, that as a Nation we have gained a world-wide reputation for initiative and imagination and the ability to carry through successfully large undertakings. Living under a form of government which has given us large freedom both to commit mistakes or to make successes, not afflicted by a bureaucratic government which has imposed a uniformity destructive of initiative, with plenty of elbow-room for the man possessing ideas and energy, always willing to learn, thoroughly democratic in spirit, possessed of large common sense, able to see means and ends and how to relate the two, and willing to follow the leadership of any one of ideas and force or to lead ourselves, we have developed independence of action as a national characteristic. In no other country have the results of national attitudes, national training, and national restraint or freedom shown to better advantage in the general intelligence, poise, good judgment, moral strength, individual initiative, and productive capacity of a people than with us.

These characteristics have carried us along very well up to recent times, and all that is valuable in them we ought to retain. Certainly the splendid initiative of our youth, never shown to better advantage than during the participation of this Nation in the recent World War, is something which we cannot afford to lose. We have, however, lacked somewhat in state and national effectiveness because we exercise our initiative in such an individual manner. It has been largely a case of each fellow for himself, and only in cases of national emergency or danger have we coöperated well. The virtue which we now need to develop to supplement this splendid national trait is a stronger sense of intelligent responsibility for the common welfare, as expressed in some form of self-imposed democratic discipline. Our most prominent characteristic has been a democratic independence and the ability to take care of ourselves. The most prominent characteristic of the German boy, on the other hand, has been a blind obedience to the authority of the State. In between the two the English and French boys have preserved their initiative and at the same time learned to respect authority and to shoulder responsibility, and the results of this training were well brought out in the recent World War. The American boy showed splendid initiative and daring, but was restive under discipline; the German boy lacked individual initiative when forced to take care of himself, but did well what he was told to do; the French and English boys exhibited, in a high degree, both initiative and an intelligent sensitiveness to leadership which contributed much to the success of their common cause.

Probably one of our greatest future educational problems is that of striving to increase our governmental effectiveness on the one hand and individual responsibility for good government on the other, while at the same time retaining our democratic life and that training which develops initiative, force, and foresight. Just where the division between personal initiative and national discipline is to be drawn is a question that must be determined somewhat by the demands made by the welfare of the State. If good citizenship is the fundamental problem, then a large place must be found for individual initiative, and much must be left to self-imposed control. If, on the other hand, the safety of the State is the important consideration, then imposed discipline must take precedence over individual initiative and liberty of action. Though we now face no great danger from the outside which seems to imperil the safety of the State, still, since the welfare of any State must depend both on civil order and security, education in a democracy must of necessity combine both liberty of action and self-imposed discipline.

Why our educational problem is difficult. Contrasted
with a highly organized nation, such as Germany was before
she attacked civilization and plunged the world into war,
we seem feeble in our ability to organize and push forward a
constructive national program for development and progress. There the State was highly organized; the people
homogeneous; the officials well educated, and selected by
careful service tests; national policies were painstakingly
thought out and promulgated; the schools were effectively
organized into uniformly good institutions for the advancement of the national interests; the teachers were carefully
trained in state institutions, and made into parts of a national army expected to follow the flag loyally; the Church
was nationalized, and in part supported by the Government; religion was taught in all schools, and the weight of
religion and the backing of the priesthood were used to support the State; and a great national army was maintained
and used as an educative force for nationalizing all elements
and training the people in obedience and respect for law and
order.

With us, on the other hand, we have only our schools.
Our government is what the people want it to be — good,
bad, or indifferent. While in a monarchy the ruling government may be much better than the people could provide for
themselves, in a democracy this can never be. The thinking
men and students of fundamental questions in any form of
government are relatively few. In a monarchy these are
usually selected to rule; in a democracy they constitute a
minority seldom selected for office and often possessing but
little power to mould majority opinion. Even in our universities professors work with a view to improving the future
rather than the present. The classroom is often a generation ahead of public opinion. Everywhere our public officials are of the people, and representative of majority ideas.
Though our States and the National Government have recently assumed many new functions, looking toward more
centralized control and better public administration, each

increase in state control has been objected to vigorously by
those who fear that the coming of bureaucratic efficiency
may reduce us to mediocrity and rob us of some of our splendid initiative. A national religion is inconceivable with us,
and a great national army we do not need or want. We are
thrown back, then, upon our systems of public education,
the public press, and our political life as the great moulding
and unifying forces in our most heterogeneous national life,
and of these three the school easily stands first as the force
which ultimately shapes the other two. Upon the public
school teacher, then, and upon those who direct the policies
of our schools, in reality rests the burden of the future of our
free democratic institutions and the welfare of our national
life. The children of to-day are the voters and rulers of to-
morrow, and to prepare them well or ill for the responsibilities of citizenship and government rests almost entirely with
the schools of our Nation. What progress we as a people
make in national character from generation to generation is
largely determined by how well the public school has seen
national needs and been guided by that largeness of vision
without which but little progress in national welfare is ever
made.

The problems our schools face. In the schools our people,
adult as well as the young, must be trained for literacy, and
the English language must be made our common national
speech. There, too, the youth of our land, girls now as well
as boys, must be trained for responsible citizenship in our
democracy, and so filled with the spirit and ideals of our
national life that they will be willing to dedicate their lives
to the preservation and advancement of our national welfare. In our high schools and colleges the more promising
of our youth must be trained for leadership and service in
the State, given a vision of our world place and relationships,
and prepared for constructive service along the lines of the
highest and best of our national traditions in statesmanship,
business, science, and government. In our common schools
and in special schools those who labor must be trained for

vocational efficiency, and given a sense of their responsibility for promoting the national welfare. The school, too, must take upon itself new duties in teaching health, promoting healthful sports, training in manly and womanly ways, inculcating thrift, teaching the principles underlying the conservation of our human and material national resources, and in preparing the rising generation for a more intelligent use of their leisure time. This last involves training for appreciation and intelligent enjoyment by developing better the musical, artistic, and literary tastes of our people.

Along with all these important aspects of the educational process must come the development generally among our people of a higher moral tone, that as a Nation we may rise and be equal to the advanced moral conceptions which we in recent years have set up in our international dealings. Our Nation has recently been accorded a prominent position in world affairs because of the high moral impulses which have characterized the various "notes" and addresses of our President on questions relating to the World War; because we took our place beside the Western Nations fighting in defense of civilization in the greatest crisis faced in a thousand years; and because our "boys" in Europe behaved in a manner which won the admiration of the people of every nation they went among. As a result the very name America stands, now, for a high and rigid code of personal and national honor, of which every American youth should not only be proud, but should also be made to feel that he must jealously guard in his thoughts, his actions, and his life. The same code of national honor must now be transferred and lived up to in our manners, our business relationships, and our international dealings with all other peoples throughout the world.

National morality is always an outgrowth of the personality, morality, and teaching of a people, and this in turn rests on proper knowledge, humane ideals, the proper training of the instincts, the development of a will to do right, good physical vigor, and, to a certain degree, upon economic competence.   Mere moral or religious instruction will not answer, because it usually does not get beneath the surface of the problem.   No nation has shown more completely the futility of mere religious instruction to produce morality than has Germany, where religious instruction was universally required.   The problem is how to influence and direct the deeper sources of the life of a people, so that the national characteristics it is desired to display to the world will be brought out because the schools have instilled into every child the conceptions and attitudes it is desired to see shine forth.   With the best of the young manhood of England, France, and Germany gone, for a generation to come, the call for our Nation to assume a new position in international affairs is one we cannot refuse to meet.   Where America will stand in the affairs of the world, and the place it will occupy in history a century hence, will be determined largely by the ability we display in shouldering the new tasks, and in subordinating every personal ambition and every sordid motive to the great ideas of international right and justice, sterling national worth, and service to mankind.   In the words of Lincoln we must "have faith that right makes might, and in that faith to the end dare to do our duty as we understand it."   How we understand our duty, and how large the duty appears, ultimately goes back to the schools and the homes of this Nation.

Education a constructive national tool.   Education to-day has become the great constructive tool of civilization.   A hundred years ago it was of little importance in the life of a Nation; to-day it is the prime essential to good government and national progress.   As people are freed from autocratic rule the need for general education becomes painfully evident.   In the hands of an uneducated people democracy is a dangerous instrument.   In Russia, Mexico, and the Central American "republic" we see what a democracy results in in the hands of an uneducated people.   There, too often, the revolver instead of the ballot box is used to settle public issues, and instead of an orderly government under law we find injustice and anarchy. When we freed Cuba, Porto Rico, and the Philippines from Spanish rule we at once instituted a general system of public education as a safeguard to the liberty we had established in these Islands, and to education we added sanitation and courts of justice as important auxiliary agencies. The good results of our work in these Islands will for long be a monument to our political foresight and our intelligent conceptions of government. In a similar way the French have opened schools in Morocco and Algiers, and the English in Egypt and India. With the freeing of Palestine from the rule of the Turk, the English at once began the establishment of schools and a national university there. In all lands where there is to-day an intelligent popular government, general education is regarded as an instrument of the first importance in moulding and shaping the destinies of the people.

In our own land, despite all our admirable progress, we still have a large task before us, and the task increases with the passing of years. We have here the makings of a great Nation, but the task before us is to make it. The raw materials — Saxon and Celt, Teuton and Slav, Latin and Hun — all are here. Our problem is to assimilate and amalgamate them all into a unified Nation, actuated by common impulses, inspired by common ideals, conscious of a moral unity and purpose which will be our strength, and so filled with reverence for our type of national life that our youth will feel that our form of government is worth dying for to defend. Never did opportunity knock more loudly at the doors of a Nation than it has at ours since 1914, and never was a Nation in better position to open its doors in response to the knocking. The place we shall occupy in history will be determined largely by how well we meet the emergencies of the present situation; how satisfactorily we solve the many new problems of the new world life after the World War; how well we respond to the calls of humanity for service; and to what extent we utilize the opportunity now presented to reorganize and unify our national life within.

Many forces must coöperate in the work, but unless our schools become clearly conscious of the national needs and the national purposes, and utilize the opportunities now presented for new and larger national service, we shall, in part at least, fail to reach the world position we might otherwise have occupied.

Importance of the educational service. Education in a democratic government such as ours is the greatest of all undertakings for the promotion of the national welfare, and the teacher in our schools renders an inconspicuous but a highly important national service. In teaching to the young the principles which lie at the basis of our democratic life; in awakening in them the conception of liberty guided by law, and the difference between freedom and license; in training them for self-control; in developing in them the ability to shoulder responsibility; in awakening them to the greatness of that democratic nobility in which all can share; in instilling into them the importance of fidelity to duty, truth, honor, and virtue; and in unifying diverse elements and fusing them into the national mould; the schools are rendering a national service seldom appreciated and not likely to be overestimated. It was to create such constructive institutions for our democratic life that we took the school over from the Church, severed all connections between it and its parent, made it free and equally open to all, and dignified its instruction as a birthright of every American boy and girl.

QUESTIONS FOR DISCUSSION

1. Does the obligation to educate impose any greater exercise of state authority than the obligation to protect the public health?
2. What would be the result were we to relieve from school taxation those who send their children to private or parochial schools?
3. While schools have, at first, been established by majority action, is it not true that much further development has been made by a small but thinking minority? Illustrate.
4. Show that art and musical education would be a legitimate extension of public educational effort.

5. Does the provision of equal opportunity for all necessitate equal or equivalent schools or school rights? Illustrate.

6. Show why the essentially democratic American school system would not be suited to an autocratic type of government.

7. Show that compulsory school attendance is the natural corollary of taxation for schools.

8. What is meant by the State increasing standards which may involve reciprocal obligations on the part of the State?

9. Show that the demands of the State on private and parochial schools, mentioned on page 494, are legitimate demands.

10. Illustrate the difference between an acceptance in principle and an acceptance in reality.

11. Are the characteristics which we have developed in our young people those of a new or an old country? Why so?

12. Illustrate what is meant by intelligent responsibility for the common welfare.

13. What kind of discipline is represented by the Army? By the Boy Scouts? Are schools of both types? Illustrate.

14. Show that the weight of a priesthood and the force of religious instruction in the schools would be strong supports for an autocratic state.

15. We do much less in the training of teachers than do homogeneous monarchical nations having an army and a priesthood. Is this right? How do you explain this condition?

16. Have we done much so far in giving our students world vision? Why? Do we need to do so?

17. What are likely to be the effects at home of the standards of national honor we have developed abroad? Illustrate.

18. Show how our educational tasks increase with the years.

19. Show how the World War is likely to be of great advantage to us in the matter of assimilating and integrating our foreign-born.

SELECTED REFERENCES

Alger, Geo. W. "Preparedness and Democratic Discipline"; in *Atlantic Monthly*, vol. 117, pp. 476–86. (April, 1916.)

An excellent article on our national problems.

Bowden, Witt. "Education for the Control and Enjoyment of Wealth"; in *Educational Review*, vol. 49, pp. 147–67. (Feb., 1915.) Also "Education for Power and Responsibility"; in *Educational Review*, vol. 49, pp. 352–67. (April, 1915.)

Two very good articles, supplemental to this chapter. Describes problems and training needed.

*Butler, N. M. *True and False Democracy*. 106 pp. The Macmillan Co., New York, 1907.

Contains three excellent addresses on the problems of democracy and the work of the school in their solution.

*Dewey, John and Evelyn. *Schools of Tomorrow*. 316 pp. E. P. Dutton & Co., New York, 1915.

Chapter XI, on "Democracy and Education," forms good supplemental reading for this chapter.

*Draper, A. S. *American Education*. 382 pp. Houghton Mifflin Co., Boston, 1909.

The first five addresses in the volume, dealing with "The Nation's Purpose," "Development of the School System," "The Functions of the State," "The Legal Basis of the Schools," and "Illiteracy and Compulsory Attendance," are able articles, supplementary to this chapter.

*Eliot, Chas. W. "The Function of Education in a Democratic Society"; in his *Educational Reform*. 418 pp. Century Co., New York, 1898.

An able address, pointing out a number of important functions.

Eliot, Chas. W. "Educational Reform and the Social Order"; in *School Review*, vol. 17, pp. 217–22. (April, 1909.)

A good article, dealing with the classes to be educated in a democratic society.

Eliot, Chas. W. *Education for Efficiency*. 29 pp. Houghton Mifflin Co., Boston, 1909.

A well-written monograph on the subject.

Hanus, Paul H. "Secondary Education as a Unifying Force in American Life"; chap. v in his *Educational Aims and Educational Values*. The Macmillan Co., New York, 1899.

The problems of democracy presented for solution, in which the secondary school can aid.

*Knight, M. M. "One Reason why our College Students do not have World Vision"; in *School and Society*, vol. VI, pp. 285–88. (Sept. 8, 1917.)

An excellent article.

Marrinan, J. J. "The Education of Youth for Democracy"; in *Educational Review*, vol. 49, pp. 379–90. (April, 1915.)

A splendid article to read in connection with this chapter.

Monroe, J. P. *New Demands in Education*. 312 pp. Doubleday, Page & Co., New York, 1912.

A very readable book, dealing with the different demands in education, such as citizenship, business, vocational training, etc., and the reasons for these new demands.

Pritchett, Henry Smith. "The Educated Man and the State"; in *Report of the United States Commissioner of Education*, 1899–1900, vol. II, pp. 1408–16.

Inaugural address as president of the Massachusetts Institute of Technology. An excellent address on the subject.

INDEX

Academies, begin teacher training, 288; early source of trained teachers, 288; state systems of, 79.

Academy, character of instruction in, 79, 187; characteristic features, 186, 188; early foundations, 185; Franklin's at Philadelphia, 185; number of established, 185, 192; Phillips Andover foundation grant, 188; semi-religious nature of, 188; transition character of, 184.

Adams, John, on education, 58.

Adams, John Quincy, on Federal Constitution, 78.

Admission requirements to colleges, table of early, 234.

Adult education, 424, 481, 503; community centers for, 429.

Agricultural colleges founded, 210. Agricultural high schools, 410, 414. Agricultural extension work, 430.

Alabama, education in before the Civil War, 250.

Albany Lancastrian School Society, 89.

Alignment of interests on free school question, 119.

Amalgamation of races, 341.

America, settlement of, 11.

Americanization program needed, 481.

Anglican Church attitude, 21.

Anglican settlements, 15.

Apperception, 317.

Apprenticeship legislation, 22; breakdown of old system, 413.

Arguments for and against free schools, 120.

Arithmetic, Colburn's, 303; first illustrated, 304; measurement of instruction in, 447; mental, 302.

Arithmeticker, an, 32.

Arkansas, education in, before the Civil War, 250.

Army draft examinations, results of, 395.

Assimilation of peoples, 341.

Attendance, compulsory, State may compel, 492. (*See* Compulsory Education.)

Attitudes, early, toward education, 15.

Average child, the, 370; average school courses, 371; effect of, 372.

Bache, A. D., 276.

Baltimore, school societies in, 88.

Barnard, Henry, *American Journal of Education*, 170, 260; first U.S. Commissioner of Education, 480; in Connecticut, 168; in Rhode Island, 169; the scholar of "the awakening," 170; visits Europe, 276.

Batavia plan, 373.

Battle for elimination of sectarianism, 171; establishment of school supervision, 155; extend the system, 184; make schools free, 147; state supported schools, 128; tax support, 129; eliminate pauper-school idea, 139.

Beecher, Henry Ward, 274.

Bell, Alexander Graham, 388.

Bell, Andrew, 90; his monitorial system, 90.

Bible as a reader, 29, 30, 32.

Binet-Simon intelligence scale, 451.

Bingham, Caleb, 174; his textbooks, 174, 218, 219.

Blackboards, first use of, 246.

Blind, education of, books for, 389; history of education for, 388.

Blow, Susan, 320.

Boston, establishes first high school, 190; schools in 1823, 226.

Braille alphabet for the blind, 389.

Breckinridge, Robert J., ancestry of, 171; work in Kentucky, 137.

ning, 252; first in New York, 193; first in Providence, 195; fitted onto graded system, 233; Massachusetts Law of 1827 for, 193; new courses in, and schools, 409; new subjects of study, 234; origin of name, 190; recent expansion of, 407, 419; rising demand for, 189; struggle to establish and maintain, 196.

History, as developed by Herbart, 313; early instruction in, 219, 222; instruction in a later development, 307; instruction first required, 307; neglected by Pestalozzi, 308.

Hofwyl, Fellenberg's Institute at, 267.

Home, changes in, 348; changes in character of, 350; effect of changes on school, 354; gains to, 351; influence of changes, 353; influence weakened, 352; the modern, 349.

Home and Colonial Infant Society, 270, 296.

Hornbook, The, 30.

Household-arts high school, 410.

Howland, John, on Providence schools, 220.

Hughes, Thomas, bequest for education, 89.

Huguenots, French, 13.

Illinois, preamble to first school law, 111; settlement of, 74, 75.

Illiterates, adult, 424; in male population, 425; who constitute, 427.

Immigration, change in character of, 337; the stream sets in, 334.

Immigrant flood in Massachusetts, 479; mixture in America, 340, 503; mixture in the Cleveland schools, 358; in our national life, 426.

Indiana, battle for taxation in, 134; early constitutional provisions in, 75, 259; referendum in, 135; settlement of, 74; university of, founded, 207.

Individual instruction, waste under, 36.

Industrial changes since 1850, 343; since Lincoln's day, 344; indus-

trial revolution, the, 343; industrial schools, state, 284; industrial transformation, after 1815, 103; after 1860, 344; types of industrial schools, 423; what industrial training paid, 356.

Infant schools, in eastern cities, 97; origin of, 96; societies, 96, 98.

Intelligence, classification of, 452; measurement of, 450; significance of measurement of, 452.

Inventions and industry, 104.

Irish immigration, 335.

Isolation and independence, early, 259.

Jackson, Andrew, significance of election of, 110.

Jay, Justice, 86; on education, 57.

Jefferson, Thomas, on education, 57; propagandist for French ideas, 258; scheme for education in Virginia, 258; helped inaugurate schools of Washington, 88.

Jena ideas in American normal schools, 317; Jena-Ziller-Rein school, 316.

Johnson, Mrs., school at Fairhope, Alabama, 446.

Jones, Miss Margaret E. M, at Oswego, 296.

Journalism, educational, begins, 260.

Journals, early American educational, 260.

Julius, Dr., 277.

Juvenile delinquency in cities, 107.

Kalamazoo case, the, 198.

Kentucky, early school legislation in, 70; education in, before the Civil War, 248; struggle in, to preserve school funds, 137.

Kidd, John, bequest for education, 89.

Kindergarten, contribution of, 322; early American schools, 319; growth of, in America, 320; origin of, 318; the kindergarten idea, 320; spread of the idea, 319; spread in the U.S., 319.

King Philip's War, effect of, on colonies, 37.